REJOICE IN MY GLADNESS

The Life Of

ṬÁHIRIH

JANET RUHE-SCHOEN

Bahá'í PUBLISHING

Wilmette, Illinois

Bahá'í Publishing
401 Greenleaf Avenue, Wilmette, Illinois 60091-2844

Printed in the United States of America on acid-free paper ∞

19 18 17 16 6 5 4 3

Library of Congress Cataloging-in-Publication Data

Ruhe-Schoen, Janet.
Rejoice in my gladness : the life of Táhirih / by Janet Ruhe-Schoen.
p. cm.
Includes bibliographical references (p.) and index.
ISBN 978-1-931847-84-1 (alk. paper)
1. Qurrat al-'Ayn, 1817 or 18–1852. 2. Baha'is—Iran—Biography. I. Title.
BP395.Q87R84 2011
297.9'3092—dc22
[B]

2011000116

Cover design by Andrew Johnson
Book design by Patrick Falso

REJOICE
IN MY GLADNESS

Contents

To my Persian teacher, Malileh Davachi Teymoorian;
to my husband, children, and grandchildren—
especially Anna Mayta, whose choreography catalyzed this work,
and to Beth, for singing to me

Acknowledgements

First of all, I must thank my Persian teacher, Malileh Teymoorian Davachi, and honor her memory. She was in her eighties when she began to teach me the Persian language. Her command of English was negligible. Yet, because of her exquisite sensibilities and unfailing empathy, she was able to impart a deep feeling for the language, for its music and its poets, and for the noblest qualities of Iranian culture in all its sublime paradoxes. When she became ill and could no longer speak, I lost so much music and joy, but now that she's released from her pain, I believe she is singing again. However, even during her illness, her heart remained so loving that she will always be, to her family, to the many friends she solaced over the years, and to her caretakers who knew her only when she was disabled, the irreplaceable *Mamika*—Grandma.

I cannot adequately express here my thanks for the providential guidance that has attended me in writing this book; I hope it reaches the reader through the text. I can, however, thank the scholars and translators who keep uncovering new facets and facts of the life of Ṭáhirih, the personalities and events surrounding her, and the revelation that inspired her. Some to whom I owe a great deal are Moojan Momen, Farzaneh Milani, Nader Saiedi, John Hatcher, Amrollah Hemmat, and Abbas Amanat. Of course, they stand on the shoulders of historians of the past, chiefly, for me, Nabíl-i-A'ẓam, Martha Root, and Marzieh

Gail. I thank Amrollah Hemmat, too, for his phone call from China to consult encouragingly with me about my translations / interpretations of Ṭáhirih's poetry.

Last, but never least, I thank my husband, Christopher Ruhe, for his belief in me, his consistent encouragement and love.

A Note on the Text

The transliterated terms in this book are based on the system used by Shoghi Effendi, Guardian of the Bahá'í Faith. Although the dominant language of Iran is sometimes referred to as *Farsi,* we've chosen *Persian* as being more consonant with English usage.

Some of the translations of Ṭáhirih's poems are my own and are intended to reflect the spirit of the poems and not the exact literal translation of the text.

Oh God, with this broken wing I desire to fly to the Divine clouds,
and with this weary heart recount the story of the world
of paradise and purity. But of course there is none except you
to be my helper . . .

—*Ṭáhirih*

Preface: Her Defining Moment

Early summer, 1848, the outskirts of the village of Badasht, northern Iran. An orchard grows, leafy and green, against a backdrop of deep purple mountains and turquoise sky. Near the fruit trees, a mountain stream flows through fallow gardens where three tents or pavilions stand. A young woman steps out from one of the tents and makes her way to the open flap of the next, from which rises a roar of men's voices, arguing.

The young woman enters and stands before the men. Silence. But only for a moment. Then—wails and screams of consternation and rage. One man slashes his own throat and staggers from the tent outside into the empty field, bleeding profusely. Another lifts his sword against the woman as if to kill her. Thoroughly serene, she faces them.

She faces them.

She stands before them unveiled. Her face is bared. She is breaking the greatest taboo of her Islamic nation. It is unthinkable that a young woman of her high status—she is a poet and scholar revered by many as a saint and dowered with wealth, impeccable lineage, and familial connections—should reveal to some eighty men who are not even related to her so much as an eye, a hair, a whisper of the curve of her cheek. Yet here she stands, her beautiful face adorned as if for her wedding, her veil torn away, warp and weft of tradition rent by her own hand,

and then by her own voice as she proclaims with ecstatic clarity, "This day is the day of festivity and universal rejoicing, the day on which the fetters of the past are burst asunder. Let all who have shared in this great achievement arise and embrace each other."[1]

Has she gone mad? Or is this the sanest, most cogent moment of her life? And if it is, what does it mean to the life of the world—her world—which is the world of Europe and the West, too, remote as it may seem? Later, during this same summer of 1848, the first Women's Rights Convention will gather in Seneca Falls, New York to demand, among other things, women's right to speak from religious pulpits, and the entire year of 1848 is one of revolution from Paris to Sicily, called by some idealists "The Springtime of the Peoples." A fateful synchronicity? As Iran's great medieval poet Rumi wrote, "Neither Eastern, nor Western—Human."[2]

Who is she then, this nineteenth-century Iranian woman standing alone, unveiled, and unafraid before a company of men? In 1852, she will be strangled and buried at night: silenced and reveiled, as if forever. Yet in 2003, on PBS television, the author Azar Nafisi will remark, ". . . Women in Iran alongside many other forces for 150 years have been fighting for their rights and for the right of their society to come into the modern world. The first woman to unveil and to question both political and religious orthodoxy was a woman named Ṭáhireh who lived in the . . . 1800s."[3]

That same year, the Ṭáhirih Justice Center in Washington D.C., founded in her name in 1997 "to protect immigrant women and girls from gender-based violence through legal services, advocacy, and public education programs" will be celebrating six years of hard-fought victories on behalf of its clients, all of them receiving pro bono assistance.[4]

And during the same era, the Iranian novelist Shahrnush Parsipur will say that she "considers Ṭáhirih a precursor of modern (Iranian) literary tradition," while the author of *Veils and Words*, a book centered around Ṭáhirih, will remark that her "contribution to the history of women's writing in Iran is invaluable: she proved that women could think, write, and reason like men—in public and for the public. Such actions set her apart from her contemporaries and confer upon her an inalienable precedence."[5]

More subtly than all that, her songs have refused to die from the voice of the winds that constantly murmur and blow through the mountains and deserts of Iran, or from the "rich culture of this great choir of poets," as Ralph Waldo Emerson described Iran's long roster of literary artists stretching back thousands of years. "If by chance I see thee face to face, I'll whisper my travail in minute detail, nuance by nuance, trace by trace" is one of Ṭáhirih's better-known refrains, yet in Iran it is often attributed to other writers, not to her. The established powers of her native land still wish to blot out all traces of her existence. Yet even if her name lives there in infamy, it lives.[6]

Ṭáhirih. The title means *the Pure One.*[7] With such an honorific, how could she have unveiled herself as if she had no shame? What forces within and without impelled her to the religious gathering in Bada<u>sh</u>t and her defining moment? We can name three of her most dominant emotions: joy, sorrow, and love.

Joy is a winged thing, poets say. Escaping gravity, it soars. The rejoicing soul can't stay earthbound but, lifted by its own warm, liberating light, rises and flies, free of all constraints. Sorrow, on the other hand, is a flightless bird, gravity's favorite child. The heart inhabited by sorrow is heavy, aching, constrained, enshrouded, imprisoned. How is it, then, that joy and sorrow can dwell simultaneously in one heart? Have they anything in common? Perhaps their possibility of cohabiting depends on their origin. If they originate in love, especially in selfless love—love for a Being greater than the self—they have a shared quality.

Strange as it may seem, that quality is emptiness. Strange, because both joy and sorrow are, at first sight, very full emotions: one bright, one dark, one a vast sunlit pool, the other a deep well, yet both brimming with water—tears of joy, tears of sorrow. And when the tears are all sobbed out: emptiness, not abysmal, but open, like the plains. The quieted soul saying: "Now tell me, God. Tell me what you want me to know. I'm ready."

Then the wind, the soul's messenger, can come out of the cave of fate and whisper the soul's story, her destiny, so the soul hears and can follow her chosen highway to her defining moment and beyond, never hesitating, never regretting, never looking back. And at road's end, the soul that has experienced both joy and sorrow to their fullest and emptiest can embrace this divine paradox, entrust the poignant relics of mortality to a friend, as Ṭáhirih did when facing her death, and say, "Remember me, and rejoice in my gladness."

A miracle? No, just love. Or rather, *yes.* For such ecstatic love is a miracle, and it was an everyday miracle in the life of Ṭáhirih, who incarnated joy and sorrow and the messenger wind itself. Ṣabá is the name of the messenger wind, a zephyr evoked by Iranian poets as restless energy, fragrances blowing hither and yon, seeking a pure heart in which to finally rest. And it would have been a perfect name for Ṭáhirih, for she likened herself, in her quest for her divine Beloved, to the zephyr. She wrote,

To see thy face, like Ṣabá I wander
 Door to door, street to street and lane to lane,
From dwelling-place to dwelling-place.

Dying of distance from thee I cry tears of blood,
 Tigris upon Tigris, stream upon stream,
Wellspring upon wellspring, sea upon sea . . .[8]

But even at her birth, Ṭáhirih already had many names.

1

News of the Birth of a Female Child

Ṭáhirih's names. Her antecedents, her hometown, her nation. Her birth. Her family's Islamic female culture.

Most historians agree that when Ṭáhirih was born in Qazvin, Iran, circa 1817, she was named Fáṭimih after the Prophet Muḥammad's saintly daughter. Her family also called her Zarrín-Táj, which means Crown of Gold, perhaps a name given to her during childhood because of her beauty and brilliance, but some cite it as part of her birth name: Fáṭimih Zarrín-Táj.[1]

Ṭáhirih's family also bestowed on her the epithet *Zakíyyih*, the Virtuous. And it is said she was nicknamed Tuti, a moniker for a pet parrot; perhaps that term of endearment became hers when she was very small, excelled at memorization and recitation, and wasn't shy about showing it.[2]

According to other authorities, her name was Umm Salmá, after Muḥammad's most outspoken and steel-witted wife whose questions catalyzed His revelatory recitations about the spiritual equality of women and men; Salmá also accompanied the Prophet on various expeditions and nursed the sick and wounded; in fact, one description of her sounds like a description of Ṭáhirih: ". . . a woman of uncommon beauty, very sound judgment, rapid powers of reasoning, and unparalleled ability to formulate correct opinions." A historian explains, "In Persia it's the custom to give a newborn the name of a family member and then, in respect for that family member, to call the child by another name. So, though Táhirih's given name was Fatima, after her maternal grandmother . . . she was called Umm Salmá."[3]

Umm Salmá is a particularly apt name, because Ṭáhirih was forthright and outspoken, rare qualities for either a female or male in nineteenth century Iran, where placation of the great and powerful, from the inner rooms of the home to the king's court, was the rule. This art of obsequiousness and manipulation involved a complex system of gift-giving called *madákhil*—labeled by a condescending British writer "the crowning interest and delight of a Persian's existence"—and a ritual etiquette called *ta'arof.*[4]

Using ta'arof, one aggrandizes the person one is addressing, especially if that person is a social superior, while belittling oneself, saying things such as, "I will put my eyes under your feet." Even between equals, ta'arof enables one to hide the secret self; it "plunges both parties, the addressee and the addresser, into a kind of factual suspense."[5]

Ṭáhirih had no use for factual suspense. She had no use for ta'arof, because her passion was *ta'arruf,* "inquiring with the view to learn; seeking knowledge; . . . instructing, teaching, notifying."[6] She swept away custom, claiming inner independence. This led her to startlingly original insights into Islamic tradition, scripture, philosophy, and literature. Using her prodigious memory and logic, she supported her insights with citations from numerous texts, and she could think on her feet, so she was an arresting debater as well as writer.

But Iran regards her more as a poet than as a religious scholar, for prevailing religionists consider her theology a heresy. In Iran she's known by the accolade *Qurratu'l-'Ayn*, Solace of the Eyes, or she's referred to as Ṭáhirih Qurratu'l-'Ayn.[7]

The soubriquet Qurratu'l-'Ayn, bestowed upon her by her mentor in Iraq, can also be translated to mean the cool luster shining from the surface of the eyes.[8] Aesthetes note that the beauty of an eye comes from its luster, the pupil glowing intensely black in its rings of color and gleaming whiteness, creating a glance of strong sensibility and depth, as opposed to vacuity. So Qurratu'l-'Ayn, like most Arabic terms, carries twin lustrous meanings: it is the title of one whose presence consoles others even while she must navigate her inner seas of spiritual passion.

In fact, the first person to call her Qurratu'l-'Ayn was her father. An unusual man for his time and place, he educated his daughters as well as his sons, but he was not alone among his class of men in doing this. He was essentially conservative; Ṭáhirih didn't come to her "heresy" because of him. He was a mullah and a mujtahid (this might be translated as a doctor of Islamic law, or an Islamic judge). His name was Muḥammad Ṣáliḥ Baraghani—the last because he came from the village of Baraghan. His father descended from a long line of mullahs from a tribe native to the mountains near the Caspian Sea; during the tenth century, his Buyid ancestors had ruled Iran and parts of Iraq, led a revival of ancient Persian culture, and instituted the tradition of the mourning processions and passion plays commemorating the martyrdom of the Imam Ḥusayn. Following family custom, Mullah Ṣáliḥ and his older brother left their home village to study Islamic theology and law for many years in different cities. In midlife, during the early 1800s, they settled in Qazvin, and so did their younger brother.[9]

Qazvin is about one hundred miles from Iran's capital, Tehran. It's an ancient town; legend has it that Princess Koz, daughter of a gargantuan mythical king, built the city as her "playground." It has since been destroyed by earthquakes, sacked by invaders, and raised as a conquering ruler's capital more than once, only to be abandoned when he moved his glories to another town. Its treasures remained at its heart, among them a sixteenth-century palace and a ninth-century mosque built by the sultan of Arabian Nights fame on the site of an old Zoroastrian fire-temple.[10]

Like all of Iran's main cities, nineteenth-century Qazvin was surrounded by an ancient pounded clay wall that had been, throughout the eras of the town's fluctuating fortunes, in various states of repair and disrepair. Tall gates punctuated the wall, and one needed a pass to travel in and out, although that was, no doubt, frequently a matter of madákhil and the whims of the guards.

As in all Iranian settlements, Qazvin's water came from an ages-old, ingenious system of underground irrigation called *qanats* that made lines of what looked like large molehills across the landscape from the mountains through the deserts. Underground reservoirs cooled by wind tunnels preserved the water brought to towns by this underground path, and Qazvin's reservoir system was the most extensive in the country, for Qazvin was known as the city of believers, and it was a pious duty to supply water—sacred substance of life in both Islam and Zoroastrianism, Iran's preceding national religion—to the populace.[11]

Also, like its sister cities, Qazvin is situated at a high altitude, so sunlight through thin air falls brilliantly clear upon its faults and graces alike, and visitors unused to heights are breathless upon arrival. Just about all of populated Iran is on an arid plateau, and travelers—at least before smog set in—reveled in the white light and the "Goodness and Purity of the Persian Air," as the seventeenth-century traveler Sir John Chardin wrote. He explained, "There is no need of stopping the Bottles, any further than just to hinder the Wine from running out: For this they make use of a Flower, as a Pink or a Rose, and put it in the Mouth of the Bottle instead of a Cork, and after they have poured any part of it out, they never stop it afterwards. The remnant of a Bottle that his been uncork'd for four and twenty hours and which one would think should evaporate and pass, is so very little alter'd that 'tis scarce to be perceiv'd."[12]

Wine? Yes, it's true that Islam forbids the consumption of wine, yet from the days of its Zoroastrian empire Iran has been famous for its wine, and the Persian tradition of sipping wine in an enclosed "paradise" (the word comes from the Persian for garden) hasn't been forgone or forgotten—hence the mystical symbolism, even for teetotalers, of a wine of astonishment, intoxication of heart and soul in thrall to a divine beloved.[13]

Ṭáhirih's father didn't approve of wine. He was a mystical drinker, a scholar known for his interpretations of scripture and Islamic law, and for his unrelenting application of legal punishments. One of his students noted, "He was rigid and firm in enjoining the good and prohibiting the evil," and this probably applied frequently to people who liked their wine. He also became known for his elegies honoring his culture's greatest martyr, the Imam Ḥusayn; perhaps in this he was conscious of following in the footsteps of his ancestors who had established the passion plays for Ḥusayn. His older brother, much more ambitious, became more famous. He was very well-connected, for he had an alliance with the nation's ruling dynasty; his first wife was a princess, a daughter of the king, Fatḥ 'Alí Sh̲áh.[14]

Fatḥ 'Alí, the second shah of the Qájár dynasty, ruled from 1798–1834, and at that time it wasn't as rare as one might think to marry royalty or be descended from it. The stupendous quantity of Fatḥ 'Alí's wives, concubines, and offspring was even more notorious than the storied length of his black beard. He wasn't the first such profligate ruler, thus the Persian saying: "Camels, fleas and princes are everywhere."[15]

In Tehran, the new capital, Fatḥ 'Alí built resplendent palaces, gardens, *maidans* (public squares), government buildings, and many mansions for his family. In Qazvin, the gateway to the Turkish Iran that he loved because it was the homeland of his tribe, the Qájárs, the shah built a bazaar with a royal mosque at its entrance. He adorned his architecture with tiles, friezes, textiles and other décor featuring the "birds and roses, vines and tulips woven into intricate patterns" typically painted in Qazvin but in the signature colors of Qájár adornment—pink and yellow.[16]

As the flashing-eyed Fatḥ 'Alí piled up treasure, European fascination with romantic Persia grew. Nineteenth-century European ambassadors to Iran busily wrote travel memoirs of the splendors of the shah's court and the rugged, haunted landscape of his kingdom—Vita Sackville-West (actually a twentieth-century traveler) described mirages of "mist and light," knowing that for the Iranians who accompanied her across the desert it was "inhabited by nymphs and monsters, chimeras, wyverns and fabulous Circean beings . . . These waterless, watered plains seemed a very breeding-ground for superstition . . . as the dust-demons . . . rose like djinns* in a column and swirled away, not obeying the direction of the wind as we conceived it to be, but hurrying off in opposite ways . . ."[17]

Preening themselves on freedom from such superstitions, the Europeans jousted with each other for the shah's favors so that their countries could control the wealth of raw materials lurking in his seas and mountains—wealth that he, seemingly unaware of the hole burned by the Industrial Revolution in Europe's stomach, did not deign to explore and exploit. They also wanted Iran as a prime strategic location for governance; because of its old empire, Iran's language was widespread, the official tongue of religious, legal, trade, and other discourse in India, Turkey, and the lands from Central Asia and Russia to China that were then called Tartary. But regardless of the great depth and influence of Persian poetry and philosophy, most Europeans saw things as Lord

* Djinns are the mysterious fire-spirits mentioned in the Qur'án, Sura 55:15.

George Curzon did: "Turkestan, Afghanistan, . . . Persia—to many these names breathe only a sense of utter remoteness or . . . romance. To me, I confess, they are pieces on a chessboard upon which is being played out a game for the dominion of the world . . ."[18]

Notwithstanding Curzon's imperial self-importance, he and rival Westerners jockeying for pride of place in the shah's court could seem comedic to Iranians—especially when they tried to practice ta'arof. European formalities were nothing compared with that intricate etiquette; Persian methods of saying one thing and doing another were so subtle that there was an adage about being strangled by a silken thread. But Iranians also knew the Europeans' tremendous power, and they were caught in a vise of competition between Russia and England, with the French often pitching in, for dominion in their territory. The shah was aware of the untrustworthiness of his European "friends," the flimsiness of their treaties, the fickleness of their alliances. He could at least impress them with his splendors, such as his absolute autocratic might and his jewels.[19]

After a first audience with the shah in 1800, Sir John Malcolm reported, "His dress baffled all description. The ground of his robes was white; but he was so covered with jewels of an extraordinary size and their splendor, from his being seated where the rays of the sun played upon them, was so dazzling, that it was impossible to distinguish the minute parts which combined to give such amazing brilliancy to his whole figure." The shah's prize jewels included the huge diamonds called Sea of Light and Crown of the Moon.[20]

As Malcolm became a bit better acquainted with the shah, Fatḥ 'Alí questioned him about England, then said it seemed to him the British king was only a sort of magistrate and that he pitied such impotency. He pointed to his ministers and courtiers ranged in rows before him and said, "I can cut all their heads off, can I not?" They chorused, "Assuredly, Point of Adoration of the world."[21]

While Fatḥ 'Alí built up Tehran as his capital, he revived Qazvin, strengthening it as a strategic site, for it was located so that anyone entering Iran, whether as an invited guest or as an invading force from Russia and other regions, had to pass through it. Qazvin was also a trade center, set on a plain between two rivers, land that produced famously delicious fruit and rich pasturage for camel fodder. Camels from Qazvin fetched prime prices, and that was no small thing. The camel was the major mode of transport, called by Persians *the Ship of the Continent.* It was able to live on thorns, run far and fast without stopping, patiently as a mountain carry a huge load on its back, and be led by music, altering pace along with the driver's singing. Excellence of fruit was a great asset, too, because fine fruit is a hallmark of Iran's exquisite hospitality and cuisine. Qazvin was particularly famous for its grapes, celebrated in springtime for its green "encircling halo of vineyards."[22]

Contrasting with Iran's age-old culinary refinement is a deep and rugged asceticism: a lady who dines on fragrantly spiced rice pilaf and tender fresh dates dripping with natural honey might lie down to sleep on nothing but a flat cotton quilt. (Of course, she may be on a rooftop beneath a dome of stars that seem to lean in for a kiss in the preternaturally clear mountain air.) As if to bespeak this asceticism, behind Qazvin rises a reddish, jagged wall of mountains, and in it lurk rocky ruins of Qazvin's legendarily swashbuckling past: eight centuries before Ṭáhirih's time, the so-called Old Man of the Mountains—leader of a branch of the Islamic sect called Ismá'ílís—carved fortress castles to house his followers. Allegedly* he brought young men to his secret garden paradise, drugged them with hashish, and sent them to kill the

* Present-day Ismailis say this legend of the Assassins is a confabulation of stories going back to Marco Polo and European knights of the Crusades (http://www.ak.dn.org/about; http://www.iis.ac.uk).

enemies of what he deemed true Islam, promising that if they died in the effort, they would return to paradise.[23]

By the nineteenth century, the Old Man of the Mountains' day was long gone, yet to some Iranians, it might have been yesterday, and the castles now in rock-piles might still have been in their glory. The passions and politics that animated the Old Man of the Mountains might be supposedly vanished, but that wasn't the case, for in the 1800s, the Ismá'ílís had a messianic revival mirroring the spirit of the era.[24]

Below the pale red peaks where Ismá'ílí palaces had towered, the hills directly behind Qazvin were tan, turning golden in sunlight. In the winter, they were snow-clad, as were their background peaks and the town itself with its maze of alleys, roofs, domes, minarets and spires; but in other seasons, Qazvin was, as Marzieh Gail describes it, "the honey-colored city of sun-baked brick, with her slim, tinkling poplars, and the bands of blue water along the yellow dust of the roads."[25]

The gold-hued city had its place in books of miracles because of its various shrines. Aside from monuments to Islamic saints and accompanying *madrassas* (religious colleges), there was a much-visited shrine for four Jewish prophets who had announced, two millennia before, Christ's arrival in Jerusalem, and a shrine for a Sufi mystic that was periodically razed by anti-Sufi forces and then rebuilt. The city had long been a center for various Christian sects, so it had churches as well as mosques. Because of all the nomads and other travelers passing through in their tribal and national costumes, the town had a distinct ethnic diversity.[26]

Ṭáhirih's father and his brothers flourished along with the city. Their success in Qazvin was both homecoming and vindication. For hundreds of years, Ṭáhirih's paternal forebears had been important mullahs in Qazvin. During the 1600s, one of them built a madrassa there that still functions today. At that time, Akhbari mullahs were the most powerful in Iran, and Qazvin was an Akhbari center. Then a less mystical, very competitive school of mullahs, the Usulis, began to gain power. During the 1750s, Ṭáhirih's paternal grandfather, an Usuli, led debates against Akhbaris. After he publicly defeated a visiting Akhbari scholar, a mob attacked his house and set fire to it, destroying his precious library, and civil authorities exiled him from the city.

He went to the village of Baraghan. It was winter, and his children died of cold during the journey. But in the village, three more sons were born to him—Ṭáhirih's father and his two brothers.[27] Meanwhile, Usuli mullahs gained dominance in Iran. They won plum positions not just through study, but by political maneuvering and inheritance, augmenting their spiritual authority with property—villages, whole quarters of cities, and richly endowed mosques. They constantly competed with the shah, his court, his princelings and officials, mullahs and mystics of other schools, and each other. The Usuli mullahs advanced materially because they interpreted holy writ using logic that could allow for human machinations.

The Akhbaris didn't allow such logic, leaning more towards mysticism, and they continued to challenge mullahs like Ṭáhirih's father and his older brother, while the royalty also tried to keep the Usulis off balance so as to remain dominant. The shah pretended or in certain cases really felt fascination with mystics. So Ṭáhirih's father and uncle, with their fellows, had to be vigilant and crafty to stay on the right side of the king and keep him from joining forces with mystics. If that happened, the populace might turn on them, for the people knew what it was to suffer betrayal by religious and political authorities who claimed concern for their welfare. They knew the horrors of famine, drought, cholera, smallpox, plague, earthquakes, and more, and they were almost hungrier for miracles than for bread.[28]

But when Ṭáhirih was born, her family was riding a wave of good fortune. Of course it would have been ideal if Ṭáhirih, firstborn of her father and his most recent bride, who was a favored child of Qazvin, had been a boy. The birth of a girl wasn't customarily a cause for rejoicing in nineteenth-century Iran, just as it was not, and still is not, in many other parts of the world.[29]

It's hard to pinpoint the year of Ṭáhirih's birth because there is no extant record of it, and perhaps there never was. Time was elastic, with two calendars simultaneously in use: the Islamic lunar one and the Persian solar one that was originally Zoroastrian and then adapted to Islamic history. Besides, the Eastern feeling for time is very different from the Western past-present-future road. Eastern time is one river, the present, in which the past is a forever-living current. This makes life easier for storytellers—"The present is always fabulous, because there everything is possible"—but harder for historians.[30]

However, the consensus among historians is that Ṭáhirih was born circa 1817. The female family members and servants attending her mother in the *andarun*, the women's quarters of the house, might have given her a bland welcome. While washing and swaddling her, they probably didn't ululate joyously and praise *Khoda*—God—but instead muttered, "God willing, the next one will be a boy." Servants in an affluent household knew the birth of a boy occasioned a feast and gift-giving, but there might be no such celebration for a girl.[31]

Yet Ṭáhirih's mother and her female relatives on both her and her husband's sides of the family may have taken a more sanguine view, for their clans had a tradition of educating their women. Ṭáhirih's paternal great-aunt, Mírzá Mah-Sharaf <u>Kh</u>ánum, was a highly admired calligrapher and writer who, after studying in Iṣfahán, worked as a scribe in the household of Fatḥ 'Alí Sháh. She "wrote most of the government's decrees in her beautiful hand," and the fact that she was addressed by the male honorific *Mírzá* was indicative of high status and respect in what was completely a man's world. Aside from slaves who were trained to dance and sing, it was rare for a woman to practice her skill so publicly, though some women excelled at poetry or served as mullahs within the andaruns.[32]

Ṭáhirih's mother, Amína Khánum,* could have been considered a mullah or even a mujtahid—though women were not usually licensed as mujtahids—for she taught in the women's wing of the large madrassa† established in Qazvin by her husband; in fact, most of the madrassa's female professors came from her family.[33]

She was seventeen when she married, and her husband was much older; records of his birthdate are dubious, but he could have been in his fifties. She wasn't his first wife. He already had quite a few sons, but Ṭáhirih was his first daughter. In all, he produced fifteen children. His house was an impressive mansion "of brick and plaster with . . . lancet bas-relief arches over the doors." The main entrance had two door knockers, one for the andarun and the other for the public, the men's part of the house. The house would have had more than one courtyard because the women would have had their own garden.[34]

These obligatory gardens reflected (literally, for they always contained water) one of Iran's most ancient traditions: on Iranian pottery dating back to four thousand BC, one can see designs of water-pools overhung by the tree of life, or the world divided into four quarters centered around a pool. This is still the standard design for a Persian garden, the pools being fed by the qanat system. Aside from their soul-feeding meditative and poetic purposes, the gardens fulfill practical needs,

---

* Khánum is a title indicating a distinguished lady.

† This madrassa was called the Ṣáliḥiyya, after its founder, and students came to it from all over Iran and as far away as India; it had some seven hundred students (Momen, "Usuli, Akhbari, Shaykhi, Bábí," p. 321).

frequently containing fruit and nut trees as well as roses, so they are called *bustan* (orchards) with the uses for the "little sea" or pool being to water the plants and lay the dust on the paths.[35]

Amína's family was very powerful in old Qazvin's religious circles. Her father was the imam of one of the city mosques, and his lineage went back to sixteenth- and seventeenth-century authors of famous Islamic texts. Her mother, Fáṭimih K͟hánum, a famous scholar and teacher in her own right, was the daughter of a revered mullah who was a *siyyid* (descendent of the house of the Prophet Muḥammad). This highly accomplished maternal grandmother very likely lived in Ṭáhirih's household when Ṭáhirih was a child. Amína was also extremely scholarly.[36]

So both she and Ṭáhirih's father could read the Qur'án for themselves, a rare ability. Most Iranian men, as well as women, were illiterate or semiliterate in their own language, and even fewer knew Arabic. The Qur'án was an Arabic book. Some people memorized parts of the Qur'án, although they couldn't read it. The Qur'án hadn't been translated into Persian. Everyone except those literate in Arabic depended on mullahs to tell them what was in the Qur'án. Over one hundred years after Ṭáhirih's era, a highly cultured Iranian woman wrote in her memoir that she first read the Qur'án for herself in an English translation given to her in India.[37]

But both of Ṭáhirih's parents knew their Qur'án and were well aware that any newborn, boy or girl, must hear whispered into her right ear upon birth or soon thereafter the *shahada* (Islamic creed) and the *azan* (call to prayer). The newborn Ṭáhirih heard, "There is no God but God and Muḥammad is the Messenger of God" and "Come to prayer . . . come to salvation . . . come to deliverance . . ."[38]

They also knew that the Qur'án forbade a father to scowl and resent fate at the birth of a daughter and deemed it worse than barbaric to kill her. Even now it is accepted practice in some places to kill newborn daughters or to misuse advances in medical technology to identify and abort them. Over one thousand years ago, in the Prophet's Arabia, girl-children were sometimes purposely buried alive in heavy desert sands. Muḥammad described and condemned the resentment and assassination of female infants:

And when news is brought
To one of them of (the birth
Of) a female (child), his face
Darkens and he is filled
With inward grief!

With shame does he hide
Himself from his people,
Because of the bad news
He has had!
Shall he retain it
On (sufferance and) contempt,
Or bury it in the dust?
Ah! What an evil (choice)
They decide on.[39]

In another reference to infanticide, Muḥammad, in a tumultuous description of apocalyptic reckoning, says it's the time when "the female (infant), buried alive, shall be asked for what crime she was killed."[40]

Ṭáhirih's mother was no doubt aware of the respect due an infant girl, yet we will never know her thoughts as she welcomed her firstborn, Ṭáhirih, into the world and looked down into her face. Was the legendary beauty already apparent? We do know that by the time she was just a few years old, Ṭáhirih's genius and questing spirit were obvious. She showed little interest in the games of other children, steeping herself in study and prayer and listening to the conversation of her learned elders.[41]

Then it's likely that she would have become aware at an early age of the rift in her family. Her mother, her mother's brother, and her father's younger brother had all gone over to the mystic side. They'd become followers of a highly controversial, vagabond Arabian saint. Her old uncle, destined to be her father-in-law, virulently opposed the saint. One day in 1822, the saint arrived in Qazvin, and Ṭáhirih's family unwittingly began its doomed wrestling match with catastrophe.[42]

2

Wine Cup in the Wilderness

The Arabian shaykh. The Youth from Bani-Hashem. Surmising salvation. The mischief of the envious one. Uncle Taqí and the saint. Love and nemesis.

The saintly traveler was Shaykh Aḥmad-i-Aḥsá'í. The title *shaykh* literally designates an elder and was sometimes applied to a high-ranking mullah. Shaykh Aḥmad was a sad-eyed ascetic with a white beard. (He apparently eschewed the black dye, usually made of cyprus and indigo, then applied by most of his contemporaries to their hair and beards.) Born in 1753, he grew up on the island of Bahrain in the Persian Gulf, quite near Iran. Most Arabians embrace the Sunni sect of Islam, but Shaykh Aḥmad's father, a nomad, was a Shiite, like the Iranians.[1]

Sunnis uphold the caliphate, the system of government established by the majority of the Islamic community after the Prophet's death. Trying to avoid hereditary succession, they elected leaders from various tribal factions. Shiites reject the caliphate, and maintain that certain descendants of the Prophet's cousin / son-in-law 'Alí and his wife (the Prophet's daughter) were hereditary, divinely guided Imams and that the succession of Imams began with 'Alí himself. However, there are fractures in Shiite Islam because of different interpretations of the identities of the Imams and how many of them there were. Sunni Islam also has its sects.[2]

As a boy Shaykh Aḥmad, devout and earnest by nature, was raised under the canopy of Twelver Shiite Islam, the dominant Shiite sect, a starry heaven from which the eyes of twelve Imams look down on humankind, and he felt a mystical intimacy with those guardian spirits. Except for his kinship with the Imams, he was a lonely soul in Bahrain, a desolate region. At abandoned sites of eleventh-century grandeur, he wept for forgotten heroes and lost glory. He disciplined himself to solitude, praying and meditating, trying to avoid music-making, the pastime of his peers that most tempted him.[3]

He accepted no one around him as his mentor, as he felt rescued by the Imams. They appeared in his dreams, interpreting Qur'ánic verses and unfolding the meanings of their own sayings as recorded in the traditions. To Islamic mystics, dreams have more authority than earthly events. His dreams sent Shaykh Aḥmad to study in Iraq. Some sources say he was twenty when he left home; others say he was forty. Quite a discrepancy.[4]

Whatever age he was, spirit sustained him. He often prayed and meditated all night, forgot to eat, and was too abstracted to don both shoes or wind his turban befittingly. He became famous for his erudition and expositions, for attracting increasingly numerous followers, and for rejecting material honors. When his enlightenment grew into an understanding of his own independent mission, he began his travels. Perhaps, given his nomadic ancestry, he rejoiced in them.

He traveled through Iran, his stated goal a pilgrimage to the shrine city of Mashhad, where the eighth imam is entombed. As he traveled, he taught and attracted followers. He wrote prolifically and produced most of his ninety-six volumes while he resided for a time in Yazd, a largely Zoroastrian city in central Iran. Yazd is an ancient mud brick settlement between Iran's two Great Salt Deserts. It's a weaving center, a town of looms and the rooftop *badgirs,* or cooling-towers, that make brilliant use of water and wind. Through its hard-baked, narrow streets came a youth who could understand Shaykh Aḥmad's secret and who would become his successor, led by a dream from his home in the north on the edge of the Caspian Sea. We'll discuss this youth in greater detail later.[5]

Then Shaykh Aḥmad journeyed from town to town, stopping for a few months to a few years in each place. He was like the tulip in a poem by Iran's beloved Hafez, who said, "On my stalk's green staff I bear a wine cup through the wilderness"—the wine is the ecstasy of mystic knowing. He attributed his knowledge to dream conferences with the Imams. "I do not say anything they would not say," he told his students. Despite his years of study, he claimed no school as the licensor of his authority as a mujtahid: each of the Imams, he reported, had licensed him. It's worth pointing out that the Arabic word for dream also connotes having a vision or bearing witness.[6]

His essential teachings were rumored to be highly controversial, even heretical, yet it was hard to penetrate the veils of mystery that surrounded them, though it was easy to see his great devotion to the Imams. Implicit in this devotion was criticism of the power the mullahs gave themselves, that of "collective deputyship" of the Hidden Imam, the Twelfth Imam who was said to have disappeared as a child, and who would return on the last day to save the world.[7]

As a group the mullahs were called *ulama.* That term is a plural of the word *alim,* which means a person who possesses *ilm,* knowledge—not mere knowledge of the Qur'án but of the inner, unspoken part of the Prophet's message. It was claimed that by imparting this knowledge from generation to generation of disciples, an alim "progressively" completed "the task of the Apostle of God (Muḥammad)."[8] So, as plural alim, the Shiite ulama claimed deputyship for the Hidden Imam and in this role prohibited anyone from naming a date for his reappearance—the Advent—and / or proclaiming himself or another as a savior bringing new religion. A title of Muḥammad's was the Seal of the Prophets, meaning, they interpreted, that there could be no other religion after His.

Yet there existed an "absolutist messianic belief in the (Hidden) Imam's eventual establishing of a utopian perfect order," and this kept the ulama from wholeheartedly supporting the government, for "every government was in theory seen as inherently oppressive." Many Islamic texts predicted the coming of the new revelator from Muḥammad's own lineage. For example, one text reads, "A Youth from Baní-Há<u>sh</u>im (the clan Muḥammad was born into, in Arabia) shall be made manifest, Who will reveal a new book and promulgate a new law . . . Most of his enemies will be the divines." Similary, Ṣádiq, the sixth imam, reportedly said, "There shall appear a Youth from Baní-Há<u>sh</u>im, Who will bid the people plight fealty unto Him. His book will be a new Book, unto which He shall summon the people to pledge their faith. Stern is his Revelation unto the Arab. If ye hear about Him, hasten unto Him."[9]

In truth, if one heard about that "Youth," it was highly dangerous to say so. Therefore, <u>Sh</u>ay<u>kh</u> Aḥmad, known by his near disciples to have heard quite a lot about him, often took refuge in *taqíyyih:* the Shiite practice of dissembling or even denying one's beliefs if one's life would be endangered by disclosing them. Like many mystics, especially the Sufis, the <u>Sh</u>ay<u>kh</u> cloaked his meanings with alchemical metaphors, such as comparing the seeker's metamorphosis into an enlightened soul to the prized alchemical transformation: base metal turning first into its primary source-self and then to gold through a miraculous mercury. If the alchemist's own base nature isn't similarly refined through love, he risks damnation, becoming infatuated with gold itself instead of the light it represents. As Hafez warned:

> Like those worthy of the path, wash your hands of the copper of existence so that you can find the philosopher's stone of love, and become gold.[10]

So Shaykh Aḥmad twirled his rhetorical, metaphysical cape, and only his nearest disciples knew what he really believed. For example, he explained the Prophet's Night Journey, described in the Qur'án as a flight on the back of a winged steed to Jerusalem and an ascent to the throne of God, as a vision or visitation, not a flesh-and-blood experience. He saw the Resurrection at the advent of the messiah not as bodies physically rising from graves but as the renaissance of the soul of humanity. And he was among those who didn't believe in a literal Hidden Imam or in his literal return. Shaykh Aḥmad's closest disciples knew he expected the imminent appearance of not just one messiah, but two.[11]

That was what had really impelled him to travel to Iran.[12] He believed that two great revelators would soon appear there, fulfilling all past prophecy. To the orthodox mullahs, even Sufi rhetoric was less threatening than this. But Shaykh Aḥmad had never identified himself with the Sufis. In fact, he disagreed with a belief of many of them: that a soul could merge with God. To the orthodox mullahs this was heresy, and Sufis had been martyred for announcing their personal oneness with God.

Shaykh Aḥmad believed the Creator was too great and too unknowable for any human to be one with it. He said humanity needed an intermediary with God, a specially endowed person who could bear the energy of the dazzling source of life and transmit its will to its creatures. The spirit of this person, like the Holy Spirit, was always alive and could be found in the world of dream, prayer, and contemplation. Shaykh Aḥmad saw the Hidden Imam as a symbol of this spirit. Only rarely, on earth, did someone (the Qur'án recognized various revelators before Muḥammad, among them Abraham, Moses, and Christ) Who was specially created, perfect in His being, manifest—i.e., show forth, radiate, demonstrate, make audible and visible—the spirit of revelation, speaking directly to people, living and dying among them, bearing a message of renewal, redemption, and salvation. Such a rare soul was, in Shaykhi lexicon, a Manifestation of God. Shaykh Aḥmad's disciples wondered if he himself was the expected manifestation of the revelatory spirit, but he only said, "Understand, for truly I have thrown unto you a key of the keys to the Invisible World."[13]

Ṭáhirih was about five years old when the charismatic, enigmatic Shaykh Aḥmad arrived in Qazvin. Her Uncle Taqí, his ear always close to the ground to detect the thundering footsteps of a rival, knew how people esteemed Shaykh Aḥmad. Uncle Taqí was sure the shaykh was a heretic and despised him as a threat to himself and his position. Yet his own brother-in-law was the one who invited Shaykh Aḥmad to Qazvin. And certain people in Uncle Taqí's own family, including Ṭáhirih's mother, became Shaykhís.[14] How could Uncle Taqí allow it? How could it be?

It seems that Uncle Taqí's relations weren't immune to the human longing for salvation so well expressed by one of Ṭáhirih's literary daughters, the twentieth-century poet Foroogh Farrokhzaad:

Someone is coming
Someone is coming
Someone who in his heart is with us
in his breath is with us
in his voice is with us

Someone whose coming
cannot be stopped . . .

Someone coming from the rain
from the sound of rain splashing
from among the whispering petunias . . .

to spread out . . . the cloth
and divide up the bread . . .

I've had a dream . . .[15]

We all have dreams. And now and then a dreamer claims to be the messiah. In Iran, such claimants often led nationalist movements. They began arising soon after the death of the Prophet and the conquest of Iran by Islamic troops. One of them was Abú Muslim. In the eighth century, he galvanized a following to avenge the martyrdoms of the Imams 'Alí and Ḥusayn. He led a revolution against the Umayyads* and established a new line of caliphs. Almost a millennium after his death, another dynasty feared his memory so much that storytellers who told his tale could have their tongues cut out, the ink washed away from the pages of their books.

Yet his influence remained pervasive. He was the poor man's martyr. He knew the story of the Imam 'Alí's magical sword. He prayed for a weapon of his own and saw the Angel Gabriel in a dream with an all-powerful axe. He had no money to buy an axe, so his friends, a blacksmith's son and other craftsmen, made him one using metal said to be from 'Alí's sword. Leading his revolt with his workman's weapon, he rode out of the eastern province of Khorasan at the head of his troops flying black banners because, according to tradition, Muḥammad said

---

* The Umayyads were the second Muslim Caliphate, established after the death of Imam 'Alí; they ruled from 661–750 from their capital in Damascus.

black standards would wave above the army of the Mahdi, the one who breaks the dawn for the Lord of the Resurrection Day, "the divine agency that brings the old revelatory cycle to its ultimate totality and potentially stands to start a new religious dispensation . . ."[16]

Abú Muslim was betrayed and murdered by the very people he set in power, yet, after him, uprisings in his name rocked Islam, and among his partisans some said he didn't die but went into hiding and would return. Some revolutionaries, in later years, claimed descent from Abú Muslim.[17]

Over half a millennium after him, during the 1400s, one who announced himself to be a new revelator abrogated Islam, saying the Arabian cycle was at an end and the Ajami (Persian) cycle had begun. He and his leading followers were killed—in Qazvin, as a matter of fact. That was when Qazvin lost its status as a throne city; the reigning shah abdicated, proclaimed the Ajami leader king for three days and did obeisance to him, then executed him, moved to Isfahan, and reinstated himself as shah, saying that in so doing he was fulfilling prophecy.[18]

But because Iran was Zoroastrian before the Islamic conquest, it has always been suspicious of its various Islamic dynasties as well as its mullahs. Zoroaster, Persia's native Prophet Who lived a millennium before Muḥammad, prophesized a messiah Who would vanquish falsehood, which He defined as the Lie, the incarnation of evil. He would rise up out of a blessed lake to defeat evil with good thoughts, good deeds, good words, not with physical weapons; he would end the old world and begin a new era. He would be the Lord of the Resurrection Day.[19]

Shaykh Aḥmad foresaw the imminence of two Manifestations of God; the first would be the harbinger of the second. Early in the 1800s, he showed his fascination with Shiraz, the town in southern Iran extolled in poetry and song, but when Shaykh Aḥmad visited Shiraz, he ignored fabled sites except for one of the city's mosques, a building that happened to resemble the shrine of Mecca, and lavishly praised it and its setting.* When disciples asked why, he merely said that some of them would live to behold a day that the prophets of the past had longed to see. Then, in November, 1817, in Tehran, he was incomprehensibly thrilled at the birth of a son to a nobleman who was close to the shah, and said his only desire was to spend the rest of his life quietly in Tehran. His students wondered who had come to Tehran, and who would come to Shiraz?[20]

They were not alone in wondering and seeking; during the nineteenth century in Iran, apocalyptic expectations hopped and burgeoned like popcorn over a flame. A man from the village of Saysan† predicted the coming of the Mahdi, withdrew for two years to a holy mountain, then met up with Shaykh Aḥmad, became his follower, returned home, and taught his fellow-villagers to expect the promised one very soon.[21]

A shepherd in a village near the northwestern town of Tabriz announced himself as the deputy of the Hidden Imam and predicted the advent within two years. When it didn't happen, he lost everything. Some say he was discredited not because his prediction failed but because he didn't gather troops and start a revolution.[22]

---

* Probably a mosque dating from 875 A.D. which had in its center "a small, square, stone building, reported to be a copy of the Kaaba at Mecca" (Curzon, *Persia and the Persian Question,* pp. 101–2). This near-replica was built circa the mid-fourteenth century to house some valuable copies of the Qur'án, and Hafez is said to have worked within its walls (*Lonely Planet Iran,* p. 273).

† A village in the province of Azerbaijan, northwestern Iran, where, in later years, nearly all the inhabitants became Bahá'ís; it was a model village in various ways, but its people were evicted and its houses razed to the ground in 1979 during the Islamic Revolution (Momen, "Social and Economic Development in an Iranian Village: The Bahá'í Community of Saysan," *Bahá'í Studies Review,* May 2009, http://www.intellectbooks.co.uk/journals/view-Article,id=8262/).

In 1807, an outcast Sufi dervish in league with a rebel government led fifty thousand horsemen against the governor of Abú Muslim's province, Khorasan, reputedly the seat of all revolution in Iran. Although he commanded his troops from a golden howdah surrounded by a 366-man guard, he died in battle.[23]

In 1817, the Iranian leader of the reviving Akhbari sect (the old enemies of Ṭáhirih's paternal relatives) was assassinated in Iraq, his death warrant issued by the mullahs of the Shiite shrine cities there. He had challenged the religious establishment in many ways, most profoundly by opposing its prohibition against seeking and perceiving the Hidden Imam, saying that anyone could encounter the Hidden Imam through intuition and that the gate of knowledge was open to all. People must free themselves from blind imitation, be independent in spirit, search for truth.[24]

Imitation was an important pillar in the faith erected by the dominant orthodoxy. Certain verses in the Qur'án laud Abraham for releasing himself from imitation of his ancestors, dispensing with idol worship. Faced with the bugaboo of those verses, the ulama ruled against what they called *bada*, innovation, but their rivals promoted intuition, feeling that divine guidance was continually present and that charismatic leadership would save the day.[25]

The leader of the new Akhbaris also indicted the ulama for misleading the people and predicted that in the Islamic year 1260 (1844 AD), a truly explosive innovation would occur: the *Zuhur*, or Advent, when the Mahdi would illumine the earth with his light. Although he was killed, his movement continued to gather adherents. In Tabriz, a city near the dangerous border with Russia, a seemingly insane old man went about painting the code Z1260 on walls and gates of houses and mosques. Asked what it meant, he said he didn't know except that it referred to the advent, and he was sure he was doing his duty. Perhaps he had heard the Akhbari predictions, or the astrologers' predictions linking 1844 with "incredible events."[26]

Among expectations for the Mahdi was that he would free Iran from the influence of foreigners, especially Russia, which delighted in invading Iran. Dervishes, the storytelling vagabonds among the Sufis, tossed their matted dreadlocks, colored bright orange with henna, and flourished their hands tipped with hennaed nails as they told rapt listeners in coffeehouses and bazaars apocalyptic tales of imminent eradication by Christians.[27]

A Sufi revival was in full swing, led by missionaries from India. One Sufi leader came to Iran because his master dreamed of the Eighth Imam instructing him to send disciples there. A man called the Sufi Killer assassinated him in 1798, and, a few years later, a poet who had accompanied him from India died under mysterious circumstances.[28] The poet's wife survived.

She was Bibi Hayati, from a Sufi family in a part of Persia that now belongs to Iraq, and she was also a poet. She lived around the same time as Ṭáhirih, but it isn't known whether or not they were aware of each other. She was a disciple of the poet's before she married him, then became the mother of his daughter and of his whole spiritual community, particularly after his death. Her poetry is still famous.[29] She had the blessing of a husband whose spirit harmonized with hers, who encouraged her poetry and scholarship; her contemporary, Ṭáhirih, even more radical in her beliefs and forced to marry a man who completely opposed her, had a chillingly different path. It was Ṭáhirih's fate to live the answer to Muḥammad's question in the Qur'án about what happens when the girl-child, "buried alive," is asked why she was killed. Ṭáhirih's life was first a search for the answer, and then the answer itself.

Ṭáhirih certainly didn't inherit any part of her radical spirit from Mullah Muḥammad Taqí Baraghání, her uncle. He was unequivocally for the status quo. In fact, as far as he was concerned, he *was* the status quo. He became an expert at issuing fatwas* that furthered his own financial gain. He expropriated properties, demanded high fees, invested avariciously, and became one of Iran's richest mullahs. One of his many ways of acquiring wealth was to charge for writing out his legal opinions; by law, he had to give fatwas orally, gratis, but written evidence was sometimes necessary. Most mujtahids supplied this type of writing for free, but Ṭáhirih's uncle often charged exorbitant amounts for it. He got into many disputes defending himself against accusations of taking bribes for his judgments, but his wealth increased. In his own opinion, he was Qazvin's most eminent religious leader, but he wasn't what he longed to be: he didn't hold the post of Friday Imam and control the Friday Mosque.[30]

Qazvin's Friday Mosque is especially large and impressive. While many Friday Mosques are entwined by the twisting byways of a bazaar, Qazvin's enjoys a sort of splendid isolation at the end of a long, wide approach that begins with a lofty ornamented gate and ends at a blue tiled grille giving glimpses of dome and minarets. From there, a narrower path leads into a grassy courtyard shaded with gigantic plane trees.[31] Uncle Taqí ardently fancied himself at the heart of that mosque, seated atop the steps of its pulpit, holding forth on Fridays beneath the high arabesques of its ancient dome.

Friday is ordained by the Prophet for congregational prayer, the Day of Gathering or Assembly. There is only one Qur'ánic verse referring to it, instructing believers that "When the call is proclaimed to prayer on Friday" they must "hasten earnestly to the Remembrance of God, and leave off business . . ." But a tradition quotes Muḥammad saying

* A fatwa is a ruling on a point of Islamic religious law (Amanat, *Resurrection and Renewal*, p. 418).

that when Friday comes, the angels stand at the door of the mosque noting all who enter and favoring, of course, the first-comers, and when the Friday Imam mounts his pulpit, the angels shut their registers and listen to him. The Friday sermon speaks for the religious authority of the nation and of Islam, and it is given before the prayer itself. This explains the original politicization of Friday assembly under the Sunni caliphate.[32]

Over the centuries, the Shiites rebelled against the tradition, considering "congregational Friday prayer . . . impermissible in the absence of the Imam of the Age." Even when Iran was a mostly Shiite nation and the mujtahids began their rise to power during the nineteenth century, some of them still said that Friday prayer had fallen into the hands of "usurpers" and was forbidden as long as the government was unjust—and that it would always be unjust until the Hidden Imam returned. The Shiites had never given godly power into the hands of their kings. Nevertheless, established religion really had no interest in the Return or Advent, and Friday Mosques flourished as lucrative properties that the Friday Imam controlled. In other words, a Friday Imam just about owned his city.[33]

The man who held the position in Qazvin had, with cruel irony, the same name as Ṭáhirih's uncle. Uncle Taqí tried fruitlessly to wrest the Friday pulpit from the other Taqí and finally issued a fatwa outlawing Friday prayer. It isn't known whether or not many people obeyed it, but perhaps he was seen by some as being very pious for doing it. However, when his rival was traveling, Uncle Taqí overruled his own fatwa, mounted the pulpit of the great mosque and led prayers. Apparently, he then kept the position of Friday Imam.[34]

Another person who made Uncle Taqí unhappy, yet seemed unconquerable, was his brother-in-law, 'Abdu'l-Vahhab, a mullah who was popular with his fellow clerics and the government even though he had a soft spot for mysticism and mystic sages. He was a friend to all. When the Baraghani brothers first came to Qazvin, he helped Uncle Taqí establish himself in the city.[35]

But Uncle Taqí was soon mired in disputes, even with 'Abdu'l-Vahhab, and then something happened to solidify his enmity. An acclaimed scholar who had mentored both Uncle Taqí and Ṭáhirih's father arrived in the city as a guest of 'Abdu'l-Vahhab. While there, the mentor praised Ṭáhirih's father as a mujtahid. This mention was equivalent to a license to practice (Islamic) law. Someone then asked if Uncle Taqí was a mujtahid. The teacher commended Uncle Taqí's knowledge. People assumed this meant Uncle Taqí also could be titled a mujtahid, and they went about saying so. 'Abdu'l-Vahhab—apparently no longer very tolerant of Uncle Taqí—heard the talk and publicly rebuked the man who had asked the original question. Public criticism is a huge affront in Iranian culture.[36] It insulted Uncle Taqí as well as the man who was rebuked. Uncle Taqí was enraged at the threat to his rank as a mujtahid, especially since he already stood on shaky ground due to his financial finagling.

The mentor then realized he'd better placate Uncle Taqí. He invited him to a special luncheon, wrote out a certificate affirming him as a mujtahid, went to the mosque with him, sat on the pulpit steps with him, praised him and titled him a mujtahid before the congregation. Yet Uncle Taqí wasn't assuaged.[37]

Nothing, it seemed, softened his heart. He simply coveted everything. The Prophet Muḥammad well knew the murderousness of envy and prayed for shelter from it:

> . . . I seek refuge
> With the Lord of the Dawn
>
> From the mischief
> Of created things;

From the mischief
Of Darkness as it overspreads;

From the mischief
Of those who practice
Secret arts:

And from the mischief
Of the envious one
As he practices envy.[38]

Of course, Uncle Taqí would have been furious if anyone had suggested that the Prophet prayed for protection against such as him. A chief trait of the envier is lack of self-awareness.* So, without considering the hypocrisy involved, when he heard that Shaykh Aḥmad was coming to Qazvin, he invited the sage to stay at his house. He knew that even in the shah's royal chambers, Shaykh Aḥmad was considered a saint. And Uncle Taqí had fallen deeply out of favor with the shah's powerful prime minister.[39] His image would be bolstered if Shaykh Aḥmad accepted his hospitality. However, the saint chose to stay with 'Abdu'l-Vahhab. This made sense because 'Abdu'l-Vahhab was the one who had invited him to the city. But Uncle Taqí didn't see it that way.

One thing that kept him insecure was the loose and improvised way in which the ulama organized (or didn't organize) themselves. They liked to keep their laws separate from the government's and they "simply did not see the need for a centralized corporate identity or for disturbing the delicate balance with the state upon which they continuously negotiated

---

* For a brilliant discussion of the effects of envy on the minds and hearts of its practitioners and victims alike, see the book *Cinderella and Her Sisters* by Ann and Barry Ulanov.

their power." They were always keeping each other, as well as the government, off balance. The government returned the compliment. "The state in turn preferred ambiguity" so it could continually negotiate anew with the ulama, jousting for power and influence in situations as they arose.[40] Uncle Taqí, like his fellows, would find himself one day on the outs with one set of clerics or one group of politicos; the next day, he would be in trouble with others.

In Qazvin, Shaykh Aḥmad became the leader of a flourishing study circle and soon established ties with Ṭáhirih's family; her youngest uncle, 'Alí, and her mother studied with him, and three of Shaykh Aḥmad's sons studied at her father's madrassa. In fact, Uncle 'Alí, a reclusive scholar who wrote prolifically, brilliantly defended the differences between Shaykhi and Sufi mysticism.[41]

So, for a time, the saint's sojourn in Qazvin was a success. When he prayed in the mosque, all the mullahs of the city prayed behind him, kneeling in rows, bowing when he bowed and rising when he rose. They paid formal calls to him at the home of his host, and he returned the courtesies.

Uncle Taqí couldn't countenance it. How could he bear to witness such honor shown to a man he considered a heretic and who based his authority on licenses conferred by the Imams in dreams, when his own authority had been publicly questioned? He knew it wouldn't take much to tip the balance against Shaykh Aḥmad. Other jealous mullahs already spread rumors about him, such as that he received land and money from royalty in exchange for "tickets to paradise."[42] One day in a public forum, Uncle Taqí led Shaykh Aḥmad to clearly state his conviction that on Resurrection Day the dead would rise in spirit, not physically. Then Uncle Taqí attacked, citing the Islamic dogma of bodily resurrection.

Shaykh Aḥmad took refuge in silence, and one of his pupils tried to change the subject, but Uncle Taqí had his weapon. He spread vicious rumors, and when Shaykh Aḥmad next went to the mosque to pray,

'Abdu'l-Vahhab was the only person with him. 'Abdu'l-Vahhab decided Shaykh Aḥmad should dissemble his beliefs and write a treatise affirming physical resurrection. Shaykh Aḥmad did so, in the veiled language he usually adopted for such feats, but no one paid any attention because Uncle Taqí continued fueling the rumor mill and issued a decree pronouncing the shaykh an unbeliever. The governor of the region, one of Iran's many princes, organized a banquet in an effort to reconcile Uncle Taqí and the saint.

At a traditional Persian dinner party, men sit on the floor around a long cloth. Fezzes, turbans, and all headgear remain in place, so everyone's stations in life are obvious. Scattered about the cloth on various receptacles are bread, white cheese, mint and other herbs, Persian pickles and relishes, radishes and scallions, grapes and melon slices. Serving men circulate with highly piled plates of pilaf, other foods, and drink. The poor are at the gate, having heard of the gathering and scented the cooking; Persian hospitality doesn't stop at invited guests; one must feed the town if it shows up on the threshold. Within the reception room's exclusive environs, however, seating is ordained by the host, and it's telling.[43]

The prince gave Shaykh Aḥmad the position of honor at his right hand and seated Uncle Taqí close by, only one person in between. Servants brought platters prepared for three people to share, so that Uncle Taqí and the saint would have to face each other and eat from the same plate. Silverware wasn't used, and plunging the fingers into food on a shared platter was a good way to instill intimacy. But Uncle Taqí ignored etiquette, turned to his right, and became a fourth in a trio of neighbors. He even went to the trouble of shielding the left side of his face with his left hand to block Shaykh Aḥmad from his sight. Naturally, it was a rather subdued meal.

But such feasts are called "conversations," or "assemblies," because they're meant for reconciliations. So the prince didn't give up. After the feast, he praised Shaykh Aḥmad as a wise man and said Uncle Taqí, also a wise man, should respect him. Uncle Taqí cried out that he was pious and that Shaykh Aḥmad was a heretic who opposed the doctrine of physical resurrection; therefore, there could never be peace between them. Despite the prince's repeated efforts, Uncle Taqí remained unyielding, and the dinner party dispersed disharmoniously into the night.[44]

Soon Uncle Taqí roused such hostility against Shaykh Aḥmad that the aged man was forced to leave the city. He went to Iraq, but some of the mullahs there denounced him to the Ottoman governor in Baghdad, and he returned to Arabia hoping to spend the rest of his days in Mecca. Before he reached his destination, he died in Medina and is buried close to the resting place of the Prophet.[45]

His successor continued to propagate his message and win adherents to it. This continuity and strength infuriated Uncle Taqí even before it magnetized Ṭáhirih into its sphere. Hatred of Shaykh Aḥmad would in the end be Uncle Taqí's nemesis, and, if we look at Ṭáhirih's life from the point of view of classic tragedy, Uncle Taqí, at last, was her nemesis. This was not, however, not because of hatred. It was because of love. Although fate took a crooked path through Shaykh Aḥmad's visit to Qazvin and Uncle Taqí's eventual, violent demise to bring about Ṭáhirih's murder, it was a route she herself chose and saw clearly. She knew, as all good romantics do, that true love is a calamity, and she gloried in the belief, as all good mystics do, that true love of the divine is the greatest calamity of all.

3

The Harp of Love and Pain

A love story. Poets and love. Love and insight. The education of a poet. Ṭáhirih's beauty. The veil. Some outspoken sisters. Solemnity and silence.

Two of Iran's most famous victims of love, that elevating and devastating passion, are Laylí and Majnún. A favorite version of their tale, which is a Middle Eastern legend predating Muḥammad, was written in Persian by the twelfth-century poet Nizami. The name *Majnún* means Madman, for the youth, torn from Laylí when her father refuses him her hand in marriage, is "enslaved by longing . . . a madman he became—but at the same time a poet, the harp of his love and of his pain."[1]

Historically, the figure of Majnún was based on the pre-Islamic Arabian poet, Prince Imru'al-Qays, who lived circa 500 AD. Expelled from his father's court for writing erotic love verses, Qays became a vagabond but then, caught in a game of political revenge, he was assassinated via an emperor's "gift": a poisoned cloak. He's considered the inventor of the *qasidah* (classical Arabic ode) with its conventions such as the poet weeping at the remains of his beloved's deserted campfire.

In the legend, Majnún, alone in the desert except for the wild animals he befriends and who become his guardians, sings his love for Laylí: "East wind, be gone early in the morning, caress her hair and whisper in her ear . . . Oh my beloved, had I not given my soul to you, trembling with desire like the wind, it would have been better to lose it . . . Yes I am a victim of the world's Evil Eye, which has stolen what was my own . . . People try to protect their children with blue amulets; even the sun, afraid of its darkness, wears a veil of pure sky-blue. But I was not protected by amulets, no veil covered my secret . . . that is why the world could rob me of it . . ."[2]

Majnún is a poet in the deepest sense, singing from his heart because he can't help it, just as the great Sufi dervish, Rumi, was "naturally an improvisator, pouring forth his thoughts as soon as they came to his lips." Rumi always wrote from the standpoint of ecstasy—called drunkenness by the Sufi poets—which was an intoxication born of contemplating God, not of opium or wine. Rumi's ecstasy was enkindled by his teacher, Shams i Tabriz, around whom his heart circled. Ṭáhirih had two such masters, and one of them called her "the Point of Ecstasy." From her ecstatic viewpoint, she wrote of Laylí and Majnún and their enviable victimization by the force that's been called the Eagle of Love,

. . . His every thieving glance
wrests wonders from the core of each
miraculous Majnún heart, pierces
Laylí's pavilion, tears her tent apart . . .[3]

Laylí's name means Night. Enfolded away from Majnún in the darkness of her father's refusal to let them marry, her moonlike face obscured by the wings of her night-black hair, she hears "her lover's voice . . . Was he not a poet? No tent curtain was woven so closely as to keep out his poems . . ." In the bazaars, children sing his verses and every passerby echoes them. Laylí, also a poet, memorizes her lover's songs, writes her replies on scraps of paper and gives them to the wind. Eventually they reach Majnún and their "two voices" are "so similar" that they sound "like a single chant." Their song, "born of pain and longing" has "the power to break the unhappiness of the world."[4]

Yet their own unhappiness grows. Laylí's father forces her to marry another man, and Majnún is consumed with grief, jealousy, and rage; finally an elderly messenger brings him a letter from Laylí: "True, I have a husband! A husband, but not a lover; for he has never shared my bed. Believe me . . . no one has yet touched the diamond; the treasure of love has remained sealed . . ."[5]

And although she knows of Majnún's agony, she envies him, telling their letter-bearer: "How I wish that I could be with him . . . But our sufferings are not alike . . . Majnún is free, walking over the mountain peaks where I cannot follow him out of my valley . . ." Laylí is "like a ruby enclosed in the heart of a stone . . ." Finally her husband, brokenhearted by her long refusal of him, dies, and she's a widow. Yet she isn't free to go her own way. She must "veil her face, seeing no one . . . for two years . . ."[6] She stays in her tent, mourning and lamenting, sad for the husband she made to suffer so severely, but sorrowing most profoundly for Majnún, able to fully express her grief for him behind the veil.

At last, her heart broken, dying, she instructs her mother to dress her like a bride for her burial. "As a salve for my eyes, take dust from Majnún's path. Prepare indigo from his sorrow, sprinkle the rose-water of his tears on my head and veil me in the scent of his grief. I want to be clad in a blood-red garment . . . Red is the color of the feast! . . . Then cover me in the veil of earth which I shall never lift again . . ."[7]

But Laylí predicts that Majnún will come and mourn at her grave, and asks her mother to have compassion on him. Soon he finds her grave and lies down there. The wild animals who have been his friends and guardians in the wilderness accompany him and keep away all who would approach him until he also dies. Even after that, they guard him until nothing remains of him but bone, strewn like pearls over the earth that hides Laylí.[8]

The transcendent moral of the fable is clear: for both Laylí and Majnún, the "veils of the satanic self". . . are "burned away at the fire of love." They "know no prudence," know of "neither faith nor blasphemy," have "no time for doubt or certainty." To them "both good and evil are the same" for they aren't good and they aren't evil, they are "living flame." True lovers can't be judged by the same standards with which we judge other people. They've leapt a boundary and inhabit another realm:

> If you could seek the unseen you would find
> Love's home, which is not reason or the mind . . .[9]

This story in many versions and ramifications was part of Ṭáhirih's literary and mystical world, as was the body of work by Iran's best-loved poet, Hafez, the fourteenth-century Sufi from the city of Shiraz who immortalized the city in his verse and made people look to it for beauty and hope. He was called the Sun of the Faith, the Praiseworthy, One who can recite the Qur'án from memory, the Tongue of the Hidden, and the Interpreter of Secrets. Iranians open his collected poetry to find personal auguries as frequently as they consult the Qur'án—possibly more frequently. Although Hafez wrote, "Behold, the world is as a shadow of a cloud and a dream of the night," he had his worldly side, saying, "The Garden of Paradise may be pleasant, but forget not the shade of the willow-tree and the fair margin of the fruitful field." And although he ignored his contemporary history, never writing about the forces that conquered Shiraz five or six times during his own life, opining, "It seems that fortune did not intend kings to be wise"—he was nevertheless a courtier, composing effusive panegyrics to each conqueror in turn. After all, poets, unless they were completely unworldly like Rumi or Ṭáhirih, depended on patronage to survive.[10]

However, it was Hafez who said, "I have estimated the effects of Reason upon Love and found that it is like that of a raindrop upon the ocean, which makes one little mark upon the water's face and disappears."[11]

For a long time, Ṭáhirih seemed to make her home in reason and the mind; one of her English translators notes that Ṭáhirih mostly wrote *ghazals* and also often employed the *kamil* meter* in a "very classical and difficult style, using rare Arabic phrases frequently . . . none of these phrases interrupts the spontaneous flow of her poetry . . ." So it would seem that her use of unusual phrases arose from joy in language and internalized fluency, not from a desire to mystify or impress. Another translator writes, "She shows herself in (her) verses to possess a rather amazing intellect—an almost other-worldly knowledge about some of the most esoteric and abstruse matters of theology, cosmology and ontology."[12]

A Pakistani professor stressed the "other-worldly" aspect. He thought "it was not necessary for her (Ṭáhirih) to practice, poetic verses were revealed to her," and she wrote "verses that are in no way inferior to those of . . . Rumi in impromptu-ness and simplicity, ecstasy and control . . ."[13]

---

* A ghazal has at least 5 couplets, each one autonomous from the others, but each line of the ghazal is the same length / meter. A refrain ends the second line of each couplet and rhymes with both lines of the first stanza; and the poet's pen-name usually appears in the last couplet. Currently, ghazal writing is a bit of a trend among English-speaking poets, but translating the flow and grace of a ghazal into English from Persian, Urdu, Arabic, etc. is extremely difficult. The kamil meter demands more complexity than a ghazal, with exacting rhyme and rhthym patterns, and is often used for didactic verse.

The Urdu poet Sabir Afaqi notes, "In my view . . . Ṭáhirih . . . was not like other poets who engage in thinking over their poems for hours and collect them into a book. Rather, she was a natural poet. Whenever her love for . . . God inspired her, she would express herself in songs . . ." He points out that Ṭáhirih lived in a time "of carnage, spoliation, and terror" and says that's why the people loved her songs and held them "close to their hearts." He went on, "In the poetry of Ṭáhirih there is light and thunder . . . and roar and flow, like that of a stream that comes down from uphill during the rainy season." He regards her as "the founder of a new cadence and inventor of a new mode of poetic expression" and feels that she should be thought of as "the founder of modern Persian poetry."[14]

Part of that modernity may come from the frustration she fearlessly expressed over the rigidity and corruption of established authorities; at one point she excoriated "the mosque (as) a shop dispensing holiness," envisioned "the tie of the (mullah's) turban* . . . cut at its source," and saw "tyranny's . . . fighting arm . . . broken" while "the garden carpet of justice unrolls . . ."[15]

Her propensity for ecstatic insight that pierced falsity probably became stronger and more dominant during the fruition of her faith in the final six years of her life, but from her earliest years it informed her intellect, which shone in everything she did and said. She was "regarded

---

* Clerics wore turbans in styles denoting their stations. The turbans were often affixed to their heads with chinstraps. They were very dramatic preachers and often physically demonstrated their rage against those they deemed heretics by tearing off their turbans and casting them on the ground. For example, Marzieh Gail writes, "In Persia, the mullahs mounted their pulpits and as a sign of their agitation, threw their turbans down on the ground, crying, 'O people! this Bahá'u'lláh is a sorcerer . . ." (Gail, *The Sheltering Branch*, p. 95). So Ṭáhirih may have been making a double allusion referring to a severing of their turban-ties.

from childhood, by her fellow-townsmen, as a prodigy . . . (and) highly esteemed even by the most haughty and learned ulamas of her country . . . for the brilliance and novelty of the views she propounded . . ." Driven by her impassioned inquiry into religious writing and thought, she wasn't prudent in expounding her views; she was unstoppable. Her brother, her father's destined successor, said, ". . . in a meeting where she sat neither I nor anyone else could say a word. It was as if all the former and future books were with her. She used to explain a subject by bringing forth demonstrations and proofs from the learned books, page by page, so that no one had the power to deny" . . . Because of her encyclopedic knowledge of "philosophy and science . . . those in her presence always considered and consulted her first."[16]

Custom dictated that girls bowed to the leadership of the men in their lives, including their brothers, especially older brothers, but Ṭáhirih was beyond such constraints. Her brother further explained, "None of us, her brothers or her cousins, dared to speak in her presence, her learning so intimidated us, and if we ventured to express some hypothesis upon a disputed point of doctrine, she demonstrated in such a clear, precise and conclusive manner that we were going astray, that we instantly withdrew confused."[17] Feminine tact, it would seem, wasn't part of her repertoire—the eagle of love left her no time for it.

Two biographers of Ṭáhirih write, ". . . early in her life, even as a child, Ṭáhirih had demonstrated an inherent capacity to decipher some of the most enigmatic passages from the Qur'án and various hadiths (traditions attributed to Muḥammad or his successors) regarding the imminent appearance of the Qá'im." The term *qá'im* means upright, and when it is used as a title, it can be interpreted to mean the one who will arise or the promised one of the previous revelator—in this case, the one prophesized by Muḥammad in sayings such as this: "He will arise to reveal the religion at the Day of the End, even as I arose at the Day of the End."[18]

Elsewhere we read, "In eloquence she was the calamity of the age and in ratiocination* the trouble of the world." Her father lamented, "Would that she had been a boy, for he would have shed illumination upon my household, and would have succeeded me." She'd shown her original genius from the time she was a child, kneeling or sitting cross-legged on the floor, her scripture text poised on her knee, yet her father couldn't envision her shedding illumination on his household, and would not flout custom so much that he'd allow her to succeed him in his duties as mujtahid.[19]

Nevertheless, in the women's wing of his madrassa, she learned Persian literature and poetry from her mother. Her father himself, along with her Uncle Taqí and two of her elder brothers, taught her Islamic jurisprudence and hadith. Two paternal cousins were her professors of philosophy, which included mystical and Gnostic thought. Her Persian and Arabic were impeccable, and she also spoke the Turkish popular in Qazvin and apparently sometimes wrote in Turkish; a book of her Turkish poetry was published in Azerbaijan in 1996. Like her mother, she became a teacher of women in Mullah Ṣáliḥ's school, and her younger sisters studied with her.[20]

In those days, printing presses revolutionized information exchange in Europe but hadn't yet found their way to Iran, so the texts Ṭáhirih and her sisters used were copied, colored, and bound by many different hands. Some were scrolls, and some were in book form with tooled leather, embroidered cloth, marbled cardboard, or delicately lacquered covers.

Pages were made of parchment, silk, or gazelle hide, and inks were compounded of dyes and sealants with ingredients kept jealously secret

---

* Reasoning leading to discovery of the cause or rationale of an Islamic ruling or injunction.

by individual calligraphers who used reed, bone, or quill pens that sang, shrilled, or crooned when they were set to the living faces of handmade papers to form letters in many styles: squared, priestly Kufic; lyrical waterfalls of Shikeste; functional, informal Nashki; arcane, entwined Thuluth; joyously dancing Ta'liq; and many more, including Taus script with letters in the forms of birds, surely delightful for child scholars.

Such manuscripts included marginal notes and parallel writings by poets, mystics, and philosophers that circled the main text like so many bees. Serious students copied classic texts word for word, memorizing them, internalizing them, to become able to recite them spontaneously and to mirror, echo, and answer them in their own writings. For Iranians, whose language was, to steal a phrase from A. J. Arberry, a "mesmeric eloquence," the study of poetry was as important as the study of the Qur'án and, anyway, the Qur'án itself is poetry, for Arabic is a rhyming tongue, as is Persian, which is one reason they are so memorizable.[21]

Ṭáhirih excelled in her grasp of Persian and Arabic literature and literary expression. In Islam, writing is the most revered art, extolled in the Qur'án in the first revelation received by Muḥammad:

Proclaim! And thy Lord
Is Most Bountiful,—

He Who taught
(The use of) the Pen,

Taught man that
Which he knew not . . .[22]

Iranians are devoted to verbal music—rhyme, rhythm, alliteration—and they justifiably rate their own language very highly. A tenth-century Persian text claims, "Persian has been understood from antiquity, from the time of Adam . . ." According to A. J. Arberry, "It is poetry that has preserved the Persian language," and Elaine Sciolino writes, "Indeed, if poetry is a connection with the beautiful and the magical, it also is . . . a means of survival. Wherever I travel in Iran, I hear poetry recited. Iranians are famous for their ability to memorize the Koran (sic) and Koranic recitation contests are popular and highly regarded by the clerics. But I often feel that if it were to be a contest between Koranic recitations in Arabic and poetry recitations in Persian, the poetry recitations would win out . . ."[23]

Of course there is some controversy. Muḥammad was scared that He was going insane when He first heard the voice of God on Mount Hiraa, terrified that He would end up wandering the desert like a deluded poet. However, the Qur'án later expressed approval of those poets who are not deluded, but "who have faith in God and do good deeds."[24]

Nizami delineated the qualities of an ideal poet: ". . . Tender of temperament, profound in thought, sound in genius, clear of vision, a powerful thinker, subtle of insight . . . well versed in many divers sciences, quick to extract what is best from his environment, of pleasing conversation in social gatherings, of cheerful countenance on festive occasions . . ." He said that "in the prime of his life and the season of his youth" the poet must memorize "20,000 couplets of poetry of the Ancients, keep in view 10,000 of the Moderns" and constantly read and remember "the divans* of the masters of his art . . . that . . . the fashion and varieties of verse may become engrained in his nature, and the defects and beauties of poetry may be inscribed on the tablet of his understanding."[25]

Even as a young girl, Ṭáhirih fulfilled his requirements, including his dictum that a poet's verse must be "written on the page of time and celebrated on the lips and tongues of the noble and be such that they

---

* Collected body of work of a single poet.

transcribe it in books and recite it in cities." It seems that her earliest poetry lamented the sufferings of the imams; if so, this shows the influence of her father, who frequently wrote such elegies.[26]

We are also told, "In addition to her virtues and knowledge, she was . . . a paragon of beauty." But, for both men and women, autobiographical and biographical writing in nineteenth-century Iran was very limited. A woman's looks, especially, wouldn't be specifically described. So we're left to wonder just what "paragon of beauty" meant in Ṭáhirih's case. The traditional rendering of beauty in old Persian illuminations is of moonfaced maidens and youths looking insipidly identical with immobile rosebud mouths, doe eyes, and little pointed fingers. Black hair and eyes were the ideal; blonde hair wasn't admired in nineteenth-century Iran, nor were blue eyes. A certain dark daringness gave the glamor that Iranians call *namak*, after a black salt. One researcher has said that Ṭáhirih's "long hair reached to her knees" and one assumes it was the desired midnight black.[27]

Her most authoritative biographer called her "a sign and token of surpassing beauty," and she'd held him in her arms when he was a four-year-old in his mother's andarun, so he actually saw her, yet his words are deep and evoke much more than mere physical charm as remembered by a person whose lifelong propensity was to look beyond appearances into people's hearts. He also noted that she loved to eat and had a sweet tooth, often helping herself to a dish of nuts and dried fruits. As an elderly sage, he told a lady who apologized for having a prodigious appetite, "Virtue and excellence consist in true faith in God, not in having a small or a large appetite for food. . . . Jináb-i-(Her Excellency) Ṭáhirih had a good appetite. When asked concerning it, she would answer, 'It is recorded in the Holy Traditions that one of the attributes of the people of paradise is partaking of food continually.'" Thus we see an example of her ready humor. People who knew Ṭáhirih also recalled that she loved fine fabrics and fragrances.[28]

But if the old Persian policies of veiled, generic description mandated that the specifics of Ṭáhirih's beauty remained undisclosed, her scholarly and mystical attainments and insights were solidly apparent, and, until her beliefs became too radical for him, her father never stopped her from expressing them, nor did he stop the circulation of her essays and poetry. But, according to custom, from the age of nine she was hidden from public view, her body swathed by the chador, her face by a veil.[29] When she spoke in her father's assemblies—and a female teacher who addressed men was rare, but not unheard-of—she did so from behind a curtain.

The word *chador* can be translated as *tent,* and it's a capacious garment made of two pieces of cloth sewn together. Some nineteenth-century chadors had ties fashioned to hold the garment in place atop the head, others had ties around the neck, and others were simply held in place by one of the wearer's hands, hidden under the chin. It was quite a balancing act to keep a chador in place, but since women were accustomed to it from childhood they could do it gracefully, and Western observers have commented on their lithe, light way of walking.

Lower class women usually wore blue cotton chadors; the middle class used dark chadors that were either cotton or silk. The upper class, to which Ṭáhirih belonged, wore black or dark blue silk chadors that sometimes had bands of gold thread woven into them. The face veil—cotton or silk—was fastened over the chador. Ṭáhirih's was most likely made of silk. One type had a slit for the eyes or a woven grid of drawn or counted threadwork, and it fastened in the back with a jewel or, in simpler cases, a knot. Another type, even more uncompromising, was made of black horsehair; and there were also face veils of black crepe, semitransparent over the eyes. Under the chador, women tucked their clothing into voluminous black outdoor trousers with sock-boots sewn onto them.

Within the andarun, women of means could indulge their taste for finery, wearing wide trousers or full skirts with brief chemises bright with embroidered motifs in sequins and gold and silver yarn. They also wore ornate, richly colored, fitted jackets, and long, jeweled belts and scarves tied around the waist. The wealthy indulged in many gems.

However, even when indoors, women usually wore head coverings, mostly scarves fastened beneath the chin, but sometimes a skullcap or snood. They frequently wore lightweight indoor chadors, including a light colored one especially for prayer.[30]

They loved cosmetics, lining their eyes with kohl, which had beneficial medicinal effects, brightening their complexions with rouge and whitening their skin with well-advertised concoctions. Women let their hair grow very long and often braided it into many plaits; they adorned hands and feet with henna, saffron and cyprus; both men and women had a great love of perfumes and used attar of roses, sandalwood, jasmine oil, ambergris, the smoke of aloe wood, and other substances to scent themselves and their garments.[31]

Outside their andaruns, women could only gather in their area of the mosque or in the public bath. All the women of a household flocked to the bathhouse weekly, accompanied by servants bearing their soaps, henna, perfumes, lotions and shampoos, along with tea, bread, pastries and fruit. They stayed for hours, taking steam baths and cool baths, being massaged by attendants, snacking and chatting. Older women appraised the looks and deportment of younger ones with an eye toward arranging their marriages. The tiled bathhouse walls echoed with their laughter and singing, and this, along with the drones and ululations of their prayers in the mosques, was about the only time women could raise their voices outside their own chambers.[32]

In nineteenth century Iran, not only were a woman's face and figure considered too seductively dangerous to be seen, but her voice was also an invitation to perdition. The philosopher Ghazali said it was wrong for a man not related to a woman to listen to her pounding food with a pestle, and "If he knocks at the door (and) . . . the woman has to answer the knock, she should stick her finger in her mouth so that her voice sounds like the voice of an old woman."[33]

We assume that Ṭáhirih did not suck her thumb (so to speak) when she sat behind a curtain or screen in "her father's and uncle's classes in the same room with two or three hundred (male) students, and . . . more than once . . . refuted the explanation that these two elderly men offered upon such and such a question."[34]

Could that uncle have been Mullah Taqí? Her more reticent uncle, 'Alí, perhaps didn't teach in large venues. If it was Mullah Taqí, that means that, to some extent, he vicariously enjoyed Ṭáhirih's reputation as a prodigy and the bit of progressive gloss it gave him. At least she was behind a curtain, observing propriety according to the Qur'án. This was the institution of *hijab*, initiated by the Prophet. He said,

> And when ye
> Ask (his ladies)
> For anything ye want,
> Ask them from before
> A screen: that makes
> For greater purity for
> Your hearts and for theirs . . .[35]

However, the teaching uncle mentioned above could have been her mother's brother, 'Abdu'l-Vahhab, to whom Mullah Taqí was bitterly opposed. At any rate, hijab didn't hold Ṭáhirih back and she was also unhindered by the prevalent superstition that a literate woman risked becoming a crazy woman.[36] This superstition existed in the western world, also, as we shall see.

But Ṭáhirih's fame as a scholar and poet wasn't unprecedented in Islam, especially among mystics. Ṭáhirih's contemporary Bibi Hayati has already been mentioned. Another contemporary was Mastura Ardalan, a noblewoman of Kurdistan. She was a poet, the only female historian in the Middle East until the end of the nineteenth century, and the author of various works, including a brief account of certain Islamic doctrine. Recently a statue of her was unveiled in Iraqi Kurdistan.[37]

Nana Asma'u, a Sufi woman of Nigeria, was another theological writer and leader. At a young age, Asma'u memorized the Qur'án. Then, during a civil war, she and her family became wanderers, carrying very few possessions with them but always preserving their library, which consisted of hundreds of manuscripts that were constantly being repaired because, although the handwritten pages were kept in goatskin bags, the parchment was quick to disintegrate. Asma'u became a renowned teacher dedicated to justice, the education of women, and peace; she wrote didactic poetry and corresponded with Muslim scholars in parts of Africa far from Nigeria.[38] Ṭáhirih may not have known of this African sister nor been acquainted with Hayati or Ardalan, but she later met and become intimate friends with several other female poets.

Their foremother was the eighth-century Sufi saint Rabi'a Basri, whose stern asceticism and ecstatic poetry set the pattern for future Sufi geniuses, including Rumi. Rabi'a had been a slave; she was freed by her master after he saw a great white light around her while she prayed in the dark of night. People believed that her presence conferred blessings (instead, it is assumed, of threatening temptation and a fall from grace) because "When a woman walks in the way of God like a man she cannot be called a woman." And, "Although she was a woman, in character she was so constant of heart that she was manifestly superior to many men."[39]

Women of today might consider the above statements backhanded praise, but until recently, a modern, aspiring female took pride in being told she thought like a man. In Ṭáhirih's time, such praise was the highest honor for a learned woman, and because of Ṭáhirih's genius and ecstatic insight, it was also accorded to her. As we've heard Laylí lament, even poor Majnún was to be envied because, as a man, he had the freedom of the mountain peaks.

So certain women of Islam and other traditions have always arrogated so-called male freedom for themselves because their spirits demand nothing less, since "spiritual experience and 'spirit' (in the sense of an animating courage) seem to go together." The first woman to be a Muslim, Muḥammad's first wife, Khadíjih, showed these qualities. She comforted Him after His first experience of revelation, when He thought He was losing His mind, telling Him that His "was no dream or delusion," and confirming Him: ". . . there's no God but He and thou art His Chosen Apostle." Khadíjih was a successful merchant, older than Muḥammad, who chose Him to be her husband "when he had no worldly resources . . . trusted him when his worth was little known . . . encouraged and understood him in his spiritual struggles" when He would ponder problems "harder and more cross-grained than the red granite of the rock around him—problems not his own, but his people's, yea, and of human destiny . . ."[40]

Khadíjíh was the mother of Fatima, Muḥammad's favorite child and the person He admitted He loved most in the world. Fatima was a spinner; she would work until her hands bled, but she alternated days of spinning with days of study, and when she spun, she allowed her servant girl to study. She was said to resemble Muḥammad, move and talk like Him, and was called the Resplendent One because of her radiant face. She had great, elevating eloquence that caused her listeners to weep with recognition of eternal truths, and when Muḥammad died, she delivered His eulogy. She also championed the right of her husband, 'Alí, to lead the Muslim community when He Himself at first ceded to the will of his fellow believers who set up the caliphate.[41]

The first Muslim martyr was a woman, too. She was the seventh person in the world to believe in Muḥammad, and although she was elderly, she was brutally killed by an Arab clan leader who opposed the Prophet. Another great early Muslim was a woman soldier of whom Muḥammad said, "Never did I look right or left but she was there defending me and fighting before me." And in the days of Muḥammad, a woman named Rufaidah, one of the first in Medina to become a Muslim, nursed the sick in a tent outside the Medina mosque and led volunteers to battlefields to treat the wounded.[42]

Yet in nineteenth-century Iran the ideal of a beautiful woman was veiled and "'Sangin o Samet' (solemn and silent)." Even in the twentieth century, a modernist Iranian writer made the romantic interest of his novel *The Blind Owl* a girl who does not speak once through the entire book, while her "demonical double" is always talking. Not that the veil is onerous in itself. It's a sign of faith and can serve as protection, which is why the Prophet told his wives to wear it after one of them was threatened. And the custom of veiling predated Islam in Iran and other parts of the world; it indicated royalty, aristocracy or sainthood, and it wasn't limited to women. Kings went veiled at times—but some said that was to hide the fact that they were drunk.[43]

Desert people used wraps over heads and faces to guard themselves from sun and sand, and men and women used veils, and the lack of veils, for dramatic effect. In the 1300s in southern Iran, a queen exposed her face to save her three sons from execution. The king had been deposed, and as she and her sons were marched, captives, through the streets of Shiraz, she lifted her veil and begged the masses to remember her husband and all his good works. The people fought her guards to release her and the princes, and drove the new government into exile. Her lifted veil was sign of her humility before them, as if she was saying she was their slave and at their mercy.[44]

It was the right of free women to wear a veil, but a veiled slave could be punished; a slave was not to aspire to a veil. Slavery was entrenched in ancient societies. The Qur'án didn't forbid it but endeavored to make it more humane. Muḥammad prohibited masters from prostituting slaves. Moreover, slaveowners were encouraged to free their slaves or allow them to work to ransom themselves. The first muezzin, or issuer of the call to prayer, was Bilal, an African slave freed by Muḥammad.[45]

The Prophet didn't name either gender or any class of people as being superior; He said, "Oh mankind! We created you from a single (pair) . . . a male and a female . . . and made you into nations and tribes, that ye may know each other (not that ye may despise each other). Verily the most honored of you in the sight of God is (he who is) the most righteous of you . . ." By advocating modest garb for every one of His female believers regardless of status, Muḥammad was promoting the equality and elevating the dignity of all women; and in the same breath, He instructed male believers to dress modestly and lower their eyes before women.[46]

However, a worldwide Islamic dress code never really came into effect and doesn't exist today. Islamic women dress differently according to their nationalities and heritages. There are various theories of just when the chador became common in Iran, but "there is little doubt about a tradition of female seclusion in pre-Islamic Iran" so that "although from the beginning Iranians rejected some elements of the invading Islamic culture, veiling and the beliefs associated with it seemed not to have provoked much—if any—cultural resistance."[47]

In fact, the greatest veils have always been *sansur* (censorship) and ta'arof. Men as well as women have to employ these behavioral veils of conformity and etiquette at all times. It's dangerous not to. Even the transcendently transparent Rumi advised keeping one's *self* a secret. And a modern Iranian poet wrote, "They sniff at your mouth / Lest you'd said 'I love you.'"[48]

Best to keep that mouth veiled. Actually, for men as well as women, veiling may be the best disguise. If a man goes so far that a smile and a gift wouldn't help him, he can flee from justice in that handiest of disguises, the all-encompassing chador and face veil, as male fugitives do in the twentieth-century novel *Savashun*, Iran's all-time bestselling novel—which is written by a woman.

When the passion plays about the Imam Ḥusayn were presented for mixed groups, women couldn't act in them, so men took women's parts, and the veil hid beards, mustaches, and hairy hands. The veiled male would also attempt to change his voice to a feminine tone and his gait to a feminine walk. However, these efforts were usually in vain, for the chador can't hide the way a person moves and speaks. Factors such as a woman's approximate age and state of health can usually be read even if she's fully veiled.

Various Islamic writers have pointed out that it isn't the veil that makes a woman pious; rather, it is the other way around. If a woman wants to be seductive, the veil won't stop her. On the other hand, Azar Nafisi wrote wonderfully of how her grandmother's use of the chador manifested chaste self-abnegation—"The shy withdrawal of my grandmother, whose every gesture begged and commanded the beholder to ignore her, to bypass her and leave her alone. All through my childhood and early youth, my grandmother's chador had a special meaning to me. It was a shelter, a world apart from the rest of the world. I remember the way she wrapped her chador around her body and the way she walked around her yard when the pomegranates were in bloom . . ."[49]

This grandmother was the ideal of solemnity and silence: true (invisible) beauty. And Ṭáhirih's obligation was to be beautiful (invisible) above all things. So, despite her erudition and eloquence, the veil and marriage at a young age to her first cousin was her lot. The bottom-line for her life-script was prudence and adherence to social mores that would preserve her family's honor, reputation, and wealth. It is said of the seeker that his "Love setteth a world aflame at every turn . . . The wise wield no command within his realm . . ."[50] But in Ṭáhirih's life, in her formative years, the worldly-wise wielded all command.

4

Drums of Ceremony

Socializing and philosophizing. Dawn prayer, Ramadan, and the drums of devotion. Muharram and the fascination of weeping. Naw-Rúz.

Though she had to follow a prudent script, Ṭáhirih's girlhood no doubt had its joys. She was a born poet, and her life was replete with things to delight a poet's heart. Qazvin had its charming gardens and stunning mountain vistas, its songbirds and snowfalls, its cold winters when families gathered around their *korsis* (in-floor stoves banked with quilts), and then the blessed *ba'arans*, the warm spring rains when fruit trees burst into bloom.

Daily life was rich with ceremony, each day punctuated five times with the call to prayer and its attendant rite. Visiting in the women's quarters was also a daily rite, with everyone immersed in the tea-taking and kalyan-smoking* of it, the ta'arof of it, and the entertainment of role-playings, jockeyings for position, stories of disasters, scandals, all

* Hubble-bubble pipe or hookah; women as well as men indulged.

the comedies and tragedies of existence. Also, vendors came to the andarun selling everything from brocades, silks and attar of roses to muslin and water jars, and there was the complex business of bargaining for the best prices.[1]

For a mind as studious, independent, and alive as Ṭáhirih's, there was always the joy of knowledge—seeking time and space alone to study and ponder, conquering a theme, then discovering a new one and delving into it while her poetic intelligence and imagination reveled in the metaphors, sonorous word music and metaphysics that coursed through her Persian and Arabic texts. Each year would roll by, marked with holidays, feasts, and festivals occurring according to the seasons, the lunar and solar calendars, and the astrologers' calculations of what was auspicious and what was not. Astrology had played a defining role in Persian life ever since Zoroastrian times; one remembers the star guiding the Three Magi (Zoroastrian priests) to Bethlehem.[2]

The travel writer Christiane Bird observed that "there certainly is fun in Persia." Part of that fun comes from a characteristic other Iranians shared with Ṭáhirih, even if they lacked her originality. "The most striking feature of the Persians as a nation is their passion for metaphysical speculation," wrote the nineteenth-century orientalist E. G. Browne, "This passion, so far from being confined to the learned classes, permeates all ranks, and manifests itself in the shopkeeper and the muleteer, as well as the scholar and the man of letters."[3]

Then, of course, there is the fun of parading and dancing in the streets for various reasons, picnicking, and horseback riding—all of which were enjoyed more by boys than girls, although women did participate in the equestrian game of polo when it originated in Persia in the sixth century. Iran has long been known for its fine breeds of horses, and its women through the ages could become equestrians, what with the prevailing rural culture and the many and diverse nomadic tribes. However, women were not welcome in the *zurkanehs*, "houses of strength" that had their heyday in the nineteenth century with men seeking spiritual as well as physical well-being while doing gymnastics to the beat of drums and the rhythmic chanting of poetry. In general, women's lot was far more solemn than men's, especially since a boy became a man at fifteen but a girl was a woman at nine. She could be married at that age. She could be made to live with her husband if she had entered puberty, and even if she hadn't, her husband could take her if her father let him.[4]

Ṭáhirih was sent to live with her husband when she was thirteen or fourteen. At age nine, she would have been obliged to don the veil, rise for dawn prayers, and fast during Ramadan.* But, given her appetite for spiritual search, it was likely that she'd already fasted and had the habit of dawn prayer. From childhood, she may have observed her mother praying in the andarun and may have imitated and joined her.

One memoirist described this, from her own upbringing: "Before sunrise Mother rose to prepare for the morning devotions. First she washed her face, then her right arm, then her left. Next she bowed her head and washed the part in her hair, then her right foot and leg, followed by her left. Over each part of her body she passed the water from the copper bowl, three times. Cleansed, she put a white band around her head entirely covering her hair. Finally she put on her semicircular white veil and pinned it under her chin . . ."[5]

Just before sunrise, the Call to Prayer rings out from the minarets. The prayer between dawn and sunrise is the first of the Muslim's five

---

* "Ramadan is the (month) in which was sent down the Qur'án, as a guide to mankind, also clear (Signs) for guidance and judgment (between right and wrong). So every one of you who is present (at his home) during that month should spend it in fasting . . ." (The Holy Qur'án, 2:185).

obligatory prayers of the day. Turning westward to the navel of the world, the Kaaba in Mecca,* the worshipper greets the morning by chanting, "God is great." She bows down and recites the first chapter of the Qur'án praising the "Master of the Day of Judgment" asking for guidance upon "the straight way." She chants a verse of her own choice from the Qur'án, bows and repeats "God is great, glory to the Greatest Lord." Standing upright she says, "God hears the one who praises him. Our Lord, all praise belongs to you."

Then she kneels on her prayer rug, hands flat on the ground, forehead to the ground. She may rest her brow on a prayer stone from the plain of Karbala, where Ḥusayn met his martyrdom. The prayer stone is a pale octagonal briquette about three inches wide containing inscriptions of the names of the twelve Imams. It has a sweet smell. She says three times, "Glory to the Lord Most High!" and "God is Most Great!"[6]

Sitting back on her heels she says, "Oh God, forgive me and show me mercy. God is great!" Prostrating herself she says, "Glory to the Lord Most High. " She'll then repeat the entire cycle, and, kneeling, recite the profession of faith, ask blessings upon Muḥammad and Abraham, and finish with an invocation, turning her head to the right and to the left, saying, "May the peace, mercy, and blessings of God be upon you."[7] If fellow believers are present, this can be addressed to them. Or it may simply be said to the recording angels hovering at the worshipper's shoulders, for according to Islam, those two angels are with us always.†

---

* Mecca is the birthplace of Muḥammad. At its heart is the cube-shaped temple called the Kaaba, which has existed since before the days of Abraham. Muḥammad's clan had the hereditary guardianship of the Kaaba (*The Oxford History of Islam*, p. 6).

† "It was We Who created man, and We know what dark suggestions his soul makes to him: for We are nearer to him than (his jugular vein). Behold,

The obligatory prayer, with variations in the number of cycles, is repeated four more times at stated periods of the day in answer to the muezzins' call from the minarets of the mosques, a chant that sends the swallows flying from the turrets, black against the sky like calligraphic script, like the very letters of the Qur'án. In Ṭáhirih's day, before clocks, newspapers, radios and cell phones, the call and the prayer ritualized the day and kept track of time. There were no hours—only dawn, morning, noon, twilight, night. Pounding kettledrums summoned people to hear a government mandate or an important fatwa or told them of portentous, perhaps calamitous, events. Kettledrums still announce sunrise and sunset in some parts of Iran, and they're beaten at shrines when a sick pilgrim is healed. Iran has its own native drums and rhythms, its own pulsing cantatas and librettos for its festivals, passion plays, weddings, good-byes. Thus, a prevalence of drum imagery exists in Persian poetry, as in these verses by Rumi, which speak of "the din of parting" and begin,

> Up, O ye lovers, and away! 'Tis time to leave the world for aye.
> Hark, loud and clear from heaven the drum of parting calls—let
> none delay!

And when Ṭáhirih, in verse, refers to love, the calamity camped at the gate of her heart, it is to the accompaniment of "drums of devotion."[8]

At the age of nine, Ṭáhirih probably heard the sunrise drum on the first day of Ramadan and was already immersed in prayer, having recited the special Ramadan prayer when the crescent moon appeared in the sky. Then she would follow the Prophet's mandate to abstain

---

two (guardian angels) appointed to learn (his doings) learn (and note them), one sitting on the right and one on the left. Not a word does he utter but there is a sentinel by him, ready to note it . . ." (The Holy Qur'án, Sura 50:16–18).

from food and drink from the very hint of day's beginning—as it says in the Qur'án, when the white thread of dawn appears, distinct from its black thread—until nightfall.

During the fasting season, Ṭáhirih's family might have had a special all-night gathering on the Night of Power, a time of mystery, guidance, and inspiration commemorating the anniversary of the revelation of the first verses of the Qur'án to Muḥammad; the only way to know its significance, it seems, is to keep it. The Qur'án says:

> The Night of Power
> Is better than
> A thousand Months.
>
> Therein come down
> The angels and the Spirit
> By God's permission,
> On every errand:
>
> Peace! . . . This
> Until the rise of Morn![9]

Also, women host their own evening religious gatherings, led by a female mullah, during Ramadan—and at other times as well. Perhaps Ṭáhirih's mother or other women in her family did that.

Frequently the story of the martyrdom of Ḥusayn would be recited, and everyone would be required to weep. As an autobiographer says, "One must be born a Persian to understand the fascination of weeping." Also, apparently, one must be born an Iraqi. The anthropologist Elizabeth Fernea tells of going to a *kraya* (women's religious gathering) during Ramadan in the 1950s in a Shiite village in Iraq: "The mullah . . . began retelling the story of the killing and betrayal of the martyr Hussein (sic) . . . At first two or three sobs could be heard, then perhaps twenty women had covered their heads with their abayahs (chadors) and were weeping; in a few minutes the whole crowd was crying and sobbing loudly. When the mullah reached the most tragic parts of the story, she would stop and lead the congregation in a group chant, which started low and increased in volume until it reached the pitch of a full-fledged wail . . ." Fernea was "frozen by the intensity of it all" but when the ceremony ended, the women immediately began "smiling and chattering," cheerily "bidding each other good night." Other observers have also been impressed by the swift recovery of Ḥusayn's mourners.[10]

The sobs are part of the rite. When Muharram comes with its days of grief for the Imam Ḥusayn, everyone dresses in black, preferably tear-stained. Ḥusayn is the primary figure of sacrifice for Shiite Muslims, but Iranians also feel he's one of them through his marriage to an Iranian princess, daughter of the king of their last Zoroastrian dynasty.

She is Shahr-bánú, said to be the ancestress of nine of the Imams. According to certain histories, she was captured during the Arabian conquest, brought to Medina, and married to Ḥusayn, who called her the Gazelle. Their descendents combine the heritage of the family of Muḥammad and of ancient Persian royalty, thus linking the Imams descended from her to Iran in a special way. There's a mountain a few miles south of Tehran dedicated to Shahr-bánú, and women go there to pray when they're in special need; men aren't allowed. She's also always the heroine of one of the Muharram passion plays.[11]

Ḥusayn was the son of Muḥammad's daughter Fatima and the first Imam, 'Alí. When the time came for Ḥusayn to take over the contested leadership of the Islamic world and assume the title of Imam, he was promised support in the town of Karbala. He began to journey there, but those who promised to help him betrayed him, and after a hard battle during which he saw his companions and family die one by one of wounds or wrenching thirst, he was slaughtered by the forces of the caliphate.[12]

For nine days, and on the actual anniversary of his death, the tenth day of Muharram, called Ashura, droves of men march through the streets rhythmically chanting and castigating themselves. Nowadays the castigation is supposed to be done in a symbolic way, but in Ṭáhirih's time, the men bled as they lashed their bare chests with whips and chains and beat themselves with stones, their leader staggering before them with hooks and pins stuck in his bleeding flesh, howling, "Oh, Ḥusayn, most great, most honored, we grieve for thee!" while the mass of men behind him wailed, "Oh, Ḥusayn!"

The men's backs turned black with blood as their bare feet on the hard-packed dust beat a counter-rhythm to chant, lash, and thud. "Oh, Ḥusayn, most betrayed, we mourn for thee!" Men fainted from exhaustion, pain, and loss of blood, but others marched on shouting, "Oh, Ḥusayn!" and men lining the streets joined in clamorously, "Oh, Ḥusayn, our beloved martyr, we grieve for thee!" On the rooftops, bodies pressed together side-by-side, the black-swathed women opened mouths hidden by face veils and shrilled high-pitched ululations, "Oh, Ḥusayn!"[13]

Ḥusayn's death was also commemorated by *ta'ziyeh*, a cycle of passion plays put on in every town, city, and village, involving every soul, it seemed, in the country with productions that included real horses and battle reenactments. In the late 1960s, the director Peter Brook attended a ta'ziyeh and reported, "I saw in a remote Iranian village one of the strongest things I have ever seen in theater: a group of 400 villagers, the entire population of the place, sitting under the tree and passing from roars of laughter to outright sobbing—although they knew perfectly well the end of the story—as they saw Hussein in danger of being killed, and then fooling his enemies, and then being martyred. And when he was martyred, the theater form became truth."[14]

During Ṭáhirih's time, these plays gained greatly in importance and splendor as royalty built special theaters and arenas for them and enthusiastically condoned them. Thoroughly veiled women attended these productions, ululating and crying out. But a princess during the time of Fatḥ 'Alí S͟háh (the shah during Ṭáhirih's childhood and youth) used to produce passion plays acted by women, for women, in her own quarters; any males needed were required to be blind, or eunuchs, or boys under a certain age. Other women in the country followed suit. Like all directors of ta'zihyehs, the princess stayed on stage throughout, instructing musicians and actors. She had her walking stick, and if a performer didn't show the requisite emotion, she'd cane her face to make her cry. [15]

It seems this insistence on ritualized grief is an effort to inoculate the self against pain, the pain of the saint's martyrdom and much more—all the wounds and losses of life. In the novel *Savashun*, named for the ancient mourning ceremony for a legendary prince to which the rites for Ḥusayn are linked, the heroine's husband is assassinated and she muses, ". . . what was the word for the shouting that comes from the pit of your stomach? It was a word that fits this kind of shouting. It must be a word that means piercing. That is, if one is unable to shout that way when faced with a flood, a thunderbolt, or one of fate's blows, one's heart will be pierced."[16]

Perhaps weariness with the insistence on linking the heart with pain is why Ṭáhirih, known for her inner radiance, refused to mourn for Ḥusayn when she was in her thirties and had found her calling—but more of that later.[17] Suffice to say that the pain of ecstasy was her métier and that she was noted for her joy; then perhaps she particularly rejoiced as a child in Naw-Rúz, the New Year, a Zoroastrian holiday that emigrated into Iranian Islam.

The echo of Zoroastrianism remains strong in Iran; it was the faith of the great Persian Empire, and Mary Boyce deems it "the oldest of the revealed creedal religions," saying that it "has probably had more influences on mankind, directly and indirectly, than any other single faith." Its prophet, Zoroaster, taught "the threefold ethic of good thought, word and act." Naw-Rúz, coming at the spring equinox, is the holiest Zoroastrian festival. An ancient text describes it: "There once lived a king who in his sovereign rule did as he pleased and had fair fortune . . . How joyous was the festival which he celebrated in the spring! All the illustrious were there . . . the king seated among the nobles like the moon among stars . . . The wine-filled cup passed among them, . . . blossoms scattered from the trees like coins showered upon the fortunate . . . To one side minstrels sang to the wine, to the other nightingales sang to the rose . . . Joyous as was the king's celebration, others were no less so . . . Each had left his house for the fields, carrying with him the means for enjoyment. From every garden and meadow and stream different kinds of song could be heard . . . Each set a crown of wild tulips on his head, each had the glowing ember of wine in his hand. One group had pleasure in racing their horses, another in listening to music and in dancing . . . All had gone out to make merry, they turned the earth's surface into a bright brocade."[18]

Of course Ṭáhirih's father and mother, both being pious mullahs, forbade wine, and it's impossible to imagine Mullah Ṣáliḥ cavorting with a crown of wild tulips on his head. Some orthodox Muslims went so far as to eschew Naw-Rúz altogether, but hopefully Ṭáhirih's family at least celebrated moderately, setting out their copy of the Qur'án alongside a volume of poetry by Hafez; just as Iranian Christian families set out their Bibles, and Jewish families their Torahs.

On the first night of the festival, perhaps the child Ṭáhirih helped arrange the symbolic foods, the *haft-seen* (seven foods with names that start with the s-sound of the letter "seen") on a special plate. *Haft* means seven, and there are many great sevens in Persian lore, among them the seven valleys through which a seeker journeys yearning for her mystic

Beloved; the stages of the universe's birth—sky, water, earth, plants, animals, humans, fire; the seven heavens; seven planets; seven seas; seven earths; seven partitions of hell; seven climates; seven tunics (layers or coatings) of the eye; seven parts of the body that touch the ground in prostration during worship; seven watery letters in the Persian alphabet; seven fiery letters; seven earthy letters; and seven airy letters.

Thus, the seven foods on the Naw-Rúz plate. They include a green herb for life, vinegar for age and patience, dried lotus fruit for love, garlic for medicine, an apple for beauty and health, sumac berries for the color of sunrise, hyacinths for spring, a sweet wheat pudding for prosperity—and to heighten the sweet taste her family might have served the famous rice cookies made in Qazvin.[19]

After the feast on the first night of Naw-Rúz come days full of visits and sweets until the thirteenth day, the grand finale, when it's bad luck to stay indoors, so everyone goes out to picnic,* preferably near a rivulet or creek. The flat dish adorned with gaily colored ribbons and full of psychedelically bright wheat grass grown for the holiday must be taken to flowing water and cast away, now that it has absorbed all impurities and sorrows from last year. The Naw-Rúz goldfish must also be released into the stream from their glass bowl.

If Ṭáhirih as a child partook of this custom, she probably saw kingfishers flashing brightly above the stream and narcissi lean over the water, admiring themselves. At that brightest season of the year the desert around Qazvin blooms with a triumphant springtime landscape of sweet-scented white wild tulips, prolific yellow tulips, tiny red and purple poppies and scarlet ranunculas, fragrant yellow squills, and Persian iris growing in pairs, one greenish-white, one bluish-white, all vivid in the light described by Vita Sackville-West as "a living thing,

* Persians invented the picnic, and the word came into English from Persian (Bird, *Neither East nor West*, p. 112).

as varied as the human temperament and as hard to capture; now lowering, now gray, now sensuous, now tender; but whatever the mood may be, it is superimposed on a basis always grand, always austere, never sentimental. The bones and architecture of the country are there, whatever light and color may sweep across them, a soft thing passing over a hard thing . . . Some complain that it is bleak; surely the rich and changing light removes such reproach. The light, and the space, and the color that sweeps in waves, like a blush over a proud and sensitive face . . ."[20]

Of course the gardens—"gardens of trees, not of flowers; green wildernesses"—are places "of spiritual reprieve . . . (places) of shadows. The plains are lonely, the garden inhabited . . . by hoopoes, crying 'Who? who?' among the branches; by lizards rustling like dry leaves . . ."[21] At Naw-Rúz time, the tree gardens bloom, crowned with the magenta flowers of judas trees, pink peach blossoms, and abundant roses.

For Iranians, their native roses are a gift very much identified with the living essence of their land, so of course roses are particularly treasured at Naw-Rúz. "In no country of the world does the rose grow in such perfection as in Persia; in no country is it so cultivated and prized by the natives," one traveler enthused, and another described roses ". . . in five colors: white, yellow, red, Spanish rose, and poppy red. Also there are 'two-faced' roses which are red on one side and yellow on the other. Certain rose bushes bear yellow, yellow-white, and yellow-red roses on the same plant." In fact, the general name for flower, *gul*, is the name for rose. Donald Wilbur says, "Many a Persian could call himself a *gulbaz*, flower lover or rosarian. Rose fragrance escapes the garden in quantities of rosewater . . . pressed from the double pink rose . . . and . . . kept in distinctive spouted vessels of blown glass and it was the custom to sprinkle guests with rose water . . . Rose preserves were much favored . . . concentrated rose water still flavors a variety of desserts, including sherbets and pastries." It's likely that the famous

Qazvin rice cookies, mentioned above as an addition to the *haft seen* plate, are flavored with rose water.[22]

In Ṭáhirih's time, by the thirteenth day of Naw-Rúz grasses and wild flowers sprouted from the mud walls and roofs of her city, and perhaps they still do—streets, even the grand mosques, all were green and blooming, scattering petals and fragrance on every breeze. The streets were also enlivened by Zoroastrian celebrants of Naw-Rúz, troubadours in makeup and bright satin costumes, and people jumping over bonfires shouting, "Give me your beautiful red color and take back my sickly pallor."[23]

Of course, the heart and soul of the festival was springtime itself. Sa'adí wrote, "God has told the chamberlain of the wafting breeze to spread an emerald green carpet and has ordered the nourisher of the spring clouds to bring to fruition the daughters of the plants in the cradle of the earth. God has had the trees put on their New Year's robes, a green-leaved clothing, and has put on the heads of the children of the branches the hat of blossoms . . ."[24]

Such were the festivals, ceremonies, and seasons that pervaded Ṭáhirih's childhood. But the looming rites were the celebration of her marriage contract and then the wedding itself. This would take her from her mother's prayer-filled, fragrant rooms, the shelter "cool like the inside of an earthen jar (with) niches in the white-washed walls of the rooms, where she set her lamp, and kept her books, wrapped up in a hand-blocked cotton cloth."[25] She would, without hesitation, abandon this shelter when her spiritual quest and her mission to impart her knowledge demanded it, but it's doubtful that she considered marriage to the son of her redoubtable uncle as likely to fulfill either of those purposes.

5

Ideal Couple, Opportune Marriage, Irresistible Moon

A marriage made in heaven. Trouble in paradise. The Atabat. Ṭáhirih's children. Progressive revelation. Claiming her path.

It seems the union between Ṭáhirih and her cousin was arranged from her earliest days. Her parents and other relatives would have repeated the old Islamic saying, "the marriage of first cousins was ordained by heaven," knowing that with such a union all property and heirs stayed within the family. Marriage, as viewed in Ṭáhirih's Iran, was nothing if not politically and financially pragmatic, a civil law contract between families, as are all Islamic marriages.[1]

Marriage for romantic reasons was ridiculed, and neither the prospective bride nor the groom were consulted about whether they did or didn't want to be married to each other. They obeyed their parents, and "the higher the status of the girl's family, the greater the degree of the family's intervention in the choice of a partner, because marriage was a means of promoting and preserving the economic wealth, authority, and prestige of all members." Besides, as a Western physician in Iran during the nineteenth century remarked, "An undutiful son or daughter is hardly known in the country . . ." And although the family's oldest male wielded absolute authority, the physician went on, "no act of serious import is ever undertaken without the advice of the mother; no man would think, for instance, of marrying contrary to his mother's advice; and by the very poorest the support of their parents would never be looked on as a burden."[2]

Even the king wouldn't sit down in his mother's presence without first receiving her consent. Everyone knew, "Paradise is at the feet of mothers." So, "in matters relating to marriage, the mother and other women played a greater role than did men. Because of seclusion and the veil, a man in search of a wife had to rely on his female relatives for information about his prospective partner. Because a bride lived in her husband's household, the women of his family took a great interest in the choice."[3]

There were cases where the bride and groom never laid eyes on each other before their wedding night, but for Ṭáhirih and her cousin, Mullah Muḥammad Baraghání, that was an unlikely scenario. Since their families were so close, Ṭáhirih probably saw her future groom when she was a little girl, and if he were near her age, perhaps they learned Qur'án together when they were very small. This actually could have allowed a bit of romantic expectation for both of them, for one or the other of them—or for neither of them!

Given her oldest brother's comments about Ṭáhirih's forthright and convincing expressions of her knowledge and theories, the cousin to whom she was betrothed was probably as awed by her genius as were her other relatives. Perhaps he resented her for it. Perhaps he was transfixed by her beauty, or by rumors of it. Perhaps he hoped marriage and childbearing would tame her. Perhaps he planned to follow the advice in a famous treatise on the management of wives and "allow his wife no musical instruments, no visiting out of doors, no listening to men's stories, nor any intercourse with women noted for such practices . . ." At least he would have expected her to follow the rules for wives which included looking contented and considering "their husbands' dignity—obey husbands and don't be recalcitrant . . . (or) disturb them with captious comments." He would have imagined that she would bend her will to his in all things, for a woman of her class was not even to leave her house without the permission of her husband.[4]

Perhaps, like many other grooms, he was a middle-aged man, while Ṭáhirih was a girl. We can find no indication of his age. He could have been near her age—the cozy relationship and affluence of their two families might have meant that he didn't have to wait to marry until he'd amassed sufficient bridewealth to pay her father. But it's likely that he was older, for his own father was nearing eighty and had married his first wife perhaps forty years before the time of Ṭáhirih's wedding.

Bridewealth was often viewed by Western observers as a purchase price paid to a bride's father for the right to wed her, but in fact it belonged to the bride herself. While she was a maiden, she was entirely the ward of her father, possessionless even in a wealthy family. But when she married, she was entitled to her inheritance, including income from resources and investments, and to her bridewealth—in fact, "bridewealth provided even the poorest woman an important asset if she became divorced or widowed. It also acted as a safeguard against divorce because a husband could not divorce his wife without its full payment." Another source of security for a woman was that her sons, and daughters, too, were bound to look after her in widowhood and old age.[5]

Considering that husbands might be much older than their wives, widowhood could come early, and because brides went to live with their husbands when they were as young as nine and perhaps bore a first child at the age of ten or eleven, the ills of aging could come fairly soon, depending on circumstances. A parallel note: although many self-righteous European male visitors to Islamic countries took great pains to disparage Islamic marriage customs and the veil, in the Christian West women often veiled for various reasons, and the age for consensual sex according to the Napoleonic Code was between ten and twelve. This didn't change until the end of the nineteenth century. Child prostitution was rampant, and without either the legality or sanctity of marriage, girls could be used by men who went unpunished. Also, when a woman in the West married, she became completely disenfranchised, ceding title to anything she might happen to own or inherit to her husband.[6]

By contrast, Ṭáhirih's marriage contract, which most likely would have been drawn up by a mullah—in her case, perhaps, her own father, who certainly would have guarded her interests—fixed her bridewealth, her right to all her assets, and could grant her the right to divorce if her husband took another wife, for "under Islamic law only the man has the absolute right to divorce and a woman's right to appeal for divorce is restricted."[7] Ideally, an Islamic marriage contract must be accepted by both bride and groom or by their proxies in a ceremony that seals lengthy negotiations between their families.

If the marriage contract ceremony for Ṭáhirih and her cousin followed the usual program, it occurred during the day in her family home. Customarily, the groom gave the bride her wedding shoes, fabric for her wedding dress, head-covering and other garb, and a large mirror with two big candles and their candleholders. The women of her household prepared two rooms for the festivities, one for men and one for women, and they sewed her bridal gown and veil. On the portentous day, the bride was bathed in hot and cold waters, massaged with various unguents, and perfumed, with her hair elaborately coiffed. Female family and friends plucked her facial hair, made up her face, dressed her, and adorned her with jewels.[8]

Traditionally, in the men's chamber, with women listening in from behind curtains, the two officiating mullahs (perhaps Ṭáhirih's and her groom's fathers?) dictated the terms of the marriage contract, and scribes wrote them down. The contract detailed every bit of property the bride brought to the marriage, right down to the ritual Qur'án and length of sewing silk; in the case of divorce, everything had to be restored to her. The groom had to say yes to the terms of the contract, and, from her curtained alcove, the bride had to do the same. She was assumed to be too shy and coy to answer for herself—few children wouldn't be—so, after a mullah asked several times and was answered with virginal silence, the women answered for her in hearty chorus. (We can have no idea if this was the scenario in Ṭáhirih's case; no accounts of her life cast her as being shy, but there is also no suggestion that she was enthused about the marriage.) Then the mullah sealed the contract, writing traditional words in the wax with a red copper pen.

In the women's room, kalyans, tea, sweets, and rice pilaf heaped on silver trays went the rounds. Perhaps, as was the custom, the women held a white cloth over Ṭáhirih's head and grated two sugar cones onto it, to ensure that her married life would be sweet; and maybe they sewed two pieces of cloth together to ensure that her mother-in-law would, to put it bluntly, keep her mouth shut.

Ṭáhirih's was a religious family, so, although the groom was her cousin, he wouldn't have been allowed to see her once she'd donned the veil, and even after the marriage contract was signed, he wouldn't see her until the actual *arusi*, the wedding, which was another huge party.[9]

The dates for Ṭáhirih's wedding are given between 1828 and 1831. If it followed custom, she spent a day being specially cleansed and groomed with henna applied to hands and feet. Beauties of Ṭáhirih's era often wore their long black hair with bangs cut across the brow, side curls against the cheeks, and numerous long braids flowing down behind. Their make-up was extremely elaborate: ". . . the face almost, it seemed, enameled, the dark brows joined, or with a vertical dark line between. The mouth, for beauty, had to be small, virtually invisible, the poets liked to say, and it was not emphasized. It was a rose unopened, the poets said; or in laughter, a rose blossoming. And there might be a beauty spot beside it—likened by poets to many things, such as the grain in the trap for the bird of a man's heart . . ."[10] As may be imagined, then, Ṭáhirih's style differed greatly from the Western concept of beauty.

If Ṭáhirih's arusi was as lavish as that of most upper class women's, she was heavily adorned, including the gems that were part of her property, from head to foot. The day before the wedding, if the dictates of custom ruled, the domestic furnishings that were part of her trousseau had been sent to her husband's house to furnish a nuptial room, along with gifts of clothing to him from her family. On her wedding morning, she walked or rode to his house accompanied by relatives, friends and musicians, but neither of her parents went along. The groom, also bejeweled and dressed in his best, and probably with henna on his hands and feet, came out to greet her, and his relatives also met her with gifts, such as deeds to property. Before crossing his threshold she threw a fistful of uncooked rice to bring good luck to girls who weren't yet married.

At this point in a traditional Persian marriage, the festivities began. Guests poured in all day with fulsome complements and, men in their room, women in the nuptial chamber with the bride, consumed sherbet, tea and sweets. Kalyans made endless rounds as Rom and Jewish musicians played and dancers danced. Several heavy meals were served, and the leftovers went to the poor gathered at the gate. As night fell, the poor also received alms. After a dinner that always included a sweet rice pilaf, the groom's father led him into the nuptial chamber, placed the bride's hand in the groom's and said, "I entrust him to you."

The couple was left alone with the night and each other. They had to consummate their union. She had to prove her virginity, and he his virility. Until they did, they were not completely bound. The bride couldn't return to her parents' house for forty days, to give her time to become accustomed to marriage; when she did come home, they had another grand celebration. She was wed. She'd vindicated and buttressed family, clan, and tribal honor.[11]

When Ṭáhirih married, her family, already covered with propriety and prosperity, could now rejoice that their daughter known as Zarrin Taj, Golden Crown, had made the perfect match. But any hope that Ṭáhirih would take refuge in solemn silence and submission to her husband, or at least the appearance of it, because of her duty to family honor and image, must have soon dwindled. Despite the fact that some other women in her family and society were educated, "her education and knowledge were most unusual among women of her time in Iran," and the combination of her erudition and eloquence with her innate fearlessness wouldn't allow her to be contained or confined.[12]

If, as some sources say, she went to Karbala with her husband shortly after the marriage so he could attend the study circle of a noted teacher there, her near relatives didn't have consistent opportunity to try to advise her, or to attempt to mediate what is thought to have been a troubled union from the start. These sources say the couple lived in a home in Karbala that was owned by their family, and for some years Ṭáhirih furthered her knowledge of Arabic and other Islamic disciplines in the shrine cities where her father and uncles had studied. If this is true, she could have attended the study circles in Karbala led by Shaykh Aḥmad's successor, for he taught women as well as men, and that would have aggravated the discord between her and her husband, who shared his father's hatred of Shaykhis and, also like his father, despotically held onto and wielded the lash of orthodox power in a society that was rebelling against it, so that chaos threatened both individual and collective psyches.[13]

In Iraq, then a province of the Ottoman Empire, Turkish (Sunni) control was wavering. In some cities, Persian (Shiite) control was stronger. Karbala was in Iraq's Shiite holy land, along with the cities of Kufa and Najaf and the town of Kazimayn. This region is called the Atabat (the Thresholds), because of all the venerated shrines within it.[14]

Kufa, on the Euphrates, is the place where the Imam 'Alí was killed, stabbed by a poisoned dagger. His house is located there, and so is the mosque where he was assassinated. Legend has it that the mosque stood on a biblical site where Abraham prayed and that Noah had lived in the vicinity; in the nineteenth century, an ancient carpentry tool hanging from the roof of the sanctuary was said to have been Noah's.[15]

But 'Alí's tomb-shrine is in Najaf. The dome of the mosque in Najaf shines with 7,777 gold bricks, and all the Imams' names are carved in the ceiling along with a poem praising 'Alí, whose mausoleum has a gate with two gold minarets and gold and silver doors; it's a square room of crystal walls covered with Qur'ánic inscriptions. The sanctuary contains a Qur'án copied by 'Alí himself, a rice grain reportedly inscribed with the text of the entire Qur'án, and a raft of jewel and gold-encrusted treasures.[16]

This for a man who slept on a skin on the ground, sat in the dark so as not to waste candles provided by the State at the expense of the people, and prayed, "How . . . can Ali lie (down) to rest, if there be yet a soul who suffereth injustice in any Muslim land?" Actually, his remains might not be in Kufa at all. Some traditions say they're in Afghanistan. Be that as it may, the cemetery of Najaf is one of the biggest in the world; Shiites travel there to die because they believe their souls are blessed if they can be buried near 'Alí, "Prince of Believers," the first Imam, "Guardian of God. . . . Interpreter of the Faith . . . Commander of the Faithful."[17]

Karbala, the city that promised to support 'Alí's son Ḥusayn but then betrayed him, has a gold-domed mosque housing Ḥusayn's immense silver catafalque. There's also a gold-domed tomb for his brother Abbas. The mosque has a huge courtyard and a wing for mullahs and students. Karbala's cemetery is another vast one. 'Alí is the most revered Imam, and he is also sacred to Sunnis as the fourth and last of the rightly-guided caliphs, but if a Shiite dies near any Imam's shrine, he believes he'll be attended at his last breaths by the Imam's spirit. If "he" is a "she," Fatima will also comfort her as she dies. The soul then doesn't go alone to meet its God; it's accompanied by saints.[18]

On a nineteenth-century map of Iran, the holy Shiite cities line up a few hundred miles from the Iranian border, with Karbala closest to Baghdad. Within Karbala's city wall, in too little space, the population burgeoned during the annual pilgrimage to Ḥusayn's tomb. Householders made money lodging pilgrims, each dwelling packing in upwards of one hundred people. Pilgrims who couldn't afford room and board jammed the courtyards of mosques or slept on the streets, which were impassable.[19]

During the 1830s and 40s in Karbala, a sage named Siyyid Káẓim-i-Ras͟htí led the S͟hayk͟hi movement. As a youth, guided by a dream, he'd made his way from his home in northern Iran, on the shores of the Caspian Sea, far south to S͟hayk͟h Aḥmad's side in Yazd, where he became his leading disciple. Appointed to create a teaching center in Karbala, he did so, his age and influence ever growing. Ṭáhirih's husband was probably linked to a virulently busy foe of the S͟hayk͟his, a mullah named Ibrahim, who also came from Qazvín.[20] Perhaps it isn't a coincidence that Ṭáhirih had a son named Ibrahim. Perhaps her husband insisted on it.

Uncle Taqí vehemently, constantly sermonized and wrote against the S͟hayk͟his. It seems Ṭáhirih's father sometimes agreed with him, but although he also had a reputation as an enemy of the S͟hayk͟his, at heart he was more peaceable.[21] He and his wife Amina chose a cousin from Amina's side of the family to marry Marḍíyyih, the sister who was closest to Ṭáhirih. That side of the family symphathized with the Shaykhis. But they also owned impressive properties, including two commanding mosques that Uncle Taqí had always coveted. Perhaps Mullah Ṣáliḥ hoped his older brother would be assuaged by a link with their wealth. If that was his strategy, it didn't work.

Meanwhile, 'Alí, the youngest Baraghani brother, encouraged his niece Ṭáhirih's connection with Siyyid Káẓim. All sources agree that by 1841–42, she was in Qazvín, was corresponding with Siyyid Káẓim and not hiding her discipleship to him, braving brutally direct, sometimes physically violent confrontations with her father, husband, and father-in-law.[22] She couldn't resist what she found in Siyyid Káẓim: the moon of millennial thought that pulled the restless tide of the times in which her fated moment glittered.

Ṭáhirih was at that point the mother of two sons, Ibrahim and Ismá'íl, both of whom were well past the age of two. In fact, they were approaching adolescence by then, so their father had absolute custody of them, and they were under his tutelage, but one historian wrote that "unusually she (Ṭáhirih) is even listed among the teachers of her sons" in her father's madrassa. She also had a daughter, named as Zaynah in one source, Ásíyih (Sara) in another. A birthdate is available for the daughter: 1837. Some mention a third son, Isháq, born in the early 1840s when Ṭáhirih's marriage was crumbling. By that time, Siyyid Káẓim had conferred upon her the accolade Qurratu'l-'Ayn and had, most likely, licensed her as a mujtahid, something her own father wouldn't do. One historian notes, "In Shi'i Islam, many families of religious scholars are known by the name of a famous ancestor . . . It is . . . testimony to her (Ṭáhirih's) prodigious abilities that, despite her heresy, her sons are called (after her) Al Qurrat al-Ayn . . . in one Shi'i biographical dictionary."[23]

We see here her tie to her children, and theirs to her; however, she had an overpowering sense of mission transcending motherhood, self-importance, and self-preservation. She was very different from her mother, who apparently feared her husband and his older brother and wouldn't mention Shaykh Aḥmad or his teachings in their presence. What Ṭáhirih learned of Shaykhi teachings from sources that included books lent from the library of a maternal cousin convinced her that Siyyid Káẓim had the guidance she craved.[24]

Her cousin, Javád Valiyani, had been afraid to lend her the books, saying her father would kill him. She had insisted, "For a long time now, I have thirsted after this; I have yearned for these explanations, these inner truths. Give me whatever you have of these books. Never mind if it angers my father."[25]

We can't be certain when she found the books. Was it before her marriage, and did she go to the Atabat with her husband ready to attend Siyyid Káẓim's study circles? Whatever the case, we know that from Qazvín, she corresponded with Siyyid Káẓim "regarding the solution of complex theological problems" and was exhilarated by the answers she received.[26]

Siyyid Káẓim was the author of over 135 texts. In them, he elucidated the radical idea of progressive revelation: ". . . how religion and religious laws have to follow the progressive maturity of humanity . . . He stated that humans at each stage of their development had a divine law revealed to them, a law that fitted their condition and time best. From Abraham to Jesus, each revelation superseded and abrogated the preceding one, until Muhammad's prophecy."[27]

He suggested "that the Muslim revelation corresponded to the time of the child's (i.e., humanity's) birth into the world, whereas all the previous ones corresponded to the stages of the child's growth in its mother's womb. As the newly born infant was still delicate in constitution, its nutritive diet was restricted to light, easily digestible meals. 'Holy law and moral principles,' he wrote, 'are the nourishment of the spirit.' It is, therefore, imperative that the laws be diverse; 'sometimes earlier commands have to be cancelled,' so that the child grows naturally in strength and ability.'"[28] He countenanced the idea of abrogating the old religious laws, implying that a new revelation was needed to teach humanity as it matured.

Progressive revelation was radical and heretical according to the ulama, unless it stopped with the revelation of Muḥammad. They would accept various revelations up to His time, although they didn't follow Muḥammad's pleas for tolerance and, as a consequence, didn't have much use for Christians, Jews, or other non-Islamic religionists. But certain Islamic philosophers had taught the idea of cycles, that "commands in this world have to change according to times and climes through abrogation." Muḥammad was also clear about progressive revelation in the Qur'án:

> God has revealed
> From time to time
> The most beautiful Message
> In the form of a Book
> Consistent with itself,
> (Yet) repeating (its teaching
> In various aspects):
> The skins of those who
> Fear their Lord tremble
> Thereat: then their skins
> And their hearts do soften
> To the celebration of
> God's praises. Such is
> The guidance of God . . .
> He also said:
> Say: "We believe
> In God, and in what

Has been revealed to us
And what was revealed
To Abraham, Ismail,
Isaac, Jacob, and the Tribes,
And in (the Books)
Given to Moses,
Jesus,
And the Prophets,
From their Lord:
We make no distinction
Between one and another
Among them, and to God do we
Bow our will."[29]

He followed this with a warning that "if anyone desires a religion other than Islam (submission to God), never will it be accepted of him . . ." The orthodox interpreted this to mean there could be no revelation after Muḥammad's. But Abdullah Yusuf Ali, the devout twentieth-century translator of the currently most-used English version of the Qur'án, commented, "The Muslim position is clear. The Muslim does not claim to have a religion peculiar to himself. Islam is not a sect or an ethnic religion. In its view all Religion is one, for the Truth is one. It was the religion preached by all the earlier Prophets. It was the truth taught by all the inspired Books. In essence it amounts to a consciousness of the Will and Plan of God and a joyful submission to that Will and Plan . . ."[30]

For ecstasy-intoxicated seekers like Ṭáhirih, immersed in that joyful submission, there was no possibility of the book of revelation ever closing. Divine revelation and sustenance was everlasting and ever-renewing, for the Creator was all bountiful, and, being creative, must always create; revelation could not progress unless it were so.

In 1838, followers of Siyyid Káẓim, knowing his messianic expectations, had asked for further explanation when he talked about progressive revelation, but he merely said, "Verily, I have announced to you the news of him who is now with me, news of him who was before me." By "him who was before me" he meant Shaykh Aḥmad, but what of "him who is now with me"? The new Messenger, the Promised One. Was it one of them, his students? Was it he, himself?[31]

By the early 1840s, he was more direct, anticipating revolutionary tumult with the Advent. In a meditation addressed to the mysterious, expected Messenger, he said, "I am apprehensive of the people, lest they harm you. I am apprehensive of my own self, lest I too may hurt you. I fear you, tremble at your authority. I dread the age in which you live . . ."[32]

He told his disciples that the Mahdi wouldn't come from the two mythic cities where it was said the Hidden Imam lived. On the contrary, "You behold Him with your own eyes and yet recognize Him not! . . . He is of noble lineage. He is a descendent of the Prophet of God, of the family of Háshim. He is young in age, and is possessed of innate knowledge. His learning is derived, not from the teachings of Shaykh Aḥmad, but from God. My knowledge is but a drop compared with the immensity of His knowledge; my attainments a speck of dust in the face of the wonders of His grace and power. Nay, immeasurable is the difference. He is of medium height, abstains from smoking, and is of extreme devoutness and piety."[33]

He lamented the blindness of most of his students. He said, "I am spellbound by the vision . . . I am powerless to divulge the mystery, and find the people incapable of bearing its weight . . ."[34]

Ṭáhirih was among the handful of disciples who could see as he saw, hear what he heard, and it was explosive within her. Even as a young girl, she must have similarly interpreted Muḥammad's utterances in the Qur'án concerning the sustained nature of revelation; that would have been one reason why, even in extreme youth, she could explain so clearly the references to the Qá'im, the Promised One. And all through her growing up, her father, despite his conservatism, had been her ally, sustaining her studies, admiring her brilliance and giving her opportunities to use it. As the pivotal year 1844 approached, she ecstatically tried to open his eyes and ears to what she perceived as a new chapter in the book of progressive revelation. Her father was enraged.

By this time, she had left her husband and was living in her father's house. Judging from later events, it would seem that she and her husband were separated but not yet divorced. One evening, she went to her father in his library and started talking about Shaykhism. Strangely, Mullah Ṣáliḥ was furious that she even knew about Shaykh Aḥmad, which leads one to wonder what he expected after the brouhaha raised by her uncle against the old sage, her mother's adherence to him, and all her own forays into mystical studies. Did her father think that his opinions with which he'd bombarded her, along with the tradition of veiling and the submission required by marriage and motherhood, would combine to act upon her genius like blinders on a horse, blocking out anything he didn't want her to know? It seems his authority and power made him the one who might as well have been wearing blinders. He blamed her cousin, Mullah Javád, the lender of the books. "Javád has made you a lost soul!" he bellowed.[35]

"The late Shaykh was a true scholar of God," Ṭáhirih answered, "and I have learned an infinity of spiritual truths from reading his book(s). Furthermore, he bases whatever he says on the traditions of the Holy Imams. You call yourself a mystic knower and a man of God, you consider my respected uncle to be a scholar as well, and most pious—and yet in neither of you do I find a trace of those qualities!"[36]

She didn't give up there. Days and weeks passed and she and her father debated about the Resurrection, the Night Journey, the Advent of the Promised One, and other questions. He droned the requisite

Usuli positions; she tried to open a door to an imminent drumbeat that she felt pounding, about to change and challenge the very heart of the world. When he couldn't best her in argument, he resorted to curses and abuse. One night, to support an argument, Ṭáhirih quoted the Sixth Imam,* and her father guffawed and ridiculed it. But the Sixth Imam was one for whom he'd always professed great reverence.

"Oh my father, these are the words of the Holy Imam, how can you mock them?" Ṭáhirih lamented.[37] With that, she stopped debating with him. She must have clearly seen the implications: the traditions she'd quoted were the prophecies about the youth from Muḥammad's lineage who would usher in the Advent, and they clearly stated that most of the youth's enemies would be the mullahs.

She devoted herself to her correspondence with Siyyid Káẓim. She urgently felt she must go to him in Karbala. Her uncle 'Alí and her cousin Javád were no doubt reporting to her on his doings. Siyyid Káẓim had become much more direct in talking about the Promised One, telling his disciples, "It is incumbent upon you to renounce all comfort, all earthly possessions and kindred, in your quest of Him who is the Desire of your hearts and of mine. Scatter far and wide, detach yourselves from all earthly things, and humbly and prayerfully beseech your Lord to sustain and guide you . . . Persevere until the time when He, who is your true Guide and Master, will graciously aid you and enable you to recognise Him. . . ." Like Shaykh Aḥmad, he foretold the imminent advent of not one, but two divine revelators. "For soon after the first trumpet-blast . . . there shall be sounded again yet another call . . ."[38]

* The Sixth Imam, Ṣádiq, made various prophecies regarding the coming of the Promised One.

In 1843, with the help of her uncle 'Alí, Ṭáhirih arranged to depart from her parents, her husband, and sons and go to Karbala accompanied by her sister and brother-in-law,* both of whom believed as she did, and her small daughter. So, from the very beginning, she risked her life for her beliefs. The murder of a female "who had the misfortune of dishonoring her family in any way, was considered legitimate and rightful," and her husband very likely thought that she was dishonoring him.[39]

On the other hand, her ever-vigilant father probably managed to cast a veil of propriety over her actions. Islamic law provides for separation between husband and wife, and, regarding her travels, she could be seen as making a pilgrimage to the Atabat with her relatives. Her uncle 'Alí could have arranged for her to receive her father's permission for such a journey, and perhaps her father hoped that time spent praying and meditating in the shrines of the Imams would change her thinking.[40] She would return a dutiful daughter, wife, and mother.

But she knew that she was journeying toward transformation. She also knew that, according to law, her sons were the concern of her husband—in fact, so was her daughter, but perhaps he had little interest in the girl. She also knew that her extended family in Qazvin had a hand in rearing her boys. More than anything, she knew her own burning, thirsting soul. Nothing could stop her.

A man, feeling such a sense of destiny, would be free to go. The poet Attar said that "a woman on the path of God becomes a man . . ."[41] So Ṭáhirih, claiming her path, claimed her right to freedom of action and full equality.

---

* The husband of her sister Marḍíyyih was named Mírzá Muḥammad-'Alí Qazvíní; he was the son of that Mullah 'Abdu'l-Vahháb whom Ṭáhirih's uncle so hated (Momen, "Usuli, Akhbari, Shaykhi, Bábí," p. 322).

6

1844, Iraq

Absence and presence. Siyyid Káẓim's farewell. Mullah Ḥusayn's leadership. Shiraz, City of Love. The pilgrim from Shiraz. Ṭáhirih's leadership. The pact of "Yes, alas."

We don't know if there was a traditional farewell ceremony when Ṭáhirih left for Karbala at the end of 1843. Perhaps her brother-in-law's family, the Shaykhi sympathizers, made sure to bestow the blessing of departure and the protective medallions on her and her party. Perhaps the travelers contemplated the tray holding the Qur'án, a flower and a bowl of water. Perhaps Ṭáhirih caressed the flower, a symbol of beauty; kissed the Qur'án, a gift of God, the Source of all beauty; and prayed while a kinswoman spilled water, a symbol of life, from a bowl and murmured, "God keep you . . . God return you to us . . . You are never alone . . . Our prayers go with you."[1] And perhaps the drums of departure beat, echoing the eagerness of Ṭáhirih's heart.

Whatever the exact circumstances of her leave-taking, the rift in her family would never be repaired. One memoirist wrote, "In Iran your place becomes empty when you leave and stays empty as long as you are away."[2] Absence is considered as physical as presence. We can only guess what Ṭáhirih's absence meant to her parents, for despite their violent disagreements, her father's love for her and desire to protect her were to be tried and proved over and over again, and as for her mother, whose spiritual feelings and hopes may have been akin to Ṭáhirih's, the voice of the heart, as a Persian poet might say, is silenced by grief. We must remember, too, that Ṭáhirih's sister went the same route as her older sibling. Sketchy records show that some communication continued between Ṭáhirih and her sons and that she maintained contact with her mother and corresponded with her father, whose network of watchful fellow mullahs in the Atabat can't be underestimated.

But her joy at being on her way no doubt overrode family concerns and complications, and she seems to have anticipated revolutionary spiritual possibilities, especially for women. She said to her sponsor, her uncle 'Alí, before taking leave of him, "Oh, when will the day come on which new laws are revealed on earth? I'll be the first to follow the new teachings and give my life for my sisters."[3]

As 1844 opened, Ṭáhirih arrived in Karbala. It was the Islamic year 1260, the year proclaimed by the drumroll of prophecy and written by the crazy old man on the walls of Tabriz. Ten days before Ṭáhirih could reach him, Siyyid Káẓim died. Just before his passing, he made the great promise of the imminent revelation of "the Beloved, the Desire of your hearts and mine." He tried to arouse in his disciples the reciprocally great commitment to begin fasting and praying immediately after his death so that, following guidance, they could set out in search of the Mahdi.[4]

Siyyid Káẓim had received tremendous veneration in his life and also suffered tremendous persecution, but at the time of his death, veneration dominated. In 1842–43, strife between Shiites and Sunnis had wracked the shrine cities, and Siyyid Káẓim had tried to mediate, but finally the Ottoman government had sacked Karbala with a reign of terror that killed thousands.[5] People had rushed to Siyyid Káẓim's home for refuge, and his status as a holy man grew.

As the city straggled back to a semblance of normalcy, the number of his followers increased. But he "had spent himself in an effort to forestall violence . . . Although only fifty years of age he became aware that his life was nearing its close." He knew that some of his recent adherents, influential men, came to him only because they sought more prestige. He addressed them as they sat in their seats of honor in his classes, "Many are those who claim to have attained union with the Beloved, and yet that Beloved refuses to acknowledge their claim. By the tears which he sheds for his loved One can the true lover be distinguished from the false."[6]

Soon after this, he left for his annual pilgrimage to the shrines in Kazimayn. When he stopped to say his noonday prayer, an Arab shepherd approached him, embraced him, and told him he'd dreamed of the Prophet Muḥammad, who had a message for him: he would die within days, and after that "He who is the Truth" would become manifest. Siyyid Káẓim's companions wept and mourned, but he said, "Is not your love for me for the sake of that true One whose advent we all await? Would you not wish me to die, that the promised One may be revealed?"[7]

Ṭáhirih arrived in Karbala to find his widow grieving and his followers in disarray, some proclaiming themselves the Mahdi, others hoping that when a certain man who was away on a mission came back to the city he would tell them what to do. He was Mullah Muḥammad Ḥusayn Bus͟hrú'í, known as Mullah Ḥusayn. He came from a village in Khorasan, the province famed both as the land where the Iranian sun rises and as the womb of revolution.

Mullah Ḥusayn, if his physique was any indication, was utterly unlike his rugged province; he was frail, with a tremor in his hands, and was said to have a heart condition. However, he was singularly determined.

He first left his native village at the age of twelve to study in Mashhad, where he became known for his fearless challenges to orthodox beliefs. He began corresponding with Siyyid Káẓim, asking questions about the Promised One.

For example, he asked if it were necessary, as some said, to learn swordsmanship to be able to assist the Mahdi. (Whatever the answer to that was, the frail scholar transformed into a champion swordsman when the time came.) He decided to go to Karbala to study with Siyyid Káẓim, but when his father died, he had to return home to help his mother and four siblings. He was restless; he wrote a verse on the wall of his home:

Your thoughts will take you out of this house,
And will lead you to the abode of mystery . . .

He dreamed of the Prophet Muḥammad, and his face became illumined with joyous purpose. He simply had to go to Karbala. His mother, a reputable poet, sold some land to further his efforts and packed her things to accompany him. His sister, a poet with the pen-name *Nightingale,* also went with him, along with his brother and nephew. They journeyed 750 miles over every kind of terrain in huge caravans, armed with guns and knives against Turcoman bandits, the shah's underfed cavalry, and other marauders.

In Karbala, Mullah Ḥusayn lived meagerly in a madrassa, earning coins as a scribe, copying treatises by Siyyid Káẓim. He ate minimally, prayed, fasted, and attended classes. His family members also attended classes, with his mother and sister seated behind a curtain. Now and then he would retire to the mosque at Kufa for a forty-day prayer vigil.[8] Soon Siyyid Káẓim chose him to undertake a long journey into Iran to confront a powerful religious dignitary and try to change his thinking.

This dignitary was one of Siyyid Káẓim's many bitter, dangerous opponents. No one volunteered for this particular mission after a student of worldly eminence offered to go and Siyyid Káẓim warned, "Beware of touching the lion's tail." But Siyyid Káẓim declared Mullah Ḥusayn equal to the task. He was. He acquitted himself brilliantly. When Siyyid Káẓim received his written report, he praised his courage and exalted his deeds above prayer because they pertained "to the essential, to the root of belief."[9]

However, Mullah Ḥusayn never saw his master again. Around the same time Ṭáhirih arrived in Karbala, Mullah Ḥusayn did, too, only to find that the one for whom he had undertaken so much was gone.

His fellow disciples begged him to teach in Siyyid Káẓim's place. Siyyid Káẓim's widow offered him the hand of her daughter in marriage; she regarded him as part of her family and free to become its head. But he didn't marry or take over the teaching circle. Instead, he reviewed Siyyid Káẓim's last wishes and asked his fellow students why they hadn't followed them. They said they expected Mullah Ḥusayn to say, "I am the Promised One." If only he would speak those words, they would all obey him.

"God forbid!" Mullah Ḥusayn cried. "Far be it from his glory that I . . . should be compared to him . . ." He immediately went out and visited each of Siyyid Káẓim's most distinguished disciples to try to persuade them to abandon every desire and pursuit and begin their search. But they were like the birds in Attar's poem, *The Conference of the Birds.* When determining whether or not to participate in the search for the magic Simorgh bird, each bird offered a different excuse. The nightingale couldn't leave his rose; the parrot couldn't leave his gilded cage; the falcon couldn't forsake his king; the partridge couldn't leave his mountains; the duck couldn't fly from his water.[10]

Not so Mullah Ḥusayn. He had always been the true seeker, searching "every face" for "the beauty of the Friend," wondering "in every country" looking "for the Beloved," and perceiving "all created things wandering distracted in search of the Friend . . ." He went to Kufa to lose himself in contemplation in the mosque. His brother and nephew accompanied him, one to pray with him, the other to serve the two of them. Forty days later, Mullah Ḥusayn prostrated himself at the tomb of Imam 'Alí, arose, and departed. He would travel the length of Iraq to Basra and take a ship across the Persian Gulf. His goal was the Iranian city of Shiraz. Why? What guidance had he received? Was it simply that, according to Islamic tradition, Shiraz was the place where the Mahdi would appear?

> Shiraz shall be full of tumult: one shall appear with lips sweet as sugar;
> I fear lest through the riot of his lips he may cast Baghdad into confusion . . .[11]

Shiraz is still known as the most poetic of cities, home and burial place of the quintessential bards Sa'di and Hafez. Pilgrims continually visit their tombs to drink wine, pour libations on the earth, and sing verses for entire starry nights. Shiraz is called *the House of Learning* and *the City of Love.* Near the city stretch the ruins of Persepolis, the mighty, historic symbol of Persia's pre-Islamic power and throne-city of the mythical king, Jamshid.* Shiraz was the capital of Fars, a province known as the original Iran. A British traveler wrote of Shiraz in 1627: "Here magick was first hatched; here Nimrod for some time lived; here Cyrus, the most excellent of the heathen princes was born: . . . hence the Magi (Zoroastrian priests) are thought to have set out towards Bethlehem, and here a series of 200 kings swayed their scepters . . ."[12]

Shiraz deserved its fame. From it and its region sprang the basic identity of the nation, including the folk tradition called *savushun*, the

---

* In Persian, *Persepolis* is translated as *Takht-i-Jamshid*, or *the Throne of Jamshid.* (Elwell-Sutten, L. P., *Persian Grammar*, p. 86).

rites of mourning for a heroically sacrificial prince that are the roots of the passion plays for the Imam Ḥusayn. In savushun, sorrow, pain, and hopelessness become salvation when, to the pervasive beat of kettledrums, women mourning men lost in battle cut off their own hair, hang it from the trees, and the breezes that are never still in Iran blow through the branches and the long black tresses.[13]

More direct guidance may have existed, though, for Mullah Ḥusayn's course to Shiraz. According to one source, a woman visited him in the mosque so that he could interpret a dream she'd had: ". . . I was in a place where . . . people were saying that ere long the sun will rise from the direction of the city of Shiraz." Of course, he knew Shaykh Aḥmad had venerated that city.[14]

As it happened, a young pilgrim he'd observed in Karbala Who had been noticed by many in that praying city for His extreme radiance, humiliation, and devotion—His "halo of innocence"—lived in Shiraz. Once, attending Siyyid Káẓim's teaching circle, the young pilgrim had been deeply moved while Mullah Ḥusayn recited poetry by Shaykh Aḥmad. This might have occurred in Siyyid Káẓim's library, which held over ten thousand volumes, where students, merchants, theologians, and artists met regularly to discuss literature and ritually mourn the Imams.[15]

When this particular young pilgrim was moved, it was evident in His entire being. People observed Him in the Shrine of Ḥusayn weeping ecstatically and lyrically chanting, "O God, my God, my Beloved, my Heart's Desire." Siyyid Káẓim's students were charmed and mystified by Him, particularly because their master treated Him with unprecedented veneration. When He first arrived in Karbala, Siyyid Káẓim took a student to visit Him, calling Him "a highly esteemed and distinguished person," and the student observed that in His presence Siyyid Káẓim was "speechless . . . with bowed head."[16]

The young man only attended Siyyid Káẓim's classes three times. The same disciple who had accompanied the master on the visit to Him reported later that during one of those classes, as soon as Siyyid Káẓim saw the young man enter, he stopped speaking. Someone begged him to finish his discourse. Looking at the pilgrim from Shiraz, who had seated Himself in the sunlight coming through a window, the teacher murmured, "What more can I say? . . . The truth is more manifest than the ray of light that has fallen upon that lap."[17]

Yet we cannot know how much, or even if, Mullah Ḥusayn knew of these circumstances when he set off for Shiraz. We only know he was obeying the behest of Siyyid Káẓim and following the deepest dictates of his heart.

And what of Ṭáhirih? One historian says that she participated in the retreat in Kufa, but, according to the rest, she did not. Instead, she stayed in the home of Siyyid Káẓim, where his widow took great comfort in her presence, revering her as her "spiritual guide and . . . affectionate companion." The widow was a gentle soul, probably in frail health (she died a short time later), who hated to have Ṭáhirih leave her side for even an hour, and perhaps this was why Ṭáhirih didn't journey to Shiraz. Many Iranian and Arabian women constantly visited the house, and they also became attached to Ṭáhirih.[18]

Meanwhile, ill-wishers from the factions that had immediately started forming among the S͟hayk͟his after their leader's death agitated against Mullah Ḥusayn, predisposing people against the possible results of his search. Ṭáhirih took on the mission of upholding him, preparing her circles of students to accept Mullah Ḥusayn's findings, for she was certain that he was on the right path. Male and female pupils flocked to her; she taught them in separate groups and spoke to the men from behind a curtain, but this didn't dim her luster as far as they were concerned. Among the women she befriended and guided were the two accomplished poets who were her literary peers, the mother and sister of Mullah Ḥusayn.[19]

And she enjoyed the opportunity to pore over the tomes of as-yet unpublished Shaykhi writings in Siyyid Káẓim's library. At one point, referring to these numerous volumes, she told her students, "Consider how much Shaykh Ahsai and Siyyid Káẓim have left: they've given us a legacy of a veritable ocean of instruction."[20]

She also fasted during the day and prayed at night, searching in spirit for the Promised One, and at last she was rewarded with a dream that came to her after a night-long vigil, as dawn broke. She saw a Youth, a siyyid* in a black cloak and green turban, standing in the air, suspended between earth and heaven, hands upraised, reciting verses and praying. She memorized one of His verses and wrote it down when she awoke.[21]

Around the same time, her brother-in-law had gone into the mosque in Kufa to keep a vigil and then, with twelve others, he too left for Shiraz. He had with him a sealed letter from Ṭáhirih for the One she was sure he'd find. She also gave him instructions:

Say to Him from me:

> The effulgence of thy face flashed forth, and the rays of thy visage arose on high;
> Why lags the word, 'Am I not your Lord?' 'Yea, that thou art,' let us make reply.
> 'Am I nots' appeal from thy drum to greet what 'Yeas' do the drums of devotion beat;
> At the gates of my heart I behold the feet and the tents of the host of calamity.[22]

Some claim this poem is by Ṭáhirih; others that it's by someone else and that she frequently recited it. It could be another poet's, adapted

---

* In Ṭáhirih's day, siyyids (descendants of the Prophet Muḥammad) wore green turbans.

and glossed with her own lines (a frequent practice in Persian poetry). In any case, it confirms her conviction that the Promised One would immediately make himself known and that the results would be anything but easy but for his followers. The phrase "Yea, that thou art," echoes humanity's response to the Creator's covenant with creation, as told in the Qur'án,

> When thy Lord drew forth
> From the children of Adam—
> From their loins—
> Their descendants, and made them
> Testify concerning themselves . . . :
> "Am I not your Lord . . . ?
> They said, "Yea!
> We do testify! . . ."[23]

The Arabic word for yes, or yea, signifying ascent, is *bala,* and it also signifies sorrow, or the sigh, *alas.* Gertrude Bell comments, "When God had created man and made him wiser than the angels,* he bound him to himself by a solemn treaty . . . and they say that the first of our fathers knew full well what a terrible gift was that life which he had received from his Lord, and sealed the treaty with a seal of grief: 'Yes, alas.' Therefore, since the earliest day, life and sorrow have gone hand in hand, bound together by the first great pact between God and man."[24]

For Ṭáhirih, mystical ecstasy would always subsume the sorrows of life, although she felt those sorrows deeply. She had already severed herself from home and family, sentenced herself to exile in her search

---

* Reference to the Qur'án, Sura 2:30–37, where God tells Adam "the nature of all things" and Adam learns "from his Lord words of inspiration . . ."

for truth, and she did not regret or begrudge the sacrifice. "The true seeker hunteth naught but the object of his quest, and the lover hath no desire save union with his beloved. Nor shall the seeker reach his goal unless he sacrifice all things."[25] Before she even knew the identity of her Promised One, she tossed her self aside and cried, "Yea!" though, with her singular prescience, she beheld calamity camped at the gates of her heart.

Freely admitting the reality of the pain of sacrifice and recognizing that its only remedy was the fulfillment of her search, she wrote in a prayer, ". . . I am effaced. I seek a splendor that could not exist by means of any save Thee . . . My God, Thine imperative is the answer to my call; Thy 'perhaps' is the salve for my misery, and Thine advent is the decree of my religion and the success of my Cause . . ."

She trusted that her search would be answered with the coming of the Promised One and she would fulfill the purpose of her life in service to Him. She only waited for Him to make His claims, name His name, and proclaim His presence on earth. His spirit was the essence that mystics call the Friend, the universal indweller of the heart. When her longed-for Friend spoke at last, Ṭáhirih would welcome Him as the ruler of her heart, and His words and His will would become her law.

In the same prayer, she said she felt that while she waited to hear the cry "'This is he!'" she had received the "undeserved" gift of "being." She said that ". . . indeed it was pure effulgence and kindness," that, in fact, she had been created "at a time when nothing existed save (that mercy)" and she "was formed whirling after a pattern that no one besides Thee had fashioned, so that Thou mightest set me in motion."[26]

So, in a state of suspense, deeply feeling her connection to her Maker and longing to be "set in motion" on the path of the Promised One, eager for the joys of spiritual rebirth and unafraid of its tribulations, Ṭáhirih awaited news from Shiraz, hoping for and trusting in the manifestation of the Friend that would unfold behind city walls, beyond a portal, within a dwelling, deeply obscure to the eyes of the world, completely dazzling to her inner eye, her waiting heart.

7

1844, Europe, and the United States

The Revolt of Islam. The Woman Clothed with the Sun. The Code and the Common Law. Female crusaders. Hijab in London. The Great Disappointment. Zion.

While concrete predictions of apocalypse rocked souls in Iran and Iraq, similar predictions played havoc in Christian and Jewish worlds during the nineteenth century. Poets, especially the Romantics, deeply felt the expectant energy. In 1817, Percy Bysshe Shelley, who named poets "the unacknowledged legislators of the world," voiced it in *The Revolt of Islam,* his long narrative of a battle for human emancipation based on gender equality.[1]

The poem has little to do with Islam except for its symbolic imagery of the veil. Its heroine, a warrior child-woman named Cythna, taught "equal laws and justice . . . to women" while "armed wrong" collapsed in her sight as her very voice repressed evil. When her multitudes of followers camped on a plain, celebrating "the banquet of the free," she passed among them and ". . . she did unwind / Her veil, as with the crowds of her own kind / She mixed . . ."[2]

When Cythna prays, she invokes a female deity: "Mother and soul of all to which is given / The light of light, the loveliness of being! . . ." and in Cythna "hearts long parted now unite . . ."[3] She's essentially a female messiah, for Shelley was apparently inspired by the fact that, in his era, the age of messianic searches, some expected a female messiah.

Among them were the Saint-Simonians. Theirs was a political movement as much as a religious one. Their French founder, a nobleman named Claude Henri de Rouvroy, comte de Saint-Simon, embraced the ideal of democracy to become an officer in the Yankee army during the American Revolutionary War. Afterwards, back in France, he foresaw an age of machinery that would bring in a new era, and he propounded a secular Christianity in which gentry and crucifix-wielding clergy would become obsolete in a civilization of equality created by science and industry.[4]

But Barthelemy Prosper Enfantin, known as Father Enfantin, took over the movement after Saint-Simon's death and made it more mystical, preaching about women's emancipation and a female messiah who would be the mother of a new savior. Confusingly, he also declared himself the Living Law and the Messiah. He believed in a Mother / Father God and advocated free love because he said marriage was a prison for women. But in 1832, he barred women from his hierarchy, saying the world's effect on them was too "hardening," and he retreated into the countryside with forty of his "sons." In reaction, some of his "daughters" published a newspaper in Paris called *La Femme Libre.* They were working-class women who all wrote under pseudonyms and addressed themselves wholly to their sister women. Meanwhile, Father Enfantin, who had been tried and convicted of "public immorality" because of his attempts to liberate womanly passions, went to Egypt to await his female messiah.[5]

His inspiration for the female messiah was the vision of the "Woman Clothed with the Sun," from the New Testament, Revelations 12:1–18, which reads, "And there appeared a great wonder in heaven: a woman clothed with the sun, and the moon under her feet, and upon her head a crown of twelve stars: And she being with child cried, travailing in birth, and pained to be delivered."[6]

This vision has caught human imagination over the centuries, with the woman being variously identified as Mary, the Church, the Nation of Israel, the Protestant Reformation, and the Virgin of Guadalupe. The vision took particular hold in the nineteenth century, and Mother Ann Lee, founder of the Shakers, was one of the charismatic figures thought to be the Woman Clothed with the Sun. Another was Joanna Southcott, who proclaimed herself to be the Woman and said she was with child, about to give birth to the savior, the Shiloh; at her peak, she gathered some twenty thousand followers in Regency, England. Although she was in her sixties and historians say she died of brain disease in 1814, today's Southcottians say she lost her life bearing a child who immediately died, and they still revere her as a prophetess.[7]

However, for some, a female messiah wasn't necessary; they just wanted equality of women and men. In 1792, in England, the same year Shelley was born, Mary Wollstonecraft published her radical work, *Vindication of the Rights of Women.* But she was among a minority of the intelligentsia. Sir Anthony Absolute, a character in the 1777 farce, *The Rivals,* voiced the prevalent view that women should not be taught to read and ". . . a circulating library in a town is an evergreen tree of diabolical knowledge . . ." Men around the world would have seconded Sir Absolute. As Jane Austen wrote some forty years later, "A woman, especially if she have the misfortune of knowing anything, should conceal it as well as she can." Political revolutions generally did nothing to remedy women's situation.[8]

For example, after the French Revolution of 1789, the supposedly egalitarian victors included women in parliamentary sessions and political meetings. Women had fought at the barricades; now they led street rallies. But within a year after the revolutionary government was established, it banned women from parliament and from forming clubs and political parties. However, *Vindication of the Rights of Women* was quickly translated into French and German, reprinted in Britain, and published in the United States. Often read clandestinely and under duress, especially because of what was deemed the scandalous nature of its author's life, the book became a talisman for aware women.[9]

The same leaps forward and backward occurred with endeavors to abolish slavery. In 1794, France granted citizenship rights and freedom to people of color in its empire, and soon afterwards, in Santo Domingo, Toussant L'overture led a slave revolt against Spain. But with the advent of Napoleon came the attempt to reimpose slavery.

The Napoleonic Code became law in 1804. It classified women in the same category as children, the insane, and jailed criminals. Soon, many other nations adopted it. But Britain didn't have to; British Common Law already classified women similarly, and it was also the norm in the United States. In Latin America, where Simon Bolivar and others managed to drive out European powers as the century advanced, women received no benefits. Until 1856, it was legal for a man to sell his wife in England, and the British law of primogeniture is well-known to all who have read Austen, Dickens, Thackeray and the like: only the oldest son inherits. He gets money, land, and house. His younger brothers are at his mercy, as are his sisters.

According to law throughout the Western world, then, the man was the head of the household, and his wife had to obey him. He decided where they lived and whether or not she could inherit or acquire property, and he had the right to scrutinize her bank accounts. She couldn't appear in court without his permission, and he had the right to read her mail. He was the sole authority over his children, and he had automatic custody of them. He could, with impunity, confine and beat his wife, and if he caught her committing adultery, he had the right to kill her. However, if she caught him, she didn't have the right to kill him.

The Napoleonic Code and British Common Law set women's legal status back from what it had been in preceding centuries, and, in a further dishonor, women's work was devalued. Formerly, men and women had worked together: house and mill, house and farm, house and artisan's shop were linked, and men knew that without women's industry, they could gain little. But with the industrial revolution, men left home to work in factories and offices. Men and women became invisible to each other for most of the day. Men brought home money at the end of the week, but women did not receive wages for their childbearing, gardening, spinning, sewing, weaving, cooking, preserving food, and compounding medicines.[10]

Man was tired, and as far as he was concerned, woman spent her days at home doing nothing. He began to instruct her from pulpit and printed page to greet him cheerfully at the end of his day in a home that was a haven, not to dishearten him with her own, implicitly petty, concerns. Wife had to placate husband; daughter had to placate father; sister had to placate brother. Suddenly woman, who had plowed and planted through the centuries, was weak. Yet this very weakness, according to Church and State, was power. Power over men. One poof of her powder puff, and he was on his knees. Well, not a powder puff in rigorously puritanical establishments: there, cosmetics were a sin. But she could still flutter her eyelashes, providing she had any left after years of constant child-bearing and weeping over the babies who succumbed to the rampant ills of the times. Many women supported this state of affairs wholeheartedly; in fact, a few made money writing about the way a model woman should behave.[11]

One woman who was a self-appointed expert on female behavior wrote that upon awakening in the morning, a lady should not ask, "'What shall I do to gratify myself or to be admired?'" On the contrary, being "the least engaged of any member of the household" . . . she should mutely devote herself to others, being wary of anything that might "draw away her thoughts from others and fix them on herself . . ." This would have been lovely if men had been exhorted to conduct themselves in an equally selfless fashion. But they had the freedom to exercise their passions, while another female adviser told women, "There are rules for all our actions, even down to sleeping with a good Grace" for "Woman owes her Being to the Comfort and Profit of Man . . ."[12]

Inevitably, there was rebellion. And rebellion demanded that its practitioners speak in public. Most women had been taught to be silent: "Let your women keep silence in the churches: for it is not permitted unto them to speak: but they are commanded to be under obedience . . . And if they will learn anything, let them ask their husbands at home . . ." This was a church stricture, but it existed forcefully in various formats and venues for women of all creeds, an exception being radical Quakers who encouraged women to speak in their meetings. The imposed silence was so pernicious that Mary Ellman remarked in the twentieth century that women trying to write were "like people looking for their own bodies under razed buildings, having to clear away debris. In their every effort to formulate a new point of view, one feels the refutation of previous points of view—a weight which must impede spontaneity." How much heavier this weight would be, then, for women endeavoring to speak from platform or pulpit.[13]

The majority of feminists started their revolt by becoming abolitionists. Sarah Louisa Forten, who wrote under the pen name of Ada, was one of them. She was the daughter of one of the most important African-American families in Philadelphia; she grew up free, and she "established the importance of women's activist poetry in the African-American and European-American abolitionist cultures . . ." She was outspoken and active personally as well as with her pen. In 1823, she was one of the charter members of the first integrated abolitionist organization, *The Philadelphia Female Anti-Slavery Society*; three of her accompanying charter members were her mother and two sisters. She worked beside Angelina Grimké, John Greenleaf Whitter, William Lloyd Garrison, and others, and with her family financed or founded some six other abolitionist organizations.[14]

Hers was a dangerous endeavor. In 1838, when the second Antislavery Convention of American Women planned to convene in Philadelphia, no church or other organization would provide space, so the participants had to build a hall. When the gathering opened, males were also present, and it was a racially integrated group. During the first sessions, mobs rioted outside. The famous Lucretia Mott, trained to believe in herself and her convictions through her radical Quaker faith, denigrated the riots as just a little bit of danger and exhorted her female friends to reject the traditional ideas of female modesty and to address the mixed audience.

Mott was a veteran campaigner, and nothing could stop her. However, one woman who delivered an address left the convention suffering from what was then called brain fever and never spoke in public again. Another followed suit. Their reactions were understandable: Mott's bit of danger grew to thousands of rioters. The mayor of Philadelphia refused to grant police protection to the gathering, so, on the second day of the convention, delegates walked to the hall in couples, black and white, arm in arm. That night, the mob set fire to the hall. Not one fireman appeared to try to stop the blaze, and the whole place burned down. Nevertheless, the women decided to increase their interracial activities.[15]

William Lloyd Garrison was one of their role models. He'd started the *Liberator*, an antislavery weekly journal, in 1831. Its motto, an adaptation of an earlier statement by Thomas Paine, was: "Our country is the world, our countrymen are all mankind." The *Liberator* had a Ladies Department headed by a picture of a chained female slave with the caption, "Am I not a woman and a sister?" Garrison backed up words with deeds. In 1835, after he was dragged by a mob through the streets of Boston, he wrote, "If persecution is the means which God has ordained for the accomplishment of this great end, EMANCIPATION, then, in dependence *upon Him* for strength to bear it, I feel as if I could say, LET IT COME: for it is my deep, solemn, deliberate conviction, that *this is a cause worth dying for.*"[16]

Two years later, he joined a group of his abolitionist women friends behind the veil at the 1840 World Anti-Slavery Convention in London. Among the ladies was Lucretia Mott. After marching through the streets in the face of mobs in Philadelphia for the abolitionist cause, Mott had to sit silently behind a curtain at the convention after the men running it voted that women must be unseen and unheard, for they were "constitutionally unfit for business and public meetings."[17]

So Mott, with Elizabeth Cady Stanton, several other women, and William Lloyd Garrison, experienced hijab. For Elizabeth Cady Stanton, newlywed to a dashing, young, abolitionist lawyer who gravely disillusioned her by voting with the majority of the men at the convention to silence the women, the experience was a great awakening. She began to see that women could only gain their spiritual and intellectual independence by exercising it. As Lucretia Mott said, both black and white female abolitionists had to rely on their own consciences, their own interpretations of scripture, "the light of truth in the soul."[18]

Certain African-American evangelical women had long since embraced the credo of independence in word and deed at all costs. In 1840, while Stanton and Mott were stuck behind the veil, the preacher Zilpha Elaw was in England, where she preached over one thousand sermons, enduring constant criticism from pundits who were sure that women weren't meant to occupy the pulpit. She felt she had a mission to people of all denominations and colors and, in the United States, had even traveled in slaveholding states, constantly risking arrest and bondage. Another preacher, known simply as Elizabeth, dared to travel and teach in the southern United States, even though she was a freed slave. As an old woman, when asked by what authority she'd dared to preach, she said, "Not by the commission of men's hands. If the Lord had ordained me, I needed nothing better."[19]

Slavery had only recently been abolished in the northern United States. In 1799, New York State legislated gradual abolition, set to occur on July 4, 1827. The master of a slave named Isabella Baumfree promised to free her in 1826, then reneged on the vow, so she took her infant daughter and escaped into the night. By 1844 she'd renamed herself Sojourner Truth and was a renowned preacher and speaker for civil rights.[20]

Ernestine Rose was another accomplished public speaker, known as the "Queen of the Lecture Platform." But she was secular. She was a Polish immigrant to the United States. At the age of sixteen she had escaped her small Jewish town in the Pale of Settlement (the part of Russia's empire where Jews were permitted to live). She ran away so that she could void her father's wedding plans for her, which included granting her inheritance from her mother to the would-be husband. She studied law and successfully argued and won her case in court. She renounced Judaism because she felt it was irrational and resisted conversion to Christianity a few years later when she was threatened with expulsion from Berlin because Jews weren't allowed to reside there. She had an audience with the Prussian king and told him, "If my reason prevents me from being Jewish, it cannot permit be to be Christian." Years later, she joined Elizabeth Cady Stanton to campaign vigorously for legislation to allow married women to own property in New York State, and she became a featured speaker for abolition. That her public stance required great heroism and took its toll is evident in her early retirement to private life in England; her youth, when she'd had to stand alone with "nothing else to support her" but "the consciousness of possessing the *might of right*" had apparently exhausted her.[21]

Another fearless female speaker was Margaret Fuller, although she preferred group discussion and didn't often take to the pulpit or the lecture platform. Influenced by Transcendentalist thinking, she supported abolition, improvement in the care of the mentally ill, and other reforms, but she is primarily known as the first real feminist in the United States for her defense of the androgyny of the human soul (mind and emotions) and therefore complete gender equality. She made her case in her book *Woman in the Nineteenth Century*, first published as an essay in 1843. The book was nurtured by the Conversation Club for Women that she led in Boston, during which she sparked philosophical discussions using the Socratic method of pointed questioning and debate.[22]

Perhaps influenced by the idea of the female messiah, Fuller asked in her book, as the fateful year 1844 loomed, "And will she not soon appear?—the woman who shall vindicate their birthright for all women; who shall teach them what to claim, and how to use what they obtain?" She wondered what the woman's name would be, and says, "Yet predictions are rash; she herself must teach us to give her the fitting name."[23]

It was Margaret Fuller's embrace of Transcendentalism and the mystical/philosophic renaissance of New England in the nineteenth century that helped her cast her intellectual and social independence in the light of optimistic prophecies of a new age, giving her "a confident belief in moral change, intuitive knowledge" that would emphasize each person's "uniqueness, potential and faith in the self." She saw religion as "the thirst for truth and good, not the love of sect and dogma," and wrote, "No doubt a new manifestation is at hand, a new hour in the day of man . . . hearts crave it now, if minds do not know how to ask it . . ."[24]

However, some minds knew exactly how to ask it; chief among them was William Miller. In his (and Margaret Fuller's) day, upstate New

York and surroundings became known as the Burned-Over District, "a psychic highway" because so many religious wildfires, lit by the rhetorical torches of evangelistic preachers and proponents of other movements such as spiritualism, swept through it from the end of the eighteenth century and into the nineteenth.[25] Miller was a beacon among those preachers. He was from Pittsfield, Massachusetts, the eldest of sixteen children born in a log cabin to a Revolutionary War veteran and a Baptist minister's daughter. By the light of long-burning pine knots that he selected and hoarded, he educated himself. In an era when the Bible and Shakespeare were the only books anyone had—if they had books at all—he read whatever he could lay his hands on.

Miller became popular in his community for his patriotic poetry, served as constable and sheriff, and was a captain in the War of 1812. He had a wife, ten children, and a fine home. He was a deist, believing in a creator who took no personal interest in creation. But after the war, his belief in a personal God and heaven and hell was reborn following a sermon he heard on the first anniversary of the Battle of Plattsburg. He realized that "the character of a Savior was vividly impressed" on his mind. He delved deeply into the Bible and, using the prophecies in the Book of Daniel, calculated that 1843 would be the year of Christ's return.

This was in 1822, around the same time that Ṭáhirih's uncle was driving Shaykh Aḥmad out of Qazvin. If William Miller and Shaykh Aḥmad could have met, they would have had much to say to each other, for the identification of Jesus with the spirit of the Advent was a familiar one in Muslim minds.[26] But of course, worlds lay between them. Like the shaykh, however, Miller, an eloquent, well-respected man, held off from public proclamation, giving his message one-on-one or in small groups of sympathizers until his sense of urgency grew. In 1832, he wrote sixteen articles in a Vermont newspaper and soon published them as *Evidences from Scripture and History of the Second Coming of Christ,*

About the Year 1843, and of His Personal Reign of One Thousand Years. He then became a full-time preacher.

After several years, all of the United States, particularly the Burned-Over District, knew William Miller's prophecy, though many scoffed at it. As time advanced, churches became afraid of his influence, and he held his large revivals outside, sometimes under threat of mob violence. He expected Christ between March 21, 1843, and March 21, 1844. The last date came and went, and no one saw Jesus descending to earth through Clouds of Glory in the way that His Advent was depicted in the Bible. Miller wrote, "I confess my error and acknowledge my disappointment, yet I still believe that the day of the Lord is near, even at the door." Another preacher called the date for October 22, 1844, which was Yom Kippur, the Jewish Day of Atonement. Miller came to believe that, too, and promoted it.[27]

On the given day, masses of people in large and small groups disposed of their worldly possessions and got ready to meet their Maker, but clouds did not roll away, no transcendent figure appeared in the heavens, and *The Great Disappointment* ensued. One Adventist wrote, ". . . such a spirit of weeping came over us as I never experienced before . . . We wept and wept, till the day dawned. I mused in my heart . . . has the Bible proved a failure? Is there no God, no heaven, no golden home city, no paradise? Is all this but a cunningly devised fable?" A doughtier soul riposted, when someone taunted him, "Why didn't you go up?" (get lifted into heaven): "And if I *had* gone up, where would you have gone?" Miller didn't lose faith, but he lost his health. He kept revising his predictions until his death in 1849, telling his "brethren" that they "must be patient, and wait for him (the Lord)."[28]

As we have seen, Miller and his Millerites were hardly alone in their expectations. In a letter written in 1844, an Englishman named John Holt wrote of a colony of "Apostles" in Malta who were awaiting the Advent: "At Athens we were joined by Mr. Frere, a brother of Rt. Hon.

J. H. Frere, the intimate friend of Canning, who in 1813 published an interpretation of prophecy and has a very confident expectation that 1847 is to be the end of the Christian dispensation—the date of the advent of our Lord and the battle of Armageddon . . . and a Mr. Fletcher who has been sent out by the Archbishop of Canterbury and who has been two years at Antioch, Damascus, etc. on a visitation to the Nestorian and other Eastern Christian Churches, mentions persuasions and appearances which convince the Turks that in this year—1260 of the Hegira*—Constantinople is to fall . . . in the East a feeling is abroad that we are in the Times of the End."[29]

Adventist expectations and their disappointment were well-publicized because Samuel Morse's electronic telegraph revolutionized media in the United States on May 23, 1844, transmitting an Old Testament quote, "What hath God wrought?"† from Washington, DC, to Baltimore, a message highly relevant to the apocryphal times. Morse's invention hastened the establishment of telegraphy, which England had begun during the 1830s, and which was already introduced into other parts of Europe, as well as India. In 1844, because of significant leaps forward in communications and other technology, even secular eyes saw the world in a crux of change. Henry Adams, political and social commentator, felt that May was the pivotal month. In his autobiography, he cited the opening of the Boston and Albany Railroad, the Cunard Steamers anchored in Boston Harbor, and Morse's telegraph, all of which gave him, when he was six years old, a "new world . . . ready for use . . ." in which "only fragments of the old met his eyes."[30]

---

* The Islamic calendar dates from the Hegira, the night of Muḥammad's flight from Mecca to Medina.

† Numbers 23:23.

During the same year, in Paris, crowds visited the first international photographic exhibition. A few years before, Samuel Morse had written, "In the winter of 1838–39 I was in Paris, and was invited by Daguerre to see his results in sun painting" (early photographs or daguerreotypes, called sun pictures). This harnessing of light to record images fascinated the world, and photography, with rapid innovations, spread quickly. Artists, awakened by photographs to the transcendence of light, began to see the world differently. J. M. W. Turner, the British master of transcendently lit canvases, is a prime example, and his 1844 work *Rain, Steam and Speed* somehow combusts the excitement of the new industrial/technological era with ecstatically romantic vision.[31]

But factories spawned by new technologies were blighting the landscape and condemning laborers—women as well as men, children as well as adults—to short, polluted, demeaning lives. Many people felt that religion and romance were no match for the power of industrial materialism and its runaway development. In 1844, Karl Marx contended that "Religion is the sigh of the oppressed creature, the feelings of a heartless world, just as it is the spirit of unspiritual conditions. It is the opium of the people."[32] For Marx, power was of the people, messianic in itself. He would soon publish *The Communist Manifesto.*

But he was preceded in 1843 by the French-Peruvian visionary and labor organizer Flora Tristan, when she published *The Worker's Union.* Tristan was an ardent Christian who urged workers to ". . . prove to your oppressors that it is by the law that you wish to triumph and not by brutal force . . . Prove that you are just and impartial; declare, you strong men, men with bare arms, that you recognize women as your equal and . . . recognize for her an equal right to the benefits of the UNIVERSAL UNION OF WORKING MEN AND WORKING WOMEN."[33]

She went on to write, "Workers, perhaps in three or four years you will have your own first Palace, ready to receive 600 old people and 600 children! Well . . . let it be written in YOUR CHARTER that you will admit . . . to receive intellectual and professional education, an equal number of GIRLS and BOYS."[34]

Traveling with financial hardship from city to city, rallying workers in factories under extremely cramped, toxic conditions, Tristan often felt like a lone savior. Influenced by the ideal of the female messiah, she saw herself as a "woman guide" and her work as "apostolic." She wasn't just radicalizing workers, she was energizing their souls. Her adherents called her the "Mother of the Workers" and the "Workers' Saint." Exhausted and ill, she died in 1844; shortly afterward, seven thousand workers in Lyons raised a monument to her with the motto "Liberty, Equality, Fraternity, Solidarity."[35]

Meanwhile, ongoing revolutions in the Americas won liberty for nations, but not necessarily for individuals. In February, 1844, Dominicans won independence from Haiti and formed the Dominican Republic. The next year, the Massachusetts Anti-Slavery Society published the autobiography of the ex-slave Frederick Douglass. Margaret Fuller, writing for the *New York Tribune* in an editorial position that was a first for a woman, proposed integration as a solution to racism and recommended Douglass' book so readers would see "a mind [that] might have been stifled in bondage" by men in whom there was "no humanity except in the outward form, and of whom the Avenger will not fail yet to demand—'Where is thy brother?'"[36]

The 1840s were also years of apocalyptic expectation for Jewish people in Europe, long subject to genocidal pogroms, excluded from full citizenship in many countries and not even allowed to reside in others. They longed for redemption from their exile "by the rivers of Babylon. There we sat down, yea, we wept, when we remembered Zion . . ." Rabbi Yehuda Alkalai, calculating the date by study of the Kabbalah, said the Messianic redemption of the Jews would begin in 1840 and urged land purchase and settlement in what is now Israel. He was considered a heretic by Jews who thought that only a miracle of God would bring about a return to Zion.[37]

So men and women of all countries, classes, and creeds felt like exiles and longingly looked homeward, felt disenfranchised and sighed for validation, vindication, and salvation. But they did not only lie down and weep; they rose in every possible type of revolution.

8

1844, Iran

Shiraz and its visitors. Civil (or uncivil) unrest. "Enter therein in peace, secure." The Most Beautiful of Stories. The arrival of the brethren. Flooded by enlightenment.

At the same time that the Millerites were retreating in despair from their unparted clouds, Mullah Ḥusayn and his companions left Iraq in pursuit of their own revolution, or, more accurately, revelation. With the prayers of Ṭáhirih and others sighing Saba-like in their ears, they endured a long, crowded, malodorous, mercilessly hot voyage on a sailing vessel from Basra to Bushehr, the port city in southern Iran that sat, sweltering, on a peninsula pointing into the Persian Gulf. When Mullah Ḥusayn alighted, he had a small tome of questions for anyone claiming to be the Mahdi. Those questions accompanied him, his brother, and nephew 155 miles overland across "raw coastal lands" and up and down the peaks and valleys of "the three-thousand foot jagged mountains of dessicated Persia" to the town of Kazerun. From there the three men continued eastward, ninety-three more miles, to Shiraz.[1]

On the morning of May 22, 1844, Mullah Ḥusayn and his companions saw Shiraz in the distance. Perhaps it was early, when "not a speck of dust has polluted the air" and "the turquoise domes of the mosques, the bazaar roofs and the houses, stand out like delicate pieces of porcelain." Perhaps they saw the charming effect of the first wood fires of the day being lighted, when "one feels that it can only be the merchants in the bazaars lighting their pipes and blowing smoke of pleasant shapes into the air." Almost instantly after that the transparent town would become opaque, subsumed with dust and ashes. Yet at any time the roses, and the peach and apricot blossoms of the city of poets would waft fragrances to greet the approaching traveler.[2]

Many travelers were pilgrims to the shrines of Hafez and Sa'adi. There were also the foreigners, the would-be colonizing or religiously-converting powers. No one trusted them. One foreigner, Joseph Wolff, a Christian missionary of Jewish descent and German origin who wandered about searching for the Lost Tribes of Israel, heard an Afghani siyyid remark, "I know those Frankee (foreign) dervishes—I know these English dervishes. They go into a country, spy out mountains and valleys, seas and rivers; find out a convenient adit [passage] and then go home, inform a gentleman there—a chief, who has the name of Company, who sends soldiers, and takes the country."[3]

Iranians had been on the watch against foreigners for years and by the 1840s saw their home industries—fabric weaving and painting, embroidery, leatherworking, pottery, and more—begin to be devalued as their bazaars filled with Manchester prints from England, along with other factory-produced European goods. The regime of Muḥammad <u>Sh</u>áh, which began in 1834 following the death of Fatḥ 'Alí, gave European merchants favored nation status. The shah's prime minister and chief engineer of Iranian policies whined about "the misery that these Farangis (Europeans) . . ." brought upon him but nevertheless kowtowed to them. In ports such as Bushehr, where Mullah Ḥusayn had disembarked, Iranians saw British and Russian commercial ships arrive complete with cannons "more accurate and deadly than any weapon they had ever seen" that, in times of tension, targeted "their merchant houses and their merchandise."[4]

And there was plenty of tension. The mullahs were on the defensive because the shah, having been influenced by Prime Minister Áqásí (his former tutor) since boyhood, thought the old man, who had once been a dervish, was a saint and modeled himself after him, eating only bread and some vinegar for lunch and dinner, abstaining from Russian sugar, wearing no European fabrics unless they were purified first.[5]

Capitalizing on his Sufi ties, Áqásí pitted a certain order of Sufis against the mullahs. Áqásí was given to encouraging factional enmities and court intrigues, along with nepotism, but he wasn't a great strategist; in fact, he was so inept that the government began to fall apart. Lands that had once belonged to the crown were awarded to private owners, and the government was unable to collect taxes, so the shah, on the verge of bankruptcy, began auctioning positions, including provincial governorships. Governors bought their posts and then used them to extort money from the populace, who were also terrorized by militia in rebellion against the governors. Also, cities had long been divided according to neighborhood gangs' territorial rights, while rivalries flourished among various tribes. This corruption fed into the escalating spiral of urban and rural violence all over Iran.

Shiraz was a case in point. After a set-to between rival government troops about their rights to quarters in the city, a British agent in Shiraz reported in mid-1844: "The majority of the houses and shops adjoining the scene of conflict were plundered and destroyed. During the two or three days that the (latest round of) the fight lasted, four persons were killed and at least 100 wounded . . . the people here come to me and say that they are in despair, that their representatives to the Court are useless . . ."[6]

So, even while reviling and distrusting foreigners, some people seemed to hope that Europeans could instill some kind of order. However, they were doomed to disappointment. And there were other ruinous forces—such as earthquakes and cholera—that were eating away at anything resembling a peaceful and prosperous reign for Muḥammad Sháh.

It's doubtful that Mullah Ḥusayn considered either the contemporary shortcomings or the fabled charms of Shiraz as he approached one of the city's main gates. However, he later said that the atmosphere of the city had "produced already an indescribable impression upon" him. He sent his companions into town to seek lodging and immersed himself in meditative solitude, pacing and walking outside the city walls. A few hours before sunset, a young man in a green turban approached him and greeted him "with tender affection as though he had been his intimate and lifelong friend."

Describing their meeting, Mullah Ḥusayn said the youth warmly invited him to his home, but "I prayed to be excused, pleading that my companions had already arranged for my stay in that city, and were now awaiting my return." The youth said, "Commit them to the care of God," and told Mullah Ḥusayn to follow Him. Inexplicably to himself, the brilliant and proud scholar, some years older than the youth and of much greater academic status, unprotestingly complied. He was "profoundly impressed by" the young man's "gentle yet compelling manner . . . His gait, the charm of His voice, the dignity of His bearing . . ."[8]

"We soon found ourselves standing at the gate of a house of modest appearance," he recalled. A young Ethiopian servant named Mubarak, opened the gate, and Mullah Ḥusayn's host quoted the Qur'án, "Enter therein in peace, secure."* Mullah Ḥusayn felt this was a good augury

---

* Sura 15:46.

as he crossed the threshold of his first house in Shiraz. He followed his host to an inner chamber. Feelings of exhaustion and anxiety that had dogged him fell away; "a feeling of unutterable joy" filled him.[9]

His host called for a pitcher of water and gave it to Mullah Ḥusayn so he could wash the dust of travel from his hands and feet. Mullah Ḥusayn wanted to go into an adjoining room, feeling it was rude to wash in front of his host, but the young man himself poured the water over his guest's hands. He handed Mullah Ḥusayn a cool drink, asked for the samovar, and made tea that he served to Mullah Ḥusayn, who then rose and politely said he must go and meet his friends for evening prayer.

"You must surely have made the hour of your return conditional upon the will and pleasure of God," the youth observed. "It seems that His will has decreed otherwise. You need have no fear of having broken your pledge."[10]

Mullah Ḥusayn had no answer. After performing ablutions, he and his host recited the evening prayer, side by side. Mullah Ḥusayn said that during the silent portion of the prayer, "I unburdened my soul, which was much oppressed, both by the mystery of this interview and the strain and stress of my search. I breathed . . . 'I have striven with all my soul, O my God, and until now have failed to find Thy promised Messenger. I testify that Thy word faileth not, and that Thy promise is sure.'"[11]

The sun went down, dusk settled over the city, and the young man asked Mullah Ḥusayn, "Whom, after Siyyid Káẓim, do you regard as his successor and your leader?" Mullah Ḥusayn said that he was searching for the "promised Beloved."[12]

"Has your teacher given you any detailed indications as to the distinguishing features of the promised One?" his host asked.[13]

Mullah Ḥusayn gave the description that had been tendered by Siyyid Káẓim: "He is of a pure lineage, is of illustrious descent, and of the seed of Fáṭimih. As to His age, He is more than twenty and less than thirty. He is endowed with innate knowledge. He is of medium height, abstains from smoking, and is free from bodily deficiency."[14]

"Behold," the youth said, his voice vibrant, "all these signs are manifest in Me!"[15]

Mullah Ḥusayn remarked with some vehemence, "He whose advent we await is a Man of unsurpassed holiness, and the Cause He is to reveal (is) a Cause of tremendous power . . ." He quoted Siyyid Káẓim's remark: "My own knowledge is but a drop compared with that with which He has been endowed. All my attainments are but a speck of dust in the face of the immensity of His knowledge . . ." In other words, he inferred, how could this relatively unlettered youth, a merchant, not a scholar, even dare to say such a thing?[16]

Then Mullah Ḥusayn was "seized with fear and remorse." He couldn't conceal his agitation or explain it to himself, but he inwardly resolved to "alter my attitude and soften my tone." Perhaps he recalled that one of the characteristics of the Promised One enumerated by Siyyid Káẓim was that he would not be highly educated? He decided that if his host again referred to the subject he would humbly ask him to substantiate his claim and free him from his "anxiety and suspense."[17]

Upon beginning his quest, before filling his notebook with questions, Mullah Ḥusayn had chosen two standards for testing whoever claimed to be the Promised One. The first was a treatise by himself full of abstruse and mysterious allusions. He felt only that wisest of souls could unravel his treatise. The second was the story of Joseph as told in Sura 12 of the Qur'án, a tale that had beguiled poets and mystics for centuries. He had previously asked Siyyid Káẓim to write about Joseph. Siyyid Káẓim had said it was beyond him but "that great One . . . will, unasked, reveal it for you. That commentary will constitute one of the weightiest testimonies of His truth . . ."[18]

While Mullah Ḥusayn inwardly considered these two conditions of his, the youth again said, "Observe attentively. Might not the Person intended by Siyyid Káẓim be none other than I?"[19]

Mullah Ḥusayn then handed him his treatise. The youth opened the book, glanced at a few passages, closed it, and began to speak, easily unraveling all its mysteries and going on to expound further verities that Mullah Ḥusayn recognized as being new, distinct from all the old references, statements that were "endowed with refreshing vividness and power." Then the youth said, "Now is the time to reveal the commentary on the Súrih of Joseph."[20]

For most Westerners familiar with the Bible, Joseph is the Old Testament hero of the story about the coat of many colors. Distinguished by this and other gifts given to him by his father, Jacob, and by the many favors and blessings bestowed upon him by nature—his great beauty, his marvelous dreams—he brought down upon himself the jealousy and wrath of his brothers, who decided to kill him. They stripped him of his coat of many colors and left him in a pit in the desert, but in the end they sold him to a passing caravan, killed a wild beast, bloodied his coat, went home and told Jacob that his favorite son was dead.

Joseph arrived in Egypt as a slave. There, he served in the household of one of the Pharaoh's chief ministers, and because he was so beautiful, the minister's wife fell madly in love with him, pursuing him while he resisted her until, by her machinations, he ended up in an underground dungeon. There, he interpreted his fellow prisoners' dreams, and finally his prowess as a seer reached the Pharaoh's ears, and he was able to interpret a strange dream of the Pharaoh's as a prediction of famine and to recommend a way to save Egypt from it. So Joseph became a great man, in charge of food supplies for a nation and more—eventually, not knowing his true identity, his brothers appeared before him, having traveled to Egypt in search of food.

Joseph still loved his brothers; when he saw them again after so many years, "he sought where to weep; and he entered into his chamber and wept there." But he didn't reveal his identity to them until he felt they were ready to go home and tell their father that Joseph wasn't dead and that Jacob, who had never ceased grieving, would be reunited with him. Then Joseph allowed himself to weep again, but this time he "wept aloud; and the Egyptians heard, and the house of Pharaoh heard."[21]

Muḥammad retold the story of Joseph in the Qur'án, as He retold the stories of Noah, Christ, Mary and many others. He called Joseph's "the most beautiful of stories" and endowed Joseph with prophetic or apostolic status. In Muḥammad's telling, Jacob was so aggrieved at the loss of Joseph that he went blind from weeping, yet he could never believe that Joseph was really dead. When Joseph at last revealed himself to his brothers in Egypt, he gave them his shirt to take to his father to prove his existence. As the brothers, still very far away from Jacob, set out for home from Egypt, "their father said, 'I do indeed scent the presence of Joseph,'" and when at last they reached his side and "cast (the shirt) over his face . . . he forthwith regained clear sight."[22]

What could that scent have been like? In the Bible, the scent of *Jacob's* raiment is described by *his* father, Isaac, as "the smell of a field which the Lord hath blessed." Isaac then blesses Jacob and says, "Let peoples serve thee, and nations bow down to thee. Be lord over thy brethren, and let thy mother's sons bow down to thee . . ."[23] Certainly Joseph was the true son of Jacob's soul, the inheritor of his qualities.

As we can see from just these few brief references, both the Old Testament and the Qur'án imbue the story with layers of meaning. Muḥammad says, "It is not a tale invented, but a confirmation of what went before it . . . and a Guide and a Mercy to any such as believe." Western artists have long been fascinated by the Biblical story—two twentieth century examples are Thomas Mann's *Joseph and His Brothers* trilogy and the 1968 musical *Joseph and the Amazing Technicolor*

Dreamcoat. Muslim mystics—in many, many works, but represented most famously perhaps by the poet Jami in his masterwork *Yusuf and Zuleika*—have for centuries longed to "find a trace of the traceless Friend" and "inhale the fragrance of the lost Joseph." Among them, of course, was Mullah Ḥusayn.[24]

So his young host, in Shiraz, unasked by him, took up a pen and, reciting aloud all the while, wrote in Arabic without pause a flow of verses that were the first chapter of his commentary on The Most Beautiful of Stories.*

Scholar Nader Saiedi points out that this commentary was not merely backward looking, focused on its story that was written in the past, but forward-looking, prophetic. It was more interpretation than commentary—a renewing, recreative, transformative and revelatory interpretation. The youth began by reciting and simultaneously writing about verse 101, one of the last verses of the sura, where Joseph, finally reunited with his entire family, prays that at his death he'll be in utter submission to God and thus united with all the righteous souls of the past. For Muslims, utter submission to God is Islam.

Mullah Ḥusayn's host wrote, "Verily, the essence of religion is none other than submission to This Remembrance . . . Whoso seeketh Islam, let him submit unto this Remembrance . . ." So He, identifying Himself as the Remembrance, immediately asserted His belief in His mission and the meaning of His existence. As the Remembrance, He described Himself as "He Who standeth concealed at the point of ice amidst the ocean of fire." He also identified Himself as "the Joseph of Divine Unity" and "the Joseph of the Supreme Origin."[25]

---

* He composed in Arabic because that was traditionally the language of revelation for Islam ever since Muḥammad had reinvigorated the language with the Qur'án. Later, he would also compose his scripture in Persian, an innovation even when used to answer questions (Saiedi, *Gate of the Heart,* p. 27).

Mullah Ḥusayn later recalled sitting "enraptured by the magic of His voice and the sweeping force of His revelation" until silence fell. Once more, now very reluctantly, Mullah Ḥusayn "rose . . . and begged leave to depart." The youth smiled and told him that if he went into the city looking and acting as he did just then, people who saw him would think he was insane. Within himself—his annihilated self, his newborn self—Mullah Ḥusayn could only agree. He felt he was bearing witness to the Creator's covenant with humanity—"Am I not your Lord? "Yea! (Balà) We do testify."[26]

In fact, to code his words with additional meanings, Mullah Ḥusayn's young host frequently used the numerical significances which can imbue Arabic letters and words, adding great weight to mystical compositions. When completed (which it was not on that first night), the Commentary on the Sura of Joseph contained 111 chapters, each chapter adding up to forty-two verses: "The number 42 is equal to the word balí (read as balá) or 'yea,' referring to the affirmative response uttered by the faithful to the primordial covenantal call of God . . ."[27]

So Mullah Ḥusayn's being resounded with "yea" as his host proclaimed, "This night, this very hour will, in the days to come, be celebrated as one of the greatest and most significant of all festivals. Render thanks to God for having graciously assisted you to attain your heart's desire . . ." He summoned Mubarak to serve dinner, which the man did with a grace and alacrity that impressed Mullah Ḥusayn and made him think that the servant's life had surely been transformed by "the regenerating influence of his Master." He then said that he "for the first time, recognized the significance of this well-known traditional utterance ascribed to Mohammed, 'I have prepared for the godly and righteous among My servants what eye hath seen not, ear heard not, nor human heart conceived.'" He became convinced that even without the brilliant verses of the Commentary on the Sura of Joseph he would have had to accept his host's claim to be the Promised One because of the "quality of hospitality and loving-kindness" that he felt "no other human being could possibly reveal."[28]

Mullah Ḥusayn had found on his journey "a trace of the traceless Friend . . ." He had inhaled "the fragrance of the long lost Joseph" and he was "dissolved in the fire of love . . ." And he was not the only listener whose life and understanding were transformed that night. Mubarak maintained a vigil outside the door, and so did the young host's wife, who told a visitor years later: "What an extraordinary night that was!" Her husband, "his whole being . . . ablaze" had told her "tonight we will entertain a dear guest." He had advised her to sleep, but, she said, "I remained awake all night and could hear His blessed voice until the morning, conversing . . . chanting the verses, and presenting proofs and arguments."[29]

All night long Mullah Ḥusayn sat at the feet of the Shirazi youth and listened to Him intone incantatory and revelatory verses interspersed with invocations and prayers. As dawn breezes began to whisper, the young man said to Mullah Ḥusayn, "O thou who art the first to believe in Me! Verily I say, I am the Báb, the Gate of God, and thou art the gate of that Gate. Eighteen souls must, in the beginning, spontaneously and of their own accord accept Me and recognize the truth of My Revelation. Unwarned and uninvited, each of these must seek independently to find me . . ."[30]

He told Mullah Ḥusayn not to tell anyone what had occurred that night. He was to busy himself in the mosque in prayer and teaching. "I . . . will join you in congregational prayer. Beware lest your attitude towards Me betray the secret of your faith."[31]

When Mullah Ḥusayn left the home of the Báb, he was transformed. He felt, he said, as if "a thunderbolt" had "benumbed my faculties. I was blinded by its dazzling splendor and overwhelmed by its crushing force . . . a sense of gladness and strength . . . seemed to have transfigured me. How feeble and impotent, how dejected and timid, I had felt previously . . . Now . . . the knowledge of His Revelation . . . galvanized my being. I felt possessed of such courage and power that were the world, all its peoples and its potentates, to rise against me, I would, alone and undaunted, withstand their onslaught . . ."[32]

He began to teach classes as instructed by the Báb. He used a text by Siyyid Káẓim and he attracted many students because of his brilliant reputation, but his companions were mystified: he had vowed not to stay in one place until he found his Promised One, yet here he was, staying in Shiraz, apparently not having found him. When they questioned him, he said, "I am stranded here." He later recalled, "My hardest time was those forty days when I was the only believer in the Báb and had to keep this secret in the depths of my heart, not being allowed to share it with my nearest friends, not even my brother."[33]

Mercifully for him, during those forty days, the Báb from time to time sent Mubarak by night to invite him to visit. Mullah Ḥusayn and the Báb would be awake until dawn, with the Báb revealing verses and the mullah sitting at His feet "fascinated by the charm of His utterance." It took the Báb forty days to reveal all of His Commentary on the Most Beautiful of Stories, it's likely that Mullah Ḥusayn was listening to Him recite it. Because he was so intuitively receptive to the Báb's eloquence, it's no wonder that he had trouble controlling his urge to tell everyone about Him, for the Báb described Himself as the "servant" interpreting text by raising "all that is motionless unto the lofty station of vibrant motion . . ." Finally, one night the Báb said, "Tomorrow, thirteen of your companions will arrive . . . Leave them not to themselves, for they have dedicated their lives to the quest of their Beloved . . ."[34]

That morning, when Mullah Ḥusayn had returned to his temporary quarters in the Ílkhání Mosque, a mullah named 'Alíy-i-Basṭámí arrived with twelve companions. Mullah 'Alí came from the outskirts of a small agricultural town in Khorasan. He'd studied with Siyyid Káẓim for years, becoming one of his prize pupils and accompanying him on his last pilgrimage to Kazimayn.[35]

He left his companions outside and met privately with Mullah Ḥusayn. "You know well how great is our confidence in you . . ." he said. "Obedient to your summons, we have forsaken our homes and have gone forth in search of our promised Beloved . . . We have followed in your footsteps . . . ready to acknowledge whomsoever you accept . . . How is it that we now see you teaching the people and conducting their prayers and devotions with the utmost tranquility? . . . agitation and expectancy seem to have vanished from your countenance. Tell us, we beseech you, the reason . . ." He inferred that perhaps Mullah Ḥusayn himself was the Promised One, and, if so, they would submit to his will.[36]

Mullah Ḥusayn replied that although it may seem that his "peace and composure" came from "the ascendancy" he seemed to have attained in Shiraz, that was far from the truth. He indicated that perhaps he'd found the object of his quest but that "God . . . according to His inscrutable wisdom" had ordered him to conceal the fact.[37]

Then Mullah 'Alí began to weep and begged Mullah Ḥusayn to tell him the name of the person he'd found. But Mullah Ḥusayn, faithful to his trust, demurred, consigning the seekers to divine guidance. Mullah 'Alí rushed back outside and told his friends that they must continue their search—praying, fasting, meditating. He began his own vigil. On the third night of it, he had a vision of a light which he followed until he saw the face of the One he sought. He knew His identity, probably from the old days in Karbala. He went to Mullah Ḥusayn, and at daybreak the two of them appeared at the house of the Báb. The servant was ready to open the door, saying the Báb had summoned him earlier and told him to expect "two guests . . . early this morning . . ." So Mullah 'Alí became a Bábí, and eventually his twelve fellow-travelers did, too.[38]

Ṭáhirih's brother-in-law* was among them. When he met the Báb, he sang Ṭáhirih's poem as she had requested him to do and presented the Báb with her letter. The Báb revealed "an exalted ordinance" for her and named her a Letter of the Living, a Dawn-breaker, one of His first followers, the only woman among them. It's interesting to note that among the first eighteen Letters of the Living, only Ṭáhirih and her two brothers-in-law† came from families of wealthy, distinguished, high-ranking mullahs. For example, Mullah Ḥusayn was the son of a dyer, while 'Alíy-i-Basṭámí, who would bring Ṭáhirih the Báb's first book and soon afterward become the first Bábí to die for his faith, was likely the son of a small landowner. Another Letter of the Living was an itinerant reciter of the Muharram passion plays.[39]

And the Letter of the Living acclaimed first in spiritual station by the Báb was the son of a poor rice farmer from Babul, then called Barfarush, a major trade center in northern Iran's Caspian region. He was Quddús—the title was given to him by the Báb, and it means *the most holy.* Quddús's family had Shaykhi affiliations, and he went to Mashhad to study in early adolescence. There he joined a small group of students that included Mullah Ḥusayn. A few years later, he was in Iraq, studying with Siyyid Káẓim, always arriving last at the classes, seating himself in the back of the room near the door, maintaining silence, always the first to leave. He was eighteen then and remained young throughout his meteoric life, brashly youthful in appearance and unconventional in his dress.[40]

---

* Mírzá Muḥammad-'Alí Qazvíní, the husband of Ṭáhirih's sister, Marḍíyyih, and the son of her maternal uncle Mullah 'Abdu'l-Vahháb (Nabíl-i-A'ẓam, *The Dawn-Breakers,* p. 81).

† Mírzá Hádí, another son of 'Abdu'l-Vahháb's, became a Letter of the Living (Nabíl-i-A'ẓam, *The Dawn-breakers,* p. 80).

He had a Christlike mystique, the freedom of selfless poverty, and wore a signet ring with part of a Qur'ánic verse on it: "If thou seest me (that) I am less than thou in wealth and children." The rest of the verse (Sura 18:39–40) reads, ". . . yet it may be that my Lord will give me better than thy garden, and loose on yours a thunderbolt out of heaven, so that it will be a slope of slippery sand . . ." So Quddús embraced detachment. In 1843, acting as a mullah in his hometown, his considerable eloquence and charisma excited the enmity of other clerics.[41]

In 1844 he made his way south, arriving in Shiraz travel-stained and disheveled. Walking down a street, he encountered Mullah Ḥusayn, embraced him, and ardently asked if he had attained his goal. Mullah Ḥusayn tried to calm and deflect him, but the Báb was walking a little distance off, and Quddús said, "Why seek you to hide him from me? I know him by his gait!" "Mullah Ḥusayn answered by repeating famous lines of Persian poetry: 'One's eyes must be of such clear sight / To know the King, wear what He might.'"[42]

Later, the Báb told Mullah Ḥusayn that He had previously communicated with Quddús in the world of dreams and had been awaiting His arrival. The Báb said "the King" had to make Himself known. In his Commentary on the Sura of Joseph, He equated His Letters of the Living, the Dawn-breakers, with Joseph's long-lost brethren: "O Concourse of Light! Verily, God hath ordained you to be the brothers of Joseph. Ye attain his presence and yet shall never recognize him except when he maketh himself known unto you." When He sent Mullah 'Alí to Karbala with his book, and others of His disciples to other places with it, it was reminiscent of Joseph sending the first sack of grain home to the bereft Jacob in famine-wracked Canaan.[43]

Ṭáhirih's brother-in-law returned to Karbala, bringing the Báb's letter to her, and in August, Mullah 'Alíy-i-Basṭámí arrived there, carrying a copy of the Commentary on the Most Beautiful of Stories, that "manifesto of the new revelation." He had friends with him, all enthused new converts. In Karbala, they found many of the Shaykhis stale and bitter with disunity and egocentric claims to leadership, but Ṭáhirih and others grasped the Báb's book with relief: it gave them direction and confirmation.[44]

Ṭáhirih recognized in it the words she'd heard in her dream of the youth in the black cloak and green turban, and she prostrated herself, forehead to the ground, in a rapture of thanksgiving. She immediately translated the text from Arabic into Persian and began disseminating it. No doubt she felt she had no choice but to translate it, given its assurance: "Whenever the faithful hear the verses of this Book being recited, their eyes will overflow with tears and their hearts will be deeply touched by Him Who is the Most Great Remembrance . . ."[45]

She embraced the Báb's book as a message to all people—not only the erudite few who knew Arabic—and she understood the transmission of that message as a heart-to-heart affair, for the "concept of 'heart'. . . is one of the most important principles in the writings of the Báb," the heart being in His lexicon not a mere seat of emotion but a sacred sanctuary, the "celestial witnessing spot." So, "the animating principle that runs through works like the Quayyumu'l-Asma* . . . is . . . a mystical love which sees in everything the Countenance of the Divine Beloved." To "everything" we can, of course, add "everyone." Ṭáhirih knew that her mission as a Dawn-breaker was universal—no one, however humble, could be excluded from a chance to consider the new teachings of the Báb.[46]

And we can imagine her joy when she read in the text of his book the Báb's instructions that His followers should gather in Karbala and He would meet them there. But, sadly, although the Báb did plan to

---

* *Qayyúmu'l-Asmá* is the Arabic name of the Commentary on the Sura of Joseph.

return to Karbala, His purpose would be frustrated, and Ṭáhirih would never meet Him. She would always be a disciple from afar—thus, her lyric, "If by chance I see Thee face to face" expressing her yearning, "I'll tell Thee my travail in minute detail . . ." In the same poem she writes:

My poor heart is wrung with anguish for Thee
  That binds my breast to the very stuff of life,
Filament by filament, vein by vein, artery by artery.

Ṭáhirih traverses her deep heart's core parting
  Veil from veil, absence from absence, and finds
Only presence, only Thee—Thee, and Thee alone.[47]

So we see her, flooded by an enlightenment that would never abate no matter what happened, writing prolifically in Persian and Arabic, "composing odes and lyrics," and praying long and ardently. She taught everyone, illiterate and learned alike, about the Báb and His message, and she sent long letters to religious leaders in Karbala "in which she ably vindicated her high purpose and exposed their malignant designs." From now on, she would be never be still; she would be homeless, a wanderer, a fugitive, a prisoner, yet forever free, her "dwelling-place in the shadow of the Essence."[48]

9

As a Slave Sitting Under a Sword

Telling the Most Beautiful of Stories. First news of the Báb in the Western world. Identifying the Báb. Khadíjih, His sweet love. Identifying Bahá.

In Karbala and its surroundings, the Báb's courier, Mullah 'Alí, taught people from the book he'd brought, the Commentary on the Most Beautiful of Stories. He was barely recovered from a beating he'd received after leaving the Báb. Just three miles from Shiraz, he'd been viciously clubbed by the irate father of a young man interested in the Báb's teachings. Nevertheless, he'd crossed the mountains, taken the relentlessly hot sea voyage over the Persian Gulf and continued across Iraq to the Atabat. The Báb had foretold that Mullah 'Alí would be the first to suffer for His cause and had said to him, "If you be slain in this path, remember that great will be your reward . . ."[1]

In obedience to the Báb's orders, Mullah 'Alí didn't disclose the identity of the author of the Commentary on the Most Beautiful of Stories. Neither did his companions, and Ṭáhirih also kept the Báb's identity a secret. That is, they said that He was the Báb, the Gate or Herald of a new era, but they didn't say that He was the young merchant from Shiraz Who had been recognized for His radiant devotion when He'd visited Karbala as a pilgrim a few years before.

However, some people remembered that young man and felt that if He had written the book, His claim must be true. Others, in response to such rumors, couldn't imagine that a self-educated youth of the merchant class, no matter how pious, could produce such an authoritative volume, one that claimed to be not only the new Qur'án, but "the Inner Qur'án." Siyyid Káẓim had told his students that their promised one would not be a recognized scholar. Until religious duties engulfed Him, the Prophet Muḥammad had been a merchant whose probity earned Him the name *al-Amin*, the Trustworthy. And He was illiterate, relying on memorization of His Qur'ánic recitations and on scribes to record them. Yet in the nineteenth century, many messianic thinkers "unanimously anticipated and were even firmly confident that the gate of the divine knowledge would come from a house of knowledge and learning and not from the ranks of the guilds and trades."[2]

This despite the fact that Persian merchants were known as "perhaps the most respectable part of the population," the Comte de Gobineau wrote. "They are regarded as being very honest . . . and as (they are) are more often than not sons of merchants who have inherited a more or less substantial fortune which they will (in turn) transmit to their sons, they are devoid of worldly ambition and above many forms of intrigue. They need public esteem and carefully cultivate it."[3] But this esteem didn't extend to theological or literary endeavor.

However, as was the case with the Qur'án, the writings of the Báb were independent of social expectations and conventions, and the Bábís relied on the Báb's scripture as proof of His claims, for He identified Himself with the text. It was His miracle, and it was His being, just as the Qur'án was Muḥammad's miracle and being.

As Islamic tradition states of its Prophet, "His character was the Qur'án." In fact, Muḥammad said that "If the whole of mankind and djinns were to gather together to produce the like of this Qur'án, they could not . . ." Yet, He went on, people continued to ask Him to "cause a spring to gush forth . . . or . . . cause the sky to fall in pieces . . . or . . . bring God and the angels before us face to face . . . or . . . have a house adorned with gold . . . or . . . mount a ladder right into the skies. No, we shall not even believe in thy mounting until thou send down to us a book* that we could read."[4]

So, knowing the odds stacked against him yet believing in the Báb's miracle just as he believed in Muḥammad's, on Oct. 6, 1844, Mullah 'Alí officially presented the Báb's book in Karbala. He didn't choose his announcement date at random; it corresponded with the 23rd of Ramadan—the Night of Power, the night that is said to be "better than a thousand months"—the anniversary of Muḥammad's bedazzlement by the first verses of the Qur'án in the cave on Mount Hira, verses called *ayat* by the Prophet. The Arabic word *ayat* means not only verses but signs and miracles; and the Báb also called his verses ayat.[5]

The next week, Mullah 'Alí went to the neighboring town of Najaf and declared "the approaching advent." He was "bearing a copy of the Koran [sic] which he stated to have been delivered to him by the forerunner of Imam Mahdi," wrote Henry Rawlinson, the British consul general in Baghdad, to his superior. Again, Mullah 'Alí consciously chose the date of his announcement: October 14, which was Eid al-Fitr, the celebration at the end of the Ramadan fast.[6]

As one of the early Bábís later recalled, after Mullah 'Alí's announcements "a body of the divines in Najaf and Karbala were seized with consternation. They arose in opposition and stirred themselves to vocif-

* Qur'ánic commentator Yusef Ali explains that they wanted a physical, parchment book, literally brought back from ethereal heaven (The Holy Qur'án, p. 721, note 2297).

erous denunciation. The Government hearing of what had transpired, became concerned lest disorders might ensue, and deemed it politic to imprison the messenger, confiscate the books and tablets in his possession and send him to the seat of the province, that is Baghdad . . . When the messenger reached Baghdad the Vali (governor) kept him in prison and placed the books and treatises in the council-chamber. My father . . . visited the messenger every day in prison . . ."[7]

Mullah 'Alí taught his visitor and, as the visitor's son remembered, "Whatever he heard he imparted to those who were seekers so that, during this short time, a large number of people came to believe." Noticing the rapid expansion of the Báb's following, the governor called "the divines of all the regions to come to Baghdad . . . They brought the messenger to this terrible assembly and asked him who the Lord of the Cause was. He answered: 'The awaited Spirit of Truth hath come. He is the One promised in the Books of God.' Then he read them some verses and prayers and called upon them to believe . . ."[8]

As the inquisitional noose, the net of a dangerous fate foreseen by the Báb, tightened around the neck of Mullah 'Alí, Rawlinson continued to issue reports on him. His letters, which reached Lord Aberdeen, the British Foreign Secretary in London in 1845, might be considered the first news of the Báb and his new faith to reach the Western world.[9]

Westerners viewed Iran as a sprawling provincial backwater. Rawlinson could have had no idea that in the Commentary on the Most Beautiful of Stories, despite the obscurity of the circumstances in which it was written, the Báb addressed the "peoples of the West," telling them to "issue forth from your cities . . . and aid God. . . . Become as true brethren in the one and indivisible religion of God . . ." Or that He summoned the "peoples of the earth," saying, "Verily His Remembrance is come to you from God after an interval during which there were no Messengers, that He may purge and purify you from uncleanliness in anticipation of the Day of the One true God . . ."[10]

Rawlinson couldn't have suspected that the Báb presented His cause as a universal religion and envisioned it being furthered by a successor who would far outshine Him. His name would be *Bahá*, meaning *glory, light, splendor*. The Báb wrote, "Indeed God hath created everywhere around this Gate oceans of divine elixir, tinged crimson with the essence of existence and vitalized through the animating power of the desired fruit; and for them God hath provided Arks of ruby, tender, crimson-colored, wherein none shall sail but the people of Bahá . . ."[11]

If Rawlinson had realized these things, he might have wondered how the inhabitants of Iran, a xenophobic land cut off from modern progress, could accept such an expansive new prophet. And it would have been worth wondering about. In fact, the intense persecution that immediately engulfed the Bábís included accusations that they were complicit with Western imperialists.

Ṭáhirih, more attuned to the Báb than most of her brethren, discerned the identity of the mystery-shrouded Bahá mentioned in the Báb's first book and wrote to Him in 1844. He was a young nobleman of Tehran who had become a Bábí in June of that year. How did she reach her conclusion? The nobleman came from an outstanding family and she must have heard about his conversion, but as we have already seen, high birth was not a qualification for spiritual superiority in her mind. However, the Báb at one point described her as "that mirror which has purified its soul in order to reflect the word by which all matters are solved . . ." And she said that after receiving the Commentary on the Most Beautiful of Stories, she "reached the state of intuitive certitude." In an ode to Bahá she wrote, "The effulgence of the Abhá* Beauty hath pierced the veil of night; behold the souls of His lovers dancing, moth-like, in the light

* A derivative of the name *Bahá*. It means *Most Glorious* (A. Q. Faizi, *Explanation of the Symbol of the Greatest Name*, p. 5, http://www.bci.orb/prophecy-fulfilled).

that has flashed from His face!" With all her beauty and erudition, she had a certain sword-thrust simplicity. And perhaps it was as Jami wrote: "Thy Beauty accompanies all the beautiful . . ."[12]

This was her magnanimity. With eyes like Henry Rawlinson's, she would have seen the Báb merely as an unsophisticated young merchant and His early follower in Tehran as an aristocrat schooled in poetry, horsemanship, politics, and well-acquainted with the intrigues and intricacies of the shah's court. Let us look at them now to see who they were in the world, and who they were to Ṭáhirih.

The twenty-five-year-old importer-exporter who said to Mullah Ḥusayn, "Verily . . . I am the Báb, the Gate of God," and prayed before him in "ethereal, subtle harmonies" was Siyyid 'Alí-Muḥammad, born on October 20, 1819 in Shiraz. He was His parents' only child, and both His mother and father descended from the house of the Prophet and from influential families who had lived in Shiraz for generations. His father was apparently a retail clothier in the Shiraz bazaar. His shop and the family ownership of it may have dated back one hundred years. Others in the Báb's family, especially on his mother's side, appear to have engaged in more widespread trade with concomitant economic results, but his father concentrated on prayer and mystical studies and was honored for his piety. The family of the Báb is now known as the Afnáns.[13]

During the Báb's childhood, His father died, perhaps during a cholera epidemic, and His mother, a very strong character herself, enlisted the help of her three brothers to rear Him. The second-oldest of these maternal uncles,* was His guardian, became like a father to Him and later was His only blood relative to become His follower during His

---

* Ḥájí Mírzá Siyyid 'Alí <u>Sh</u>írází.

lifetime. He knew that he had on his hands a handsome boy who was quiet but not at all diffident. The Báb showed His mettle at an early age, when He was five years old, on His first day at a thoroughly conventional *maktab*, or Qur'án school.[14]

In later years, an older pupil who sat with the Báb on that day recalled the child's unusually dignified and courteous manner, which matched His equally independent thinking. He was told to recite, along with the rest of the small boys, the first lines of a primer that had been set in front of him, and He absolutely refused to open His mouth. The older pupil asked the Báb why He didn't join in the recitation. The Báb maintained silence, and the questioner remained mystified until the voices of two students nearby reached their ears. The students were reciting Hafez: "From the pinnacles of Heaven they call out unto thee; / I know not what hath thee herein entrapped." The Báb looked up at the older boy and said, "There is your answer."[15] From this, it would seem that even as a very young child the Bab felt a higher calling and didn't easily tolerate being "entrapped" by the world, especially the conventional trappings of school with its rote learning.

The Báb referred to Hafez again when He overheard some older students questioning their teacher on a particular subject. The teacher told them he'd look up the answer at home that night and bring it to them the next day. Then the Báb spoke, answering the question Himself, and when the teacher asked Him how He knew the answer, He smiled and recited the following couplet by Hafez: "Should the grace of the Holy Spirit once again deign to assist, / Others will also do what Christ could perform."[16]

The teacher, who was a follower of Shaykh Aḥmad, saw in the child signs of the expected promised one, and felt inadequate to teach Him. He brought the Báb to His guardian-uncle, saying, "He . . . stands in no need of teachers such as I." Although the uncle inwardly agreed, he sternly instructed the Báb to return to school, "to observe silence, and to listen attentively" to the teacher's every word. It is likely that the Báb's guardian wished to protect Him, cloak Him in commonality until the inevitable day when that would no longer be possible.[17]

The Báb tried to obey His uncle, but He wasn't interested in child's play and was sometimes late for school. Other students sent to fetch Him at His family home would invariably find Him immersed in prayer. When His teacher asked Him about this, He would say that He'd been in the house of His Grandfather. (Siyyids often referred to the Prophet Muḥammad as their Grandfather.) The teacher said that a boy under ten was under no compulsion to pray so rigorously, and the Báb replied, "I wish to be like my Grandfather."[18]

When He was finally relieved of school, where the only subject He'd really enjoyed had been calligraphy, the Báb went to work in Bushehr, running his uncles' trading house there. He was fifteen, the age of maturity according to Islamic law, and He had apprenticed for His uncles in the bazaar and in their offices for many years.[19]

Despite His generous spending of capital to assist the poor and His absorption in prayer to the denigration of his practical concerns, "His scrupulous attention to detail and His undeviating fairness in transactions became widely known in the region." In that, as well as in His prayerfulness, He was like His "Grandfather."[20]

However, unlike Muḥammad, the Bab was literate. He knew Persian and Arabic, and He used them with much more eloquence than can be attributed to a maktab schooling "often described by himself and others as archaic, monotonous and cruel." In two of His most important books, the Arabic *Bayan* and the Persian *Bayan*, He mentions how His former schoolmaster flogged students and says that teachers are "forbidden" to "cause any grief" children under five years old. Of course, He didn't countenance brutal treatment of older children, either.[21]

He began revealing His philosophy even before Mullah Ḥusayn and other seekers became aware of Him. He wrote treatises at least as early as His sojourn in Bushehr. In fact, His guardian-uncle enlisted a friend to advise him "not to write certain things which can only arouse the jealousy of some people: these people cannot bear to see a young merchant of little schooling show such erudition, they feel envious." However, the friend had refused to give that advice, quoting a poem, "The fair of face cannot put up with the veil; shut him in, and out of the window will he show his visage."[22]

To some, the Báb's probity as a merchant—and His piety—indicated great virtue, but to others, His lack of attachment to material things and His devoutness indicated insanity. There must be something wrong with Him, they reasoned. Even in the intense heat, under the bullet-like sun of Bushehr, He would spend hours on His rooftop praying; at sunrise, He'd gaze northward toward Tehran and pray with such ardor that people said He was worshipping the sun. He also regularly attended gatherings eulogizing the Imam Ḥusayn, where fellow worshippers were deeply moved by the unusual sincerity of His tears. He was, of course, aware of the frequent showmanship involved in mystical weeping, and later quoted an Arab poet who said that everyone cries for Layla all night, but when tears actually drip down from soaked cheeks onto necks and clothing, then we know "who weeps and who pretends weeping.'"[23]

But if He was detached from success in business, His uncles were not—though His guardian-uncle would soon lose His mercantile enthusiasm. Besides their offices in Shiraz and Bushehr, His uncles also had one in Yazd. They traded along a southern route with ports in Arabia, India, Zanzibar and Java, and they imported English fabric, tea, sugar, coffee, and other processed goods—what we now call value-added products. However, their exports were mostly unprocessed: dried fruits, grains, spices, tobacco, raw silk, and livestock. Of course, the prices of the value-added imports, such as highly finished English damasks, hardly evened out with the lower prices of the raw cash crops, so Iranian traders suffered. Also, during the 1830–40s, a northern trade route opened up, competing with the southern one.

Adding to the economic instability, while the Báb was in Bushehr, the British pressed their gunboat diplomacy. In 1837, they tried to occupy Bushehr, landing with their navy. The people of the city rioted against them, and they withdrew to Kharg Island. In 1839, they again tried to enter Bushehr, and this time a religious authority and the governor led the protesting rioters. Again, the British went back to the island. In 1841, they finally managed to establish their official Residency* in Bushehr.[24]

As for the Báb, His prayers, visions, dreams, and heartfelt longings led Him away from his uncles' offices and trade routes. He wrote to His uncles, asking them to take over the Bushehr office for Him so he could go on pilgrimage to the Atabat, but when they procrastinated, He balanced His accounts with the help of Mubarak, locked His office, wrapped His black cloak around Himself, and left. By the time His guardian-uncle—sent by the Báb's mother, who had meanwhile arranged the Báb's marriage—came to Iraq to retrieve Him in 1841, He had a reputation as "the Ecstatic One" and "the praying siyyid," and this stayed with Him after His return to Shiraz and His marriage.[25]

He was twenty-three in 1842 when He married Khadíjih-Bagum,† the woman to whom He always referred as His well-beloved. She was His cousin, had known Him in her childhood, and had grown up in the house next door to his guardian-uncle's. She'd dreamed of Him when he was about sixteen, seeing Him "in a verdant plain, with flowers in profusion, facing towards . . . Mecca . . . in an attitude of prayer . . . (and wearing an outer coat) on which Qur'ánic verses were

* Office of the British governor-general's representative, as distinct from an embassy, which is an ambassador's office.

† *Bagum* is an honorific denoting a lady of high rank.

embroidered with threads of gold." Around the time of their marriage, the Báb's guardian-uncle, his life also touched by intimations from proximity to his enigmatic nephew, withdrew from trade and from the public to await the Advent.[26]

Khadíjih found herself happy and harmonious with her gentle husband, and her mother-in-law also treated her with wonderful kindness, but her contentedness was interrupted one night by a dire dream, and when she told the Báb about it, He predicted that they would enjoy, in all, only two-and-a-half years together.

Khadíjih became pregnant and then almost died while giving birth. The Báb wrote a prayer on a mirror and told His mother to hold the mirror in front of His wife. His mother did so, and Khadíjih and the baby survived—but the infant, a son, died shortly afterwards. The Báb's mother scolded Him: if you're so powerful, why didn't you make the birth easier, spare your wife such suffering, and also spare the child's life? The Báb replied that He wasn't destined to leave progeny. His mother was furious, but He would say nothing more. The child was buried under a cypress in the tomb of a medieval holy lady thought to have been a Christian nun.[27]

The Báb mostly spent His days in contemplative strolling outside the city walls and visits to His uncle's office, coming home at sunset to spend part of the evening writing letters or meditations, frequently in a state of prayer. One day, He came home before sunset and requested an early dinner. He and His wife dined with His mother in her room. Later that night, Khadíjih woke and realized He'd left their bed. After an hour, she went looking for him, trying the street door of the house to see if He'd gone out, but it was locked from within. Then, she said, "I walked to the western side of the house, looked up at the roof-top, and saw that the upper chamber was well-lighted . . . I had never known Him to go to that part of the house at that hour of the night, unless He had guests. And He always told me when a visitor was expected. He had not said that He was to have a guest that night. So, with both astonishment and trepidation, I went up the steps at the northern side of the courtyard."[28]

She continued, "There I saw him standing in that chamber, His hands raised heavenwards, intoning a prayer in a most melodious voice, with tears streaming down His face . . . and His face was luminous; rays of light radiated from it. He looked so majestic and resplendent that fear seized me and I stood transfixed where I was, trembling uncontrollably . . . I was on the point of screaming, when he made a gesture . . . telling me to go back . . . and I returned to my room . . ."[29]

Yet she barely slept. At dawn, when she heard the muezzin's call to prayer, she went to her mother-in-law's room. There sat the Báb, drinking tea. His mother wasn't present. When Khadíjih remembered how overwhelming the Báb had looked the night before, she "paled and shuddered involuntarily." The Báb gave her His cup and told her to drink what was left of His tea. She did, and recovered her composure. She was able to tell Him, "You are no longer . . . the same person I knew in our childhood. We grew up together, and we have been married for two years . . . and now . . . you have been transformed . . ."[30]

He smiled and said He hadn't wished her to see Him like that, but it must have been God's will so that when He made His great announcement she would accept it "with absolute certitude."[31]

In truth, she was, from that point on, His first follower. A later historian wrote, "No one except Táhirih, among the women of her generation, surpassed her [Khadíjih] in the spontaneous character of her devotion nor excelled the fervor of her faith." Soon after this incident, she and the Báb were separated by circumstance and never reunited. Whenever she spoke of Him then, she'd be overwhelmed by sorrow and become mute. He wrote to her, "My sweet love, may God preserve thee." Years after His brutal early death, she became a follower of Bahá, Who said, after she passed away, that she had ". . . before the creation of the world of being, found the fragrance of the garment of the Merciful."[32]

But from now on, we'll refer to Bahá by His full title, Bahá'u'lláh. He was two years older than the Báb and gifted with the same ineffable tenderness and kindness. He was born Mírzá Ḥusayn-'Alí on November 11, 1817, in Tehran, but His childhood home was the mountainous, wooded region of Núr, a name that means *light.* The area reputedly was named for a saint who lived there in ancient times and, it was said, radiated light when he spoke. According to legend, a celestial tree would grow in Núr, with branches touching heaven and fruit nourishing the world. It was also said that Zoroaster retreated there to pray and meditate and that one day the mountains of the region would forever imprison the king of hatred and war. Núr was in the province of Mazandaran, a large and storied region known as the last part of Iran to surrender to Islam during the Arabian conquest.

On His father's side, Bahá'u'lláh was descended from Yazdigird III, the last Zoroastrian king of Iran. On his mother's side, the line of descent went back to Zoroaster Himself. His lineage also connected to sons of Abraham who, in Biblical times, migrated to Iran and Afghanistan.[33]

Bahá'u'lláh's father was a calligrapher of such artistry that he'd received a robe of honor from Fatḥ-'Alí-Sháh. He was vizier to the chief of the shah's imperial guard and was known for sagacity and generosity. The shah titled him Mírzá Buzurg (great prince). He had three wives, three legal concubines, and sixteen children.

Bahá'u'lláh's mother was the second wife. She was a widow who already had a son and two daughters. And Bahá'ulláh wasn't His father's firstborn son, yet His parents favored Him. His mother remarked that, as an infant, He never cried. Later, when He was about seven, she and His father were watching Him walk about the garden, and when she said it was a shame that He wasn't taller, Mírzá Buzurg snapped that it didn't matter, for He had stature granted by brilliance, perception, and rare maturity.

His gifts are apparent in some of the anecdotes that survive from His boyhood. Bahá'u'lláh Himself wrote of how sad He felt as a child when He read the story of the Banu Qurayzah, a Jewish tribe in the time of Muḥammad whose men were all executed by decree of a leader of their Jewish and Muslim alliance because they violated a pact. The tribe had risen in arms against the alliance—and by Jewish law, in such a case, everyone in the tribe, including women and children, should have been killed. So the slaughter of the men was relatively merciful. However, Muḥammad did not want it to occur at all. He bowed to the Jewish leader's decree. The young Bahá'u'lláh lamented that such a tragedy had taken place and prayed for trust and love to unite all the people of the world.[34]

He also described his childhood reaction to a wedding feast for one of His older brothers where the entertainment included a puppet spectacular with trumpet fanfares, guns emitting real smoke, a bejeweled puppet king, his minions of richly garbed nobles, and puppet troops engaged in war, apparently shedding real blood. The young Bahá'u'lláh was fascinated with the play and afterwards stayed in the tented pavilion watching the puppet master pack up his actors—mere tinseled dolls now—and all of his equipment. Everything fit into one box. Bahá'u'lláh later recalled that the puppet master told him, "All these lavish trappings, the king, the princes, and the ministers, their pomp and glory, their might and power, everything you saw are now contained within this box." To Bahá'u'lláh, as He later said, "ever since that day, all the trappings of the world . . . seemed . . . akin to that same spectacle . . ."[35]

Yet the boy grew up immersed in these worldly "trappings." His father owned a huge mansion-compound in Tehran, various country estates, and entire villages. Having dreamed portentously of Baha'u'llah's future, and feeling that "amongst all his sons and daughters, this son . . . was one apart," he inscribed, in his own inimitable calligraphy, in a mansion where the family usually spent the summer, ". . . this is the vale of Love, hold thy steps; / This is holy ground, shed thy foot-gear." Reportedly, that was what Moses heard on Mount Sinai when he neared the Burning Bush.[36]

For His part, Bahá'u'lláh rejoiced in mountains and forests, meadows and gardens, and His green province of Mazandaran was replete with all those. He had the education common to aristocrats of the day—literature, etiquette, falconry. Hunting was, of course, the sport of kings. Fatḥ-'Alí-Sháh loved it—there are many paintings of him and his courtiers hunting, for they were expected to ride with him as he proved his prowess. Growing into adolescence, the sons of noblemen were expected to win his favor by becoming part of his hunting and camping entourage. There is no mention of Bahá'u'lláh ever joining this activity. It's doubtful that He wanted to; in later years, He grieved His gardener by telling him not to bother the locusts that were devouring the leaves of His trees—after all, they had to eat, too. But His gardener's distress became too great, so at last Bahá'u'lláh went and stood beneath the trees, remarked that the gardener did not want the locusts and saying, "God protect you," lifted the hem of His robe. The locusts rose in a cloud and flew away.[37]

He did love horseback riding, the long treks through the mountains down into the city of Tehran and back again. As He grew into adolescence, people began coming to Him to resolve their problems, and He became chief mediator and judge in His sprawling family. He had a sunny disposition, and children were drawn to him. And despite the fact that He hadn't been educated as a theological scholar, He didn't hesitate to expound on religious questions.[38]

Sometimes during His country ramblings, He visited a popular religious class run by a distant relative. He'd sit cross-legged on the floor among the large gathering of students and eventually speak up and answer some abstruse question with simple logic. One day the instructor gave the students a riddle: What does Islamic tradition mean when it says Fáṭimih was the best of women except the one born to Mary? The students bandied about various solutions until Bahá'u'lláh said the answer was that there wasn't any woman better than Fátimih, since Mary didn't have a daughter.[39]

The teacher was highly offended that a youth who wore the black lambskin kolah, a high, slant-crowned sort of top hat used by princes and courtiers, knew more than his turbaned students did. He related to his students a dream he'd had that he wandered into a room full of trunks—all the property of Bahá'u'lláh, he was told. He opened one and saw it jammed with books so bejeweled that their blinding light woke him. He interpreted the dream to mean that Bahá'u'lláh was honored by association with himself and his publications.[40]

No doubt Bahá'u'lláh's father would have interpreted the dream differently. Most people who had known Bahá'u'lláh since childhood held him in high regard. His father, too, was steeped in esteem: the shah had made him governor of a mountainous region populated by warlike, rebellious, bandit tribes. Mírzá Buzurg dealt with them wisely, as he also dealt with the enmities and rumors of the king's court. Then Fatḥ-'Alí-Sháh died.[41]

In 1835, the new monarch, Muḥammad Sháh, started purging the old administration, installing his own people. His Prime Minister, Áqásí, a conniver with a scanty double-pointed beard and rapier fingernails, knew that Mírzá Buzurg had once said of him, "May this satyr be kept away" from a position of authority. In fact, he had the letter where Mírzá Buzurg had written it. He summoned the eighteen-year-old Bahá'u'lláh to his office and showed him the letter, ranting that he didn't know what he'd done to deserve such libel. Bahá'u'lláh preserved a discreet silence.[42]

Soon afterwards, Bahá'u'lláh's marriage to his fifteen-year old cousin was lavishly celebrated. That was the last great event Mírzá Buzurg hosted. A flash flood destroyed one of his most valuable properties; he lost his position as vizier and his generous stipend; he had to mortgage and sell much of his remaining property; he was mired in exorbitant debt and entangled in legal claims engineered by Áqásí. Eventually he was placed under house arrest. Bahá'u'lláh rode to Tehran and managed to have him freed, but in 1839, Mírzá Buzurg died, having maintained patience and charity despite his ruin, even to former friends who betrayed and abandoned him.[43]

After his father's death, government positions were offered to Bahá'u'lláh, but He refused them. Áqásí, who hated Him, said, "Leave him to himself . . . He has some higher aim in view," and proceeded to try to destroy His reputation by attacking His "feasting and banqueting," saying he was meditating a plot to overthrow the government.[44]

It happened that Bahá'u'lláh and His wife rarely participated in aristocratic social life, preferring to care for the needy, so much so that they were called "The Father of the Poor" and "the Mother of Consolation." Bahá'u'lláh responded to the prime minister's accusations: "Gracious God, is the man who, out of the abundance of his heart, shares his bread with his fellow man, to be accused of harboring criminal intentions?"[45]

So it happened that when Mullah Ḥusayn arrived in Tehran in 1844, having come straight from the Báb in Shiraz and bearing a message for an unnamed personage who was to meet certain standards and possess certain characteristics, the answers to his questions led him to Bahá'u'lláh. Mullah Ḥusayn was staying in a madrassa in the city, discreetly teaching the Báb's message to those he deemed receptive. Late one night, he was speaking with a young man who, he found out, came from the province of Núr. Mullah Ḥusayn asked him if there was one among the late Mírzá Buzurg's sons who was similar to his father, superior to his siblings. The young man named Bahá'u'lláh—i.e., Mírzá Ḥusayn-'Alí of Núr.[46]

"What is His occupation?" Mullah Ḥusayn asked. "He cheers the disconsolate and feeds the hungry," came the reply. "What of his rank and position?" "He has none, apart from befriending the poor and stranger."[47]

Mullah Ḥusayn asked more questions, and all the replies confirmed that this was the person the Báb intended him to find. He gave the young man a scroll wrapped in cloth; the scroll contained some of the Commentary on the Most Beautiful of Stories. He asked that it be brought to Bahá'u'lláh at dawn. The young man did so, finding both Bahá'u'lláh and one of His brothers awake, for this was the hour when the poor frequently came to the house for help. In fact, the brother, Mírzá Músá, was standing in the doorway of the house, and it was he who later related the history of the delivery of the Báb's scroll.[48]

Bahá'u'lláh unsealed the scroll, unfurled it, and began to read aloud. Almost immediately He asked His brother: "Músá, what have you to say?" As for Himself, the words of the Báb were, He felt, of "divine origin," like the Qur'án, and were "endowed with the same regenerating power." He gave the young messenger a gift of Russian sugar and some fine tea to bring to Mullah Ḥusayn.[49]

Fine tea and that particular variety of sugar were rare in Iran at the time and were considered very luxurious gifts. However, when the staid, ascetic Mullah Ḥusayn clasped the gifts and kissed them, the messenger wondered at such an uncharacteristically emotive reaction, knowing it wasn't because of the material value of the sugar and tea.[50]

Ṭáhirih would not have wondered. And her conviction, like Mullah Ḥusayn's, would have been affirmed when news reached her of Bahá'u'lláh's first actions after receiving the message from the Báb: He traveled to his home region of Núr to share it. There, He found both belief and skepticism. His charisma was so great that, like Muḥammad before him, and like the Báb, He was accused of sorcery. A religious leader in Núr said of Him, "A youth, a layman, attired in the garb of nobility, has . . . invaded the stronghold of orthodoxy, and disrupted the holy faith of Islam . . . Whoever attains his presence falls immediately under his spell, and is enthralled by the power of his utterance. I know not whether he is a sorcerer, or whether he mixes with his tea some mysterious substance that makes every man who drinks it fall victim to its charms."[51]

Bahá'u'lláh's life, like the Báb's, was now in constant danger, and indeed all the Bábís operated as if under a death warrant. Bahá'u'lláh would come to describe it in these words: "I have been, most of the days of My life, even as a slave, sitting under a sword hanging on a thread, knowing not whether it would fall soon or late upon him."[52]

This sense of threat was never a deterrent to Bahá'u'lláh, the Báb, or to those who followed in their footsteps such as Ṭáhirih, who was, from the first, one of the chief leaders of the Báb's disciples. In fact, danger spurred her to action, and she urged others to allow it to goad them onward, too.

10

Fire and Ice

Ṭáhirih's "secret of secrets." Mullah 'Alí's fate. Lost promise. The London Times reports. Al-Ṭáhirih's command. The posterity of the Prophet. In the abode of the enemy.

The veils that constructed Ṭáhirih's family unity and the security they gave her were rent asunder when she left for Karbala at the end of 1843, and they completely vanished when she became a Bábí in 1844. But she felt a wholeness and assurance in the "divine norm" or standard that she said differed greatly from "the human norm." With insights from the Báb's first book flooding her heart, she said only inner awareness of the divine standard could lead the seeker to unravel "the secret of secrets," progressive revelation. From Karbala, she wrote to her cousin Javad that the Báb was "the Grand Divine Proof," the fulfillment of Shaykhi teachings; she said spiritual endeavor, not rational thought, had liberated her vision: "With an insight free from intruders, I observed God's power and omnipotence (and realized) that this great cause most definitely needs a locus of manifestation." How could the Creator "leave the people to themselves," she reasoned, when "it is necessary for

His grace to increase, His benevolence to broaden and His blessing to mature . . . And day after day the cycle of universe is in progress . . ." and "there is no suspension in his emanation."[1]

As has been stated previously, the term "manifestation" is used to signify a shining forth, an appearance. The Báb referred to himself and other Prophets, or divine educators, as Manifestations of God revealing the Creator's will and attributes, harking back to the story in the Qur'án of God teaching Adam "the nature of all things." Qur'ánic commentator Yusuf Ali says that the literal words in Arabic are *"the names of things . . . "* 'Abdu'l-Bahá,* the son of Bahá'u'lláh and His designated interpreter of Bahá'í teachings, later explained, "'The Objective Point of all is the Manifestation of God. And whoever directs his attention in prayer to that Focal Point has directed his attention, verily, to God.'" For the Creator is beyond human reach, although Its life-force and intent are in the human just as an artist's brush strokes and life-force are in the painting. Thus the thin but absolutely unbreakable line between a Revelator and His God; He cannot *be* God, but speaks for God, manifests His Maker's radiance.[2]

Circa 1910, 'Abdu'l-Bahá told pilgrims from the West who were staying in His home a story of Ṭáhirih, calling her, as He frequently did, by her well-known title, *Qurratu'l-'Ayn* ("Solace of the Eyes"): "On a certain occasion the famous heroine of this Movement, Qurratu'l-'Ayn, chanced to meet a devout Muhammedan who was praying and questioned him thus, 'To whom art thou praying, may I ask?' 'I am praying to the very Essence of Mercy and the Reality of Divinity.' And she, smiling, said, 'Oh away with your god! Away with him. Come, and I will show you the God of today. It is the Báb! Your god is a phantom, while *this* is certainty. Can the Sea be contained in a little glass?'"[3]

---

* The title *'Abdu'l-Bahá*, which He took for himself in his maturity, means *Servant of Glory.* His given name was Abbas, and He was born on in May, 1844, in Tehran, on the same night that the Báb declared His mission to Mullah Ḥusayn.

Not that she believed the Báb was God. 'Abdu'l-Bahá would later explain that the Creator could "never be comprehended" because It is "comprehensive," so the "'reality of Divinity is . . . beyond comprehension," and Ṭáhirih knew this. For the Bábís, and now the Bahá'ís, the Creator is a mystery surpassing perception for any human, including a divine Revelator. Many are the passages in the scriptures of all religions in which a Revelator expresses His own mystification before God, as in this one by Bahá'u'lláh: "I swear by Thy glory, O Beloved of my soul! I am bewildered when I contemplate the tokens of Thy handiwork and the evidences of Thy might, and find myself completely unable to unravel the mystery of the least of Thy signs, how much more to apprehend Thine own Self. . . "[4]

However, the Manifestation, according to Bahá'u'lláh, has a dual nature. He wrote that humans have "the unique distinction and capacity" to know and love God, "a capacity that must needs be regarded as the generating impulse and the primary purpose underlying the whole of creation." He said that God had "shed the light of one His names . . . upon the inmost reality of each and every created thing," but "He hath focused the radiance of all of His names and attributes" upon human reality.[5]

However, He likened the "energies with which the . . . Source of heavenly guidance" endowed human reality to the flame latent in the candle and the light latent in the lamp. He wrote:

> The radiance of these energies may be obscured by worldly desires even as the light of the sun can be concealed beneath the dust and dross which cover the mirror. Neither the candle nor the lamp can be lighted through their own unaided efforts, nor can it ever be possible for the mirror to free itself from its dross. It is clear and evident that until a fire is kindled the lamp will never be ignited, and unless the dross is blotted out from the face of the

> mirror it can never represent the image of the sun nor reflect its light and glory.
>
> And since there can be no tie of direct intercourse to bind the one true God with His creation, and no resemblance whatever can exist between the transient and the Eternal, the contingent and the Absolute, He hath ordained that in every age and dispensation a pure and stainless Soul be made manifest in the kingdoms of earth and heaven.[6]

This Soul was the Manifestation of God, a "subtle, mysterious and ethereal being" with "a twofold nature; the physical, pertaining to the world of matter, and the spiritual, which is born of the substance of God Himself." Bahá'u'lláh writes that the Manifestation has a "double station." He goes on to say:

> The first station, which is related to His innermost reality, representeth Him as One Whose voice is the voice of God Himself. To this testifieth the tradition: "Manifold and mysterious is My relationship with God. I am He, Himself, and He is I, Myself, except that I am that I am, and He is that He is. . . ." The second station is the human station, exemplified by the following verses: "I am but a man like you." "Say, praise be to my Lord! Am I more than a man, an apostle?"
>
> These Essences of Detachment, these resplendent Realities are the channels of God's all-pervasive grace. Led by the light of unfailing guidance, and invested with supreme sovereignty, They are commissioned to use the inspiration of Their words, the effusions of Their infallible grace and the sanctifying breeze of Their Revelation for the cleansing of every longing heart and receptive spirit from the dross and dust of earthly cares and limitations. Then, and only then, will the Trust of God, latent in the reality of man,

> emerge, as resplendent as the rising Orb of Divine Revelation, from behind the veil of concealment, and implant the ensign of its revealed glory upon the summits of men's hearts . . . [7]

Shaykh Aḥmad and Siyyid Káẓim had characterized the Manifestation as the Perfect Man and "the manifestation of the Muḥammadan Truth," yet certain Shaykhis feared that to accept the Báb might be disloyal to those two teachers. Ṭáhirih's answer to their doubt was her view that in fact the only person who had truly recognized the spiritual greatness of Shaykh Aḥmad and Siyyid Káẓim was the Báb Himself, whom she called "the point of the point in the circle of being." The Shaykhi writings held the key for understanding her "secret of secrets"; namely, the oneness of all divine revelation and the need for it to be continual, unceasing, and progressive. With her deep understanding of the Báb's purpose from the time of his first book, The Commentary on the Sura of Joseph, in which he summoned "people of the West" to His Cause, she saw beyond the borders of her nation and her time to envision the ultimate purpose of divine Revelation as the establishment of world unity. And 'Abdu'l-Bahá later said, "The holy Manifestations of God were sent down to make visible the oneness of humanity."[8]

Ṭahirih was among the first of the Bábís to really see this universal purpose and to believe in and teach progressive revelation. She immediately perceived and championed the unified reality that had been the heart of Shaykhi theology and was now the heart of the Báb's theology. In the Báb's interpretation of the story of Joseph, the well into which Joseph's brothers cast him is "the well of Absolute Unity . . . deep and dark . . . " In it, "all differentiations and distinctions are obliterated . . . " It is "the unfathomable realm of utter effacement and nothingness."[9]

The ecstatically mystical Ṭáhirih embraced self-effacement and nothingness, tossing away egocentric, institutional formulae that made one religion superior to another and one intellect superior to another.

She began to disseminate the Báb's proclamation of equality in His Commentary on the Most Beautiful of Stories—that "each and every Prophet . . . established a separate Covenant concerning the Remembrance of God and His Day," and His assertion that His new creed was "the essence of the Faith of Muḥammad."[10]

She rejoiced in the Báb's conception of how "phenomenal history and the Sacred Word" related to each other to express "the principle of progressive revelation." This was the heart's logic, her logic. With the revelation of the Báb, all her life's doubts and questions were resolved. She wrote:

I bound my heart to Your curls of flowing hair
  And now from the bonds of both worlds I'm set free.

Religion to me has always seemed dusty, old.
  Only the light of Love has marked my path.
With this eternal covenant I hold
  To love You—chosen freely and in faith. . .

In her teaching circles under the sponsorship of Siyyid Káẓim's widow she presented progressive revelation using reason and logic, while urging her listeners to pray that their hearts might accept it.[11]

She grasped and imparted how the principle of progressive revelation propelled people past dire prophecies of the end of the world into a dawn of discovery. Instead of turning around and around and inward, Bábí vision spiraled forward and opened outward. Hers was the clearest and freest Bábí voice in Karbala. She deeply internalized how the Báb's Commentary on the Story of Joseph affirmed Joseph's declaration of the oneness of religion to his fellows in Pharaoh's dungeon, as told in the Qur'án: "O my two companions of the prison! (I ask you): Are many lords differing among themselves better, or the One God, Supreme and Irresistible? If not Him, ye worship nothing but names . . . for which God hath sent down no authority . . ." And the Báb warned His followers that when the time came for the one He heralded to arise, that "true Joseph," they must not barter Him away for "a paltry price."[12]

The Báb's claims agitated and attracted many, augmenting for Iraq's authorities the problem of what to do with Mullah 'Alí, his courier who had brought the Commentary on the Sura of Joseph into the country. They brought him to trial before a court of Sunni and Shiite mullahs (a mix of sects that was unprecedented). The court examined the Báb's book and issued a fatwa against it, saying it was blasphemous and anyone who believed in it should be put to death. It attempted to imitate the Qur'án, and this was forbidden; the author took liberties with Qur'ánic texts and made the book innovative—also forbidden; and finally, the author claimed He brought the Advent, a criminally extreme stance that undermined religion itself and *sharia*, the body of Islamic law. Perhaps worst of all to the mullahs, the Báb summoned them to leave their institutions and join Him.[13]

Each signer of the fatwa then answered the question: "And so is he (the Báb) an unbeliever (in Islam) by virtue of what we have mentioned or not? And is the one ('Alíy-i-Basṭámí) who has believed in him and has lent him credence in this matter and has assisted him in spreading and propagating it and has preached it to the people an unbeliever or not?"[14]

The decision was inconclusive. The Sunnis wanted to sentence Mullah 'Alí to death for apostasy, while the Shiites recommended exile from the shrine cities for him and anyone like him who openly proclaimed "a belief in the expected immediate advent of the Imam." Ultimately the Ottoman government had to make a final decision.[15]

At the same time, the Bábís in the shrine cities eagerly awaited the arrival of the Báb Himself. He had made His pilgrimage to Mecca, fulfilling Qur'ánic prophecy as He saw fit, and soon, they expected, He would be en route to them. But when He came to the port of Bushehr in southern Iran, the governor of Fars province sent horsemen to arrest Him. Instead of waiting to be accosted, the Báb rode out to meet His destiny. About forty miles from the port, as His party began to mount from plain to plateau, He spotted the governor's men and sent Mubarak ahead to summon them. They didn't want to approach Him, but, finally, one of their officers rode forward. When the Báb inquired as to their mission the officer answered evasively, but the Báb said, "'The governor has sent you to arrest Me. Here am I; do with Me as you please.'"[16]

So the Báb returned to Shiraz in custody, while Mullah 'Alí spent more months in prison in Baghdad as the Persian and Ottoman governments fought over him. The Shiites had no soft spot for him or his beliefs, but they feared that if an Iranian mullah was killed on Ottoman soil, the already rebellious and frequently violent Iranian populace would find even more cause to revolt, so the Iranian prime minister, Áqásí, wanted him deported to Iran. Finally, in April, 1845, Major Rawlinson wrote his superiors that "'the Persian Priest of Shiraz so long detained in confinement at this place was sent to Constantinople (Istanbul).'"[17]

After that, no one knows exactly what became of Mullah 'Alíy-i-Basṭámí. Passing through Mosul, he apparently raised a stir by openly proclaiming the Advent. Then, some said, he was ill from his long imprisonment and died on his way to Istanbul, while others said he was killed. But it seems, from the most reliable report, that he actually reached Istanbul and was condemned to hard labor. A month later, Iranians again protested his sentence and demanded his deportation. They won, but when they went to find him, they discovered that he had died. Even if he'd survived, who in Iran would have granted him life?[18]

No matter how he died, we know that to him, death was a blessed end. When he first left the Báb in Shiraz, he was accosted and clubbed outside the city. He managed to tell his attacker, "Stay your hand, for the eye of God is observing you . . . I mind not the tortures you inflict upon me, for I stand prepared for the most grievous afflictions in the path I have chosen to follow. Your injuries, compared to what is destined to befall me in the future, are as a drop compared to the ocean . . ."[19] The attacker didn't stay his hand, but continued the beating until that hand was exhausted.*

Despite his own acceptance of his fate, the disappearance of Mullah 'Alí was a blow to the Bábís in the shrine cities, and then they received news that the Báb wouldn't be coming to them. This was a great test of faith. Even when the Báb was in Mecca "with the word," He said, that would "split asunder whatever is in the heavens and the earth," He had forecast that He would "commence the new Cause" in the "hinterland of Kufa."[20] Some of them had expected that He'd appear even while Mullah 'Alí was still in jail and ride to the rescue, then go on to lead an insurrection. Anyway, how was it possible that a Revelator could break His promise?

Certain Bábís abandoned the cause. The Báb wrote to Mullah Ḥusayn that "for every person in the Book of your Lord there is a written destiny . . ." It wasn't His destiny to visit Karbala and its surroundings at that time, and He invited Mullah Ḥusayn and others who could to come to Him in Shiraz. He also reminded them that "God is above the interpretation that oppressors make of the great, supreme word" and advised them not to be "intimidated by the Baghdad verdict (against His book and His messenger). Struggle in the path of your Lord by (means of) wisdom and firm arguments, in which there is a remedy for the denials and the denunciations of the ulama, if you are conscious of the Divine cause and believe in it."[21]

---

* The attacker was named 'Abdu'l-Majíd, and later, in Baghdad, he met Bahá'u'lláh, received His forgiveness, and became a Bahá'í. This was after his son, whom he'd been trying to keep from the new religion, died for it in Tehran (Nabíl-i-A'ẓam, *The Dawn-Breakers*, pp. 89–90).

For the Báb, these words were more than easy encouragement; they arose out of great suffering. He did not use the word "struggle" lightly. He "explains in one of his works (that) each act of denial by the people was like the blow of a sword cutting his heart in pieces—a spiritual martyrdom far more painful than any physical death."[22]

In prayer, He addressed His Maker, "O Lord! . . . You know what I heard in the Mother of the Cities (i.e. Mecca) of the opposition of the ulama and the denial Your servant encountered . . . Therefore, I gave up my goal, and did not travel to that land, hoping that the sedition . . . would settle and those who were obedient to You would not be humiliated, and no one would find a chance to inflict the slightest harm upon someone else . . . My Lord, this is Your decision and this is Your command . . . and You directed me toward what I understood from Your Book . . . This was not my initiative but it was Your will . . ."[23]

The Báb was trying to mitigate pain for His followers; He didn't cancel His plan to go to Karbala out of fear of danger to Himself. He walked into danger upon His return to Iran; He didn't run from His arrest, and within months, He was under sentence of death in Shiraz. His was a message of fire, but His own nature was so gentle and empathetic that if the tears He shed over His followers' sufferings could have put out the fire, they would have. However, His own nature was of necessity subsumed by His mission, and at one point He referred to Himself as "He who standeth concealed at the point of ice amidst the ocean of fire." And fiery was the response. In November, 1845, such a response—literally—was reported in the London Times.[24]

It was the first public mention of the Báb in the West. It called Him an imposter and described him as "a merchant who had returned from a pilgrimage to Mecca, and proclaimed himself a successor of the Prophet." It told how "Four persons being heard repeating their profession of faith according to the form prescribed by the imposter, were apprehended, tried, and found guilty of unpardonable blasphemy. They were sentenced to lose their beards by fire being set to them . . . "The next day "each of them was led by an executioner who had made a hole in his (the victim's) nose and passed through it a string, which he sometimes pulled with such violence that the unfortunate fellows cried out alternately for mercy . . . and for vengeance from heaven." Onlookers gave the executioners money in return for the spectacle, and "in the evening when the pockets of the executioners were well filled . . . they led the unfortunate fellows to the city gate, and there turned them adrift."[25]

This report, which came from British merchants in Shiraz, was reprinted in 1846 in a U.S. publication called *The Eclectic Magazine of Foreign Literature, Science, and Art,* and also in the *Literary Gazette of London.*

One of the afflicted was Quddús, who had accompanied the Báb on His pilgrimage to Mecca and afterwards was sent before Him to Shiraz to convert the Báb's guardian-uncle and also disseminate the contents of a new book by the Báb. The book was taken up earnestly: another Bábí whose beard was burned off was a mullah* who obeyed its injunction to insert a phrase into the call to prayer: "I bear witness that He whose name is the Báb is the servant of the Remnant of God" (referring to Bahá'u'lláh). This caused a riot. Quddús was arrested along with the proclaimer of the new call and one other (possibly two others, as in the report, but that isn't certain), and they underwent even more than the torments described in the Times.[26]

The mullah, a seemingly frail man of advanced years, had also proclaimed from the pulpit passages of the Báb's Commentary on the

* He was Mullah Ṣádiq-i-<u>Kh</u>urásání, and this was the first of his afflictions, for he would again give the Báb's call from the pulpit, and would again be beaten (Nabíl-i-A'ẓam, *The Dawn-Breakers*, p. 186–87).

Sura of Joseph; when he was brought before the governor, the governor read the opening sentence of the book— "Divest yourselves of the robe of sovereignty, for He Who is the King in truth hath been made manifest"—and was enraged, demanding to know if Muḥammad Sháh himself was expected to abdicate. The mullah said, "If the words be the Word of God, the abdication of Muḥammad Sháh and his like can matter but little. It can in no wise turn aside the Divine Purpose . . ."[27]

The governor ordered that the mullah be stripped of his clothing and lashed one thousand times. Surprising all onlookers, the man survived the torture. Afterwards, his beard was burned off, and so was the beard of Quddús. It had taken the governor some time to turn his attention to Quddús; he'd first been dismissive of Quddús because of his "youthful appearance and unconventional dress."[28] Perhaps he thought he was merely a holy fool who had wandered in to see the show.

The Báb, meanwhile, was under surveillance, confined in Shiraz. After riding out to meet the party sent to arrest Him, He had ridden at the head of the troops straight to the city's citadel, instead of entering Shiraz in chains as the governor had envisioned.[29]

When the governor roared at him, ranting that he was a disgrace to Islam and to the shah, the Báb quoted the Qur'án, "O ye who believe! If a wicked person comes to you with any news, ascertain the truth, lest ye harm people unwittingly, and afterwards become full of repentance for what ye have done." As the governor and the clerics present likely knew, the quote continues, "And know that among you is God's Apostle: were he . . . to follow your (wishes), ye would certainly fall into misfortune . . ."[30]

The governor barked at an attendant to strike the Báb. The blow was a hard one—it bruised the Báb's face and knocked His turban off—a severe impact, especially if the turban were fastened with a chin strap. The Friday Imam of the city gently picked up the turban and replaced it on the Báb's head, but another cleric assailed the Báb verbally and physically. The Báb's uncle, alerted by Mubarak, who had ridden ahead to inform him when the Báb was intercepted by soldiers, rushed to the scene, posted the Báb's bail, and took His nephew home. The Báb had to stay under house arrest. During this time, and until the end of His life, He showed the transformation in His nature wrought by the mantle of mission enveloping Him. He may have been confined, but He constantly welcomed visitors. Mubarak led them to His presence via a secret "interior door leading from the home of the mother-in-law of the Báb," and Mubarak, as always, delivered letters and messages from Him to various recipients. The stone had been thrown in the pond, so to speak, and nothing could stop its outward ripples.[31]

But, far away in Karbala, the Bábís felt abandoned. It fell to Ṭáhirih to rally whom she could. She did so with exhilaration. On Ashura, the day of lamentation for the Imam Ḥusayn, which fell on December 30 in 1845, she refused to wear mourning. Instead, she dressed festively and urged her sister and other women companions to do the same. She had a reason: it happened to be the Báb's birthday, and she thought it was time to celebrate. Out with the old, in with the new! Righteous Shiite denizens of the shrine cities were scandalized, and so were a lot of S͟hayk͟his and Bábís.[32]

The Shiites of the shrine cities lived as if washed up on an island in a sea of enemy Sunnis. Sunni Muslims observe Ashura the way Muḥammad observed it—to them, Ashura is a day of voluntary fasting declared by the Prophet when He established His community in Medina. Of course, Ḥusayn's tragedy didn't occur during the Prophet's lifetime. Some fifty years after the Prophet's death, Ḥusayn challenged the Sunni-installed caliphate, and Sunnis don't recognize Ḥusayn and his fellow Imams.[33]

Sunnis regard Ashura as a day of rejoicing because they say Muḥammad took it up as a tradition from the Jews of Medina, who fasted on that day to commemorate the liberation of the Hebrew slaves from

Egypt when God parted the Red Sea and let Moses lead them across. Muharram is one of the four holy months when Muslims are not to engage in warfare. (But that prohibition is constantly broken, as it was when Ḥusayn was attacked.) Also, the first day of Muharram is the Islamic New Year, the day Muḥammad arrived in Medina in 622 A.D., day one of year one of the Islamic calendar. But Shiite Iran clings to the Zoroastrian (and pre-Zoroastrian) New Year on the spring equinox.[34] Perhaps a wisdom in the Báb's setting the New Year of His calendar* on the ancient Naw Ruz was to avoid the roiling controversies linked with Muharram. Certainly He revered Ḥusayn. In His Commentary on the Sura of Joseph, He condemned "such as waged war against Ḥusayn" and said "God knoweth well the heart of Ḥusayn, the heat of his burning thirst and his long-suffering . . ."[35]

Ṭáhirih, translator of that book from Arabic to Persian, was in complete accord with Him. There was nothing irreverent in her festive garb. In fact, there was reverence: she was leaving institutionalized sorrow behind and embracing the joy of a new day. This is from a poem of hers that many Persian-speaking Bahá'is currently chant when they celebrate the Birth of the Báb:

> Dawnbreak! Daybreak! Blessed be today!
> Revived, renewed, fresh off the loom, blessed be today!
>
> Sun ascending! Day of dominion! Dwell in joy today!
> Spin raw silk of happiness and dance, this blessed day . . .
>
> Why wait? My robe is re-embroidered on this very morn.
> Why hesitate? The veil splits, sun's up, splendor is born . . .[36]

---

* That calendar is now in use worldwide by the Bahá'ís.

Given such eloquent jubilation, by 1845, Ṭáhirih had a following of Bábí women and men called the *Qurratiya,* after her title Qurratu'l-'Ayn, (Solace of the Eyes). The women came from different backgrounds, but many were highly accomplished. Among them were her well-educated sister Marḍíyyih; a Shaykhi scholar titled Shams-i-Duha (Morning Sun); the widow of Siyyid Káẓim; the poet Bibi Kuchak, who was Mullah Ḥusayn's sister; the poet mother of Mullah Ḥusayn; and Ṭáhirih's devoted maid Qánitih. Meanwhile, several Shaykhis had set up their own teaching circles, asserting themselves as authorities, even claiming prophethood.[37]

At the beginning of 1846, Ṭáhirih lost a firm friend and defender when Siyyid Káẓim's widow died. One of the Shaykhis began teaching in Siyyid Káẓim's house, concurrent with Ṭáhirih's classes. His group was small, about twenty-three people, most of them related to him. But his tongue and his letters to authorities did a huge amount of damage. He called Ṭáhirih "bint-i-talih," daughter of evil, a pun on "bint-i-Ṣaliḥ," daughter of Mullah Ṣaliḥ.[38]

Because of him and others like him, in August of 1846, Ṭáhirih moved to the town of Kazimayn and spent about six months there, fearlessly continuing her very public teaching. Some Shaykhis wrote to the Báb. Should they give credence to her opinions? What was her station, was she above them, did she have the right to lead and to innovate?[39]

The Báb responded, "Concerning what you have inquired about that mirror which has purified its soul in order to reflect the word by which all matters are solved: she is a righteous, learned, active, and pure woman; and do not dispute al-Ṭáhirih in her command for she is aware of the circumstances of the cause and there is nothing for you but submission to her since it is not destined for you to recognize the truth of her status."[40]

Seventy Bábís in Kazimayn heard the Báb's letter read aloud. Some were satisfied by it; others disclaimed the Báb. The chief instigator of the anti-Ṭáhirih scandal had written to the Báb on his own, and in reply the Báb called Ṭáhirih "the pure leaf" and upheld her implication that she herself was proof of God's liberating greatness, saying, "Let none of those who are my followers repudiate her, for she speaks not save with evidence that has shown forth from the people of sinlessness (the Imams) . . ." The Bábís also knew that the Báb had given her the title *Siddiqih*, "the Truth." Even with this, and Ṭáhirih's offers of conciliation and cooperation, her enemies weren't assuaged but kept up their ruthless criticism and vilification.[41]

And what of the feelings of her private heart? From what we have of her prose and poetry, we can see no political or intellectual machinations within her. Her radicalism arose from love, ecstasy, the impulsion of an inborn mission that allowed her no hesitation or fear: the purity that the Báb discerned. She wrote:

You're the milk and you're the honey
You're the tree and you're the fruit
You are the sun and you are the moon
A speck, an iota, I am.

You're the palm and you're the date
You are the nectar-lipped beloved
A distinguished master, you, dear love,
An insolent slave, I am.

You are the Mecca and you are the One
You're the temple and you're the shrine
You're the beloved, the honored one
The miserable lover, I am.

"Come to me!"
Love said alluringly
"Free of pride and pretense,
Manifestation of the One, I am."

Táhirih is but floating dust at your feet
Drunk by the wine of your face.
Awaiting your blessing
A confessing sinner, I am.[42]

In this spirit—humble as dust yet daring all—Ṭáhirih invited the religious authorities of Kazimayn to debate her in public. None were willing to risk it. She then challenged them to *mubahala*, a practice defined by one historian as "mutual execration by means of sincere praying to God for the annihilation of the other party. An ancient religious test." The intent of participants in mubahala is to invoke "divine arbitration between good and evil." The gauntlet was often thrown down "as a last resort for settling doctrinal disputes between two unyielding parties with opposite views." The practice is referred to in the Qur'án (note the inclusion of women in Line 8):

If any one disputes
In this matter with thee,
Now after (full) knowledge
Hath come to thee,
Say: "Come! Let us
Gather together, —
Our sons and your sons,
Our women and your women,
Ourselves and yourselves:
Then let us earnestly pray,

And invoke the curse
Of God on those who lie. . . "[43]

This comes from an incident in the early days of Islam when a deputation of Christians visited the Prophet. They liked His teachings about Christ, and they wanted to establish ties with the new Islamic state, yet they wouldn't accept Islam as a religion. The Prophet offered mubahala, but the deputation refused. The Prophet sent them home unharmed, though He did exact what were called the wages of rule in return for protection by his State.[44]

Ṭáhirih's attackers also refused to accept her challenge. In February, 1847, she returned to Karbala, but not for long. Her enemies incited the ulama to issue a fatwa demanding her death, and a mob swarmed through the streets to find Ṭáhirih and kill her. But the mob attacked the wrong house. Dragging out of it a veiled woman, they assumed she was Ṭáhirih. But she was Shamsu'ḍ-Ḍuḥá. The mob, aided by police and other guardians of the law, dragged her through the streets into the bazaar, vilifying, clubbing and stoning her. At last her father-in-law rushed into the melee, shouting that she was not Ṭáhirih. Challenged to produce a witness, he couldn't, so local gang members, religious students and others kept beating her. Finally a voice penetrated the riot, shouting that Ṭáhirih had been arrested. Shamsu'ḍ-Ḍuḥá, half-dead, was delivered.[45]

Ṭáhirih had notified the governor, "I am at your disposal. Do not harm any other." The governor confined her to her house with guards at her door; no one could go in or out. She lived in a state of siege, isolated. All she said in her own defense was that she made no claim except to learning. She again issued a challenge to mubahala, adding, "Assemble the doctors both Sunni and Shiite, that we may confer and dispute, so the truth and falsity of either side, and the wisdom of both parties may be made apparent to all persons of discernment." Once again, none of them were willing to face her.[46]

She was sentenced to house arrest and her jailers in Karbala reported on her to the Ottoman government. But no reply came. For three months she lived in isolation, surrounded by guards. At last she herself sent a message to the governor: "No word has come from either Baghdad or Constantinople. Accordingly, we will ourselves proceed to Baghdad and await the answer there." She summoned one of her chief enemies and told him she was going to Baghdad to prove the truth of the Báb's claim. Three days later, the governor ordered her immediate departure from Karbala.[47]

As she left the city, accompanied by her staunchest friends and followers, a mob followed, stoning her. She was a woman claiming the same freedoms as a man, and even worse, in the mind of the mob, a heretical man. Her enemies started and fueled slander, accusing her of outlandishly licentious behavior, so the mob considered her a completely reprehensible prostitute.[48]

Rumors that she was immoral reached Qazvin. She wrote to her father, "I plead with you! This humblest of people is your daughter. You know her, and she has been brought up and educated under your supervision. If she had, or has, a worldly love, that could not have remained a secret to you. If you want to inquire into her affairs, God who holds the scale and is the remover of the veils would testify for her." She said that when she'd shared with him her "declaration of the word of God," he'd accused her of paganism and faithlessness. She warned him that if he kept opposing "the glorious cause of the great living Imam," he would end in sorrow. She asked her father to recognize the spirit of the Báb's words, and concluded, "Dear father! So many times when I visit the holy shrine of the Imam, may peace be upon him, in the flood of my tears I pity you and pray for you that perhaps you may be saved." In another letter she told him, "If you fail to recognize the cause, there will be no benefit for you in all your acts of devotion."[49]

He, no doubt, felt that she was utterly lost. And now she was far from him, in Baghdad. But at first, she stayed in the home of a friend who honored her and her entourage with fine and spacious hospitality that included a site for her teaching circles.[50]

Baghdad, once a center of world civilization, was in the nineteenth century a dilapidated city decorated with date palms and orange trees with the half-mile wide Tigris River at its heart, its waters nourishing the gardens on its banks. Brightly tiled cupolas and minarets rose over the tops of the city's palm trees with storks, sacred birds to the Muslims, nesting in them. Lattices, verandas, and gardens of riverside buildings hung above the Tigris on either side, while a variety of boats traveled the river, among them round crafts of cowry-shell ornamented wickerwork ferrying men, sheep, and horses.[51]

On closer look, one found that the ill-maintained banks of the Tigris and those of the Euphrates combined with the abandoned state of the city's canals to cause frequent flooding, making the land around the city marshy and malarial. Plague had killed huge numbers of the city's residents in 1831, and other illnesses were rife, so many of the narrow streets were drab and deserted, walls and houses falling into ruin.[52]

The city's mosques were crumbling; its heart was its bazaar, crammed "from daybreak to nightfall with Arabs, Kurds, Persians, Indians, and men of every color and clime . . . a horse with difficulty made his way through the crowd; and the mounted officers of the Pasha and the Bedouin on his mare, with his spear tufted with ostrich feathers, were assaulted with loud or muttered curses as they attempted to force their way through the dense mass of human beings."[53]

The human beings were mostly male, of course. Women were at home in their andaruns. The men sat on platforms in front of their kiosks smoking their water pipes, drinking coffee, and awaiting customers, or they sat in the myriad coffeehouses—smoking, sipping, playing chess or draughts or a bean game. They sported colorful garb, while any women venturing abroad were enveloped in white or black burkas, their faces hidden by black horsehair veils.[54]

Ṭáhirih's male followers went into those streets and brought back inquirers to attend her teaching circles. Among her listeners was a Jewish physician* to the shah, accompanying the king as he traveled to Karbala for a pilgrimage. The physician heard Ṭáhirih addressing a group of mullahs from behind a curtain. Not happening to catch her mention of the Báb, he thought that she herself was the Promised One, but later, in Tehran, he learned who she actually was, and became a Bábí.[55]

People who had known her previously noted a transformation, an increase in her eloquence, and commented, "This is not the woman we knew before." With all her knowledge of complicated doctrines and texts, she spoke with "an almost shocking plainness, and yet when she spoke . . . you were stirred to the bottom of your soul, and filled with admiration, and tears came from your eyes."[56]

Supporting her increased certitude was a new book by the Báb, a commentary on the 118th chapter of the Qur'án, the Sura of Kaw<u>th</u>ar (Abundance).† The Báb's commentary was some two thousand verses, but the Sura has only three verses: "We verily have conferred upon Thee the Kaw<u>th</u>ar fountain of abundance. Therefore pray unto thy Lord, and sacrifice. Verily, it is thine enemy who will be without posterity." Tradition has it that on Resurrection Day, the true believer will drink from the fountain of Kaw<u>th</u>ar and never thirst again.

Muḥammad's enemies had taunted him, saying He'd be without posterity because all His sons died in infancy. Shiite Islam finds His heirs, however, among the descendants of His daughter Fáṭimih and

---

* Hakim Masih (Mohabbat, *Paisajes del Alma*, p. 137, note 1).

† Kaw<u>th</u>ar is the fountain of all good (The Holy Qu'rán, p. 1798), a river in paradise from which all other rivers flow and which leads to the lake whose shores are home to the faithful souls that attain heaven (Bahá'u'lláh, The Kitáb-i-Íqán, pp. 243–44).

His kinsman 'Alí. The line of Imams and also the siyyids are His posterity. The Báb, a siyyid, was among the heirs of Muḥammad and, with His claim to be the One Who Would Arise, also claimed to fulfill the promise of the Sura of Abundance.[57]

In His interpretation of the sura, the Báb equates the true fountain of plenitude with His own heart and tells the reader that if she would "Behold . . . with the glance of thy heart, the loftiest outpouring of divine creation within thine own soul, thou wouldst find naught but the crystal river of the incorruptible water of Kawthar at the sublime station of divinity."[58]

And of Himself as both the herald of a Prophet-to-come, and a Prophet in His own right, He said His was "the hour of the coming together of the two worlds of descent and ascent . . . manifesting both Viceregency and Prophethood with one and the same soul . . ." The Báb knew His life and mission were short; His life was in His death. Out of His descent, the "arc of ascent" would arise.[59]

Elaborating on this "Divine Unity" in which one Prophet follows another in progressive revelation, the Báb equated *kaf*, the first letter of the word kawthar, with the primordial Word (*kalima*) that "cried out in praise of its Creator" and said it signified "the Word which shone forth on Mount Sinai . . . above the Ark of Testimony in the Pillar of Fire upon Mount Horeb . . . (and) upon Mount Paran . . . "* Unfolding His

---

* Bahá'u'lláh later mentioned Mount Paran in The Hidden Words: "Call ye to mind that Covenant ye have entered into with Me upon Mount Paran. . . " (The Hidden Words, Persian no. 71). Later, 'Abdu'l-Bahá explained remembrance of Mount Paran, saying "in the sight of God the past, the present and the future are all one . . . whereas, relative to man, the past is gone and forgotten, the present is fleeting, and the future is within the realm of hope . . . " The Covenant, then, is forever unfolding and we might say it is part of our collective consciousness. He writes that every Prophet establishes a covenant "with all believers . . . until the promised day when the Personage stipulated at the outset of that Mission is made manifest . . ." ('Abdu'l-Bahá, *Selections from the Writings of 'Abdu'l-Bahá*, no. 181.2.)

abundance, or unity, He said the "Sinaitic Tree" had "sprung up" or "had been planted . . . in his bosom" and predicted tribulations for those who remained "oblivious" of it. In support of her beloved "secret of secrets," her fount of beneficence, Ṭáhirih cited the Báb's new book frequently during her exchanges with her opponents, "leaving her adversaries in a state of complete desperation."[60]

Finally, with public curiosity growing about her and animosity against her keeping pace, fueled by jealous S͟hayk͟his and Bábís, among others, the *válí* (governor) of Baghdad called Ṭáhirih before him. He was the same man who had put Mullah 'Alíy-i-Basṭámí on trial. But he did not publicly try Ṭáhirih. Instead, he personally questioned her before witnesses; further details are unknown. He then sent to the Sublime Porte for guidance about her. His relatively gentle tactics might have resulted from his fears because the Shiites had actually won a little victory in the case of Mullah 'Alí when they prevented his outright execution. Also, it was unprecedented to put a woman on trial. Besides that, he might have felt that Ṭáhirih's oratory during a hearing could increase her following. After he interrogated her, he placed her under house arrest in the dwelling of Ibn Álúsí, the *mufti* (judge) who had wanted Mullah 'Alí condemned to death.[61]

The judge took it upon himself to debate with Ṭáhirih about the Resurrection Day, the Balance, the Reckoning and other topics from the Qur'án. He was trying to make her recant her beliefs, but she was unshakeable, and over the months that she stayed in his house, he apparently came to agree with some of her views and even allowed her, on several occasions, to continue her large teaching circles at the home of her former host.[62]

The judge was a tremendously erudite man and a prolific writer—one of his works consisted of fourteen volumes. Years later, he said Ṭáhirih had discussed her convictions with him with "no dissimulation or apprehension" and he found her more worthy of respect than most men. "She was a wise and decent woman who was unique in virtue and chastity," he said. He admired the extent of her knowledge and he observed that, far from being hedonistic and impious, she rose at dawn to pray and meditate, and she frequently fasted.[63]

He realized her so-called "followers" were Bábís, followers of the Báb, as she was, and that they believed in progressive revelation, but according to him the purpose of that was to understand "what has been previously laid down." It's possible that Ṭáhirih's meeting with Sunni ulama, observed by the Jewish physician who later became a Bábí, was hosted by the judge.[64]

One day he told her a dream he'd had and asked for interpretation. He dreamed he saw the Shiite authorities breaking into the tomb of the Imam Ḥusayn, opening the grave and beginning to lay hands on the body—which was unsullied, for a saint's remains are always inviolate. "I cast myself down on the corpse," he told Ṭáhirih, "and I warded them off." Ṭáhirih said his dream meant that he was about to free her from the hands of her Shiite enemies. "I too had interpreted it thus," he said.[65]

Soon afterwards, his father came to the house and asked to meet Ṭáhirih. Forgoing courtesies and greetings, he attacked her with curses and mockery. The judge apologized to her on his father's behalf and announced that the answer had arrived from Istanbul. "The King has commanded that you be set free, but only on condition that you leave his realms . . ." (The judge was really many faceted; a few years later he praised the governor for driving the "group of Shiite extremists calling themselves Bábís" out of Iraq, and added that "all those who possess wisdom would testify to their blasphemous beliefs.")[66]

Ṭáhirih knew that her father expected her to return to Qazvin. During her stay in the judge's home, an envoy from her family had visited, arguing for her release with the faint praise that she was a "chaste woman" who had been "overwhelmed with Satanic temptations." The envoy later reported back to her family, "The entire nobility and the ulama of Baghdad greatly respect her and confer on her highest praises. Whatever has been relayed to you . . . (about her) is slander and fabrication."[67]

No doubt the governor and judge expected Ṭáhirih to return to Qazvin immediately upon her release. And in fact her brothers were en route to meet her. However, when her order of deportation came, although she left Baghdad right away, she traveled slowly, accompanied by her entourage, taking time to gather villagers and townspeople, proclaiming her message. As if knowing the further confines and dire straits that awaited her in her native city, while it was still possible she made the most of the freedom she so urgently claimed for herself and her cause.[68]

11

Murder

People of the Absolute. Debate and debacle. The Zindiq in the inimical city. The cutting edge. Sacrificial lambs, unappeased hunger. Flight.

Accompanied by her female contingent and surrounded by about thirty armed male followers, Ṭáhirih was escorted by Ottoman guards to the Iranian border. It was around March, 1847. No doubt she traveled in a howdah, "a sort of curtained cage balanced on a horse"—or camel, or donkey—and so did her accompanying sisters. A howdah could be big enough to seat two people, so we can imagine her maid, Qánitih, or another female companion jouncing along beside her. Her male friends and the guards rode horses and other beasts, or walked. It must have been quite a procession through the rugged, mountainous terrain.[1]

Her journey, lasting about three months, took her through regions where many people belonged to the Ahl-i-Haqq ("People of the Absolute, the Real, God"), a very antiestablishment sect mainly characterized by extreme reverence for the Imam 'Alí, but with beliefs and practices that varied from group to group. The People of the Absolute were mostly concentrated in eastern Iraq and western Iran; they were highly messianic, and hardly pacifists. During the 1830s, twenty thousand of their armed men flocked to a prophesizing preacher in Azerbaijan who promised "restoration of 'the ancient purity'" and "opposition to 'the vices of the people, and the unfaithfulness of the priests.'" During the 1840s, a Kurdish poet named Timur prophesized to the People of the Absolute near Kermanshah of a "crystal tower" where "the king of blessing," the "white-clad shah," resided. "He shall come," Timur promised, "the true distinguisher, like a two edged blade. He will divide the sincere from the deceitful . . ."[2]

The same people who welcomed those seers warmly drew Ṭáhirih into their midst in the village of Karand, "that most picturesque town of the mountains, built on terraced slopes at the mouth of a great gorge, and facing a broad and fertile intermontaine valley . . ." Karand was an especially passionate and militant community: a few years before her visit, the people of Karand had killed a governor along with two hundred troops because of his "'misconduct, immorality, excessive killing, numerous rapes,'" and his "'difference in religion.'" Ṭáhirih stayed with them for three days, and when she left, 1,200 of them wanted to go with her, but she couldn't accept the offer.[3]

She went on to Kermanshah, an ancient city set against fierce, red rock peaks and populated by Kurds, Loris, and other tribes, many of them People of the Absolute. She stayed for forty days, setting up a teaching center where her deeds included translating and reciting the Commentary on the Sura of Abundance. The governor of the province and his wife "acknowledged the truth of the Cause and testified to their admiration and love for Ṭáhirih." Princes and clerics attended her teaching circles, fascinated by her profound knowledge, her eloquence and élan.[4]

Finally, pressured by orthodox mullahs, the city's chief mujtahid asked the governor to expel Ṭáhirih and her entourage. Through the governor, Ṭáhirih relayed a message to the mujtahid challenging him to either debate her or stand for mubahala. The mujtahid was unwilling to face her in either situation, so he wrote to her father and uncles, asking them what to do. Meanwhile, troops attacked her and her retinue one night, beating them, looting their possessions and arresting about twenty-five Arab Bábís. They carried Ṭáhirih, in an uncovered howdah, into a barren field and left her there with certain of her friends. They had no food, water, shelter, nor any means of traveling on.[5]

Ṭáhirih, however, had her writing materials. One of the Bábís took a letter from her to the governor: "We were guests in your city. Is this the way you treat your guests?" He read it and said, "I knew nothing of this injustice. This mischief was kindled by the divines." Ṭáhirih refused to go back to Kermanshah, so the governor ordered the travelers' possessions returned and provided means for her to continue her journey.[6]

She proceeded to Hamadan. En route, she stopped in the village of Sahnih, where—as in Karand—the entire population became Bábís and wanted to travel with her. Had Ṭáhirih wished, her retinue could have appeared to be a small army by the time she reached Hamadan. She thanked the villagers, stayed with them for two days, but didn't accept their offer to accompany her. However, a deputation of her brothers, sent from Qazvin by her family, awaited her in Sahnih, and she consented to return home with them on condition that they allow her to take as much time as she required for her teaching purposes in Hamadan.[7]

Hamadan, six thousand feet up in the Zagros Mountains, is one of the world's oldest cities. Near it lie the ruins* of a temple to Anahita,

* In August, 2010, the ancient ruins were destroyed and hundreds of trees cut down so an Islamic *mosalla*, a prayer place, could be built. Access to the public had been denied for two years. No archeological investigation was ever made at the site (http://www.cais-soas.com/News/2010/january2010/20-01.htm).

a symbol sacred to Zoroastrians, related to an ancient Persian water and warrior goddess identified with various other deities of the ancient world, chiefly Artemis. At one point, the entire temple complex—nearly a mile around—was entirely covered with silver and gold. In Ṭáhirih's time it was a pilgrimage site for women and had been since its glory days long, long ago.[8]

Hamadan is also the location of the tomb-shrine of the Jewish heroine Queen Esther* and her uncle Mordecai. A photograph taken circa 2007 shows that the Jewish star over the gate of the shrine has been riddled with bullet holes and that two of its points have broken off. There are now only three or four Jewish families still living in Hamadan, yet women from diverse religions come to the shrine to pray for children. They bring textiles to put on the tombs, and, believing that the cloth is blessed by the contact, needy visitors take the cloth and use it. Legend has it that Esther's tomb and the land around it was a refuge for people trying to escape the Arab invasion circa 621 A.D.[9]

During the nineteenth century, Hamadan had a large Jewish population. But even in places where there were relatively big settlements of Jews, living in Iran was highly risky for those of Jewish descent. They were branded as unclean infidels who couldn't enter Muslim shops and homes, so they lived apart and were not to venture out on rainy days because the rain might wash their impurity onto Muslims. Jews weren't allowed to learn Persian, couldn't testify in court even to defend themselves, and had to wear special hats and patches on their clothes. At times Jewish women were forbidden to wear chadors, which meant

* Ancient Persia, under the regime of Cyrus the Great, had a morality based on Zoroastrian monotheism and tolerance; Jewish people benefited, and Esther could wed the legendary King Ahashuerus (Grousset, René, *The Civilizations of the East*, Vol. 2, p. 118).

they had to go unveiled like prostitutes.* Some were forced to convert to Islam, and they were subject to beatings, rape, torture, expulsion, murder. During the 1830s a massacre in Tabriz wiped out the entire Jewish population of the city.[10]

But, as in the case of the Jewish physician to the shah who became a Bábí, members of the Jewish community managed to circumvent their circumstances, take active roles, and exert influence in their world. And because the universal spirit of the Báb's creed didn't limit Ṭáhirih to teaching only Muslims, in Hamadan the son of a Jewish rabbi† attended Ṭáhirih's teaching circles and became a Bábí. It was to this rabbi's house that Ṭáhirih went for refuge when she was under attack after a virulent debate with clerics in Hamadan.[11]

This debate took place after admiring aristocratic women helped Ṭáhirih contact the governor, who was a brother of the shah and "an effective member of the princely ruling elite." She convinced him to convene a relatively ecumenical gathering of divines at his residence so that she could address them and they could debate her. She spoke to them from behind a curtain, setting forth "three rules for the disputation: reliance on prophecies; abstinence from smoking . . . and . . . adopting decent language and avoiding abuse and execration." Then she told them of her belief in progressive revelation and in the Báb as the inaugurator of the Advent and a new cycle or age in human development.[12]

One of the clerics broke the agreed-upon rules of civility and launched a violent argument against her. The governor scolded him furiously and dispersed the meeting. Ṭáhirih sent a messenger with a

---

* We see here Ṭáhirih's daring, and perhaps her identification with the outcasts of society, when she chose unveiling to symbolize the purity and freshness of the Báb's Faith; she knew how that classed her, paradoxically, with those considered depraved and fallen.

† Rabbi Hakham Ilyahu and his son Il'azar.

letter to the city's chief mujtahid, who beat the messenger* to the point of death. The messenger was carried back to her, seemingly breathing his last. She instructed him, "Come, get up . . . Happiness and peace be upon you that you have suffered in the path of your Beloved! Rise up, and continue to work for Him!" He opened his eyes and she smiled at him. ". . . For one beating you became unconscious; this is the time we are ready to give our lives . . ." She said it was his good fortune to sacrifice his life "to exalt the word of the Best Beloved." She must have been referring to his fated martyrdom in Qazvin, for although he was ill for a week, he didn't die just then.[13]

After that, Ṭáhirih went to stay in the home of the rabbi, and the next day transferred to a village owned by a certain tribe of nobility whose ladies were sympathetic to her cause. She then consented to go with her brothers to Qazvin. She sent many of her Arab followers back to Iraq, and traveled on with a mostly Persian retinue.[14]

By July, 1847, she was in Qazvin, facing the city fathers and the men of her family. Her hometown was, according to one historian, "inimical" to the Báb's new faith; it "prided itself on the fact that no fewer than a hundred of the highest ecclesiastical leaders of Islam dwelt within its gates . . ."[15]

Of course some of her relatives were Bábís, such as her younger uncle, 'Alí, but he was an introverted scholar, and while he "confessed submission" to the Báb, testifying to "the veracity of the Great Remembrance," he was no activist. Her mother, as we have seen, studied with S͟hayk͟h Aḥmad and became a S͟hayk͟hi, but no one knows if that led her to become a Bábí or not, so, if she did, she kept it secret. Her cousin Javad had begun as a Bábí zealot, but now he was an enemy.[16]

---

* Mullah Ibrahim Mahallati.

At first he'd declared, "Now is the time to take our revenge on Baraghani" (Ṭáhirih's uncle, Mullah Taqí), and had proclaimed the Báb's religion from the pulpit of a mosque; then, after the Báb cancelled his trip to Iraq, Javad took a group to Shiraz. There, he became angry at the Báb's unwillingness to mount an armed insurrection, and he was also jealous of the unassailable position of Mullah Ḥusayn as the Báb's trusted first disciple. He became venomous in his destructiveness and derision.[17]

Also, in 1847, a manual on Shia theology was lithographed in Iran and became popular. According to E. G. Browne, since it was written during the time of the Báb, it was intended to disprove Him. In about 483 pages, it insisted that of God's numerous Prophets announcing His will and law, Muḥammad was the last and greatest, and it said the Qur'án and hadiths were the basis of true faith, listing heresies that included communism (Mazdak taught a form of communism in sixth-century Persia and various groups, including the Bábís, have been accused of communism since then); deification and adoration of the Imams; denial of bodily resurrection and life after death; and use of musical instruments.

The book proclaimed, "God is just" and went on to say, "This is a fundamental article of our Faith, and whosoever holds the contrary is eternally damned." It asserted that humans have free will but added, "God created the hearts of believers, unbelievers, and waiverers each from a different clay." Affirming all the revelations that antedated Muḥammad's from the days of Adam to the time of Jesus, it said that after Muḥammad, anyone "who claims to be a prophet is an unbeliever and should be killed by the Muslims" and avowed that no human or djinn could produce anything to equal even one chapter or verse of the Qur'án. In deciphering prophecies, it employed a term other than "gate" to deflect interest in the Báb as the Gate or Portal of new revelation. However, it speaks of the Return, giving over forty-eight signs of it, among them "the appearance of a figure in the sun; the multiplicity of misleading lawyers and poets; the abounding of tyranny and oppression . . ."[18]

In such a prevailing atmosphere, for Ṭáhirih, reunion with her family must have been similar to being stuffed into a bag of cats. Her father was unmoving in his disapproval of her beliefs; her husband and father-in-law violently, publicly opposed her; and her mother was as pacifistic as Uncle 'Alí, although she did, in her quiet way, stand by Ṭáhirih.* So, when Ṭáhirih's brothers wanted to escort her into the city without her entourage, she insisted on bringing her friends with her. However, in her family, she did have some forthright fellow-believers: her sister Marḍíyyih, her brother-in-law who was one of the armed men that traveled with her from Iraq to Iran, and a kinsman named Siyyid 'Abdu'l-Hádí who had been betrothed to her daughter and was also one of her armed companions. If we accept the historical reading that her daughter was with her in all her travels, then her daughter also returned with her from Karbala to Qazvin. Her daughter at this time would have been about ten years old.[19]

Among the Arabian companions who stayed in Qazvin was an older man named Mullah Ṣaliḥ Karami. He was a theologian who became a Bábí in Karbala after meeting Mullah 'Alí, the bearer of the Commentary on the Most Beautiful of Stories. He upheld Ṭáhirih during her disputations with her husband. He, Ṭáhirih, and other Bábís often met in the house of the Farhadi family. Many members of the Farhadi family had become Bábís through a visit of one of the Letters of the Living† to Qazvin; he had been the first Bábí to stay in their home.

---

* Martha Root, a journalist from the United States, traveled to Iran in the early years of the twentieth century and interviewed some of Ṭáhirih's relatives there. They told her "this mother and daughter had always been close to each other" (Root, *Táhirih the Pure*, p. 72).

† Mullah Jalíl-i-Urúmí.

This family had already endured great hardship for its beliefs; among other things, while their first Bábí visitor was with them, Ṭáhirih's bitter uncle ordered their house attacked and their visitor kidnapped, then chained him in a cellar and tortured him. A dauntless Farhadi son-in-law rescued him.[20]

At Ṭáhirih's father's house, women sent by her husband arrived to convince her to return to him. Were these women his sisters, his mother and grandmother, other wives? In all available sources, specifics aren't given. Whatever their position, the women couldn't intimidate Ṭáhirih. "Say to my presumptuous and arrogant kinsman," she told them, "'If your desire had really been to be a faithful mate and companion to me, you would have hastened to meet me in Karbala and would on foot have guided my howdah all the way to Qazvin. I would, while journeying with you, have roused you from your sleep of heedlessness and would have shown you the way of truth. But this was not to be. Three years have elapsed since our separation. Neither in this world nor in the next can I ever be associated with you. I have cast you out of my life forever." So, in fact, she finally dissolved the marriage, although that wasn't the woman's prerogative according to Islamic law, and her husband in the end divorced her.[21]

But before he did that, Ṭáhirih's friends found places to stay in the city, and her family gathered in her father's mansion to confront her and try to persuade her to resume her marriage, but she categorically refused to have anything to do with her husband, saying that he was "unclean."[22]

Her father, objecting to her new religion, couldn't understand how she, with all her learning and brilliance, could choose to follow a "lad" from Shiraz. She told him that all her "knowledge and attainments . . . were . . . as an insignificant mote beside that mighty and radiant luminary" (the Báb). He replied, "Though you regard your excellence and learning of such small account in comparison with the virtues of the Shirazi lad, still, had you been my son . . . and had you put forward this claim (of being the Báb), I would have accepted it."[23]

Uncle Taqí cursed the Báb and struck Ṭáhirih several times. Her response was a strange prophecy: "O Uncle, I see your mouth fill with blood!"[24]

Undaunted, claiming as she always did her inviolable freedom, she continued her teaching activities just as she had in Karbala, Kazimayn, Baghdad, Karand, Kermanshah, Sahnih, and Hamadan. Important ladies of the city, wives of influential mullahs and other authorities, came to learn from her. She strengthened the Bábís while attracting more converts. Some two decades later, in Europe, in 1866, the *Journal Asiatique* wondered, "How could it be that a woman, in Persia . . . and above all in a city like Qazvin, where the clergy possessed so great an influence . . . how could it be that *there*. . . . a woman could have organized so strong a group of heretics? There lies a question which puzzles even the Persian historian, Sipihr, for such an occurrence was without precedent!"[25]

The chronicler Sipihr (panegyrist to three shahs and official State historian whose pen-name means *Celestial Sphere*) couldn't believe that a beauty with "a moon-like face and hair like musk" could be such a genius, so he attributed her success to licentiousness, giving free reign to his own lust in his descriptions of her and saying that she promised immunity from hellfire for anyone who touched her. He said she told her followers a woman could marry nine husbands; a later historian stretched that to ninety.[26]

Autumn came—October, 1847—and a young man with a decisive and violent nature arrived in Qazvin. He was a baker, a Shaykhi who was on his way to visit the Báb and decide for himself if His claim was true. He later said, "On the day of my arrival at Qazvin, I became aware that the town was in a great state of turmoil. As I was passing through the market-place, I saw a crowd of ruffians who had stripped a man of his head-dress and shoes, had wound his turban around his neck, and by it were dragging him through the streets. An angry multitude was tormenting him with their threats, their blows and curses."[27]

The young man asked why they were persecuting the fellow and was told "his unpardonable guilt" was that he had publicly praised Shaykh Aḥmad and Siyyid Káẓim, so that one known as "the Proof of Islam" (none other than Uncle Taqí) had pronounced him a heretic and demanded that he be kicked out of town.[28]

The young man went to Uncle Taqí to find out if this was so. What was heretical about Shaykhi beliefs? To him they were utterly true to Islam. He asked Uncle Taqí if he actually had condemned the mistreated man. Yes he certainly had, the aged mullah replied, asserting that the god that Shaykh Aḥmad worshipped was "a god in whom I can never believe. Him as well as his followers I regard as the very embodiments of error."[29]

The baker wanted to kill the old mullah with his bare hands then and there, but restrained himself, deciding it would be better to ram a knife down his throat "so that he would never again be able to utter such blasphemy."[30]

He left Uncle Taqí to finish teaching what would be his last religious classes, and went to the market where, he said:

> I bought a dagger and a spear-head of the sharpest and finest steel. I concealed them in my bosom . . . I was waiting for my opportunity when, one night, I entered (his) masjid (mosque) . . . I waited until the hour of dawn . . . I saw an old woman enter . . . carrying with her a rug, which she spread over the floor of the mihrab (prayer niche). Soon after, I saw Mullah Taqí enter alone, walk to the mihrab, and offer his prayer. Cautiously and quietly, I followed him and stood behind him. He was prostrating himself on the floor, when I rushed upon him, drew out my spear-head, and

plunged it into the back of his neck. He uttered a loud cry. I threw him on his back and, unsheathing my dagger, drove it hilt-deep into his mouth. With the same dagger, I struck him at several places in his breast and side, and left him bleeding in the mihrab.

I ascended immediately to the roof of the masjid and watched the frenzy and agitation of the multitude. A crowd rushed in and, placing him upon a litter, transported him to his house. Unable to identify the murderer, the people . . . rushed at one another's throats, violently attacked and mutually accused one another in the presence of the governor.[31]

Remembering the chaos and despoliation, a Bahá'í of Qazvin later wrote: ". . . a crowd of theological students entered the house of Haji Siyyid Asadu'llah (the elderly uncle of the Farhadi family). He and his nephew . . . were arrested and taken to prison. The mob plundered the houses of everyone known to be related to the believers. I was a very small child but I remember well the time that . . . a persecutor and murderer of Bábís,* accompanied by many officers and executioners knocked at our door. No one opened it, so they climbed over the wall and entered, investigating and wishing to break into some rooms that were locked. The master of the house opened the doors, while all the family was shaking with fear . . ."[32]

Many other such raids occurred, and the leader "would say to the women, 'Your husband has left his religion and this means you can be married to anyone whom you wish.'"[33]

Men arrived at the door of Ṭáhirih's house to arrest her; when her father refused to let her go, they took her by force along with other women, including her maid, Qánitih. The governor accused Ṭáhirih

---

* Siyyid Muhsin, known as the Bábí killer (Amanat, *Resurrection and Renewal*, p. 323).

of conspiring with the Farhadi family patriarch to murder her uncle. She insisted that she was innocent, but her husband kept urging severe punishment. Hadn't she said to her uncle, "I see your mouth fill with blood"? What was that, if not a threat? Ṭáhirih's mother defended her, saying that it had not been a threat but an example of her daughter's prescience and intuition.[34]

Hoping to force a confession, but apparently afraid to touch Ṭáhirih, the governor ordered his executioner to bring hot irons for branding and had his henchmen "put the hands of Qánitih under a sliding door, intending to brand them from the other side."[35]

Ṭáhirih uncovered her face and turned it westward in the direction of the mountains where the Báb, after shifts of fortune that will be described later, was by that time a prisoner in a fortress. She "began to pray and supplicate . . . Then on the air outside a voice arose, crying: 'The murderer is found!' . . . No branding was done."[36]

The murderer had confessed. Sickened by watching the melee in the streets below, he abandoned his rooftop, went to the authorities, and asked, "If I deliver into your hands the author of this murder, will you promise me to set free all the innocent people who are suffering in his place?" He received the promise, but then his confession wasn't accepted. Why would he kill such a learned man? The assassin replied, "He was not a learned man; he . . . only stole a little bunch of grapes from a cultural garden . . ."[37]

The governor finally took the murderer to the bedside of the dying Taqí, who pointed an anguished finger at him and gestured that he should be removed at once from his presence. The murderer then confessed to Ṭáhirih's husband and father. But Ṭáhirih's husband said he was lying. "This man is not worthy to be the murderer of my father." The assassin said, "Bring a suit of fine clothes for me so that your father's murderer may appear worthy." He was chained and jailed, but other prisoners weren't released.[38]

Ṭáhirih was confined in the andarun of her husband's house. She was haloed, or horned, by words her murdered uncle used to utter, quoting a tradition: "'When the signs of the promised One appear, the Zindiq (Heretic) of Qazvin will also appear, and the words of the Zindiq will be the words of a woman's religion!' Now this woman and her religion have appeared."[39]

Her father persisted in his efforts to protect her. When her virtue was attacked at a meeting led by the new Friday Imam, Ṭáhirih's ex-husband, he rose to her defense, and her ex-husband taunted him mercilessly, reciting a verse, "No glory rests upon that house / From which the hens crow like cocks." Tears streamed down Mullah Ṣáliḥ's face, soaking his beard.[40]

It was Ṭáhirih's discarded husband, with several of his male kin, who organized the raids of Bábí houses. Then they brought some of their prisoners to Tehran, and these included the confessed murderer and several of Ṭáhirih's friends who had guarded her during her travels.[41]

Bahá'u'lláh was in Tehran at the time. Hearing that the captives were in chains and suffering from hunger and the unusually cold autumn weather, He gave them money for their relief. Then Bahá'u'lláh was arrested, accused of complicity in the murder of Ṭáhirih's uncle, and Himself imprisoned for several days. The confessed assassin managed to escape with the help of the son of the shah's chief stableman.[42]

He disappeared without a trace, and the shah refused to sentence any of the other prisoners to death, citing the case of Imam 'Alí, who told his disciples that if he were killed, "the murderer alone should . . . be made to atone for his act . . . no one else but he should be put to death . . ." He asked if the late Mullah Taqí could possibly have claimed superiority to Imam 'Alí? (It serves to remember here that Uncle Taqí had long since lost favor with the royal family.)[43]

Nevertheless, Ṭáhirih's former husband and his fellows found a way. They claimed that Ṭáhirih's outstandingly loyal friend, <u>Sh</u>ay<u>kh</u> Ṣaliḥ

Karimi, was the assassin, and though the chief mujtahid of Tehran refused to ratify the sentence, Ṭahirih's husband finally managed to persuade the shah to order his execution. He was blown from the mouth of a cannon in one of the city's main squares, becoming the first Bábí to die for his faith on Iranian soil.[44]

The elder uncle of the Farhadi family was also sent to Tehran, because he was so well-respected in Qazvin that there would have been huge objections to his "punishment"—for an uncommitted crime—there. He died en route to Tehran or upon arrival; either the journey, chained and on foot in the cold, was too much for him, or he was murdered by night. In the morning, his death was announced, attributed to illness.[45]

Ṭáhirih's ex-husband brought the other prisoners back to Qazvin and incited a mob to kill them. One of them—the same man who had been so severely beaten in Hamadan that he almost died—was struck on the head with a hatchet by a carpenter, then stoned and burned. The other was beaten with sticks, burned, and finally stoned to death. These things occurred in front of Ṭáhirih's ex-husband's house, and it is possible that she was still imprisoned there at the time and saw her friends tortured and murdered.[46]

Eventually, she was removed by her father from her husband's house and secluded in the basement of her girlhood home. Her father must have hoped to insure her safety. She suspected that agents of her husband might poison her while she was in his andarun, and couldn't be sure that they weren't infiltrating her father's kitchens. "She was . . . heavy of heart, grieving on the painful events that had come to pass . . . watched on every side . . ."[47]

However, she saw beyond her immediate predicament. She sent her husband a message quoting Sura 9:33 of the Qur'án: "Fain would they extinguish God's light with their mouths, but God only desireth to perfect His Light, albeit the infidels abhor it." So she inferred that his father, stabbed in the mouth for his verbal invective, was an infidel; and she inferred progressive revelation in citing the perfection—presumably ongoing—of God's Light. She must have known, too, that her husband would be familiar with the rest of the chapter as a reference to his father's avariciousness; it condemns priests who falsely take men's goods and block their spiritual path.

She went on, "If my Cause be the Cause of the Truth, if the Lord whom I worship be none other than the one true God, He will, ere nine days have elapsed, deliver me from the yoke of your tyranny. Should He fail to achieve my deliverance, you are free to act as you desire. You will have irrevocably established the falsity of my belief." Her husband ignored the message and went ahead with his machinations against her.

But a plan for her rescue was in motion. Ṭáhirih had a close friend named Khatun Jan, the daughter of the Farhadi patriarch who had died in Tehran. Khatun Jan, though sorrowing for her father and living in hiding in a ruined shrine because her house had been sacked by mobs, managed to stay in touch with Ṭáhirih by entering her quarters disguised as a laundress or under some other pretext. In this way, she could get news to Ṭáhirih and bring her food that was safe to eat. Khatun Jan's husband, accused of complicity in the murder of Mullah Taqí, had escaped to Tehran, where he was in touch with Bahá'u'lláh who, undaunted by his own contretemps with the authorities, sent him back to Qazvin with money and supplies so that he and Khatun Jan could liberate Ṭáhirih.[48]

On the night of Ṭáhirih's escape, Khatun Jan, dressed as a beggar, stayed near the house and managed to convey the message that it was time to go. Ṭáhirih somehow slipped away from her house. She and Khatun Jan got past the city gates, found Khatun Jan's husband waiting with three horses in a secluded spot, and "by an unfrequented route" reached Tehran by daybreak, which means they rode hard and fast all night long. As soon as the city gates opened, they managed to pass through and reach the home of Bahá'u'lláh.[49]

Ṭáhirih would never return to Qazvin. She was parted from her family forever. She might have sung, with Hafez,

Since we gave up our heart and eyes to the storm of affliction
Say, "Come, flood of sorrow, tear this house from its foundations."[50]

Her older brother, her father's designated heir, was so impressed by the fulfillment of her own prophesy of escape that he immediately "acknowledged . . . the truth of the Revelation"—but later, he did not prove stalwart. It's known that she had some contact, later, with at least one of her sons. And if indeed her daughter was always with her, perhaps the child escaped with her that night, or else joined her soon afterwards (a theory that would mean Ṭáhirih's mother, father—someone—quite quickly knew her whereabouts).[51]

Today, her uncle Taqí's tombstone bears a relief carving captioned, "The Martyrdom of Mullah Taqí by a Babí heretic." It shows a mullah kneeling in a prayer niche being stabbed by a masked man while a woman watches from behind a curtain, a piece of paper in her hand demonstrating her evil: she is literate.[52] At present, that is Ṭáhirih's only monument in her homeland.

12

The Price of a Cashmere Shawl

The Báb in custody. Choler, cholera, a drink of water. The transformation of an oppressor. Vaḥíd. "The mountains of Azerbaijan too have their claims."

In general, monuments are few for any Bábís in Iran, and it is hard for them to be preserved in the face of persistent opposition. For example, although the Bahá'ís managed over hard-pressed years to gain ownership of the home of the Báb in Shiraz and maintain it for pilgrims and visitors, it was razed after the Islamic Revolution in 1979. Such misfortune might have saddened but not surprised the Báb—His life was, as He'd known it must be, a greater tragedy. Let us look at what He underwent while His devoted Ṭáhirih endured her travails of 1844 through 1848.[1]

For a while after His return from Mecca and His arrest, the Báb was apparently able to live in His own quarters as well as His uncle's. One night, His home in Shiraz was raided and He was summarily arrested. His wife, Khadíjíh Begum, later recalled that it was during the month of Ramadan, a hot night, so that she and her husband were sleeping on the roof; her mother-in-law was asleep in the courtyard. Suddenly, the

Báb was roughly awakened by constables who had marched across the city's rooftops to His residence. He sent His wife downstairs and stayed with the arresting officers while they entered an "upper chamber" and "took away every book and every piece of writing that they found . . ." The Báb repeatedly asked the reason for the invasion until they finally told Him, "It has been reported to us that some people have assembled in this house."[2]

By that time, they could see that no one except the small family was in the house, so the Báb suggested they "go away in peace." However, they took Him with them. <u>Kh</u>adíjíh said, "God knows what His mother and I suffered that night. We were thankful that His grandmother, an elderly lady, was not home. It was close to dawn when He came home. They had demanded money and, as He had no cash with Him, they had laid hands on the cashmere shawl round his waist and cut it up." The chief constable got half the shawl, and the others got bits.[3]

Soon afterwards, they arrested the Báb again and locked Him up in the chief constable's house. Rumors flew that He was to be killed within that house. His guardian-uncle, now one of His most ardent followers, had been beaten up by persecutors and was not at all well, but He determinedly planned to rescue the Báb with the assistance of <u>Kh</u>adíjíh's sister. She managed to relay news of the Báb to His family by disguising herself in a ragged chador, hiding in the shadow of a mosque near His house and, when the coast was clear, appearing at the His gate to whisper her information, probably to the faithful Mubarak. Another friend, the wife of a merchant* who had met the Báb on the boat crossing the Persian Gulf to Mecca, consistently took <u>Kh</u>adíjíh's sister to the home of a relative, the Friday Imam, trying to convince

* The merchant was Hájí Abu'l-Ḥasan, who became a Bábí and remained one in the face of lifelong persecution (Balyuzi, *<u>Kh</u>adíjíh Bagum: The Wife of the Báb*, p. 18).

him to intervene on the Báb's behalf. As a result, when the ulama of Shiraz condemned the Báb to death and the requisite officials signed the decree, the Friday Imam refused to ratify it. He persuaded religious and civic authorities to bring the Báb to a certain mosque and give Him the opportunity to repudiate His claim.[4]

The Báb's wife and mother sent a woman to the mosque to bring them news of whatever happened, but women were not allowed in. Nevertheless, Khadíjíh said they heard that the Báb had "ascended the pulpit and spoken words which had kindled once again the wrath of the Governor and the divines, whereupon they had led Him back to confinement."[5]

During 1845 and 1846, the Báb was not only kept in government quarters but was also remanded to his guardian-uncle's care, so Mullah Ḥusayn and others who had journeyed to Shiraz were able to meet with Him, and people who had been struck by His presence in the mosque could learn more about His message. In fact, for a short time, the Báb enjoyed a certain amount of tranquility, but He told His wife, and no one else, of overwhelming sufferings to come. He gave her a prayer and said, "In the hour of your perplexity recite this prayer ere you go to sleep. I myself will appear to you and will banish your anxiety." She lived a long time after his death and found that His prayer was always "unfailing."[6]

The Báb's final arrest in Shiraz occurred when He was staying with His uncle. By that time the governor was livid because the agents he'd assigned to keep watch on the Báb told him, "The eager crowd that gathers every night to visit the Báb surpasses in number the multitude of people that throng every day before the gates of the seat of your government." So the chief constable and his men forced their way into the guardian-uncle's house and once again took the Báb and some of His followers into custody.[7]

The governor had received orders from Tehran, from Prime Minister Áqásí, to kill the Báb immediately. But on the night of the Báb's arrest, the governor heard ululating wails and saw the emaciated, blue-tinged, pallid dead, killed by cholera, being carried out into the streets. He fled the city. Then the chief constable discovered his own sons dying of the disease. He pleaded with the Báb to work a miracle and save them. It was dawn by that time. The Báb made His ablutions before saying His first prayer of the day and gave the water He had used to the constable, telling him to have his sons drink it. Then, He said, they would recover. They did, and the constable found the governor and asked him to liberate the Báb. He released the Báb on one condition: He must leave Shiraz.[8]

The Báb's wife remembered, "One day, to our indescribable joy, He came home and stayed two or three days . . . these were the last days of my life with Him." Another year had gone by. Ramadan would soon arrive again. The Báb told his wife He would leave the city that night. She could only pray and hope that He would reach a safe haven. It was the end of September, 1846, and the Báb took the road to Isfahan.[9]

Despite his travails in Shiraz, the Báb left behind, in southern Iran, a diverse Bábí community consisting not only of religious scholars and well-off merchants, but of a stirrup-maker, a baker, a keyholder to a shrine, a quilt-maker, a poet, and others. After He went away, the governor, furious at losing the chance to execute Him and longing to find out where He'd gone, mercilessly beat His guardian-uncle and brother-in-law for information that was not forthcoming, and warned people that "if a single sheet of the writings of the Báb was found in their possession, they would be severely punished." Years later, a Bábí woman remembered how people sank bundles of the writings of the Báb into huge copper colanders to wash away the ink, then buried the paper or threw it into wells.[10]

Meanwhile the Báb made his way to Isfahan, a city once so resplendent it was said, "Isfahan is half the world." By the nineteenth century, however, the city, despite its huge public square (the largest in the world), its mosques and madrassas, was in disrepair, and its sprawling province was home to the rebellious Lur and Bakhtiyari tribes along with a "semi-independent Arab population."[11]

The governor of the region, Manúchihr Khán, was a Georgian eunuch who was a favorite of the shah's. He'd been assigned his post because he was known as a merciless administrator, "hated and feared for his cruelty." He'd once been an official in Shiraz where, after quelling an uprising, he erected a tower made of the mortared-together living bodies of eighty prisoners.[12]

Now the Báb wrote a letter to Manúchihr Khán requesting asylum. He received a favorable response. His letter alone had transformed Manúchihr Khán. He had been forcibly made a Muslim and a eunuch in his childhood, and his cruelty was his vengeance upon the world. Upon meeting the Báb in person, he announced, "Never until this day have I in my heart been firmly convinced of the truth of Islam . . ." He believed the Báb had "superhuman power . . . a power which no amount of learning can ever impart." He communicated his enthusiasm for the Báb to the shah, who ordered him to send the Báb to Tehran so he could meet him.[13]

Meanwhile, Isfahan's mullahs passed sentence of death on the Báb. Manúchihr Khán managed to secretly keep the Báb in the city under his own protection, fearing to send Him to Tehran because of what the shah's prime minister, Áqásí, might do to Him. He offered the Báb his huge fortune and his entire army, even removed his own rings and tried to give them to the Báb, hoping the Báb would march in triumph to Tehran, sweep Áqásí aside and convert the shah, but the Báb said His cause would only be advanced "through the poor and lowly of this land . . ." Manúchihr Khán, in the end, realized that his wealth had come from oppression and repented his misdeeds. He died soon afterwards.[14]

The shah again ordered the Báb to come to Tehran. He was to depart in secrecy and travel in disguise, under guard. The prime minister was apprehensive about the inevitable adoring crowds that the Báb attracted, and also thought nothing would be worse for the shah than to be in the Báb's presence, but the shah was most curious to meet Him.[15]

While the Báb was still in Shiraz, the shah had sent the man* he considered "the most learned, the most eloquent, and the most influential of his subjects, to interview the Báb and to report to him the results of his investigations." This man, known for his "sagacity, his unsurpassed knowledge and mature wisdom," was a person of such "pre-eminence among the leading figures in Persia" that in any gathering, no matter how erudite, he was the chief speaker and his listeners sat in "reverently observed silence." Yet it was he who sat in silence before the twenty-four-year-old Báb as the Báb revealed the Commentary on the Sura of Abundance. The Báb titled him Vaḥíd, the Unique One, and Vaḥíd wrote to the shah that he was now a Bábí.[16]

The Báb had a similar effect on the soldiers taking him to Tehran. Like the villagers who welcomed Ṭáhirih as she journeyed through their mountains en route to Qazvin, their captain was of the People of Truth, and many of the horsemen were of another sect that was very close in sentiment to the People of Truth. When they reached the city of Qom, the second most holy city in Iran, these guards wanted to disobey their orders to circumvent the town.[17]

They wanted to give the Báb the opportunity to take refuge in the sacred shrine there. The captain told the Báb that they had been "particularly directed . . . to keep away from the Tomb of the Immaculate (the sister of the Eighth Imam), that inviolable sanctuary under whose shelter the most notorious criminals are immune from arrest. We are ready, however, to ignore utterly for Your sake whatever instructions we have received . . ."[18]

---

* Siyyid Yaḥyáy-i-Dárábí.

The Báb quoted the following tradition: "The heart of the true believer is the throne of God.'" He added that He preferred "the way of the country rather than to enter this unholy city . . . The immaculate one whose remains are interred within this shrine, her brother, and her illustrious ancestors no doubt bewail the plight of this wicked people . . . Outwardly they serve and reverence her shrine; inwardly they disgrace her dignity." So the captain took the Báb to a village populated by members of the People of Truth, where the Báb "was touched by the warmth and spontaneity of the reception . . . accorded Him."[19]

But the Báb deeply felt His loneliness; His face was drawn with sorrow, for He had wept and prayed long nights since leaving Shiraz. He appeared to be headed straight into the mouth of the enemy—as He reached Tehran, His guards were instructed to pitch a tent for Him near a village that belonged to Prime Minister Áqásí—but that didn't seem to concern Him. In fact, "the peacefulness" of the place, "the luxuriance of its vegetation, and the unceasing murmur of its streams greatly pleased the Báb." But what pleased Him most was a sealed letter and gifts brought by a messenger from Bahá'u'lláh. His companions later recalled that as soon as they were put into His hands, relief and joy illumined His face, and after that His weeping and His despairing prayers "gave way to expressions of thanksgiving and praise, of hope and triumph."[20]

Then one night, in a never-explained, mysterious incident of that journey, the guards discovered that the Báb's tent was empty. They searched the camp and couldn't find Him anywhere. The captain said He must have gone out into the countryside to pray and meditate, and set out on foot looking for Him. One by one, other guards went along, some on horseback. But they came upon no sign of Him until, as dawn approached, they saw Him walking toward them alone from the direction of Tehran. "Did you believe me to have escaped?" He asked. They felt He was filled with new confidence, His voice strengthened by new power. He never gave any reasons for this further elevation of His soul.[21]

The Báb remained in the pastoral spot where the prime minister had consigned Him, enjoying it greatly, for about two weeks, but then received a letter from the king: "Much as we desire to meet you, we find ourself unable, in view of our immediate departure from our capital, to receive you befittingly . . . We have signified our desire that you be conducted to Mah-ku . . ." He asked the Báb to "continue to pray for our well-being and for the prosperity of our realm"—an apposite request, given the constant rebellions against his rule. Those in the know were certain that the instigator of the Báb's invitation to the fortress of Mah-ku, in other words, His sentencing to imprisonment, was none other than the prime minister. The presence in Tehran, by the side of the shah, of the governor who had exiled the Báb from Shiraz, no doubt had its effect, also.[22]

The town of Mah-ku was in the mountains of Azerbaijan, and above it loomed the dungeon euphemistically known as *the castle*. It was another old stomping ground (so to speak) of Áqásí's; he had been born in Mah-ku.[23]

It would have been hard for anyone who knew Áqásí in the days of his power to imagine him as a newborn. An Englishman described him as "a quizzical old gentleman with a long nose . . ." He had the changeable, whimsical temper of a real despot and a tendency to disguise his malicious plots with jocular sarcasm and practical jokes, appearing the buffoon while all the time his bony hands trembled on his stick waiting to pounce. In reality, he wasn't very astute. He assumed a pose of Sufi mysticism, and the shah thought he could work miracles. However, he didn't seem able to miraculously cure the shah's gout. The shah hoped the Báb would do that.[24]

The shah promised to summon the Báb to Tehran later and sent Him money for the expenses of His journey to Mah-ku, but the Báb gave the royal funds to the poor and paid His way with His own savings. Spring found Him encamped in a village now called Takistan, near Qazvin. He revealed tablets specifically directed to the leading mullahs of the city, including Ṭáhirih's father, her uncle Taqí, and her uncle's old enemy 'Abdu'l-Vahhab. (This was before Ṭáhirih had returned to Qazvin from Iraq.)[25]

Her uncle tore up the Báb's letter. 'Abdu'l-Vahhab went to Ṭáhirih's father and suggested they go to meet the Báb, but her father reportedly advised his in-law, "Two of your sons are accused of being attracted to and believing (in the new movement) and two of my daughters also. If we were to make this move (meet the Báb), my fear is that other ulama will accuse us of betrayal and we will completely lose our position of respect . . ."[26]

Though he may have been worried about his own prestige, it's more likely, given his increasing tendency to withdraw from worldly affairs, that Mullah Ṣaliḥ wanted to maintain influence simply to better protect his children. Whatever the reason, he didn't take the opportunity to meet the person who so enthralled his beloved daughter.

Others from the city, including two of 'Abdu'l-Vahhab's sons, did go to meet the Báb. A contingent of Bábís from Tehran, Qazvin, and the nearby town of Zanjan arrived by night, circumvented His sleeping guards, and tried to convince Him to escape with them, but He refused, saying, "The mountains of Azerbaijan too have their claims."[27]

He went on to the city of Tabriz, second city of the nation, where the Crown Prince presided. As His cavalcade passed through a village called Milan, many of its residents turned out to get a glimpse of Him, and an old woman approached Him holding a sick child whose hairless head was covered with scabs. The Báb put His handkerchief over the child's head, said a few words, and the child was cured. According to a contemporary history, about two hundred people saw this and were immediately converted. The same history recounts that when the Báb left Milan, He suddenly began galloping His horse, a sorry nag, at such a swift pace that His guards couldn't catch up with Him. He at last reined in and said, smiling, and that if He'd decided to escape they couldn't have stopped Him. The guards also noticed His superhuman endurance. They were strong, seasoned horsemen used to cold and fatigue, but they reported that when they flagged, the Báb showed no sign of tiredness, and from morning to night, He didn't even seem to shift His posture on the saddle.[28]

As he approached Tabriz, the Bábís of the city all went to greet Him, but a cordon of officials halted them. However, one of them, a youth, "broke through the cordon . . . (and) barefooted . . . ran more than a mile till he reached the Báb . . . fell prostrate on the ground and unrestrainedly wept." The Báb dismounted, lifted the young man up, enfolded him in His arms, and wiped away his tears. When the Báb actually entered the city, crowds lined the streets, among them His followers. Most of the masses were not Bábís, yet as He passed, they raised the cry, "Allah-u-Akbar!" (God is Most Great), alarming the authorities, who sent out town criers to warn people that they mustn't by any means seek to personally meet the Báb.[29]

He was secluded in Tabriz for forty days, then taken into Azerbaijan and imprisoned in the castle of Mah-ku. Azerbaijan was wild mountain terrain; in ancient times, it had been a center of Zoroastrianism, then Christianity, then Shiite Islam, and a refuge for religious fugitives of all kinds seeking shelter in its trackless hills. It was said that Czar Alexander, who died in 1825 while visiting the Black Sea, wasn't dead but had become a wandering ascetic living on alms and speaking in prophecies and riddles, a Fool-in-Christ, somewhere in Azerbaijan.[30]

The name Azerjaibajan springs from *azer* or *azar,* meaning *fire* in Persian. The word is also the name of the Zoroastrian angel presiding over fire, and it forms part of the titles of Zoroastrian fire-temples. Azar was the original name of the city of Tabriz, and the Prophet Abraham's idol-worshipping father was named Azar. In Persian, azar also signifies the hue of flame as well as "trouble, misfortune, calamity, ruin, slaughter." An *azaras* is a salamander (regarded by magical thinkers as a magical animal) and *Azarshasp* is a name for not only the angel of fire, but its demon.

Azerbaijan got its name because from earliest memory, its prodigious, constantly spurting, flooding, and pooling supply of oil and natural gas often spontaneously set fire to hillsides and the Caspian Sea, where it caused exploding waves. Oil from the sludgy land of the capital region lit Zoroastrian temples, was a mainstay for Silk Road traders, and was used in patent medicines. Stoic mystics sat before eternal flames lit by oil and starved themselves to death trying to live on the energy of fire.[31]

During Russia's conquest of the Caucasus in the 1820s–30s, Azerbaijanis began to espouse modern European influences, but in the 1850s, when Alexandre Dumas visited, he found the medieval, swashbuckling spirit of his musketeers alive and well in the fortress-style capital, Baku. Azerbaijanis were tough warriors. From the sixteenth century on, Azerbaijani tribes conquered other rugged folks to become the ruling Persian dynasty.[32]

No doubt Prime Minister Áqásí, the would-be engineer of the Báb's destruction, felt that the young phenomenon would simply vanish and be forgotten in the mountains of Azerbaijan. But, as Ṭáhirih's affirmative unveiling at the conference convened in the Báb's support and other events of 1848 abundantly proved, nothing could have been further from the truth.

13

1848, Iran—Love's Amplitude

Refuge in Tehran. A providential garden. Pilgrimage of the great seeker to Mah-ku. A new "gate" in the city of the Eighth Imam. Onward to the Verdant Isle.

When Ṭáhirih fled her father's basement prison in Qazvin and reached the home of Bahá'u'lláh in Tehran, she was in a greatly weakened state. Besides her heavy grief over the brutal killings of her friends, she'd been extremely ill, "had suffered enormously," and she suspected her ailments came from poison administered by her ex-husband that she'd imbibed despite all caution.[1]

However, she seems to have quickly regained vitality. No doubt her nearness to Bahá'u'lláh, Whom she already saw as the successor to the Báb, had a salutary effect. Bahá'u'lláh wrote in later years that she was one of His most fiery followers, calling her "the Point* of Ecstasy Jináb-

---

* In Persian and Arabic calligraphy, the point is the beginning of the word, the first mark of the pen on paper. For mystics, it symbolizes the intermediary between

i-Ṭá [Ṭáhirih]"* and saying, "For a long time she was nigh unto this Servant and would not have bartered a moment of her visit with this Servant for the kingdoms of this world or the next. Indeed, she did not wish to be separated from Me for even a moment, but what happened was destined to occur. And so many were the verses and poems she uttered regarding this wondrous Faith.'"[2]

In this excerpt, for example, perhaps inspired by the Commentary on the Sura of Abundance, she speaks of Bahá'u'lláh as "love's amplitude"—

. . . Baha's sun glows high above the Prophet's mount.
Before the lustrous beauty of His unveiled face
Earth trembles, men flee, heavy rains pour down
Leveling all except His rising place.

In gold links of His language, chained by the sun,
Hundreds of prophets, love's multitude,
Over the wastelands presciently run
To Him, haven of havens, love's amplitude.[3]

She urged him to "drum out: 'Am I not your Lord?'" She swore that the drum of human hearts would reply, "Yea, verily." The generous and safe hospitality provided by His wife and the affection of His small

---

the physical and spiritual worlds; it comes forth from nothingness into being. Then the letters issue from the first point. So the Báb was the point. His Letters of the Living found Him and thus emerged from a hidden, waiting, searching state into a state of fulfillment. Ṭáhirih was not only a letter but a point, a burgeoning heart (National Spiritual Assembly of the United States, "Letters of the Living," at http://www.bahai-encyclopedia-project.org).

* *Jináb* is a courtesy title for men and woman that can be translated as *Her Honor* (Gail, *Bahá'í Glossary*, p. 24).

children must have helped revive the drum of her own heart. His four-year-old son Abbas, known to us as 'Abdu'l-Bahá, spent a lot of time with her and was a great favorite of hers. He later recalled that among her characteristics was her love of good food; she was often munching on dried fruits and nuts. When 'Abdu'l-Bahá was an old man, he told a lady at his table who had apologized for her large appetite, "Virtue and excellence consist in true faith in God, not in having a large or small appetite for food . . . Jináb-i-Ṭáhirih had a good appetite. When asked concerning it, she would answer, 'It is recorded in the Holy Traditions that one of the attributes of the people of paradise is 'partaking of food, continually . . .'" So here we have a glimpse of her sense of humor.[4]

Although word of her escape quickly spread and authorities launched a search for her, the Bábís "kept arriving to see her in a steady stream, and Ṭáhirih, seated behind a curtain, would converse with them." 'Abdu'l-Bahá recalled the day when Vaḥíd, for whom the Báb had revealed the Commentary on the Sura of Abundance, came to talk with her. He said, "I was then a child, and was sitting on her lap. With eloquence and fervor, Vaḥíd was discoursing on the signs and verses that bore witness to the advent of the new Manifestation. She suddenly interrupted him and, raising her voice, vehemently declared: ". . . Let deeds, not words, testify to thy faith, if thou art a man of true learning. Cease idly repeating the traditions of the past, for the day of service, of steadfast action, is come. Now is the time to show forth the true signs of God, to rend asunder the veils of idle fancy . . . to sacrifice ourselves in His path . . ."[5]

Outside the windows of the upper chamber where Ṭáhirih sat, Tehran's turquoise sky gave jubilant background to the mud-colored town, its mansions as well as its most wretched little streets with their streams of reeking water.[6] On the horizon rose the perfect peak of Mt. Demavand, symbol of Iran just as Mt. Fuji is symbolic of Japan. During the day, Ṭáhirih and her visitors most likely drank tea in glasses with silver holders; a server filled each glass with chunks of sugar hammered from a cone, poured strong tea essence over it, and followed that with the bubbling, steaming water from the samovar.

Since Ṭáhirih would have been quartered in the andarun of Bahá'u'lláh's home, we can assume that her hostess was Ásíyih Khánum, wife of Bahá'u'lláh, an intelligent and saintly woman known for her pure-hearted charity. Besides their son, she and Bahá'u'lláh had a daughter who would have been a toddler at the time; this daughter later said of her mother, "I wish you could have seen her as I first remember her, tall, slender, graceful, eyes of dark blue . . . her very presence enfolding . . . all . . . in the fragrance of gentle courtesy . . ." The daughter, who was very like her mother, grew up to be a bulwark of support for her brother and later for his grandson. 'Abdu'l-Bahá also had blue eyes, but they were lighter, flecked with brown. Perhaps his devout earnestness reminded Ṭáhirih of something she might have been told about the Báb, that the Báb's father had told a friend, when the Báb was small, how the child rose at midnight "to offer His obligatory prayers, in the midst of which he weeps . . ."[7]

But, much as she loved Him and His family, Ṭáhirih couldn't stay indefinitely in the home of Bahá'u'lláh. His own situation was precarious because He'd been accused of complicity in the assassination of Ṭáhirih's uncle, Taqí, and of course the hunt was on for Ṭáhirih. He sent her to stay at the home of a relative of His who had been exiled from a government post during one of the frequent upheavals in the shah's administration. The women of the exile's household made her welcome, and Bahá'u'lláh and His family visited her, along with other old and new friends, for her contacts were not confined only to Bábís; irresistibly, people were drawn to her and her teaching of the new faith continued.[8]

Then the Báb issued a call that His followers must gather in Khorasan. It wasn't the first time He'd told them to go to that province said to be the seat of all revolution in Iran. He'd been saying it almost from the very beginning, and Ṭáhirih had it in her mind to go there when she first went back to Qazvin from Baghdad, but events intervened.[9] Now was her time to try again.

Khorasan had a large Bábí community, established by Mullah Ḥusayn a few years since when he returned to his native town in the region after discovering the Báb in Shiraz and delivering his message to Bahá'u'lláh in Tehran. Nearly two thousand people used to attend each of his lectures, and other mullahs became jealous. After all, Mullah Ḥusayn didn't come from the priestly elite; he was only a dyer's son, so why should he win such a following?[10]

Meanwhile, Khorasan continued to be tumultuous, as usual. Muḥammad Sháh was ailing, so popular revolts and civil wars broke out even more frequently than before. As always there were, among other challenges, bandits to contend with; roiling caravans of people bearing the rotting corpses of their relatives for burial in the shrine city; and, for the superstitious, ghouls and other monsters haunting the vast wildernesses. Ṭáhirih, being fearless and a flouter of superstition, no doubt had no qualms about traveling there immediately to help promote the Cause of the Báb.[11]

Besides, Bahá'u'lláh realized she was no longer safe in Tehran and He must send her away. Planning to leave for Khorasan soon, Himself, He put her in the care of His loyal brother, Mírzá Músá.* Supplying Músá with food and money, He assured Him of God's guidance and warned Him to be very careful at the city gates, for Ṭáhirih didn't have a permit to pass through, and the guards were on the lookout for a fugitive woman. But with Músá and his outriders she went through the

* Also known as Áqáy-i-Kalím. Bahá'u'lláh said he was his "staunch supporter and the ablest of His brothers and sisters" (Gail, *Bahá'í Glossary*, p. 33).

city's Shimiran gate, and the guards didn't even ask where they were going.[12]

Mírzá Músá remembered afterwards, "'. . . At a distance of two farsangs* from the capital, we alighted in the midst of an orchard abundantly watered and situated at the foot of a mountain, in the center of which was a house that looked completely deserted. As I went about in search of the proprietor, I met an old man who was watering his plants . . . He explained that a dispute had arisen between the owner and his tenant . . . those who occupied the place had deserted it . . . I . . . invited him to share with us our luncheon. When, later in the day, I decided to depart for Tehran, I found him willing to watch over and guard Ṭáhirih and her attendant . . .'" (The attendant would have been the faithful Qánitih.) The next day, another Bábí came out from the capital to be Ṭáhirih's protector. He told her that Bahá'u'lláh was so glad to learn of her safety that He called the orchard a garden of paradise and said the house had been "providentially" prepared for her."[13]

Ṭáhirih stayed in the garden for seven days, and one hopes it was full of Persia's signature roses—"huge bushes, compact . . . spattered with flame-colored blossom; the ground carpeted with fallen petals . . . the interior of the petal red, but lined with gold, the two together giving a glow of orange . . . (and) side by side with these . . . the yellow rose . . ." Then she journeyed on toward Khorasan but halted on its borders to gather with fellow Bábís for the volatile Conference of Badasht. And so ended any peace she could hope to know during the rest of her short

---

* Unit of measurement for distance, usually three to four miles. In various parts of Iran, the length of a farsang differs depending on the terrain and how far locals say a laden mule can walk in an hour (Nabíl-i-A'ẓam, *The Dawn-breakers*, Glossary, p. 674).

life. However, she was not expecting peace, just as her brother-in-faith, Mullah Ḥusayn, the great seeker, didn't expect it.[14]

Not that Mullah Ḥusayn wanted to foster war. However, the large community of Bábís in Khorasan had attracted the favorable attention of a rebel warlord who had the allegiance of three major cities; he had already defeated the shah's army and massacred all prisoners. He misunderstood the aims of the Bábís and wanted to meet with Mullah Ḥusayn to win more fighting men for his forces. Mullah Ḥusayn knew he could never convince the warlord that the Bábí "insurrection" was a spiritual one, so he felt he'd better absent himself from the region. What better time to make a pilgrimage to visit the imprisoned Báb in Azerbaijan?[15]

The journey was 1,200 miles. Mullah Ḥusayn vowed to walk the entire distance. And he wanted to go alone. But a loyal attendant* insisted on accompanying him. At the beginning of 1848, the two left Mashhad in the middle of the night without a word to anyone. When the Bábís found out where Mullah Ḥusayn had gone, they hurried after him with horses and supplies. He refused to take anything and again pleaded with his friend to return to the city, but the man refused.[16]

All along his route, Mullah Ḥusayn met with Bábís in towns and villages, but he would not accept the pack animals and food they offered him. In Tehran, he was able to meet Bahá'u'lláh face-to-face. He'd delivered the Báb's message to Bahá'u'lláh through an intermediary in 1844 and had never seen him. No one knows how much he intuited of Bahá'u'lláh's destiny, but from his earlier reaction to the tea and sugar Bahá'u'lláh sent him in Tehran, and other implications in his words

* This was Qambar-'Alí, who would meet his death within a year of the momentous pilgrimage, on the same night that Mullah Ḥusayn was also killed (Nabíl-i-A'ẓam, *The Dawn-Breakers*, p. 417).

and actions, it is evident that his feelings for Bahá'u'lláh were deep. However, his emotions upon meeting with Him can only be imagined, for theirs was a private talk, and there's no extant record of it.[17]

Qazvin lies ninety-three miles west of Tehran. According to one author, when Mullah Ḥusayn passed through Qazvin on his pilgrimage he met with Ṭáhirih for the first time. However, it seems more likely that they would have become acquainted when Mullah Ḥusayn came to Karbala while she was teaching in the home of Siyyid Káẓim's widow, where she had befriended Mullah Husayn's mother and sister. Another source says they met before the murder of Ṭáhirih's uncle, probably in the home of the man who would later rescue Ṭáhirih from Qazvin. Whatever the circumstances, "We know that Ṭáhirih was certainly impressed by Mullah Ḥusayn . . . she wrote a long letter in Arabic to him. On several pages she expresses exuberant praise of the first believer, such as a humble servant might express to her Lord."[18]

Trekking onward, Mullah Ḥusayn and his companion reached Tabriz on March 21, 1848, where they "were obliged to change clothes so as not to be recognized as they approached Mah-ku." They had heard that the Báb's warden, the governor* of the province, appointed by the hostile prime minister, was a Turkish Sunni famed for his relentless ferocity. They planned to approach the fortress-prison as cautiously as possible, hoping to evade this man's keen eye.[19]

However, the governor had already succumbed to the Báb's charisma and had come to believe in Him. First of all, He hadn't been able to prevent the Kurdish Sunnis living in the vicinity of the prison from coming, in their curiosity, "to the foot of the mountain to obtain a glimpse of the Báb," and now they gathered "daily at the mountain's base to gaze upwards in the hope of obtaining His blessing." Then, one

* 'Alí Khán.

day while riding through the wilderness, he saw the Báb "standing by the side of the river" praying. He waited for the Báb to finish praying so he could scold Him for leaving the prison. But the Báb remained enraptured. The governor approached Him, and the Báb showed no awareness of his presence. Going to the prison, the governor found that all of its gates were properly closed. He entered, and the guards ushered him to the Báb, where, "utterly confounded," he told the Báb what he'd seen and added, "I know not whether my reason has deserted me." The Báb said, "What you have witnessed is true and undeniable . . ."[20]

Now Mullah Ḥusayn and his companion, nearing the prison, couldn't evade that governor's dreams. The governor later said:

> In my sleep, I was startled by the sudden intelligence that Muḥammad, the Prophet of God, was soon to arrive at Mah-ku . . . to visit the Báb and to offer Him his congratulations on the advent of the Naw-Rúz festival. In my dream, I ran out to meet Him . . . hastened on foot in the direction of the river . . . and . . . saw two men advancing towards me . . . I thought one of them to be the Prophet Himself . . . and was bending to kiss the hem of His robe, when suddenly I awoke. A great joy had flooded my soul . . .
>
> I performed my ablutions, offered my prayer, arrayed myself in my richest attire, anointed myself with perfume, and proceeded to the spot where, the night before in my dream, I had gazed upon . . . the Prophet. I . . . instructed my attendants to saddle three of my best and swiftest steeds and conduct them immediately to the bridge. The sun had just risen when, alone and unescorted, I walked out of the town of Mah-ku in the direction of the river. As I approached the bridge, I discovered, with a throb of wonder, the two men whom I had seen in my dream walking one behind the other . . . advancing towards me. Instinctively I fell at the feet of the one whom I believed to be the Prophet . . .[21]

That one was Mullah Ḥusayn. The governor offered him a horse so he could proceed in style into Mah-ku, but Mullah Ḥusayn refused because he'd vowed to go the entire distance to the Báb on foot. The governor then walked after Mullah Ḥusayn to the prison gate.[22]

When Mullah Ḥusayn reached the gate, he looked up and saw the Báb waiting to greet him. Mullah Ḥusayn bowed humbly, then stood motionless. The Báb embraced him and led him into the prison, which must have seemed to the pilgrim like the most luxurious of mansions.[23]

Mullah Ḥusayn, his attendant, and fellow Bábís of the region, celebrated that Naw-Rúz with the Báb, the fourth new year since the Báb had declared His mission. It was the first time in His nine-month imprisonment at Mah-ku that the Báb was able to receive a number of disciples. One of them later recalled being "at the foot of the mountain" and listening to "the voice of the Báb, as he dictated the teachings and principles of His Faith" to one permitted to be His amanuensis. "The melody of His chanting, the rhythmic flow of the verses which streamed from His lips caught our ears . . . Mountain and valley re-echoed the majesty of His voice . . ."[24]

The Báb commented to Mullah Ḥusayn that the crumbling mountain fortress of Mah-ku overlooked the Araxes or Aras River, which was the border between Iran and Russia. The Qur'án mentions that river as "Ras" in a prophetic passage, and it is said that Zoroaster walked and taught on its banks.[25]

The Báb quoted a tradition: "'Treasures lie hidden beneath the throne of God; the key to those treasures is the tongue of poets.'" He said that poets inspired by "the immediate influence of the Holy Spirit" sometimes uttered words "the significance of which they themselves are often times unable to apprehend," and He illustrated this by adding, "That is the river, and this is the bank thereof, of which the poet Hafez has written: 'O zephyr, shouldst thou pass by the banks of the Araxes, implant a kiss on the earth of that valley and make fragrant thy breath.

Hail, a thousand times hail to thee, O abode of Salma! How dear is the voice of thy camel-drivers, how sweet the jingling of thy bells!'"[26]

Perhaps the Báb also knew by then of the eulogy written in His honor by a noted poet* from Shiraz who was ostensibly not His follower. The poet included in his eulogy that quote from Hafez and wrote at the head of it: "In praise of the manifestation of the Siyyid-i-Báb."[27]

The Báb said the "abode of Salma" mentioned by Hafez indicated the town called Salmas by the Turks. It was near a place named Chihriq. There, He said, He would soon be imprisoned in another mountain. Mullah Ḥusayn must be on his way before that happened. The Báb told him to journey on foot, but said that his time for peerless horsemanship was coming.[28]

Every other time that Mullah Ḥusayn had taken his leave of the Báb, the Báb had promised they would meet again. This time, He did not. He said, "The Feast of Sacrifice is fast approaching . . . let nothing detain you from achieving your destiny. Having attained your destination, prepare yourself to receive Us, for We too shall ere long follow you." Mullah Ḥusayn interpreted this to mean that he'd be called upon to give his life for his beliefs, and so would the Báb, and that their next reunion would not be in the corporeal world.[29]

On April 9, 1848, the Báb was transferred to Chihriq. One of the Letters of the Living wrote, presumably to an uncle of the Báb's, that the "Russian Envoy had heard that He was in Mah-ku, and, being afraid of disturbance, told the Vizier . . . Aqasi" to send the Báb "'to some other area . . . because Mah-ku is on the frontier and close to our territory, and we are afraid of disturbances; a few years ago, a certain Mullah

---

* Mira Habib-i-Shirazi, known as Qa'ini or Qaani. "Qaani (d. 1853), the best Iranian writer of the 19th Century and perhaps the most outstanding since Jami, was one of Iran's most brilliant and melodious poets" ("A Brief History of Persian Literature," http://www.iranchamber.com/literature/articles/history_literature.php).

Sadiq claimed to be the deputy [of the Imam] and within a month gathered 30,000 followers round him.' The Russians had witnessed that and had taken fright."[30]

The Báb had told Mullah Ḥusayn to retrace his steps as far as Tehran, revisiting various villages and towns, and then to go to the province of Mazandaran. Looking at a map, this seems a roundabout route, but even now, the slanting roads over the Elborz Mountains, the Middle East's highest range, are so difficult that some people still go through Tehran. Mullah Ḥusayn, on foot, of course, followed the Báb's instructions and had the good fortune to be able to meet once more with Bahá'u'lláh in the capital.[31]

Then he started for Mazandaran, the fabled, forested region where Bahá'u'lláh had grown up. There, the Báb had told him, he would find "God's hidden treasure."* He believed that he found it when he became reacquainted with his fellow Letter of the Living, Quddús, in Babul.[32]

In the home of Quddús, Mullah Ḥusayn was given the seat of honor while Quddús occupied a lowly position by the door. Quddús asked his guest if he'd brought with him any of the Báb's new writings. Mullah Ḥusayn had not. Quddús then handed him some manuscripts. The power and clarity of the writing so impressed Mullah Ḥusayn that he said, "I testify to my whole-hearted recognition of the sublimity of these words . . ."[33]

Quddús said nothing. Mullah Ḥusayn, realizing that it was his host who had written the texts, left his seat of honor and went to where Quddús sat on the threshold of the room. Bowing before Quddús,

* This is an evocative echo of what He said in 1844 when He sent Mullah Ḥusayn to Tehran deliver His special scroll: "A secret lies hidden in that city. When made manifest, it shall turn the earth into paradise. My hope is that you may partake of its grace and recognize its splendor" (Mehrabkhani, *Mullá Ḥusayn: Disciple at Dawn*, p. 90).

he said, "The hidden treasure of which the Báb has spoken now lies unveiled before my eyes. Its light has dispelled the gloom of perplexity and doubt. Though my master be now hidden amid the mountain fastnesses of Azerbaijan, the sign of His splendor and the revelation of His might stand manifest before me. I have found in Mazandaran the reflection of his glory."[34]

We can only wonder at the remarkable wisdom and humility of Mullah Ḥusayn, a man of such outstanding erudition and personal power that he would have been accepted by most of his fellow Shaykhis as the Promised One if he'd chosen to make such a claim, yet who was able to bend his will and give his heart to the young reed that was the Báb and again to Quddús, who seemed to him to be the Báb's mirror image.[35]

When the Bábís of the region came to Quddús's house the next day to meet Mullah Ḥusayn, they found he'd gladly ceded his seat of honor to his host. They heard Quddús tell Mullah Ḥusayn to go and speak directly about the message of the Báb with one of the ulama who had become the chief enemy of the Bábís in Mazandaran, and then travel onward to Mashhad and build a center of teaching and hospitality. Upon his return to Mashhad, Mullah Ḥusayn did just that, and Quddús soon arrived there to work with him. The center came to be known as the Bábíyyih, and after Mullah Ḥusayn's mother and sister left Ṭáhirih's side, they went to Mashhad to teach the many female students. The center was a great success, infuriating the city's religious establishment, who reacted to it murderously.[36]

Mullah Ḥusayn remained the front man for the teaching campaign, walking all over Mashhad with enthusiastic companions and also visiting towns and villages surrounding the city, holding classes not only in the Bábíyyih but in a certain madrassa, winning people of all classes and positions to the Báb's cause, including the captain of the prince's artilleries.[37]

The population of Mashhad was unusually diverse. Behind its turreted and towered but disintegrating mud wall, the city was a crossroad of the oriental world. Its unusually wide and straight main street (with a canal for sewage, drinking water, bathing, and laundry running down its center) was lined with elm, willow, mulberry and plane trees, and crowded with Afghans, Arabs, Turks, Tartars, Bedouins, and more. The streets were noisy with the sounds of livestock, beggars, and vendors. Side streets were the "familiar labyrinth of intricate alleys wandering between mud walls, turning odd corners that seem to lead nowhere, occasionally stumbling upon a small piece of bazaar, now emerging upon open spaces and heaps of rubbish." Wealthy homes flourished behind high walls, while hovels had "low doorways often below the level of the street."[38]

The city's vast graveyards reeked, overloaded with the bodies of people who had died near the Shrine of the Eighth Imam or were transported to it already dead and moldering. The cemeteries were also constantly plundered for granite and other saleable items, leaving the corpses exposed.[39]

At the end of the main street, an arch in a wall led to the shrine and its mosques, madrassas, library, and souvenir shops. It was said that the Eighth Imam, within his gold-laden, jewel-ornamented, marble-paved, and richly carpeted tomb was still alive and would miraculously answer prayers if a suitable fee was paid to one of the mullahs. For their piety, pilgrims received various amenities: three days room and board and "wives"—women available for temporary marriages. The purportedly still-alive Imam (or his representative, the guardian of the shrine) could well-afford this generosity for he owned extensive properties all over Iran.[40]

To protect their worldly power the authorities demanded mass conformity. The Jews of Mashhad had been made to convert to Islam in 1838, although most of them continued practicing Judaism in secret, calling themselves Anusim, the Compelled Ones.[41] This name served as an ironic reference to the fact that the Qur'án says there is no compulsion in Islam.*

But the folkloric tradition that the Eighth Imam still lived also said that everyone in the country must embrace the same faith. And it predicted that of the two Promised Ones (Qá'ims) to arise at "the end of time" in Iran, one would appear in Khorasan in a mosque next to the one dedicated to the Imam. The Bábís had not yet directly declared the Báb as the author of their message; they "taught only that a new 'gate' to the Hidden Imam had opened."[42]

Then, one day, Mullah Ḥusayn walked to the destined mosque. From the pulpit, which was dedicated to the Lord of the Age, he proclaimed a new revelation. At the same time, the Báb wrote His letters to His followers in Iran and Iraq "instructing them to go to the aid of Mullah Ḥusayn and Quddús." So Ṭáhirih, Bahá'u'lláh, and others set out in their direction.[43]

More and more people flocked to the Bábíyyih, and the ulama (those who didn't become Bábís) were increasingly infuriated. At one point Mullah Ḥusayn sent them some scripture with words by the Báb written in black ink and words by the Imam 'Alí written in red ink. It was widely known that Bábí scriptures were always written in red ink. So, when the mullahs saw them, they wrote under the black ink text that it was inspired and under the red ink text that it was "full of grammatical errors and blasphemy against God." They hadn't bothered to read, they'd merely condemned out of hand.[44]

Sadly, many of the Bábís hadn't yet learned the peaceful means employed by Mullah Ḥusayn, nor had they absorbed the Báb's example

* "Let there be no compulsion in religion: truth stands out clear from error . . ." (The Holy Qur'án, Sura 2:256).

of long-suffering. Raised in a Shiite tradition that lauded the strength of its martyred warriors and glorified their battles, they believed the Promised One's first act would be "to raise an army and wage war . . . cause rivers of blood to flow in retribution for the wrongs done to the true believers."[45]

Consequently, violence erupted between the Bábís and their enemies. One day on a Mashhad street, a passerby was heaping insults on Mullah Ḥusayn and his cause. A Bábí named Ḥasan heard him, grabbed him, and beat him. Ḥasan was captured and bastinadoed,* after which his nose was pierced, and he was led through the city by a rope thrust like a halter through the holes. The Bábís ran to Mullah Ḥusayn to tell him about it, and he promised to rescue their companion by the next day.[46]

However, that wasn't quick enough or retributive enough for the Bábís. They marched through the streets shouting "Ya Sahibu'z-Zaman!" ("Oh Thou Lord of the Age") and came face-to-face with a crowd that was still tormenting Ḥasan. Fighting broke out; Ḥasan escaped, and one of his tormentors was killed.[47]

The prince-governor of the region then ordered the arrest of Mullah Ḥusayn. But the captain of the prince's artillery, one of his most prized officers, interceded. The prince then changed his tone, inviting Mullah Ḥusayn to come and stay in "a highly ornamented tent next to his own"—ostensibly for Mullah Ḥusayn's protection. Quddús advised Mullah Ḥusayn to accept the "invitation," though they both knew it would make him a prisoner. Quddús, meanwhile, left the city.[48]

Now, as the Bab had foretold, Mullah Ḥusayn's time for horsemanship arrived. He traveled on horseback to the prince's camp. The prince made him so welcome that he was even able to preach from a pulpit that the

* Torturing a person by tying him down and repeatedly lashing the soles of his feet with a rod (Mehrabkhani, *Mullá Ḥusayn: Disciple at Dawn*, p. 164).

prince set up for him. But he knew the ulama of Mashhad wouldn't stop persecuting the Bábís, who were now leaderless. He offered to make a pilgrimage to Karbala, and the prince, who had no idea what to do about the whole situation, was happy to accommodate him and to let him return to the city to get ready for his journey.[49]

He had seven days to leave the city. The Báb sent him His own turban with the message: "Adorn your head with My green turban, the emblem of My lineage" and told him to ride out of Khorasan leading his brethren with the black standards unfurled, flying high above them, and "hasten to the Verdant Isle" to rejoin Quddús.[50]

By verdant isle, the Báb meant the green province of Mazandaran. The black standards would fulfill Islamic prophecy about the Promised One: "Should your eyes behold the Black standards proceeding from Khorasan, hasten toward them, even should ye have to crawl over snow, inasmuch as they proclaim the advent of the promised Mahdi . . ."[51]

Mullah Ḥusayn's erstwhile host, the prince, offered him money for his travel expenses, and so did the captain of the artillery. Mullah Ḥusayn accepted a horse and sword from the captain, who was a fellow believer, rejected all the rest, and rode away with 202 companions.[52]

A farsang's distance from the city, he hoisted high his black flags, donned the Báb's green turban, and led his small army forward, stopping to "fearlessly proclaim" his "message of the New Day" in every village and town. At every place they stopped, men joined their march.[53]

Simultaneously with these events, the imprisoned Báb was summoned to Tabriz for the trial where He would confound the tiger-eyed prince regent, and Quddús met up with Bahá'u'lláh and made camp in the orchard-gardens of Badasht, where Ṭáhirih—with spiritual revolution restless in her heart—also had a pavilion. Some eighty other believers surrounded them, hoping that through their consultations, they'd come up with a plan to free the Báb. However, most of them were unable to visualize their true purpose and destiny, which was entirely different than anything they would have been able to imagine. It would be Ṭáhirih's role to stand before them as their Siddiqih, Truth, as the Báb had called her three years before, and unveil to them their path.

14

1848, Iran—The Golden Looking Glass

The Conference of Badasht and its aftermath.

Badasht was a nondescript hamlet on a major route leading into Khorasan. It was near the large town of Shahrud, a halfway point on the highway from Tehran to Mashhad, about 250 miles northeast of the capital where travelers joined big caravans of horse, camel, mule, and donkey trains to journey together and thus ward off raiders. "The already dusty highway traversed the treeless rolling country along the foothills of the southernmost range of the Elborz Mountains. It was the upper edge of the great Persian desert, with the salt sink of Kavir to the south, lofty Mount Demavend in sight to the north." On that road, Ṭáhirih in her howdah would have covered perhaps fifteen to twenty miles per day.[1]

When she reached Badasht, she found that Bahá'u'lláh had rented "three fallow gardens with a mountain stream flowing through them." Though the gardens were not cultivated, it was June, and the fruit trees were green against the "blue-purple backdrop" of the mountains. Each of the three gardens had its pavilion, arranged by Bahá'u'lláh, and Ṭáhirih settled into one with her maid Qánitih attending her and Khatun Jan's husband, who had helped her escape from Qazvin, as her doorkeeper. Bahá'u'lláh had another pavilion, but no one knew who was to occupy the third until one day Bahá'u'lláh brought Quddús from Shahrud. Fellow conferees pitched tents in the surrounding orchard. All were guests of Bahá'u'lláh, and all were men except for Ṭáhirih and Qánitih. A new book composed by the Báb in the prison of Mah-ku was to be shared with them; it was the Bayan (Utterances or Exposition), and the Báb had written both Persian and Arabic versions.[2]

Since April 10, 1848, the Báb had been imprisoned in Chihriq. Although His new warden was a brother-in-law of Muḥammad Sháh, who at first determined to keep Him strictly hidden, this proved impossible, and the Kurdish inhabitants of the nearby village came to the fortress each day "to prostrate themselves in adoration." A "European eyewitness" wrote that people entered the prison courtyard until it was too crowded, so the overflow "remained in the street and listened with rapt attention to the verses" chanted by the Báb. Among the outstanding converts of that period were "a prominent official of high literary repute"* and "a dervish, a former navvab,† from India, whom had seen the Báb in a vision in which the Báb told him to renounce wealth and position, and hasten on foot to meet Him in Azerbaijan."[3]

During His imprisonment, the Báb maintained "continual correspondence" with Bahá'u'lláh. Although the Bábís hoped the purpose of their gathering in the orchard in the foothills of the mountain ramparts was to liberate the Báb, His purpose, in collaboration with Bahá'u'lláh, was to liberate them from "the past—with its order, its ecclesiasticism, its traditions, and ceremonials."[4]

---

* Siyyid Asadu'lláh, also called Dayyán.

† A high government official, an aristocrat or noble, also transliterated as nabob (Gail, *Bahá'í Glossary*, p. 38).

The eight thousand verses of the Báb's recent scripture, the Bayan, abrogated certain Islamic laws and ceremonies and gave new interpretations to terms such as Paradise, Hell, death and Resurrection, while upholding the prophetic truth of Muḥammad. In the twentieth century, Shoghi Effendi, the Guardian* of the Bahá'í Faith, would write that the Bayan was "revolutionizing in the principles it instilled, calculated to awaken from their age-long torpor the clergy and the people."[5]

First the Bábís had to be awakened. It was Ṭáhirih's task to make sure they could not escape understanding the Báb's true meaning. Galvanized by Bahá'u'lláh and aided by Quddús, she would show them the passing of the centuries-old order, the blaze and heat of the newborn day, the change in laws they'd taken to be eternal.

Ṭáhirih felt herself deeply integrated into that process of change; her very presence at Badasht as a leader among the Bábís showed that a new social law was coming into being. It included the principle that would be clearly, unmistakably stated by Bahá'u'lláh: men and women are equal. While religious women frequently have to rebel against what is seen as divine will in order to assert their rights to speak and act, Ṭáhirih, claiming her freedom, felt deeply obedient to her Creator and her faith. Although she is rightfully seen as a pioneer for women's rights, Ṭáhirih did more than proclaim equality for her gender; she embodied the liberating reality of her religion. As 'Abdu'l-Bahá later explained:

> The truth is that all mankind are the creatures and servants of one God, and in His estimate all are human. *Man* is a generic term applying to all humanity. The biblical statement "Let us make

---

* Shoghi Effendi was 'Abdu'l-Bahá's eldest grandson. His first name means "yearning" and *Effendi* is a Turkish title meaning *sir* or *master*, sometimes used for scholars in the Middle East (Gail, *Bahá'í Glossary*, p. 47).

man in our image, after our likeness" does not mean that woman was not created. The image and likeness of God apply to her as well. In Persian and Arabic there are two distinct words translated into English as man: one meaning man and woman collectively, the other distinguishing man as male from woman the female. The first word and its pronoun are generic, collective; the other is restricted to the male. This is the same in Hebrew.

To accept and observe a distinction which God has not intended in creation is ignorance and superstition . . .[6]

So it was that, as summer of 1848 unwound its golden days in the orchard that seethed with the restless energy of men longing for quick and decisive action against their enemies, Ṭáhirih, their sister, opened the door to their new path under the guidance of Ḥusayn-'Alí of Nur, Bahá'u'lláh. Each one of the Bábís present acquired a new name, conferred by Bahá'u'lláh. This was when Ḥusayn-'Alí took the designation *Bahá*; it was also during these days that Ṭáhirih took her title and Quddús took his. Later, participants each received a special letter from the Báb affirming their titles. Every day, new passages of scripture were chanted aloud to the assemblage, and each day an Islamic law or tradition was abrogated. During this time Quddús maintained a conservative stance, resisting innovation, while Ṭáhirih was radically revolutionary and Bahá'u'lláh preserved a moderating neutrality. Shoghi Effendi said this occurred by previous agreement among the three of them, as an effort to safely canalize the inevitable passionate emotions aroused in the Bábís by the necessarily "sudden . . . complete and dramatic break with the past."[7]

One day Bahá'u'lláh was resting in His pavilion because of a slight illness. Quddús came to Him, and others gathered there, too. A messenger from Ṭáhirih appeared and summoned Quddús to her pavilion. He said, "I have severed myself entirely from her. I refuse to meet her."[8]

The messenger went to Ṭáhirih, returned, and said, "She insists on your visit. If you persist in your refusal, she herself will come to you."[9]

Quddús again refused.

The messenger unsheathed his sword, laid it on the ground before Quddús, and said, "I refuse to go without you. Either choose to accompany me to the presence of Ṭáhirih or cut off my head with this sword."[10]

Quddús lifted the sword as if to comply. The messenger "stretched forth his neck to receive the fatal blow, when suddenly . . . Ṭáhirih, adorned and unveiled, appeared before the eyes of the assembled companions. Consternation immediately seized the entire gathering."[11]

The French chronicler A. L. M. Nicolas wrote that the effect of Ṭáhirih's countenance on the men was "astounding . . . Some hid their faces with their hands, others prostrated themselves, others covered their heads with their garments so that they could not see the features of her Highness, the Pure One. If it was a grievous sin to look upon the face of an unknown woman who might pass by, what a crime to let one's eyes fall upon her who was so saintly!"[12]

However, Shoghi Effendi reminds us that some of the men at that moment probably "recalled with throbbing hearts the Islamic tradition foreshadowing the appearance of Fatima herself unveiled while crossing the Bridge (Sirat) on the promised Day of Judgment." It is possible that even Bahá'u'lláh was surprised by the moment that she chose for her announcement. He later wrote, "We fell ill one day, and were confined to bed. Ṭáhirih sent a message to call upon Us. We were surprised at her message, and were at a loss as to what We should reply. Suddenly We saw her at the door, her face unveiled before us." He cited the prophecy regarding Fáṭimih, recalling that His amanuensis later mentioned the tradition, "The face of Fáṭimih must needs be revealed on the Day of Judgment and appear unveiled before the eyes of men. At that moment the voice of the Unseen shall be heard saying: Turn your eyes away from that which ye have seen."[13]

So we don't know to what exact extent the activities of the three major players—Bahá'u'lláh, Quddús, and Ṭáhirih—were scripted at the Conference of Badasht. Perhaps it was what theater people now call a structured improvisation, where the course of action has been decided, but not down to precise means and moments: those are left to the judgment of the individual players. We do know that the unveiled Ṭáhirih calmly seated herself to the right of Quddús. One of the men was "so gravely shaken that he cut his throat with his own hands. Covered with blood and shrieking with excitement, he fled away from the face of Ṭáhirih. A few, following his example, abandoned their companions . . .* A number were seen standing speechless before her . . . Quddús, meanwhile . . . remained seated . . . holding the unsheathed sword . . . It seemed as if he were waiting for the moment when he could strike his fatal blow at Ṭáhirih."[14]

Neither the tumult nor the sword moved her. "A feeling of joy and triumph . . . illumined her face." She rose to her feet and addressed "the remnant" of the assembly. Her message was directly related to the Báb's new book, the Bayan, with its emphasis on the One he harbingered. She quoted the Qur'án, "'Verily, amid gardens and rivers shall the pious dwell in the seat of truth, in the presence of the potent King.'" So saying, she glanced at both Bahá'u'lláh and Quddús, thus keeping veiled the identity of the "King," (but, as we know, she recognized Bahá'u'lláh as the one promised by the Bab). She then declared, "I am the Word which the Qá'im is to utter, the Word which shall put to flight the chiefs and nobles of the earth!" She concluded, "This day is the day of festivity and universal rejoicing, the day on which the fetters of the past are burst

* The man who cut his throat, 'Abdu'l-Kháliq-i-Iṣfáhání, remained a Bábí and later gave his life for his faith. Ṭáhirih gave him the title *Dhabih,* which means *the Sacrifice* in Arabic (Nabíl-i-A'ẓam, *The Dawn-breakers*, p. 422).

asunder. Let those who have shared in this great achievement arise and embrace each other."[15]

Bahá'u'lláh, Who also had maintained absolute serenity, then called on a man who was still in possession of his faculties to recite from the Qur'án a chapter called *The Inevitable*; it's also called *The Resurrection.* It describes calamity: "When the Event Inevitable cometh to pass, then will no (soul) entertain falsehood concerning its coming. (Many) will it bring low; (many) will it exalt; when the earth shall be shaken to its depths, and the mountains shall be crumbled to atoms, becoming dust scattered abroad . . ." And it describes reward, a shelter for the righteous who ascend to heaven, "No frivolity will they hear therein, nor any taint of ill,—only the saying, 'Peace! Peace!'"[16]

In the ensuing hours and days, the conferees regained a measure of composure, but Bahá'u'lláh later recalled, "How great was the consternation that seized the companions . . . A few, unable to tolerate that which was to them so revolting a departure from the established custom of Islam, fled in horror from before her face. Dismayed, they sought refuge in a deserted castle in that neighborhood." Bahá'u'lláh sent word to those shaken souls that their flight was "unnecessary."[17]

Quddús and Ṭáhirih continued to express bitter disagreement with each other, and the opinions of their companions were split between them. She said of Quddús, "I deem him a pupil whom the Báb has sent me to edify and instruct." He said she was a heretic and that anyone who followed her grievously erred. To some, the conference seemed a complete failure. All must have been relieved when, after several days, "Bahá'u'lláh intervened and, in His masterly way, effected a complete reconciliation between them (Ṭáhirih and Quddús). He healed the wounds which that sharp controversy had caused and directed the efforts of both along the path of constructive service." Whether or not Ṭáhirih and Quddús had slipped from their pre-planned roles as opponents to fall into a state of real anger, or whether they had been continuing their roleplay, we can never know. But they did canalize and embody the conflict of opposing camps of men at the gathering and unity between them made harmony possible for the rest of the proceedings.[18]

Whatever their previous feelings, in mid-July, by the end of the 22-day gathering when they, with Bahá'u'lláh, rode away northward, Ṭáhirih and Quddús shared a howdah "which had been prepared for their journey by Bahá'u'lláh." A procession of Bábís followed them, chanting the odes that Ṭáhirih composed daily. They went by way of the mountains, avoiding a main road through an area where there might be arrest warrants out for them, and ". . . mountain and valley re-echoed the shouts with which that enthusiastic band . . . hailed the . . . birth of the new Day."[19]

What did Ṭáhirih feel in her emancipation that day when she entered Bahá'u'lláh's pavilion free of the hijab? Women who discard their veils often describe "the feel of the wind and the sun on . . . hair and skin—it was so startling . . ."[20] Perhaps such sensations were, to her, welcome refinements on her sweet exhilaration of spirit.

Whatever its effects on her own soul, her selfless action had opened paths to a new definition of humanity for both men and women that future generations have yet to truly find and embrace. Her deed was truly of the sort Bahá'u'lláh described when he later wrote, "One righteous act is endowed with a potency that can so elevate the dust as to pass beyond the heaven of heavens. It can tear every bond asunder, and hath the power to restore the force that hath spent itself and vanished . . ."[21]

But in the aftermath of Badasht, a few of the Bábís, perhaps inevitably, took the unveiling of Ṭáhirih and the abrogation of old traditions as license to misbehave. As they followed "the track . . . upward along the Mojen River and over a high pass into the headwaters of the Nika River's long valley to the Caspian Sea . . . some unstable members of the party were ripe for trouble. Along the mountain valley road through the village of Niyala, these few were guilty of provocative acts toward the village women."[22] The results were disastrous.

Bahá'u'lláh later said, "'We were all gathered in the village of Níyálá and were resting at the foot of a mountain, when, at the hour of dawn, we were suddenly awakened by stones which the people of the neighborhood were hurling upon us from the top of the mountain. The fierceness of their attack induced our companions to flee in terror . . . I clothed Quddús in my own garments and dispatched him to a place of safety, where I intended to join him. When I arrived, I found that he had gone. None of our companions had remained in Níyálá except Ṭáhirih and a young man from Shíráz, Mírzá 'Abdu'lláh.* The violence with which we were assailed had brought desolation into our camp. I found no one into whose custody I could deliver Ṭáhirih except that young man, who displayed on that occasion a courage and determination that were truly surprising. Sword in hand, undaunted by the savage assault of the inhabitants of the village, who had rushed to plunder our property, he sprang forward . . . Though himself wounded in several parts of his body, he risked his life . . ."[23]

But although Bahá'u'lláh lauded bravery and self-sacrifice, He didn't condone violence. He went on, "I bade him desist from his act. When the tumult had subsided, I approached a number of inhabitants of the village and was able to convince them of the cruelty and shamefulness of their behavior. I subsequently succeeded in restoring a part of our plundered property."[24]

Bahá'u'lláh sent Ṭáhirih, with her female attendant, under the protection of another trusted Bábí, into His home province of Nur, where

---

* It's possible that this young man was the escaped assassin of Ṭáhirih's uncle; the name is the same. If so, his fierceness was certainly innate.

he arranged shelter for her. Now she was a fugitive not only from her murderous husband, but from the law, homeless.[25]

To most people, her very name was scandal. A Muslim polemicist, giving his version of her story, wrote, "It seems God created women as a sort of test for men. As it is forbidden to go near the wine, so it is forbidden to go near the other, women. When beautiful women discard their modesty they bring rains of devastation. There was such a woman, Qurratu'l-'Ayn, in Iran . . ."[26]

This writer attributed all of Ṭáhirih's appeal to her beauty. He credits her with being a well-educated poet and says "oration was her special art," yet "to lure the people into the fold of new religion she renounced Purdah and began to mix up with people showing her beauty and preaching . . . She succeeding in gaining a hold over a large number of people on account of her beauty . . ."[27]

He fantasized that it was Ṭáhirih's "lover" who "martyred the Mujtahid (her uncle) in the state of prayer . . ." and that after this, "her prime opponent was removed. She became bold enough to preach her hedonism with more gusto."[28]

It's hard to see any hedonism in being locked in solitary confinement by her husband and then in her childhood home under constant threat of poisoning or death by some other means, or in becoming a homeless fugitive, cut off entirely from family and almost entirely from friends. This writer, however, felt free to imagine what he wished and eagerly objectified Ṭáhirih as no more than a beautiful thing, like Keats's Grecian urn.

If he knew about the "calligram of the hidden beauty of Allah" attributed to the human face by the members of the Hurufi sect, he certainly didn't relate it to Ṭáhirih's beauty. The Hurufi believed "the invisible beauty of God vibrates in the body of each prophet and is extended to the human countenance," which manifests the seven verses of the first chapter of the Qur'án, the Muslim profession of faith, in seven lines—two pairs of eyelashes, two eyebrows, and the hairline.[29]

Nevertheless, human distrust, fear and envy of beauty, spiritual or physical, too often overcomes admiration of it. Despite the protection accorded her by Bahá'u'lláh and the unflagging approval of the Báb, Ṭáhirih from day to day had to bear the burden of her beauty alone, whether she was veiled or unveiled, especially as Bahá'u'lláh could not yet take open leadership of the Bábí movement, and the Báb was a prisoner. Once she removed the veil, exposing the sacred calligram of her face, even if she afterwards donned her chador and face-covering as usual, in the minds of her countrymen she was utterly vulnerable. She wrote,

> He turns, returns, the Primal Point—He proclaims ascendance,
> Yet He veils his radiance, His beloved countenance.
>
> Multitudinous eternal veils in sun's ascent abide—
> Alas, alas, Ahmad,* for your new-minted, beautified, unveiled bride.[30]

However, despite being a homeless fugitive of questionable reputation, she preserved the invulnerability of mission. 'Abdu'l-Bahá would later say, ". . . the trials of homelessness and adversity in the path of God . . . are blessed by the divine favor . . . Abraham's migration from His native land caused the bountiful gifts of the All-Glorious to be made manifest, and the setting of Canaan's brightest star unfolded to the eyes the radiance of Joseph . . ."[31]

* *Aḥmad* is another name for Muḥammad, meaning the Friend (The Holy Qur'án, Sura 61:6). Islamic philosophers use the term *Ahmadi* to refer to the light or spirit of Muḥammad; Ṭáhirih used it to refer to what she saw as the new manifestation of that light in the Báb and Bahá'u'lláh (Hatcher and Hemmat, *The Poetry of Ṭáhirih*, p. 189, note 327).

She also preserved her innate fearlessness. She was afraid of nothing, especially not beauty. As the Báb wrote in the Persian Bayan, "No created thing shall ever attain its paradise unless it appeareth in its highest prescribed degree of perfection. For instance, this crystal representeth the paradise of the stone whereof its substance is composed. Likewise there are various stages in the paradise for the crystal itself . . . So long as it was stone it was worthless, but if it attaineth the excellence of ruby—a potentiality which is latent in it—how much a carat will it be worth?" And how subject to greedy, grasping hands. Yet Ṭáhirih, the ruby, shone unflinchingly. Gods of ancient religions were jealous of beauty and sought to destroy it; other interpretations of the Deity curse beauty as a temptation; but Ṭáhirih knew that her beauty, unveiled in the service of the Báb, was approved by Providence and safe beneath Its gaze:

I unloose my ambergris hair across the desert plain:
one curl the wild gazelle ensnares.

With kohl I darken my narcissus eyes and I darken
day itself: I am the world's demise.

Every dawn to see my face the sphere of heaven shifts,
uplifts its golden looking-glass . . .[32]

15

1848, Iran—Under the Tiger's Eye

The Báb's trial in Tabriz.

In her poetry, Ṭáhirih inevitably represented herself as being alone except for her Divine Beloved. Although she was perhaps accompanied by her daughter and Qánitih most of the time, there was no help for her aloneness. Her unveiled beauty, as well as the beauty she saw in the two men she cherished as Revelators, and her dedication to them, cut her from her roots and the mundane world. Other Bábís necessarily suffered the same fate. Like her, they willingly accepted it as a destiny larger than each one of them, a whirlwind forcing them to create, forget, recreate and lose themselves time after time. It carried them far from families and homes on a trajectory completely opposed to every expectation of their culture.

"We Iranians," one memoirist wrote, "value family above all else and spend our whole lives within its hot, protective walls . . . From it we derive our very being, our deepest and most meaningful sense of self. Through it we define who we are, to the world and to ourselves. As long as the family is intact, secure, and complete, we know that we are somebody instead of nobody."[1]

Ṭáhirih's family was shattered. The forces that did it went deeper than her own actions, for they were part of a fate that was much larger than herself. When she was a child, the explosion began with her uncle Taqí's persecution of Shaykh Aḥmad. Now Mullah Taqí was slain by one of Aḥmad's followers while Ṭáhirih was ranged with the one she believed had been predicted by Aḥmad. Her sister Marḍíyyih, her brother-in-law, various members of her brother-in-law's family, her younger uncle, the man to whom her daughter was betrothed, and perhaps, at heart, her mother Amina—all had also become followers of the Báb, and had to bear estrangement from their kindred in proportion to the profundity of their devotion to their new faith.

The families of the Báb and Bahá'u'lláh were also divided, with some against and some for their prophetic scions, and the families of all the Bábís suffered similar disruptions, many of them bitter and bloody. Adding to this unrelieved trial was the pain the Bábís suffered when they couldn't immediately know each other's fates or the state of their beloved Báb because of vast, mountainous distances and lack of technology—the telegraphs and trains burgeoning in other parts of the world hadn't yet reached Iran.*

However, Iranians had long-since evolved high-speed long-distance horseback riding for message delivery.† So when the Báb, on trial in Tabriz shortly after the Conference of Badasht, publicly declared His

* Iran's first telegraph line was installed between Tehran and a site near Zanjan in 1857 (http://www.tct.ir/pagecontent.php?rQV). The country's first railway was a short, horse-drawn line within Tehran built toward the end of the nineteenth century (http://www.msedv.com/rai/history.html).

† Cyrus the Great established the world's first postal system in Iran during the sixth Century BC, with horsemen carrying messages day and night throughout the Persian Empire. Post offices with stamps and such didn't appear in the country until 1851 (http://www.persi.com/history/history.htm).

mission as the Qá'im in the presence of the crown prince word carried relatively quickly.

At the time of the trial—early July, 1848, possibly simultaneous with Ṭáhirih's unveiled appearance at Badasht—the crown prince, Násiri'd-Dín, was seventeen years old and had recently been appointed governor of Azerbaijan. Muḥammad S͟háh was dying, and his formerly redoubtable prime minister, Áqásí, with no one to shelter him, cowered in a village from which he wrote to the crown prince begging "harmony and friendship," but he received no answer. Nonetheless, Áqásí was the moving spirit behind the Báb's trial; he hoped to terrorize the Bábís with it.[2]

He knew the prince's ascension to the throne wasn't assured. There was stiff competition and the prince's mother, a ruthless political manipulator, had many enemies. Rumors circulated that Násiri'd-Dín wasn't really Muḥammad S͟háh's son but the product of one of his mother's romantic liaisons during one of her scandalous all-night parties. She'd long been estranged from her royal husband; he had been twelve and she fourteen when they were married in an effort to force unity on the many factions of their Qajar tribe.[3]

The king hated her and hated her son. He banished the prince to Azerbaijan and kept him impoverished so that he grew up as a classic poor little rich boy, his prime wish in winter a pair of wool socks. Among his few prize possessions was a diamond aigrette for his hat presented to him by the Czar of Russia.[4]

Nevertheless, even as a rather ragged teenage prince with a haphazard court, Násiri'd-Dín had strange and challenging eyes—huge, dark, glittering. After his ascent to the throne, it was said that to meet him face-to-face was to look "the tiger in the eyes" for he had an "'imperial stare' . . . of such magnetic power that . . . neither man nor beast could stand before it." Now he wanted to fix his gaze on the Báb, who definitely interested him, for the Báb was phenomenal and new, and the prince loved the latest sensations. In 1844, watching a French photographer demonstrate what were then called sun-pictures, the prince had been enraptured; later he became known as the photographer shah. Soon after seeing the sun pictures, he had embraced a survey called *Display of the World*, translated from French, describing geopolitical life on the five continents, and then another work, *Geography of the World*, by an Englishman, Edward Burgess.[5]

After being appointed governor of Azerbaijan in 1848, the prince turned to Burgess, a businessman who had become a translator and tutor, to teach him about natural sciences, history, and geography. They both lived in Tabriz, the gray stone town that was then Iran's largest city, an amazing fact considering its predilection for destruction by epidemics, Ottoman invaders, and earthquakes. Its renowned Blue Mosque, the flower of a medieval Turkman dynasty nicknamed the Black Sheep, collapsed in an earthquake in 1773, and in the Báb's time it remained a pile of rubble; four years later, seventy-seven thousand people died in another quake. Yet denizens of Tabriz were famous for their robustness; they seemed indestructible, like the town's massive gray fourteenth-century citadel, called the Ark.[6]

The city's bazaar, about one-thousand years old, was a center for trade with Europe and also an information center. Reform-minded Iranians gathered in its coffeehouses, and innovations from nearby Russian and Ottoman territories flourished within Tabriz's frequently demolished walls against its unchanging backdrop of dry, ridged, red clay mountains.[7]

In 1848 Edward Burgess wrote to his brother, "You will perhaps be surprised to hear that we have now in Tabriz no less than 16 printing establishments, and more in Tehran; in fact books have become so cheap in Persia that it has done much injury to the trade of the copyists . . ." Of course the Bábís used this to advantage in disseminating their literature.[8]

In Tabriz, Burgess could buy the English daily newspaper *Gallignani's Messenger*, also the *Illustrated London News* and *Punch*. He could get French newspapers, brought from Turkey. He provided translations from these papers to his Iranian friends. After revolution broke out in France in 1848, he told his brother, "the affairs of France have as you may suppose made a great impression in this country and my translations of the newspapers are looked for with much eagerness."[9]

American missionaries in Azerbaijan prodded this interest in the latest news. They'd been active in Tabriz since 1834, establishing schools and hospitals. Now they were, Burgess said, "much pleased with the news from Europe," where revolution had spread from France to many other countries. They were hopeful that the entire world would overthrow its monarchies.[10]

Overthrow of monarchies couldn't have had much appeal to Prince Násiri'd-Dín. To his relatively open but feral and completely self-absorbed mind, the only being who could assert monarchy over his Qajar Dynasty would have to be divine. Could it be the Báb? In that case, he would cede his throne to Him.

In fact, at the Báb's trial, he did just that; at least, he gave Him his seat. He must have been dazzled by the reputation for miracle-working that preceded the Báb to the city. It was the Báb's inexplicable powers that particularly discomfited authorities. After His transfer to the prison of Chihriq, He'd been kept under newly rigid surveillance, but devotees found Him nonetheless. People had heard about the once wealthy dervish from India who arrived in Chihriq and told Kurdish leaders, "In the days when I occupied (an) exalted position . . . in India, the Báb appeared to me in a vision. He gazed at me and won my heart completely. I arose, and had started to follow Him, when He looked at me intently and said: 'Divest yourself of your gorgeous attire, depart from your native land, and hasten on foot to meet Me in Azerbaijan. In Chihriq, you will attain your heart's desire . . .'"[11]

The Báb had been imprisoned in Chihriq for three months when he was summoned to Tabriz. En route, he stopped in Orumiyeh, or Urmia, an ancient city on a huge, deep-blue salt lake. Civilization at Urmia dates back to 2000 BC, and legend has it that Zoroaster was born there and that two of the Magi who welcomed the birth of Christ were buried there. The founder of Iran's Ilkhanid dynasty kept his treasury on an island in the middle of the lake and was buried on it in the thirteenth century, a rite complete with the sacrifice of virgins. One of the highest lakes on the Iranian plateau, it's thousands of miles in width and length and has been a UNESCO Biosphere Reserve since 1976.[12]

The Báb was the prisoner / guest of an official in the town who reverenced Him and even had a painter make a portrait of Him,* yet also wanted to test Him. The Báb was going to go by horseback to the public bath one Friday, and His host had his groom supply one of the wildest horses in his stable. The groom secretly advised the Báb not to ride the horse, but the Báb told him, "Fear not. Do as you have been bidden and commit Us to the care of the Almighty."[13]

The population of the town, knowing about the official's ruse, gathered to witness the result. The Báb approached the horse, took hold of the bridle, caressed the animal, put His foot in the stirrup, and mounted. The horse was calm, and the Báb rode it to the bath, followed by the multitude who now pressed forward to touch His garments and kiss His stirrups. Returning from the bath, He rode the same horse. His host, on foot, accompanied Him, while the people rushed into the bath to take away vials of the water He'd used. The Báb remarked on a tradition regarding the lake of Orumiyeh, that it would rise, overflow, and flood the town. Later, when He learned that the majority of the

---

* A watercolor now in the International Archives of the Bahá'í Faith in Haifa, Israel (Balyuzi, *The Bab*, pp. 138–39).

townsfolk now swore they were His followers, He quoted the Qu'rán, "Think men that when they say, 'We believe,' they shall be let alone and not be put to proof?'"* Soon afterward, following His trial and attempts to discredit Him, all but a few of those sudden converts deserted Him.[14]

However, before that happened, rumors of His supernatural powers swept the country, and Tabriz was so fraught with expectation that the mullahs feared insurrection when the Báb arrived in the city.[15]

Shaykhis were quite dominant in Tabriz—in fact, the crown prince's tutor was a Shaykhi—but they were hostile to the Báb and demanded his execution. Yet many clerics reneged on attending the trial because they actually feared the Bábís and didn't trust Áqásí, while government authorities, fearing the Báb was too popular to be put to death, wouldn't allow the mullahs who most ardently demanded His execution to attend the trial. They housed the Báb outside the city gates. No one could enter His presence unless He specifically wanted to see them.[16]

On the day of the trial, the army had to force a passage for Him through a surging multitude eager for a glimpse of His face. The Báb entered the official residence of the prince-governor, took the prince's seat, and, before the jury of Shaykhis and other mullahs, his trial began. The spokesman asked the Báb, "Whom do you claim to be, and what is the message that you have brought?"[17]

"'I am the city of knowledge and 'Alí is its gate,'" the Báb said, quoting a famous tradition. He added, "It is incumbent on you to obey me, by virtue of 'Enter the gate with reverence!'† But I did not utter these words . . ."

"Who then is the speaker?"

* The Holy Qur'án, Sura 29:1.

† The Holy Qur'án, Sura 4:153.

"He who shone forth on Mount Sinai . . ."

The questioner insisted on more clarity.

The Báb said, "I am that person whom you have been expecting for more than a millennium . . . I am the Lord of Command . . ."

A mullah rebuked Him asking how He could possibly be the Promised One. After all, He was only the son of a Shirazi clothier.[18]

The Báb then declared, "I am, I am, I am the Promised One! I am the One whose name you have for a thousand years invoked, at whose mention you have risen, whose advent you have longed to witness, and the hour of whose Revelation you have prayed to God to hasten. Verily I say, it is incumbent upon the peoples of both the East and the West to obey My word and to pledge allegiance to My person."

"You wretched and immature lad of Shíráz!" yelled an old one-eyed Shaykhi whose enmity toward the Báb had been foreseen years ago by Siyyid Káẓim. "'You have already convulsed and subverted 'Iráq, do you wish to arouse a like turmoil in Azerbaijan?'"

"Your honor," the Báb replied, "I have not come hither of My own accord. I have been summoned to this place."

"Hold your peace, you perverse and contemptible follower of Satan!"

"Your honor, I maintain what I have already declared."[19]

The spokesman intervened, saying that if he became convinced of the Báb's claim, he'd beg to be the Báb's shoeshine boy. He was being sarcastic, but the young Crown Prince apparently didn't catch the sarcasm because he volunteered that yes, if the Báb's claims proved to be valid, he would cede his monarchy to the Báb.[20]

Now the spokesman had to switch tracks. Mockery and jokes wouldn't work; he demanded "incontrovertible evidence." The Báb said His proofs were in His writings, His revelation. He began to reveal verses, but the mullahs immediately attacked his Arabic grammar. The Báb said, "The Qur'án itself does in no wise accord with the rules and conventions current amongst men. The Word of God can never be subject to the limitations of His creatures. Nay, the rules and canons which men have adopted have been deduced from the text of the Word of God and are based upon it. These men have, in the very texts of that holy Book, discovered no less than three hundred instances of grammatical error, such as the one you now criticise. Inasmuch as it was the Word of God, they had no other alternative except to resign themselves to His will."

Someone shouted out the question, "To which tense does the word Ishtartanna belong?"

The Báb quoted the Qur'án, "'Far be the glory of thy Lord, the Lord of all greatness, from what they impute to Him, and peace be upon His Apostles! And praise be to God, the Lord of the worlds.'"* He then rose and exited the gathering.

The old one-eyed Shaykhi, quaking with rage, thundered, "I warn you, if you allow this Youth to pursue unhampered the course of his activities, the day will come when the entire population of Tabríz will have flocked to His standard . . ."[21]

The gathering ignored him and merely argued about how to punish the Báb for taking the prince's seat and for leaving the court without asking permission. They decided He should be brought before a similar assemblage and bastinadoed. The crown prince opposed that. They called upon a soldier to privately administer the beating, but he refused. Finally a leading cleric of the city volunteered.[22]

Soon afterwards, in the cleric's house, the Báb endured the torture of the bastinado. The mullah tied the Báb's ankles and beat the soles of His feet with unyielding rods, also striking Him across the face in the process.[23]

* The Holy Qur'án, Sura 37:180.

Official transcripts of the trial were disseminated, written in a way that made the Báb and His inquisitors seem idiotic and also claiming that the Báb had recanted His faith. A British physician residing in Tabriz, Dr. William Cormick, was called in to treat the Báb's injuries from the bastinado and also to ascertain if He was sane.[24]

Dr. Cormick wrote to a missionary friend of his that the injury to the Báb's face was "a great wound and swelling." The doctor had to come more than once to tend it. He reported of the Báb:

> He only once deigned to answer me, on my saying that I was not a Musulman (sic) and was willing to know something about his religion, as I might perhaps be inclined to adopt it. He regarded me very intently on my saying this, and replied that he had no doubt of all Europeans coming over to his religion . . . In the interviews consequent on this I could never get him to have a confidential chat with me, as some government people were always present, he being a prisoner. He was very thankful for my attentions to him. He was a very mild and delicate-looking man, rather small in stature and very fair for a Persian, with a melodious soft voice, which struck me much . . . Of his doctrine I heard nothing from his own lips . . . He was seen by some Armenian carpenters, who were sent to make some repairs in his prison, reading the Bible, and he took no pains to conceal it, but on the contrary told them of it . . .[25]

Dr. Cormick did not find that the Báb was insane, nor did two Iranian physicians called in for the same purpose.[26]

In early August, the Báb was returned to his prison in Chihriq. He wrote a letter to Áqásí, a closely-written scroll now known as the Sermon of Wrath. In September, a Bábí named Hujjat (the Proof), delivered the long message personally to Áqásí, reciting the sermon aloud to him from memory. Bahá'u'lláh was in Tehran then, and He later admiringly remembered how Hujjat visited His home and reported delivering the scroll.[27]

So the Báb's sunrise reached its zenith in His countenance when He proclaimed, "I am the Promised One" in Tabriz and, almost simultaneously, in Ṭáhirih's unveiled face at Badasht. Sparks from these brilliant events would speed over the ready ground of Iran, lighting wildfires of faith and persecution everywhere as the new sun approached its noonday splendor. Contemporaneous with these events, a handful of women in the United States, led by Elizabeth Cady Stanton and inspired by the spread of revolution throughout Europe, convened the first Women's Rights Conference. Iran wasn't the only spot on earth made incandescent by the fiery energy of renewal.

16

1848, the United States and Europe

From tea table to speaker's platform. "Bread or death." Progressive Friends. Truth speaks. Improvisation. "Mankind is one and beats with one great heart."

When we last observed our restless souls of the United States and Europe, back in Chapter 7, they were protesting their exile from an ideal world by rising up to prophesize as well as fight their way out of their world of loss where they wept by the rivers of Babylon. By 1848, they were more interested in battle than prophecy.

That year is known as the Year of Revolutions. One of its most significant events occurred almost simultaneously with the Conference of Badasht and the Báb's trial in Tabriz. On July 19, 1848, half a world away, Elizabeth Cady Stanton addressed the world's first Women's Rights Conference in Seneca Falls, New York.[1]

For the first time in her life, she mounted a speaker's platform. Raised in a strict church-going family, she'd been taught from the cradle that it was sinful for a woman to speak in public. As a child she had been "chilled to the very core by listening to sermons on . . . eternal damnation" and since she frequently fell asleep during such preaching and committed other childish crimes day in and day out, she was sure she was "a veritable child of the Evil One" and felt the devil at night "crouching in a dark corner of the nursery" waiting to take her to hell. She credited her own "animal spirits . . . reasoning powers and common sense" with freeing her from the terror, but it had been a tough fight. She had certainly come a long way by the time it fell to her to read the convention's Declaration of Sentiments, which she and several friends had composed a day or two before based on the Declaration of Independence. It began, "We hold these truths to be self-evident: that all men and women are created equal; that they are endowed by their Creator with certain inalienable rights . . ." and went on to say that, such rights having been denied to women by their government, ". . . it is their duty to throw off such a government" and "demand the equal station to which they are entitled."[2]

The conference itself had been planned just a week before at a tea party in the home of Jane Hunt, a wealthy Quaker, where Elizabeth Cady Stanton and Lucretia Mott were both guests. Stanton and Mott hadn't seen each other since they met behind the veil at the antislavery convention in London in 1840. Stanton let loose to the tea party what she later called "the torrent of my long-accumulating discontent."[3]

She was restless despite the fact that she, Ernestine Rose, and others had recently, after twelve years of hard petitioning, celebrated the passage of an act to protect the property of married women in New York State. But her confinement to home and seven children on a muddy lot in a malarial, one-horse town while her unsympathetic husband spent most of his time on the road had taught her that women needed much more. As the famous, popular wit and poet Frances Osgood (married, mother of three and a much-desired cosmopolitan presence in artistic salons) pointed out, in response to New York State's granting of property rights for women:

Alas for those, whose all of wealth
Is in their souls and faces,
Whose only "rents" are rents in heart,
Whose only tenants—graces.

How must that poor protection bill
Provoke their bitter laughter,
Since they themselves are leased for life,
And no pay-day till after![4]

Nevertheless, it was progress. Also, news of revolutions in Paris, Italy and Austria galvanized Stanton and her friends. They decided to launch a woman's rights convention as soon as possible, and that meant the next week.[5]

Along with their fury at being put in hijab in London and their hopes for outcomes positive to women if the European revolutions succeeded, Stanton and Mott were also inspired by women of the Iroquois Nation, near Seneca Falls, who played leading roles in tribal life. Mott and her husband had arrived in Seneca Falls fresh from a visit to the Iroquois. Mott had observed women and men planning governmental change together, with the women arranging the accompanying Strawberry Ceremony. Stanton had often dined with Iroquois women at her cousin's dinner table in Peterboro, NY; her cousin's daughter had recently "shed the 20 pounds of clothing that fashion dictated," along with the corseting, to adopt bloomers, a style that promised comfort like that enjoyed by the Iroquois women in their tunics and leggings.[6]

Stanton knew the Iroquois Nation was structured around a powerful matriarchy. She was mocked for comparing herself to Native American women who, she said, gave birth without exorbitant pain and could return quickly to their daily chores. She credited the relatively easy births of her seven children to her habits of open-air exercise and wholesome eating, and her refusal to wear corsets. Contrary to established belief within Victorian society, child-bearing, she insisted, did not have to be a curse, and giving birth without difficulty did not indicate a lack of proper delicacy. [7]

Other factors were that the United States had become the first nation in the world to recognize the new French Republic, and Stanton, Mott, and their associates were heartened because France had abolished slavery on May 9, 1848. Mott addressed her fellow abolitionists, ". . . when we see human freedom engaging the attention of the nations of the earth, we may take courage."[8]

They couldn't help hoping that women would be men's equal partners in the new revolutionary regimes in Europe, where women fought in the streets or threw stones, furniture, boiling oil and such out the windows on enemy troops—"such means of warfare as the household may easily furnish to the thoughtful matron," Margaret Fuller reported from Italy. *The London Illustrated News* featured a drawing of two Frenchwomen atop a barricade with a banner: *Bread or Death.* The accompanying article reported that both women were shot shortly after leading the charge.[9]

During the first months of 1848, a German woman radical said, "It seemed in those days as if the world awakened to a new morning, something springlike and festive coursed through the air. All the old antiquated customs fell with one blow, for once there was no bureaucracy and no social prejudice, no more barriers to companionable dealings between the sexes."[10]

Women dressed in their national colors and sewed flags for their newly independent countries. They left the "quiet circle of the home," as the newspaper of a women's association in Berlin put it, to be present where crowds gathered whether for the funeral of a fallen hero or heroine, or for celebrations of liberty in public squares. French feminists asserted, "Men's liberty and equality are clearly those of women as well."[11]

However, as had happened following the French revolution of 1779 and other glorious storms, governments new and old put the kibosh on women's hopes. As a result, disappointed European feminists began expecting great things from their sisters in the United States, but they probably didn't picture ladies in Quaker gray gathered at a tea table.[12]

Except for Stanton, the ladies who planned the first women's rights convention were all Progressive Friends, a branch of the peaceable Quakers who also happened to be radical abolitionists. Jane Hunt's husband owned a textile mill that produced wool but not cotton, because cotton was cultivated by Southern slaves. In fact, back in 1840, when William Lloyd Garrison joined the ladies in hijab at the anti-slavery convention, he wore a suit of wool cloth made by Hunt's mill and was proud that his clothing hadn't been made by enslaved hands. Another of the ladies around the table was Mary Ann M'Clintock, whose husband's store only sold goods not produced by slave labor. And the Progressive Friends differed from other Quaker groups by allowing men and women to meet together and giving women equal voice.[13]

Immediately after the tea party, the five women secured the Weslayan Chapel for their event and put an ad in the Seneca Falls Courier inviting all to discuss "the social, civil and religious condition and rights of women." Known speaker Lucretia Mott was the main draw for the convention. Other papers also immediately ran ads, including Frederick Douglass's antislavery *North Star*, where the invitation to the convention appeared in the midst of a report about a festival in Rochester, NY, commemorating the end of slavery in the West Indies.[14]

Three days before the convention, the planners met to draw up a statement of resolution and an agenda, and write a Declaration of Sentiments. All at once they felt "as helpless and hopeless as if they had suddenly been asked to construct a steam engine." They immersed themselves in "faithful perusal of various masculine productions," such as reports of peace, antislavery, and temperance conferences, but all seemed "too tame and pacific for the inauguration of a rebellion such as the world had never before seen." Finally they settled on the Declaration of Independence as the basis for their core document.[15]

They stated that human history is "a history of repeated injuries and usurpations on the part of man toward woman, having in direct object the establishment of an absolute tyranny over her." They listed the wrongs: women had no right to vote and therefore wasn't represented in her nation's government and had to obey laws she hadn't chosen; if she was married, the federal government gave all her property and other material goods to her husband, including any wages she might earn; and as far as civil rights went, she was as legally dead, or else a child. This declaration of independence for women linked them with the rebellious colonists of the American Revolution and males to the oppressor, that poor old madman, King George III.[16]

It claimed the spiritual independence of women, saying that man "claiming Apostolic authority excluded her from the ministry, and, with some exceptions, from public participation in the affairs of the Church . . . He has usurped the prerogative of Jehovah himself, claiming it as his right to assign for her a sphere of action, when that belongs to her conscience and to her God."[17]

Elizabeth Cady Stanton was the one who insisted that the Declaration demand women's right to vote. Her husband threatened to boycott the convention if this was included, and even Lucretia Mott said, in her antiquated Quaker English, "Why Lizzie, thee will make us ridiculous!" Stanton was adamant. She won. However, Mott, the seasoned speaker, felt it was "unseemly" for a lady to chair the meeting, so her husband James did the honors. Stanton's husband, true to his word, left town.[18]

On Wednesday, July 19, the ladies arrived at the chapel to find the door locked, and no one had the key. But there was an open window. Stanton's enterprising nephew climbed in and unbarred the front door. The pews filled with three hundred participants, including forty men.

The planners had meant the first day to be "exclusively for women," but in a spirit of tolerance, they let the males stay.[19]

Almost every participant was shocked that the Declaration called for women's suffrage. Stanton defended it: "To have drunkards, idiots, horse-racing rum-selling rowdies . . . and silly boys fully recognized, while we ourselves are thrust out from all the rights that belong to citizens, is too grossly insulting to be any longer quietly submitted to. The right is ours. We must have it." Frederick Douglass was one who firmly supported her, saying that "right" was genderless. The suffrage resolution passed, but just barely.[20]

By the second day of the session, Stanton, in full voice, was proclaiming against women's imprisonment as so-called angels, made only for domesticity, unable to tolerate public life, dependent on men for all succor, "care and protection—such as the wolf gives the lamb—such as the eagle the hare he carries to his aerie! Most cunningly he entraps her, and then takes from her all those rights which he cleaves to as life itself—rights which have been baptized in blood—and the maintenance of which is even now rocking to their foundations the kingdoms of the Old World . . ."[21]

And she added another resolution: "The speedy success of our cause depends upon the zealous and untiring efforts of both men and women, for the overthrow of the monopoly of the pulpit, and for securing to women of equal participation with men in the various trades, professions, and commerce." It passed unanimously, and one hundred people, thirty-two of them men, signed the declaration and its resolutions.[22]

This small convention in upstate New York received huge notice. The press picked it up and gave it everything they had—that is, all their ammunition against women's rights. "A woman is a nobody. A wife is everything," said the *Philadelphia Public Ledger and Daily Transcript.* Speaking on behalf of "the ladies of Philadelphia" it said they were determined to "maintain their rights as Wives, Belles, Virgins and Mothers."

Others joined the chorus of ridicule, but there was a great undertone of seriousness in the men, for important issues were involved—the *Oneida Whig* newspaper asked perhaps the most pressing question: "WHERE, GENTLEMEN, WILL BE OUR DINNERS?[23]

Only the *New York Herald Tribune* conceded that the demand for suffrage made sense, even if it was "unwise and mistaken." That paper wrote, "This is the age of revolutions. To whatever part of the world attention is directed, the political and social fabric of the world is crumbling to pieces . . . the revolution is no longer confined to the Old World, nor to the masculine gender . . ."[24]

Dismayed by the unladylike publicity, some women dropped out of the fray and asked that their signatures be removed from the Declaration, but Elizabeth Cady Stanton welcomed the attention. "It will start women thinking, and men, too," she said. Lucretia Mott dubbed her the leading "pioneer in the work."[25]

Two-weeks later, the pioneer was at a follow-up meeting in Rochester, New York. This meeting had been planned before the press attacked the first convention, and many of the newly emancipated got cold feet. However, the convention forged ahead, led by those who still believed "the gift of tongues had been vouchsafed to them" in Seneca Falls. Hecklers called "Louder, louder" as the Rochester conference's female secretary tried to read the minutes from Seneca Falls. The female chair, apparently forgetting for a moment the "gift of tongues," rose and appealed, "Friends, we present ourselves here before you as an oppressed class, with trembling frames and faltering tongues, and we do not expect to be able to speak so as to be heard by all at first . . ." But a schoolteacher used to projecting her voice offered to read the minutes and did so in fully audible tones.[26]

Soon afterwards, in 1851, on the second day of a feminist convention in a church in Akron, Ohio, Sojourner Truth ripped the meeting out of the hands of male clergyman who threatened to usurp it while boy hecklers from the gallery goaded them on. Amidst the fulminations, one minister claimed that women could not have rights because of "the manhood of Christ."[27]

Truth had been crouching in a corner of the pulpit since the first day, when she had entered, tall and gaunt in "gray dress and white turban surmounted with an uncouth sunbonnet." As she swept down the aisle, there were whispers of "Women's rights and niggers!" "I told you so!" Truth maintained her silence that first day, only breaking it during intermission to circulate among the crowd and sell copies of her *Life of Sojourner Truth* while people pressed up to the chairwoman, Francis Gage, and begged, "Don't let her speak, it will ruin us, we shall be utterly denounced."[28]

On the second day, amidst the invasion by the male ministers, Truth finally rose from her corner and fixed her eyes on the chairwoman. "Don't let her speak," the murmurs continued. But Gage stepped forward and said, "Sojourner Truth."[29]

Truth was about six feet tall, an astounding height for a woman in those days. Her voice, deep and resonant, penetrated every ear in the packed church while she proceeded to orate, as Gage said later, taking "us up in her strong arms and carry(ing) us safely over the slough of difficulty turning the whole tide in our favor."[30]

Truth said, "That man over there says that women need to be helped into carriages, and lifted over ditches, and to have the best place everywhere. Nobody ever helps me into carriages or over mud-puddles, or gives me any best place! And ain't I a woman? Look at me! Look at my arm! I have ploughed, and planted, and gathered into barns, and no man could head me! And ain't I a woman? I could work as much and eat as much as any man—when I could get it—and bear the lash as well! And ain't I a woman? I have borne 13 children and seen them almost all sold off to slavery, and when I cried out with my mother's grief, none but Jesus heard me. And ain't I a woman?[31]

". . . That little man in black there, he says women can't have as much rights as men, because Christ wasn't a woman! Where did your Christ come from? Where did your Christ come from? From God and a woman! Man had nothing to do with Him."[32]

At every sentence, she elicited thunderous applause. She ended, "If the first woman God ever made was strong enough to turn the world upside down all alone, these women together ought to be able to turn it back, and get it right side up again." The crowd cheered, and people had tears streaming down their cheeks as Sojourner Truth returned to her corner. She was fulfilling her chosen mission of "testifying . . . concerning the wickedness of this here people."[33]

She had added her voice to the chorus of women who could no longer remain quiescent and unquestioning. "The work of revolution," as the *Herald Tribune* newspaper had said regarding the 1848 convention, was "no longer confined to the masculine gender."[34]

Margaret Fuller, the writer of *Women in the 19th Century* and leader of famous, liberating "conversations" for women, had been a groundbreaking reporter and editor for that very paper. She was known to the organizers of the women's rights movement, and her presence was sorely missed among them. She would have been happy to be at Seneca Falls, but she wasn't in the United States at the time, and never would be again. In July, 1848, she was in Europe, at war.

In the Europe of Fuller's day, Italy and Germany (dominated by Prussia) were haphazard patchworks of states with various duchies, kingdoms, etc. Poland as we know it now didn't exist; it was divided among Austria, Prussia and Russia. Austria's Hapsburg monarchy claimed much of Italy. The European revolutionaries of 1848 demanded freedom from empires and overlords, independence for their own nations and cultures, and sovereignty of the human soul. They were fired by nationalism, unemployment, bad harvests, and oppressive government.

The revolutionaries had no pan-European unity; their uprisings were separate and spontaneous. Like the Women's Rights Conference, the anti-slavery struggle, Ṭáhirih's epoch-opening deed at Badasht, the Báb's declaration in Tabriz, and Mullah Ḥusayn's hoisting of the Black Standards, the revolutions were unplanned or only loosely planned—structured improvisations, so to speak. They ignited from ready timber, lit by news that flew from one city in revolt to another via quickened and expanded communications. Increased literacy in Europe and the United States demanded ever proliferating numbers of books, newspapers, and magazines; monthlies ran up to fifty pages of small print, and newspapers also packed in the words. Numerous feminist journals started appearing in 1848, and all information flowed faster along steam, train, and telegraph lines.[35]

The revolutions were volcanic—befitting the times, for during the 1840s, Mount Etna in Sicily and Vesuvius near Naples erupted periodically. This didn't escape writers and revolutionaries seeking metaphors; Italian dissidents sidetracked Austrian censorship with code based on terms of volcanic eruption, and a group of French feminists named themselves the Vesuviennes.[36]

There was constant tug of war between repressive and expressive powers, and feminists, as we have seen, suffered fierce backlash, but innovation continued. At the end of summer, 1848, the French Parliament swore in Mathieu Luis of Guadeloupe. He was a conservative monarchist, but he was, nevertheless, the first Black member.

In Italy, Margaret Fuller, transcendentalist turned revolutionary, pursued her radical star, undaunted by antifeminism. In 1846, after a disastrous love affair in New York, she'd sailed for Europe as a tutor to the son of some friends and also, in a first for a female journalist from anywhere in the world, as a foreign correspondent. In Europe, she immersed herself in culture and also went down into mines, toured prisons, and examined factories. She saw dire poverty and described "persons, especially women, dressed in dirty, wretched tatters, worse than none, and with an expression of listless, unexpecting woe upon their faces . . ."[37]

Editorializing freely, as was her wont, she summoned those "who have eyes and see not, ears and hear not," to open up and respond to "the convulsions and sobs of injured Humanity!" In London and Paris, she befriended exiled revolutionaries. Guisseppe Mazzini, of Italy, was one she particularly understood. She felt his passionate commitment to freedom and loved the depth of old world culture that informed his every gesture.[38]

In spring, 1847, she went to Italy secretly carrying Mazzini's messages to his family and fellow revolutionaries. She was instantly welcomed as a compatriot. She wrote, "Italy receives me as a long-lost child and I feel myself at home here." She called Rome "*my* country, city of the soul." She also met her soul mate, an aristocrat in rebellion against his title. (Nevertheless, he was universally referred to as *the Count*). He was younger than she, and devastatingly handsome. Now she was happy in love as well as in war. Militantly she cried, "It is vain to cry peace, peace, when there is no peace." She manned the barricades, she nursed the wounded, and she saw citizens with homemade weapons drive thousands of Austrian troops out of their country. She said, "'I have seen the Austrian arms dragged through the streets of Rome and burned in the Piazza del Popolo. The Italians embraced one another and cried, 'Miracolo, Providenza!'"[39]

Miracle! Providence! That was the problem with the revolutions of 1848. It was all very well to salute miracles, but why burn the weapons when arms were so few; why not keep them to use against the enemy? By the end of 1848, the revolutions all over Europe were disintegrating while governments renewed their rigidity. As 1849 began, Fuller saw her revolution in its death throes.

She wrote of "Thirty-seven braves . . . buried beneath a heap of wall that fell upon them in the shock of one cannonade. A marble nymph, with broken arm, looked sadly that way from her sun-dried fountain, some roses were blooming still, some red oleanders amid the ruin . . ."[40]

She noticed "a pair of skeleton legs" protruding "from a bank of one barricade." In another place a dog had scratched away the "light covering of earth from the body of a man" leaving the corpse "lying face upward, all dressed . . ."[41]

She begged the "men and women of America" to "*do something*. . . send money, send cheer—acknowledge as the legitimate leaders and rulers those men who represent the people, who understand its wants, who are ready to die or live for its good . . . Friends, countrymen, and lovers of virtue, lovers of freedom, lovers of truth!—be on the alert, rest not supine in your easier lives, but remember 'Mankind is one, and beats with one great heart.'"[42]

Her revolution ignominiously collapsed as foreign troops bombarded Rome and restored the Pope, who had been exiled, to his Vatican. Fuller braved enemy fire to nurse the wounded and dying, and she briefly ran the government's military hospital.[43]

Yet she was not cast down. She and her Count now had an infant son. She felt hope for the future, but it would be a fiery future. "It proves possible for the wickedness of man to mar to an indefinite extent the benevolent designs of God," she wrote, yet she foresaw another, apocalyptic revolution and also said, ". . . The wishes of Heaven shall waft a fire that will burn down all, root and branch, and prepare the earth for an entirely new culture . . ."[44]

She said that clergymen's influence was "too perverting" and that monarchs must fall, for "every man who assumes an arbitrary lordship over fellow man must be driven out." Her coming revolution was "uncompromising . . . England cannot reason nor ratify nor criticize it—France cannot betray it—Germany cannot bungle it—Italy cannot bubble it away—Russia cannot stamp it down nor hide it in Siberia. The New Era is no longer an embryo: it is born . . ."[45]

But Fuller had to leave her Italy that had "bubbled away" one revolution, for its government kept her and her Count under police surveillance. Meanwhile, Horace Greeley, in New York, despite his radical sentiments, fired her from her reporting position with his newspaper because he'd heard about her liaison and her child, and although she claimed marriage to the Count, Greeley didn't believe it. He refused to publish her history of the Italian revolution.[46]

In 1850, she sailed for the United States with the Count and their son. She didn't know what she'd do in the United States or how she and her child and young Italian husband would fit in. However, she did know she'd be derided as a scandalous harpy and worse, and she feared her younger husband would be wooed by dewier women attracted by his title and good looks. But she would never have to face these problems. Her ship broke up in a storm on a sandbar off Fire Island and sank in sight of the U.S. shore. All aboard were lost.

Witnesses recalled her clutching her baby, clinging to a mast. Wind and waves washed her husband overboard. The storm ripped her son from her arms. Water and gales also destroyed her manuscript of Italian history. After her death, rumor spread that she could have saved herself but chose suicide. A contemporary called her "a heathen priestess, though of what god or goddess we will not pretend to say . . ."[47]

Over fifty years after her death, Henry James, who didn't like her writing style and generally had nothing good to say of any woman writer, praised her as an improvisatrice who lived brilliantly—unlike other great speakers, who only talked brilliantly. He lamented the "unquestionably haunting Margaret-ghost."[48]

She is one of the many revolutionary, romantic ghosts of 1848 haunting our twenty-first century, constantly demanding that we see her vision of equal rights for all humanity and hear her voice of burning purity and love. She was caught by the same passion that would lift Ṭáhirih and her fellow dawn-breakers, in the few short months or years remaining to them, away from the shifting sands of time into a heroic eternity.

17

"And I Will Bury My Soul With My Own Hand"

Fugitive wanderings. The master-stroke. Ṭabarsí. Bahá'u'lláh in Amul. The death of Mullah Ḥusayn. The death of Quddús. Renewed captivity.

Whoever hath washed his hands of living
Utters his mind without misgiving.

In straits which no escape afford
The hand takes hold of the edge of the sword.

—Sa'adi[1]

Not a great deal is known of Ṭáhirih's path as a fugitive following the Conference of Badasht, although her last refuge was a farm where she stayed for about a year. While she was there the men she'd urged so ardently to action were using their swords to beat off the shah's army, and she pined to join them. In fact, according to one Bahá'í historian, during the final days of the conference she had rallied the men, flourishing an unsheathed sword in her hand, "Wrap up this spectacle. The time for prayer and liturgy is over. Now is the time for devotion and sacrifice."[2]

Reading the story of what followed, the battles-to-the-death fought during 1848–50 by some of the Bábís, we can see, once again, her prescience, but we may wonder at her and her brethren's hawkish qualities. After all, their mission was to be dawn-breakers for a new day or epoch in the life of humanity, and we now know that when Bahá'u'lláh proclaimed Himself to be the sun of that day, He adamantly commanded abstention from violence. It helps to remember that the Bábís were not His disciples; most of them had no inkling of what His future role would be, but all of them believed the Báb was the fulfillment of prophecy, and most of them expected Him to lead a bloody insurrection in accordance with the widely accepted hadith. They'd grown up in a culture that believed in defensive holy warfare, according to the Qur'án: "Fight in the cause of God those who fight you, but do not transgress limits . . . And slay them wherever ye catch them and turn them out from where they have turned you out . . . But fight them not at the Sacred Mosque, unless they fight you there, but if they fight you, slay them . . ."[3] After Bahá'u'lláh began to establish the Bahá'í Faith, He abrogated the provision for such warfare, but the Báb had not done so.

In the time leading up to the siege at the Shrine of Shaykh Ṭabarsí, which was the first battle, Ṭáhirih, after fleeing the villagers at Niyala, the mountain hamlet, went briefly into Bahá'u'lláh's home province and then to Babul, the native town of Quddús. Perhaps she and he had been en route there to teach their faith together before their party was dispersed. But by the time she got to Babul, it was September, 1848, and Quddús was once again a guest / prisoner in his influential relative's house in nearby Sari. There he would remain for ninety-five days.[4]

Nineteenth-century travelers described Babul as a humid, squalid, muddy dump and also as a balmy paradise of orange trees. It was a trade center near the Caspian Sea, but its population had been decimated by plague during the 1830s and had barely recovered since. It was "surrounded by rich rice, sugar and cotton plantations" but "so buried in forest trees as to be invisible from the exterior." There was a small lake in town with an island on which stood a ruined villa, property of the shah. Houses in Babul were not close together and the town didn't have fortifications; everything was scattered through the forest—this was typical of settlements in Mazandaran.[5]

In Babul, Ṭáhirih stayed in the home of a sympathetic mullah and preached to his congregation. Was she also able to visit Quddús? We know that "though confined, Quddús was treated with marked deference, and was allowed to receive most of the companions who had been present at the gathering of Badasht." It seems that Quddús's warden / relative, though antipathetic to the Bábís to such an extent that he would soon demand their extermination, "was withheld by an inner power from showing the least disrespect to Quddús while the latter was confined in his home." Despite this mysterious respite, Quddús didn't allow any of his visitors to remain in Sari but encouraged them to "enlist under the Black Standards hoisted by Mullah Ḥusayn."[6]

We know Bahá'u'lláh met with Quddús in Sari. Bahá'u'lláh had just been propitiously sprung from a lethal trap. While traveling, He'd had to stop in the town of Gaz because He was ill. An edict from Muḥammad Sháh for His arrest and execution caught up with Him. As he was being marched toward Tehran by the highly reluctant arresting officer, who had actually been planning a reception in His honor before receiving the imperial summons, they met a horseman galloping in their direction and received the news that Muḥammad Sháh was dead. The summons was nullified, Bahá'u'lláh was freed, and the reception was duly held.[7]

He resumed His journey. He later said that while He was in Sari, He was "again exposed to the insults of the people." He and most of the town notables were on friendly terms, but when the populace saw Him walking with Quddús, they began hurling the word *Bábí* as an invective, and He and Quddús were "unable to escape their bitter denunciations."[8]

If Ṭáhirih was able to see Quddús, it would only have been fleetingly, before she went into hiding. Under the protection of different Bábís designated by Bahá'u'lláh, she moved from village to village, frequently changing her dwelling-place. After about a year, she came to the farmhouse south of Amul where she was able to remain for a time, frustrated at her inability to join Mullah Ḥusayn and his companions. Apparently she "gave her signet ring to a woman to be eventually sent to Quddús . . . The verse on the signet ring read, 'Lord of Ṭáhirih, remember her.'"[9]

Bahá'u'lláh, too, was kept by destiny from throwing in his lot with Mullah Ḥusayn. As one of the Báb's followers, He said, referring to the Báb as the Primal Point: "I stand, life in hand, ready; that perchance, through God's loving-kindness and grace, the revealed and manifest Letter may lay down his life as a sacrifice in the path of the Primal Point, the Most Exalted Word."[10] Bahá'u'lláh's prayer would, in fact, be answered—but His sacrifice would extend over long years, instead of occurring in one magnificent moment.

It's actually amazing that Ṭáhirih and Bahá'u'lláh survived their journey to Babul. Religious leaders there were lethally opposed to their cause and were the ones who drove Mullah Ḥusayn and his retinue into siege and battle. Anti-Bábí sentiment was rife all over the country as mullahs, who previously "had never agreed on any religious matter, large or small, now united against a common enemy." They labeled the Bábís atheists, communists, cannibals, and said they married their own sisters. They even said that it was Bábís who had killed the Imam

Ḥusayn centuries before at Karbala. They told people not to speak with Bábís because they were sorcerers. They warned against taking tea with Bábís because they would mix something in the tea that would make a person go mad. The mullahs also said it was praiseworthy to kill a Bábí and that the killer's sins would be forgiven for doing so. Mothers told children that if they didn't behave, the Bábís would come and eat them up.[11]

Nevertheless, along his way from Mashhad, flying his black standards as a sign to his countrymen that the promised day had come, Mullah Ḥusayn converted the populations of several villages. The village of Miyamay was so sympathetic that he was able to lead the Friday congregational prayer in the mosque, and thirty men and boys then joined his march.[12]

After a few weeks he made camp beside a stream, beneath a big tree. As the Imam Ḥusayn had done centuries before on the journey to Karbala, he told his companions he was awaiting guidance. They were a large and sometimes unruly group of mullahs and religious students, carpenters and other craftsmen, farmers, masons, merchants, some on horseback, others on foot. Mullah Ḥusayn addressed them twice daily, keeping their spirits up and their minds focused during the march.[13]

Now they camped in the fields around the sheltering tree, keeping vigil night and day while Mullah Ḥusayn prayed and meditated. One day, a heavy wind knocked a branch from the tree. Mullah Ḥusayn said, "The tree of the sovereignty of Muḥammad S͟háh has, by the will of God, been uprooted and hurled to the ground." Three days later, they heard that Muḥammad S͟háh was dead.[14]

Mullah Ḥusayn pointed toward the region the Báb had called the verdant isle. He said, "This is the way that leads to our Karbala. Whoever is unprepared for the great trials that lie before us, let him now repair to his home and give up the journey." A few days later he issued the same warning, saying that the Báb was the only one "in the East and in the West" with a "rightful claim" to be the path to God, again calling upon those who were willing to die for the Báb to stay with him while those who weren't willing should leave. Of the 232 men present, 212 remained.[15]

Ever since he'd learned that the Báb had been tortured with the bastinado in Tabriz, Mullah Ḥusayn had dressed in mourning. Now he donned brighter garments and led his companions forward through "roads . . . like swamps" where the men, "unused to this kind of weather . . . suffered terribly . . ." On October 10, 1848, they reached Babul.[16]

The city's chief cleric, an inveterate enemy of Quddús who was responsible for his being under house arrest, was sure Mullah Ḥusayn had come to attack him. He sent out a crier summoning the town to his mosque. A huge crowd assembled. The black-garbed priest climbed the steps to the top of the pulpit, ripped off his turban and hurled it to the ground, tore open his shirt and howled, "Awake, for our enemies stand at our very doors, ready to wipe out all that we cherish as pure and holy. Should we fail to resist them, none will be left to survive their onslaught. . . . the protecting hand of Muḥammad Sháh has been suddenly withdrawn! . . . Tomorrow, at the hour of dawn, let all of you arise and march out to exterminate their forces."[17]

The next day at dawn a mob eager for both plunder and salvation grabbed guns, swords, axes, scythes and spades and thundered out to vanquish the Bábís, who had, on Mullah Ḥusayn's orders, divested themselves of plunderable property, and who met the mob as it blocked the road to the city. They reached for their swords, but Mullah Ḥusayn admonished them, "Not yet." The mob opened fire, and six Bábís fell. "The time is not yet come," Mullah Ḥusayn said. "The number is not yet complete." Then a humble soul who had insisted on walking beside Mullah Ḥusayn's horse for eighty-three days was shot down. Mullah Ḥusayn offered a prayer and charged.[18]

His special object was the enemy who had shot his foot soldier. Seeing the infuriated rider bearing down upon him, the enemy hid behind a tree and lifted his musket. With one sword stroke, Mullah Ḥusayn halved tree trunk, musket, and man.[19]

This same feat is attributed to various heroes of Middle Eastern history. In fact, warriors trained for it. One novelist describes an Arab emir saying that his father didn't allow his servants to launch his falcons, but launched them himself, and even landed eagles himself—he was "very strong. With a sharp sword he could cut a man in half with a single stroke. The bird is always held on the right arm. This strengthens it for the sword."[20]

But Mullah Ḥusayn had never practiced falconry. And although people like the Farhadi brothers in Qazvin allegedly forged swords in their basement and trained recruits to fight in the prophesized Insurrection, Mullah Ḥusayn hadn't rehearsed swordsmanship or warfare and in fact was said to have a palsy in his right hand, which trembled as he wrote. He was described by one who, as a child, met him in Tehran: "Lean and fragile to look at, but keen and bright as the sword which never left his side. For the rest, he was not more than thirty or thirty-five years old, and his raiment was white." But from the time he unsheathed his sword in Mazandaran, he was a warrior whose name struck terror in the hearts of his opponents.[21]

After his first master-stroke, he slashed his way through the mob and a rain of bullets, galloped at top speed into Babul and rode three times around the home of the chief cleric. Having instigated the riot, this mullah was hiding in his house. "Have you forgotten," Mullah Ḥusayn thundered for the benefit of his enemy's ears, "that he who preaches a holy war must himself ride at the head of his followers?" [22]

Meanwhile, his companions also galloped into town roaring, "Ya Sahibu'z-Zaman!" (Oh, Thou Lord of the Age!)[23]

"Peace! Peace!" the cowed townspeople called out, and Mullah Ḥusayn gave them peace. He stood before them and addressed them: "O followers of the Prophet of God, and shi'ahs of the imams of His Faith. Why have you risen against us . . . Did we ever repudiate the truth of your Faith?" He questioned their spirit of hospitality and pointed out to them, "Both my person and my horse have escaped unhurt from your overwhelming attack. Except for the slight scratch which I received on my face, you have been powerless to wound me. God has protected me . . ."[24]

He took his band to stay in a caravanserai and sent some of them out to buy provisions. He soon found out that the town's protestations of "peace" had been insincere; no one was willing to sell them anything. The Bábís were ready to rush into battle again but Mullah Ḥusayn controlled them. By sunset, a crowd of people surrounded the caravanserai ready to shoot down Bábís on sight. Mullah Ḥusayn asked if any of his companions would go to the roof top and offer the call to prayer. Knowing that he would most likely be killed, a youth complied and had just cried out, "God is Most Great" when he was shot down. Two other youths then tried, one after the other, to utter the call from the rooftop, and they were also shot and killed. The mob shouted challenges and obscenities. Mullah Ḥusayn mounted his horse and led a charge. The well-armed crowd fled.[25]

After sustaining other attacks by the people of Babul, including the burial-alive of one of the Bábís in a well, an attempt to burn down the caravanserai, and efforts to keep food and water from entering its walls, Mullah Ḥusayn accepted the plea of a so-called peace delegation that offered him and his men safe passage through the woods away from town. However, the delegation had a plot. Deep in the woods, the guards who were supposedly to help the Bábís turned on them, murdering and robbing them until one of the Bábís stabbed the leader of the guard to death and others vanquished the rest of the escort. Mullah Ḥusayn forbade them to take any plunder from the enemies, only the swords and horses.[26]

They then proceeded through the forest until they reached an old shrine called Shaykh Ṭabarsí, named after a cleric regarded as a saint. The shrine's caretaker threw himself at Mullah Ḥusayn's feet. He had dreamed the night before that the Imam Ḥusayn himself had arrived at Ṭabarsí with seventy-two warriors and other companions, that they fought a heroic battle and were visited one night by the Prophet Muḥammad. He eagerly gave them refuge.[27]

The shrine was surrounded only by a hedge with a weak fence of sticks and cane and a shallow ditch, to keep animals out. Mullah Ḥusayn started the Bábís building a new wall, some watchtowers, another entrance to the grounds, and some huts of wood and grass. Attackers from surrounding villages constantly interrupted this project.[28]

When the work was finished, Bahá'u'lláh arrived at the fort. Mullah Ḥusayn greeted Him with such solicitude, reverence, and forgetfulness of all else around him that his companions were amazed. Was Mullah Ḥusayn paying homage to Bahá'u'lláh's social status and wealth, and the fact that He brought supplies for the fort? The companions knew their leader better than that. But they were mystified.[29]

Bahá'u'lláh had just been with Quddús in Sari. He told Mullah Ḥusayn that now it was time to bring Quddús to the fort. At his instructions, Mullah Ḥusayn sent a certain Bábí with six others to demand the release of Quddús. Then Bahá'u'lláh went on His way, hoping to gather more help for the fort, promising to return.[30]

Mullah Ḥusayn told his friends that they must treat Quddús as they would the Báb. "As to myself," he said, "you must consider me as his lowly servant . . . but refrain from kissing either his hands or his feet, for his blessed heart dislikes such evidences of reverent affection." Mystified again, the companions could only obey this wish of their revered commander.[31]

When he learned that Quddús, on horseback, was drawing near, Mullah Ḥusayn put two candles into the hands of each Bábí, lighted them himself, and led a candlelit march to meet Quddús. As they escorted him to the fort, they all chanted, "Holy, holy, the Lord our God, the Lord of the angels and the spirit."[32]

Quddús dismounted at the fort and leaned against the walls of the ancient shrine. He said, "The Remnant of God will be best for you if ye are of those who believe." Immediately afterward, he asked Mullah Ḥusayn about Bahá'u'lláh. By doing this, Quddús, representing the Báb, fulfilled a tradition, "And when the Promised One is made manifest, he shall lean His back against the Kaaba and shall address the 313 followers who will have grouped around him these words, 'The Remnant of God will be best for you if you believe.'" It happened that by that time there were 312 men there, and then suddenly a young man arrived from Babul, begging to be admitted.[33]

Quddús handed Mullah Ḥusayn some of his writings to be read aloud. The first celebrated the Báb, the second Bahá'u'lláh, and the third Ṭáhirih. So it was that with dignity and ceremony the Bábís conducted themselves within the walls of Ṭabarsí, a place that was outwardly obscure, rain-soaked and doomed, but in their eyes and within their hearts a center of sunlit, glorious, and eternal blessing.[34]

As the days passed in the forest fort, Quddús led recitations and prayer sessions, and continued writing. Meanwhile a new shah ascended the throne: the teenager, Násiri'd-Dín, finally brought to power via the machinations of his mother and the man who became his first prime minister.[35]

He soon received word from a vengeful mullah that the Bábís were about to proclaim their own kingdom, "a sovereignty that shall abase to the dust the imperial diadem of your illustrious ancestors. I feel it my duty to warn you that the day is fast approaching when not only the province of Mazandaran but the whole of Persia . . . will have repudiated your authority and . . . surrendered to their cause."[36]

The shah referred the situation to his army in Mazandaran. An officer reported that the Bábís in the fort were a "handful of untrained and frail-bodied students." He predicted that within two days, a brother officer of his, leading a small detachment, could annihilate them.[37]

A "small detachment" of twelve thousand men was therefore raised, armed, and stationed in the village of Afra near Ṭabarsí. The commanding officer immediately stopped all bread and water from reaching the entrenched Bábís. He barricaded the fort and opened fire on anyone who left its gate. Quddús forbade anyone to try to leave and said, "God willing, this very night a downpour of rain will overtake our opponents, followed by a heavy snowfall, which will assist us to repulse their contemplated assault."[38]

Snow was highly unusual in that part of the Caspian region, but that night it rained, and the next night it snowed. In the fort, the Bábís collected water to last them a long time, while the army camped outside was flooded and much of its ammunition ruined.[39]

On the third day, two hours after sunrise, Quddús, Mullah Ḥusayn, and three others charged out of the fort, riding abreast, followed by their troops on foot, all roaring "Oh thou Lord of the Age!" Their bared swords, raised high, glittered in the sun, blinding the enemy. The Bábís, not even at their full strength of 313 because some had been left behind to guard the fort, pursued the army to the village of Afra. In forty-five minutes, all the officers were dead, and the army scattered.[40]

The shah's army lost 430 men, and only one Bábí was wounded. Word of the prowess of the Bábís buzzed around Iran, crossing silence-inducing mountains and vast salt deserts, and myths grew about their terrifying ferocity. Mullahs preached that their power came from Satan and that the hosts of hell rode with them.[41]

During the resulting lull in hostilities, Quddús, knowing that a stronger army would soon mass against them, commanded his companions to dig a moat around the fort. It took them nineteen days. They also built stronger walls, strengthened by entire tree trunks, to replace the first ones, which had been ruined by the army's cannon balls and bullets.[42]

Now a new army, headed by a prince, marched on Ṭabarsí. He sent a messagenger to Mullah Ḥusayn, who said, "Tell your master we utterly disclaim any intention either of subverting the foundations of the monarchy or of usurping the authority of Násiri'd-Dín Sháh. Our Cause concerns the revelation of the Promised One . . ."[43]

The messenger burst into tears and cried, "What are we to do?" Mullah Ḥusayn told him to tell the prince to send the mullahs of Sari and Babul to the fort to debate with the Bábís. The prince could judge the outcome. This convinced the messenger, but not the prince.[44]

The shah had sent an edict demanding that the army "efface" the Bábís "from the pages of time and . . . wipe them off the face of the earth . . . This is not a trifling amusement. The fate of our religion and of Shiite doctrine hangs in the balance. You must cleanse the realm of this filthy and reprobate sect, so that not a trace of them remains . . ." The prince planned to attack Ṭabarsí three days later.[45]

Before dawn, on December 21, 1848, the gates of Ṭabarsí opened. Quddús called out, "Mount your steeds, O heroes of God!" and Mullah Ḥusayn with 202 companions followed him through snow, mud, and darkness toward the enemy. They forded a river that had no bridge and rode through four villages to the prince's army in Vas-Kas. When they arrived, Bábís from Mazandaran called out in local dialect, so the guards thought they were reinforcements awaited by the prince. Then the Bábís shouted, "Oh Thou Lord of the Age!" and charged.[46]

The army opened fire, but no bullet could stop Mullah Ḥusayn. He and some companions rode to the prince's quarters and burst inside. The prince fled through a back window and escaped barefooted. Two of his brothers, however, kept fighting the Bábís until one of the Bábís found a jar of gunpowder and set fire to the house, killing its defenders. The Bábís took none of the stores of gold and silver in the house but did give Mullah Ḥusayn the prince's sword, because his had been broken by a bullet.[47]

Much of the prince's army panicked and fled, but others fought on, and the battle lasted into the day. Suddenly the shah's men discharged one thousand bullets. One of them hit Quddús in the mouth. This caused the Bábís to fight even more fiercely, and in the end, they repulsed the army. But Mullah Ḥusayn, who had forbidden looting, blamed the wounding of Quddús on certain Bábís who had insisted on remaining and trying to plunder the army's stores instead of leaving when he ordered them to do so.[48]

Quddús, carried back to the fort, held a cloth to his mouth with one hand and wrote a message with another, "The stone of the infidel broke the teeth of the Prophet of God; mine have fallen as a result of the bullet of the enemy . . . my soul is immersed in gladness . . ." He begged his weeping companions (among the loudest ones were those guilty of plundering) to be quiet.[49]

While Quddús tried to staunch his flow of blood, Bahá'u'lláh, who had been waylaid in the forest while trying to return to the fort, was in Amul, suffering the blows of the bastinado. At the beginning of December, He'd left Tehran determined to supply the fort and fight beside its defenders despite His antipathy to violence. However, He indicated to one of the Bábís that He thought He wouldn't get there. Later He wrote that it simply wasn't to be; He had a different destiny.[50]

He was arrested on orders of the prince-governor of Amul. The governor's men stole His fine horse and the horses of His companions. His friends had to walk, handcuffed, to the town of Amul, but because of His aristocratic status, Bahá'u'lláh wasn't handcuffed and was given an old nag to ride.[51]

As they straggled down forest paths under tall oaks, and through meadows in misty and balmy air under a blue and white sky, they came to a river, and Bahá'u'lláh told His friends to throw into it any Bábí documents they might possess. The water would wash away the ink, for most of the copies were handwritten. If they were tried, lack of evidence that they were indeed Bábís might spare their lives. All but one man obeyed.[52]

The prince-governor, who had ordered the arrest, wasn't even in Amul when the prisoners arrived. He'd gone to Ṭabarsí to see and deride the fort. The acting-governor of Amul wasn't happy to act as warden to Bahá'u'lláh, the impressive heir to a noble house that he greatly respected. But he had his orders. He put Bahá'u'lláh and His party on trial in the courtyard of the mosque. Four thousand people gathered there, and more watched from surrounding rooftops. The mood was extremely hostile toward the Bábís.[53]

The acting-governor, to assuage the mob, chastised Bahá'u'lláh for riding to the aid of the Bábís in Ṭabarsí. Bahá'u'lláh said, "We are innocent of the guilt they impute to us . . . I would advise you to act in a manner that will eventually cause you no regret."[54]

The mullah-in-charge asked about the Báb's mission. Bahá'u'lláh said that He personally "cherished . . . a great affection for Him" and was sure that "He had, under no circumstances, acted contrary to the Faith of Islam."[55]

The mullah replied that this was twisting the truth. Meanwhile, guards searched the Bábís' pockets and found a manuscript apparently by the Báb. He handed it to the mullah-in-charge, who read some of it aloud and then trumpeted to the masses that it contained spelling mistakes. Bahá'u'lláh told him that the words he'd just read were a quote from "the Imám 'Alí, the Commander of the Faithful . . ."[56]

No one seemed to have anything to add. The acting-governor, trying to assuage the mullahs while doing the least possible damage, ordered that the Bábís be bastinadoed. However, he did not want this torture applied to Bahá'u'lláh.[57]

But Bahá'u'lláh kept each man from being beaten and finally said, "If you insist on inflicting your punishment, I offer myself." He was put on His back on the ground, His bare feet bound to a bar above Him. One of His companions, who happened to be His maternal uncle, threw himself in front of the torturer, trying to shield his nephew. The torturer hit out at him with the bastinado rods, slashing him all over until he fainted from the pain. Then the torturer beat Bahá'u'lláh until His feet bled. Leaving a bloody trail, Bahá'u'lláh and His companions were taken to a room in the mosque.[58]

The mullahs planned to attack and kill them, so the acting-governor engineered their escape by night and had them escorted to his house, where they lived for some days under siege. Their host dreaded the return of the prince-governor from Ṭabarsí, but he came home a changed man, won over by the heroism and self-abnegation of the Bábís. He gave Bahá'u'lláh and His companions safe passage—but not to the fort.[59]

Now the Bábís in Ṭabarsí had no hope of receiving food, ammunition, or anything. A huge army led by the previously routed prince gathered against them, and they were cut off from all aid. The army surrounded the fort with barricades and armaments and marched through military exercises, trying to terrify the Bábís.[60]

Rumors of the Bábís' prowess included an overestimation of their numbers. Prince Dimitri Dolgorukov, Russian Minister in Iran, sent an official dispatch to his superiors saying there were some fifteen hundred men defending Ṭabarsí. Even if this had been so, it was far fewer than the shah's troops, and Dolgorukov knew it. He mentioned that the shah's army was made up of untrained local regiments; he said they had "several cannons but it seems that no one knows how to use them." Did he know that the Bábí force was a motley crew of men and boys with even less training and far fewer armaments? He insisted the Bábís were dangerous and must be destroyed.[61]

By February 1, 1849, the Bábís finished digging a well, and Mullah Ḥusayn said, "Today we shall have all the water we require for our baths. Cleansed of all earthly defilements, we shall seek the court of the Almighty . . . This night, ere the hour of dawn, let those who wish to join me be ready to issue forth from behind these walls and, scattering once again the dark forces which have beset our path, ascend untrammeled to the heights of glory."[62]

He bathed and spent the night chanting prayers and conversing with Quddús. At first sight of the morning star, he rose to lead his charge. He wore clean garments and the Báb's turban. With 313 men, he rode out of the fort crying, "Oh Thou Lord of the Age!"[63]

He charged the first barricade, then the second and the third, dodging huge volumes of bullets, scattering soldiers left and right, while some Bábís attacked the army from the rear. The army was so confused that its soldiers were killing each other in the dark. Then part of the army camp burst into flames, and by this grim light the soldiers could see to aim their guns. Still, the Bábís pressed forward. The army began to flee.[64]

Mullah Ḥusayn's horse got tangled in the ropes of a tent, and several Bábís tried to free him. The prince-general, hidden for the duration of the battle high in a tree, saw the entangled horse. He didn't know who the rider was, but he aimed and fired. Mullah Ḥusayn took the bullet.[65]

He tried to ride back to the fort but eventually fell, and his companions carried him the rest of the way. In an inner chamber of the shrine, they laid him down before Quddús and left the two alone. Although Mullah Ḥusayn had seemed to be unconscious by that time, the Bábís outside the door heard two voices conversing within. At last, Quddús came from the room and allowed the Bábís to say farewell to their fallen hero. Mullah Ḥusayn lay dead with a tinge of a smile on his lips.[66]

Quddús clothed Mullah Ḥusayn in his own shirt, kissed his eyes and brow, and laid the body in the tomb the Bábís had made. Thirty-six other Bábís also died that day. They, too, were carefully buried. "Take heed of the example of these martyrs of our Faith," Quddús said. ". . . In life, be and remain as united as these are now in death."[67]

A year later, the prince who shot Mullah Ḥusayn said that anyone present at Ṭabarsí would understand what had happened centuries before at Karbala, and anyone who had seen Mullah Ḥusayn would believe that the Imam Ḥusayn had returned to earth. He compared himself to Shimr, the reviled assassin of the Imam. He said that he could recognize those cut down in battle by Mullah Ḥusayn by the nature of his sword strokes, which he thought must be like the incomparable sword strokes of the Imam 'Alí, and he said, "I forbade all who were aware of this thing to mention it or make it known, lest the troops should be discouraged and should wax faint in the fight."[68]

Marveling at the courage of the Bábís, he said, "I know not what had been shown to these people, or what they had seen, that they came forth to battle with such alacrity and joy . . . And the astonishing thing was that all these men were scholars and men of learning, sedentary recluses of the college and the cloister . . . During the last three months of the siege, moreover, they were absolutely without bread and water, and were reduced to the extreme of weakness through lack of even such pittance of food as is sufficient to sustain life . . ."[69]

There he was referring to the forty-five days it took him, after the battle in which Mullah Ḥusayn died, to reorganize his army and muster new forces. During that time he allowed no supplies to enter Ṭabarsí. The Bábís tried to keep the death of Mullah Ḥusayn a secret, but turncoats revealed it to one of the prince's officers, who tried a new attack, alone, without the prince, so he could get the credit for it. With only eighteen men, the Bábís deterred his first sally. The officer fell off his horse and ran away, leaving his boot dangling ignominiously from a stirrup.[70]

Now the Bábís were reduced to eating horseflesh from the army's abandoned steeds. When there was no more meat, they ate grass and leaves. The army of twelve thousand started bombarding Ṭabarsí with cannons fired over the fortifications from towers. The Bábís, driven underground, still managed to destroy the cannon towers and scatter the snipers. Then their enemy's store of ammunition exploded, causing a month-long halt in the battle.[71]

The Bábís subsisted again on horseflesh, on the leather of saddles and their own shoes, on boiled grass. At last they had nothing but a bit of water. The army attacked again. Despite starvation, the Bábís kept repelling them.[72]

Finally, in desperation, the prince sent a delegate promising amnesty to the Bábís if they surrendered. Although they knew it was probably a trap, they decided to accept the agreement and lay down their arms. So Quddús, leading the tattered remnant of Bábís in mounted formation, left the fort. But first, a survivor later recalled, they "went to the tomb of Mullah Ḥusayn to say farewell to him. We were all weeping." When at last they began to move away, Mullah Ḥusayn's nephew said that he would never leave his uncle's tomb. Quddús was already on horseback, and he ordered the men to put the nephew on a horse and take him along. But the young man fainted and fell. When he came to, he was again put on a horse, but "he fell again, and died." His body was washed and buried nearby.

Mullah Ḥusayn's brother, who was also accompanying Quddús, was recognized in the prince's camp and put to death, for the prince immediately reneged on his word. He had almost all the Bábís killed and took Quddús prisoner. He then put it about that he'd devastated the Bábís in battle, but most people knew the truth. Dolgorukov reported that the prince resorted to "trickery" and said the Bábís' victory had aroused "the spirit of a new and even more dangerous resistance."[73]

It also aroused horrible repercussions. During the battles of Fort Ṭabarsí, Babul's religious authorities had stirred the people into an even greater frenzy of hatred and fear than before. They inflicted various torturous deaths on survivors of Ṭabarsí, and on May 16, 1849, in Babul, they finally laid hands on Quddús, tearing away his clothes, trampling his turban (a green turban which had been his gift from the Báb) in the mud, weighting him down with chains and parading him naked through the streets. The populace spat upon him, cursed him, pierced his body, mutilated him. All the time, they heard him praying for their forgiveness. They dragged him into the public square, and Quddús cried, "Would that my mother were with me, and could see with her own eyes the splendor of my nuptials." The mob tore him limb from limb, built a fire, and burned his remains. He was twenty-seven years old. He had foreseen his end in a sermon called "The Eternal Martyrdom," where he wrote, "and I will bury my soul with my own hand."[74]

In all, 173 men died during or immediately after the siege at Ṭabarsí. The youngest was fourteen, and the oldest was seventy-nine. Some of them also suffered ignominy and torture. They included distinguished scholars as well as merchants, masons, and a sifter of wheat. Among them were Dhabíḥ, who had cut his own throat at Badasht; thirty-two of the thirty-three volunteers from the village of Miyamay, along with volunteers from other villages Mullah Ḥusayn had passed through; and nine Letters of the Living, including Mullah Ḥusayn and Quddús, Mullah Ḥusayn's brother and nephew, Ṭáhirih's brother-in-law, and Mullah Jalíl-i-Urúmí, the first to bring the Bábí message to Qazvin. The brother-in-law of Mullah Ḥusayn also gave his life.

During their long separation from their loved ones, Mullah Ḥusayn's sister, Bíbí Kúchik, along with his mother, had continued the teaching circles in Mashhad. After the tragic deaths, they eventually returned to their home village and devoted themselves to the care of the families of some forty men from there who had died at Ṭabarsí. They suffered constant attacks and persecution; after the mother's death, their home was razed and the family had to take shelter in a ruin outside of town. At last, the widowed Bíbí Kúchik traveled on. Wherever she found herself, in whatever conditions, this sister poet and loyal friend of Ṭáhirih's distinguished herself by her faith and constancy. She lived to become a Bahá'í, and she received a title from Bahá'u'lláh: Leaf of Paradise.[75]

The emotions she and her mother endured can scarcely be imagined. When the Báb, in His prison, learned of the catastrophe at Fort Ṭabarsí, "He was crushed with grief . . . for nine days he refused to meet any of his friends . . ." He couldn't eat. "Tears rained continually from His eyes, and expressions of anguish dropped unceasingly from His lips . . ." His amanuensis tried to record His lamentations, but the Báb told Him to destroy what he'd written down. His intense mourning lasted for five months.[76]

After this, the first thing the Báb wrote was dedicated to Mullah Ḥusayn, then He wrote of Quddús and the others who had died at Ṭabarsí. He sent a Bábí on a pilgrimage to Ṭabarsí to circumambulate the shrine, recite the prayers and praises He had revealed, and bring back to Him a handful of earth from the spot.[77]

Mullah 'Alíy-i-Basṭámí had been the first Letter of the Living to give his life, and now nine more had fallen. Ṭáhirih was among the handful who survived. Then, someone in or near her farmhouse refuge gave away her whereabouts to agents of her ever-vigilant former husband. The farmer who had protected her was murdered, and in January, 1850, she was arrested, taken to Tehran, and charged with collaboration in the murder of her uncle. Two far more powerful men than her former husband waited to meet her: Násiri'd-Dín Sháh and his prime minister, who, it seems, had listed her among his most-wanted criminals as a Bábí rebel.[78]

18

Thralls of Yearning Love

Great Commander. Pivot of the Universe. ". . . that magic can only captivate the pure in heart . . ." The Plains of Karbala again. The death of the Báb. Women to the barricades.

When Ṭáhirih reached Tehran in January, 1850, each of Iran's two most powerful men separately summoned her. Apparently no reports exist of her interview with the prime minister, but he probably didn't find her very pleasing because she undoubtedly responded to him as challengingly as some of her co-believers did, and he had them killed soon afterward.[1]

Áqásí was gone, and the new prime minister, Mírzá Taqí Khán, was so powerful that the shah gave him the title *Regent*. However, Mírzá Taqí Khán preferred his title of *Amír*—Commander—for he'd been the commander of the shah's army. The people called him Amír Kabír, Great Commander. Formerly Násiri'd-Dín Sháh's tutor, he was the man who had secured the throne for the shah. He had risen to his eminence not because of family connections—his father was a cook in the royal kitchen—but because of his abilities and assertiveness. He was an ambitious reformer who had traveled outside of Iran on diplomatic missions and wanted to free Iran from its growing dependence on European powers. He tried to modernize the army, to actually pay the soldiers instead of letting officers siphon off their salaries, and he prohibited the army from plundering towns and villages for supplies. He endeavored to develop the Iranian arms industry, exerted himself against the ancient system of bribery, started urban renewal projects and cooperatives for artisans, began publishing an official gazette, and in his prose style avoided traditional bombast and rhetoric so that he's now known as the father of modern prose in Iran. At the time of Ṭáhirih's arrest, he was working on his greatest achievement, the government's military-technical university staffed by professors from abroad whose classes, mostly in French, covered "medicine, pharmacy, military tactics, engineering, mineralogy . . . history, mathematics," other foreign languages, etc.[2]

He was a secularist seeking to curb the power of the ulama and ensure rights for religious minorities. However, he considered the Bábís "a threat to public order," both state and religious. He particularly feared the spread of the Bábí Faith among public officials. So he became an inveterate enemy of the Báb and his followers.[3]

He was a man old in experience and set in his views and ways. The shah, however, was young and novelty-loving, and he was quite taken with Ṭáhirih. There are sketchy versions of their meeting. Although he'd had a coldly wretched childhood and was new to kingship, the shah had the arrogance and self-possession inevitable in a youth hailed as "the pivot of the universe," the "king of kings," and "the shadow of God." He possessed a growing harem, the peacock throne, and a mother titled "the sublime cradle"—bearer of the pivot of the universe—who knew all there was to know about playing for power. She'd run an interim government after the death of her estranged husband; she'd seen herself as his equal, and now she saw herself as her son's equal, and also as his guardian angel.[4]

In her layers of clothing so heavily brocaded with jewels that they stood out stiffly from her body, making her look strangely like a wooden Russian babushka doll, and with her plain, aging face, she didn't look very angelic.[5] But as "the sublime cradle" who oversaw all her son's business, she was likely present when her son met the dangerously beautiful, scandalous Ṭáhirih.

Did Ṭáhirih come unveiled into the shah's presence, whether she wanted to or not? It is reported that the shah's tiger eyes under his astonishingly heavy black brows appraised her and that he said, "I like her looks. Leave her, and let her be."[6]

Though he was nineteen and she was in her mid-thirties, he likely assumed that his royal presence and richly embellished throne room would dazzle her. They dazzled everyone else (except his mother). He was surrounded by sycophants, not the least among them being his poets, who constantly sang him flowery panegyrics. Kings and other patrons of poets constantly exacted and expected such tributes. But the shah knew Ṭáhirih was a mystic poet in the tradition of Rumi, and he might have suspected she'd be like Rumi in her response to him. Indeed, she was. She echoed Prince Seyavash, a hero of that epic weave of Persian fables and history, *The Book of Kings.* Seyavash rebeled against his father and lost his throne because of his adherence to a higher will, saying:

> . . . nothing—not motes, not lions or elephants—
> can rise against God's will; the man who disobeys
> His God has wandering wits, he's lost himself . . .[7]

Perhaps the shah imagined tempting Ṭáhirih away from her austerity, breaking her pride. She was imprisoned in a small room high up in the home of Mahmud Khan, the *kalantar* (mayor) of Tehran; there weren't any stairs going to the room, so it had to be reached by a ladder. The shah sent her a letter there, offering to marry her and make her the guardian of the ladies of his harem, and she wrote her reply on the back of the message:

> Kingdom, wealth, and power for thee
> Beggary, exile, and loss for me
> If the former be good, it's thine
> If the latter is hard, it's mine . . .[8]

She chose, she said, "'the thralls of yearning love'" which constrained her in "'the bonds of pain and calamity.'" The shah's reputed remark upon receipt of this message was, "'So far, history has not shown us such a woman.'"[9]

Apparently he didn't know about the great Sufi, Rabi'a Basri, or remember the stories of the Imam Ḥusayn's redoubtable sister Zaynab, the Prophet's daughter Fáṭimih, her mother Khadíjíh, and others. Certainly, Ṭáhirih did. And like those brilliant foremothers, she had to submit to restraints imposed by petty and envious enemies. However, she had her loyal upholders, both male and female. But almost all of them were torn from her as heroic deaths decimated the Bábí community. Like the Báb, she was heartbroken by the tragedies.

Right after her imprisonment in the mayor's home, authorities brought fourteen other Bábí prisoners to the house and incarcerated them there for twenty days, torturing them, trying to force them to recant their faith and admit complicity in a false accusation: they were said to be plotting the assassination of the prime minister. All fourteen Bábís were highly influential men. Seven of them recanted and were set free, but seven would not break. The prime minister, Amír Kabír, met with each of the seven, trying to persuade him to reject and so disprove the Báb. The shah, meanwhile, remained distant from decisions regarding the Bábís, giving absolute authority to his prime minister.[10]

The first to stand before Amír Kabír was the Báb's guardian-uncle, Ḥájí Mírzá 'Alí Shírází, who had been arrested in Tehran after visiting the jailed Báb in Azerbaijan; friends offered to pay his ransom, but he didn't let them. Ḥájí Mírzá 'Alí was a siyyid, of course, like his nephew. The prime minister said he was "loth to inflict the slightest injury upon the Prophet's descendants" and promised that Ḥájí Mírzá 'Alí would live the rest of his life under the protection of the shah if only he would deny his faith.[11]

Far from doing that, the Báb's uncle said, "My repudiation of the truths enshrined in this Revelation would be tantamount to a rejection of all the Revelations that have preceded it . . . to deny the Divine character of the Message which Muḥammad, Jesus, Moses, and all the Prophets of the past have revealed. God knows that whatever I have heard and read concerning the sayings and doings of those Messengers, I have been privileged to witness the same from this Youth, this beloved Kinsman of mine, from His earliest boyhood to this, the thirtieth year of His life . . . I only request that you allow me to be the first to lay down my life in the path of my beloved Kinsman."[12]

Amír Kabír, "stupefied by such an answer . . . motioned that he be taken out and beheaded." He was taken into the great public square near the palace that was surrounded by the homes of foreign ambassadors. An interested mob gathered. Raising a prayer of gratitude, the victim told them that the Promised One they'd awaited for over a millennium had come yet they'd imprisoned Him and "risen to exterminate His companions . . . I pray that the Almighty may wipe away the stain of your guilt . . ."[13]

He knelt to be beheaded. The executioner brought his sword down on the outstretched neck then left the scene, saying his sword needed to be sharpened. He never returned. He spent his life repenting of killing a man whom he considered as holy as the Seventh Imam. He took up other work, in another town, and wept every time he recounted how Ḥájí Mírzá 'Alí Shírází died or even when he heard his name.[14]

The next of the seven was a famous and popular dervish named Mírzá Qurbán-'Alí. Even the shah's mother was a fan of his, and she pleaded on his behalf saying he couldn't possibly be a Bábí. He was offered royal patronage and a pension if he recanted but said he only wished he had one thousand lives to give for the Báb. When he stood before Amír Kabír and the prime minister expressed reluctance to have him killed, he said, why not? He reasoned that his name, Qurbán, meant sacrifice, and 'Alí was the given name of the Báb—Siyyid 'Alí Muḥammad. Therefore it was his destiny to die for the Bab.[15]

Amír Kabír cried, "Take him away! Another moment and this dervish will have cast his spell over me!"[16]

The dervish replied, "You are proof against that magic that can only captivate the pure in heart."[17]

"Nothing but the edge of the sword can silence the voice of this deluded people," Amír Kabír raged. He gave orders that no more Bábís were to be brought before him; if they wouldn't recant, just kill them.[18]

In the square where the body of the Báb's uncle lay, the dervish addressed the multitude, ". . . though my soul brims over with ecstasy I can, alas, find no heart to share with me its charm . . ." He knelt before the mutilated corpse and as he held it in his arms, the executioner struck his blow. But it only threw Qurbán 'Alí forward and knocked his turban to the ground. The dervish recited,

> Happy he whom love's intoxication
> So hath overcome that scarce he knows
> Whether at the feet of the Beloved
> It be head or turban which he throws.

The executioner struck again, and Qurbán 'Alí died.[19]

After that, one by one, the remaining five were brought into the square and killed. After the last martyr had been killed, the executioner's block was running with blood and gore—reeking, sticky, sickeningly glossy. Yet the orgy of blood continued. For three days and three nights, the bodies of the seven martyrs remained in the great square, and "thousands of devout shí'ahs gathered round their corpses, kicked them . . . and spat upon their faces. They were pelted, cursed, and mocked by the angry multitude. Heaps of refuse were flung upon their remains by the bystanders, and the foulest atrocities were perpetrated upon their bodies . . ." Finally the remains were thrown into one grave outside the consecrated grounds of the public cemetery.[20]

"Minds are in an extraordinarily excited state due to the executions which have just taken place in the great square of Tehran," the Russian envoy Dolgorukov reported to his minister of foreign affairs in February, 1850. Although he believed the Bábís were communist brigands who wanted to take over Iran, he couldn't help but condemn the "injustice" and "cruelty" of the establishment and remark that "one can only regret the blindness of the shah's authorities," because ultimately the martyrdoms would create more sympathy for the Bábís.[21]

The Báb, already grief-stricken over the tragedy of Ṭabarsí, revealed a prayer recognizing the seven martyrs as the ones prophesized in Islamic tradition whose deaths would immediately precede His own. He longed for deliverance. But He had to bear news of one further horror.[22]

He had an especially loved disciple, Vaḥíd, the distinguished cleric who had been sent to Him by the shah to ascertain the truth of His claims, and who had immediately become a Bábí, telling the shah that only God could have changed his heart. For Vaḥíd, the Báb had revealed the Commentary on the Sura of Abundance; and Vaḥíd was the man told by Ṭáhirih in the home of Bahá'u'lláh in 1848 to abandon words for action. He did. Denounced by fellow mullahs as being bewitched and insane, he journeyed all over Iran teaching about the Báb. He was also one of the few, like Ṭáhirih, who sensed the mission of Bahá'u'lláh.[23]

Having been a man of power and influence, Vaḥíd had several residences. One was in Yazd, the ancient Zoroastrian center of Iran. In 1850, while there, his fearless eloquence aroused great enmity, and a fatwa was issued against his life. He escaped by night, but his house was plundered, and one of his servants was captured and killed. Hunted by a posse, Vaḥíd went by way of obscure mountain tracks south to another of his houses, in Nayriz, a town near Shiraz. He didn't hide himself; during his journey, he stopped in every mosque to announce the Advent from the pulpit.[24]

As he approached Nayriz, a mass of his friends, rich and poor, came out to welcome him. But the governor tried to block his entry into the city. He failed, and Vaḥíd went to the Friday Mosque and preached to about fifteen hundred people, all of whom became Bábís. For a few days, he held revivals in the mosque, winning more adherents. Then he wanted to leave the city, fearing the new Bábís would be harmed, but his converts wouldn't let him go. However, when the governor recruited one thousand soldiers against Vaḥíd, some of the new converts broke away and became Vaḥíd's enemies.[25]

Now Ṭabarsí repeated itself, just as savagely, but on a smaller scale. Vaḥíd, with seventy-two companions, took refuge in a fort; regiments laid siege to the fort, blocking water and food; the Bábís built a cistern, reinforced the fort, received more volunteers; enemy troops were augmented yet failed to rout the Bábís and suffered many casualties; within a month, the military commanders, bested various times by small, motley Bábí bands that included a ninety-year-old shoemaker, had to resort to trickery. They were terrified not only by the fierceness of the Bábí men, but by their women, who stood on rooftops during the routs, yelling along with the men, "Allah'u'Akhbar!" God is Most Great![26]

On June 29, 1850, in an eerie replay of what had happened to the Imam Ḥusayn on the plain of Karbala so long ago, Vaḥíd was bound to a horse by the green turban that marked him as a siyyid. He was dragged through the streets and trampled by a multitude of horsemen. Women of Nayriz danced around his corpse to the beating of drums and cymbals. His head was cut off, stuffed with straw and sent to the prince-governor of Shiraz, who received it while feasting in his summer house.[27]

The army ransacked and burned the houses of the Bábís of Nayriz and marched to Shiraz with captive Bábí women and children, some stripped almost naked. On their spears, the soldiers carried the decapitated heads of relatives of the captives—the heads of their fathers, sons, and brothers who had been publicly tortured and killed. These were the very poor Bábís. The rich were kept back to be tormented more slowly for the pleasure of the pious—crucified, branded with hot irons, starved, and worse. Two Bábí women, rather than subject themselves to inevitable rape, drowned themselves in a well.[28]

Four years later a cleric with a conscience wrote—high up on an inner wall of the Friday Mosque—a full report of what had happened to Vaḥíd and his companions. He used veiled language, but he told how Vaḥíd had been deceived and the homes of the Bábís demolished, a whole quarter of the city decimated.[29]

Soon after the tragedy of Nayriz, the Báb also relinquished His life. Compared to the torments of His disciples, which had tortured His heart to its farthest limits, His end was relatively civilized, if a regiment of seven hundred fifty soldiers shooting at one man and one of His disciples strung up against a wall can be called civilized.

If we appraise the Báb's death and the deaths of His followers from a non-mystical point of view, we can quote Azar Nafisi, "The worse crime committed by totalitarian mindsets is that they force their victims to become complicit in their crimes. Dancing with your jailer, participating in your own execution is an act of utmost brutality."[30]

We have witnessed this brutality throughout our human history, and some of us have been victims of it in multiple settings, from public arenas to private households, all over the world. Although the Báb and many Bábís longed to give their lives for their beliefs, and did so with Christly resignation and radiance, this does not mitigate the brutality of the death-dealing authorities. However, there was a certain consolation for the Báb during His execution: He didn't die alone. A youth named Anís died with Him, holding Him, with his head pressed against the Báb's heart, a sign and symbol of mercy and love in the midst of slaughter.

The Báb and Anís were killed in Tabriz by the orders of Amír Kabír. Modern-day travel-writer Christiane Bird describes the site of the Báb's death:

> In the center of Tabriz stands a gloomy, hulking structure known as the Arg-e Tabriz, a sheer brick citadel shaped like an inverted U. Built in the early 14th Century, it was at one time used as a prison. Criminals were hurled from its rooftop, and legend has it that one woman was saved from death when her chador filled with air and lowered her gently to the ground.
>
> It was also at or near the Arg-e Tabriz that Mirza Ali Muhammad, better known as the Báb, founder of a faith which led to the Bahá'í religion . . . was . . . suspended by ropes before a firing squad.[31]

The governor-general of Azerbaijan refused to have anything to do with it. He said, "I am neither Ibn-i-Ziyad nor Ibn-i-Sa'd (two of the men involved in the martyrdom of the Imam Husayn at Karbala) that he (Amír Kabír) should call upon me to slay an innocent descendant of the Prophet of God."[32]

Of course someone else willingly complied. The Báb had been brought from prison in Chihriq to Tabriz and lodged in a government house. Now he was marched, with a small retinue of attendants, from that house to a cell in the citadel. His captors made sure to remove His green turban, indicative of His lineage. They made every attempt to keep the populace from contact with Him, but Anís, a young man whose stepfather had imprisoned him at home because of his beliefs, escaped the house, managed to throw himself in the Báb's path, and begged never to be parted from Him. The Báb raised him to his feet and told him, "Rest assured, you will be with me." Two years earlier, Anis had dreamed of the Báb, and in his dream, the Báb had said those same words to him.[33]

That night, in His cell, the Báb was happy, rejoicing in His approaching martyrdom. But He told the little group accompanying Him that He would prefer to meet death at the hand of a friend, rather than that of an enemy. They wept copiously, unable to contemplate taking His life. But Anís leapt to his feet and said he would comply with any wish of the Báb's. His fellows restrained him. However, it was for this spirit of fearless obedience that the Báb chose Anís to share "the crown of martyrdom."[34]

In the morning the Báb's captors took him to the homes of the city's three leading mullahs. All had death-warrants signed, sealed, and ready. They didn't deign to meet the Báb.[35]

Then the Báb and Anís were led into the barracks square before the citadel. When the commander of the firing squad saw them, he didn't want to carry out his assignment. He was a Christian, and his regiment was made up of Armenian Christians. He went to the Báb and said he had no reason to hold anything against Him. "If your Cause be the Cause of Truth," he begged, "enable me to free myself from the obligation to shed your blood."[36]

"Follow your instructions," the Báb told him, "and if your intention be sincere, the Almighty is surely able to relieve you from your perplexity."[37]

The Báb and Anís were suspended by ropes from a nail in the wall of the citadel, with Anís' head resting on the breast of the Báb. Seven hundred fifty soldiers in three files aimed rifles at them. Masses watched from the roofs of surrounding buildings. At the command, each row of two hundred fifty soldiers fired their guns. The pall of smoke and dust rose so thickly that no one could see anything. When it cleared, the Báb was gone, and Anís was standing, unbound and unharmed, beneath the nail in the wall.[38]

Years later, in 1909, a Christian missionary's wife wrote of this event: ". . . indeed, a miracle had been performed, for in spite of the many bullets which had been aimed at him not one had touched the Báb, but had only brought him deliverance by severing the ropes which bound him, so that he fell to the ground unhurt . . ."[39]

A contemporary observer, Queen Victoria's envoy to Iran, Sir Justin Shiel, wrote to his officer in charge of Foreign Affairs, "When the smoke and dust cleared away after the volley, the Báb was not to be seen, and the populace proclaimed that he had ascended to the skies. . . ."[40]

Finally, the Báb was found in the barracks cell, deep in conversation with His scribe. This conversation had been interrupted the first time the soldiers came to take the Báb. Now the Báb announced to the guard who found Him that His conversation was finished and the soldiers were free to carry out their orders. But the guard was terrified and fled the scene, while the leader of the firing squad that had failed to shoot the Báb told his superiors that he'd done what he could and he wasn't about to try again.[41]

Another regiment replaced his. The Báb and Anís were suspended from ropes attached to the same nail. The Báb addressed the onlookers on the rooftops, "Had you believed in me . . . every one of you would have followed the example of this youth, (Anís), who stood in rank above most of you, and willingly would have sacrificed himself in My path. The day will come when you will have recognized Me; that day I shall have ceased to be with you."[42]

Seven hundred fifty soldiers fired their rifles. It was noon, July 9, 1850. "A gale of exceptional severity arose and swept over the whole city. A whirlwind of dust of incredible density obscured the light of the sun and blinded the eyes of the people. The entire city remained enveloped in that darkness from noon till night . . ."[43]

The bodies of the Báb and Anís were shattered, but the Báb's face remained whole. An artist from Tabriz, brought by an officer of the Russian consulate, made a sketch of it. A man who saw the sketch said, "it was such a faithful portrait of the Báb . . . No bullet had struck His forehead, His cheeks, or His lips. I gazed upon a smile which seemed to be still lingering upon His countenance. His body, however, had been severely mutilated. I could recognize the arms and head of his companion, who seemed to be holding Him in his embrace. As I gazed horror-struck upon that haunting picture, and saw how those noble traits had been disfigured, my heart sank within me. I turned away my face in anguish and . . . locked myself within my room. For three days and three nights . . . I tossed upon my bed, writhing in agony and pain."[44]

Guards dragged the bodies of the Báb and Anís through the streets and dumped them on the edge of the moat outside the city walls. One soldier kept watch over them. But two Bábís near the moat, disguised as hapless madmen, also kept vigil. The next day, a disciple of the Báb who had hoped to rescue Him from execution arrived in Tabriz. He went to the mayor, who was a friend of his, and said he was going to attack the guard and carry the bodies away. The mayor said there was a better way, and found a man to accomplish the task. The disciple then had the bodies shrouded and hidden in a silk factory in the town of Milan. Under the guidance of Bahá'u'lláh, they were soon put in a sepulcher and taken to Tehran as the Báb had wished.[45]

It was falsely reported that wild animals had devoured the corpses. Clerics thundered: Didn't this prove that the Báb's claim was a sham? Wild beasts can't destroy the remains of a saint, much less a Messenger of God.[46]

But the effect of this was countered by the true tale of how the first firing squad missed the Báb, an event picked up by the Western press and reported in Europe and the United States. It was subsequently written up in the *Journal Asiatique* after the Bábí movement was profoundly covered in Arthur Comte de Gobineau's book *Les Religions et les Philosophies dans l'Asie Centrale.* Over fifty years after the Báb's death, Jules Bois, a French writer, said, "among the litterateurs of my generation, in the Paris of 1890, the martyrdom of the Báb was still as fresh a topic as had been the first news of his death. We wrote poems about him. Sarah Bernhardt entreated Catulle Mendes for a play on the theme of this historic tragedy."[47]

In Iran, people were also impressed by the fates of the executioners. A third of the men in the regiment that killed the Báb died in an earthquake that same year. The remaining five hundred mutinied and met the same death the Báb did, dying by firing squad—and not only that, their bodies were subject to further mutilation. Within a few years, the prime minister, Amír Kabír himself, was ousted from power and assassinated, his veins and arteries slit by his killer in a public bath.[48]

Even before those downfalls, immediately following the Báb's execution it seemed nothing could quench the Bábí flame. The wildfire blazed everywhere, and the town of Zanjan, in western Iran, became a flashpoint. Zanjan isn't far from Qazvin, and it's the capital of a small province east of the Mountain of the Tiger between Iraq and Azerbaijan. Situated near the huge Soltaniyeh Mausoleum, which has the world's tallest brick dome and dominates the vacant skyline of the countryside, Zanjan, a mostly Turkish speaking town, was very lovely in its time, surrounded by relatively prosperous villages with populations that swelled seasonally with visitors from powerful nomadic tribes.[49]

The conflict in Zanjan started at the same time as the siege in Nayriz, while the Báb was still alive, and it lasted into 1851. It's mentioned in *Lonely Planet's* 2004 travel guide to Iran as "Zanjan city's moment of infamy . . . a bloody siege ordered by Persian prime minister Amír Kabír." Since the Báb's cause is now understood as the birth of the Bahá'í Faith, the guidebook goes on, "The resulting massacre was part of the relatively successful campaign to crush the nascent Bahá'í religion . . . [which] was spreading much too rapidly for Tehran's liking." Describing the city's old, twisting streets for the tourist, the guidebook adds that "the 1851 Bahá'í massacres were perpetrated in lanes behind where you now see philosopher Soravardi's bust on a library wall."[50]

Perhaps the reason the guidebook mentions this and not the other nineteenth century massacres of Bábís is that it was "the most violent and devastating" of the three run-ins the Bábís had with the military.[51]

The leader of the Bábís of Zanjan was Mullah Muḥammad 'Alíy-i-Zanjání, whose title, Ḥujjat, given by the Báb, means *the Proof.* Ḥujjat had been a militant Akhbari mullah, inheriting his position from his father, who was known as a miracle-worker. He was very popular, even after his brother mullahs turned against him, saying he was heretical because he believed the prophets and the twelve imams were like anyone else in appearance—born just like other human beings but superior morally and spiritually. The mullahs also denounced him because he expected the Advent to be ushered in by a living man on earth, born of a woman. He was tremendously forthright and eloquent, and whenever he was summoned to Tehran to be examined by a conclave of mujtahids before Muḥammad Sháh, he inevitably vanquished his opponents with his superior reasoning.[52]

When he heard about the Báb, he sent a representative to meet Him, to report on Him and bring back some of His writings. As soon as he read a few words of the writings, he "went mad" (in the eyes of onlookers): he shut up his own books and said, "The season of spring and wine has arrived. . . . Search for knowledge after reaching the known is heresy." He wrote a letter of faith to the Báb and publicly urged his congregation to become Bábís.[53]

He thought it heretical *not* to be a Bábí, but of course others disagreed. Denounced as an apostate for his open proclamation of the Báb's message from the pulpit of the Friday Mosque, he was exiled from

Zanjan to Tehran where he continued to radically oppose corruption and proclaim the Advent. While in Tehran, he heard that the Báb was en route to prison in Azerbaijan, and he sent a messenger to the Báb with a petition: he begged the Báb to allow him to organize His escape. But the Báb replied that no one could escape the decree of God. Nevertheless, Ḥujjat then dispatched some Bábís to try to convince Him to let them rescue Him, but He couldn't be persuaded.[54]

This was during the lifetime of Muḥammad Sháh. The ever-restless and outspoken Ḥujjat aroused the severe enmity of the shah's prime minister, Áqásí, yet he retained the favor of the shah, who refused to let him leave Tehran, declaring him a prisoner of the city. When the siege of Fort Ṭabarsí began, Ḥujjat longed to join his fellows there, but he was not allowed past the city gates. His comfort was "his close association with Bahá'u'lláh." After Násiri'd-Dín took the throne, Amír Kabír decided to assassinate Ḥujjat. But the prisoner managed to disguise himself and escape home to Zanjan, where the Bábís rallied around him and his enemies eagerly awaited a chance to attack.[55]

It came when Ḥujjat intervened on behalf of a Bábí child who had been arrested for quarreling with another child. Ḥujjat wrote an appeal to the governor saying the child should be disciplined, if necessary, at home. He was too young, Ḥujjat argued, to be in the hands of legal authorities.[56]

The appeal was ignored, and another Bábí, brandishing his sword, forced his way into the governor's house and released the child. The town mullahs, infuriated, compelled the governor to arrest Ḥujjat. The two men who marched to his house to take him wore suits of armor, complete with helmets, and brought with them thugs from street gangs. But one of the Bábís, with seven companions, all carrying swords, met them before they reached Ḥujjat's house.[57]

"Where are you going?" the Bábí asked the helmeted leader of the posse. Receiving an insult in reply, he cried, "Oh Thou Lord of the

Age!" and, despite the helmet, stabbed the leader in the brow. This facile overwhelming of the armor sent the posse fleeing.[58]

"Oh Thou Lord of the Age," was recognized as the cry of the latter day, the end time. When he heard the Bábís raise that cry as their byword, the governor was severely shaken. But he was also presented with the corpse of a Bábí to rejoice over: the posse that had been scattered by the Bábí with the sword encountered a Bábí who was unarmed and broke his head with an axe. They carried him to the governor's house, where one of the leading mullahs of the city stabbed him in the chest with a pen-knife. The governor added a sword blow. Others, using weapons they had at hand, completed the carnage. The Bábí, thanking God for the honor, died. This occurred on May 16, 1850—forty-five days before Vaḥíd was slaughtered and fifty-five days before the execution of the Báb.[59]

Then the governor sent out the town crier with a message to the city's populace: anyone who remained in the quarter of the city where Ḥujjat and most of the Bábís resided would be risking his own life and the life of his family, and anyone with any common sense should flee this area. Some left, and some didn't. Many families grieved at parting from loved ones who either refused to stay with them or refused to leave with them. Three thousand new recruits from other towns and villages swelled the troops assembled against Ḥujjat. From his pulpit, Ḥujjat said that God's hand had separated "truth from falsehood and divided the light of guidance from the darkness of error." However, knowing that he himself was the chief target, he didn't encourage anyone to remain with him.[60]

The Bábís ended up besieged in a citadel, deprived of food and water, and the conflict of Zanjan followed the bloodily implacable pattern of Ṭabarsí and Nayriz, except that a larger number of people died on both sides, and, because the citadel was within the city walls, many old mud-brick houses crumbled under the weight of cannon balls. As at Ṭabarsí and Nayriz, Bábís repeatedly routed the enemy despite their smaller numbers. As at Nayriz, Bábí women arose to aid their men.[61]

At first, the Bábí women didn't bear arms, but a young woman named Zaynab changed that. She was Ḥujjat's sister-in-law. As far as she knew, the Báb didn't prohibit women from fighting, so she cut her hair, donned a male tunic and headdress, armed herself with musket, shield and sword, and joined the fray. She was assumed to be a man by her companions and by the enemy, but Ḥujjat knew who she was. He gave her a man's name—Rustam-'Alí, for a hero from The Book of Kings. He told her, "'This is the Day of Resurrection, the day when 'all secrets shall be searched out.'* Not by their outward appearance, but by the character of their beliefs and the manner of their lives, does God judge his creatures, be they men or women . . ." But he reminded her that they were only fighting in self-defense, not to wage holy war.[62]

For five months, Zaynab's sword never left her side. Some say it was her pillow during the brief moments when she slept. She used her shield as a blanket. Some say she commanded a retinue of nineteen men, but most agree that she operated freely, joining in sorties or leading them wherever she was needed. Eventually, she was killed in battle, but shortly afterward, in utterly dire straits, other Bábí women in Zanjan donned male clothing, took up weapons left by their dead male kin, and fought. E. G. Browne later wrote that he "subsequently heard it on good authority that, like the Carthaginian women of old, they (the Bábí women of Zanjan) cut off their long hair, and bound it round the crazy guns to afford them the necessary support."[63]

The war in Zanjan continued for eight months. Finally, on January 8, 1851, Ḥujjat, who had resisted an effort at trickery foisted upon him as it had been upon Vaḥíd and Quddus, already severely wounded in

* The Holy Qur'án, Sura 86:9.

the face, and having witnessed the death of his wife, was shot while he was praying. He died soon afterward. This left two hundred Bábí men and five hundred women to defend the Bábí section of Zanjan.[64]

The death of Ḥujjat greatly emboldened the enemy. The Bábís resisted bravely, but they were eventually overrun and massacred. The dwellings were pillaged, and the women were captured, robbed, and stripped of all but rags. Although we don't know for sure, it's likely some were raped and held as prisoners unless they recanted. Men who had survived siege and massacre were blown from guns; stripped naked, soaked in ice-cold water and whipped to death; suffocated in boiling oil; and smeared with treacle and put out in the snow to die. Ḥujjat's body had been hidden by the Bábís, but it was found, dragged through the streets, exposed in a public square, and mutilated. Years later, visitors to Zanjan could still see bloodstains on city walls and streets.[65]

19

The Solitude of the Sun

"Lord of Love thyself proclaim . . ." The princess. Attempt on the life of the shah. "Candle decoration" and "retaliation by blood." Eclipse. Diamonds. "Thee, and thee alone . . ."

Ṭáhirih was a captive in the home of the mayor of Tehran. The Báb was no more, and Mullah Ḥusayn and Quddús were gone, consumed by calamity along with so many others of her fellow dawn-breakers. Perhaps a solace for her was the presence, in the same city, of Bahá'u'lláh, although He wasn't there all the time, as we shall see. She hailed Him as the Lord of Love in poetry and song and had no fear of the death she knew awaited her in His path—

Lord of Love, thyself proclaim, let clamor
rule the path to Thee. Thou must do it,

for my pen can't name thee, Manifold Light;
before Thy face my pen is shamed. Like all

who sense Thy secrets I can but blush
and cast my life away, a sacrifice.

Longing to fill myself with thee, I dance
at the sun—calamity! A mirror

turned toward thy brilliancy . . .[1]

It is not known whether she was able to see Bahá'u'lláh during her almost three years of imprisonment in Tehran, but she certainly was not wholly cut off from the Bábís, and her influence as a teacher, particularly of women, continued to grow.

One channel for her communication with her friends who were not in Tehran was a Bábí poet in Qazvin titled Bihjat (meaning *joy*, *grace*, *excellence*, or *exaltation.*). He and Ṭáhirih corresponded and exchanged poetry, aided by Bábí women who adopted humble disguises to be able to have contact with her. Amír Kabír had ordered that Ṭáhirih be closely watched, and the mayor didn't permit her to have pen and paper. However, she made ink from vegetable juice and dipped broom straws in it to write on torn pieces of paper that had been used to wrap food. This, of course, complicated future transcription of her poems, especially since her modes of expression were so complex.[2]

She needed this complexity, not only because she often coded her allusions and used symbolic language to protect the recipients of her writings, but because she called upon an uncommon depth of "theology, religious history, and Islamic philosophy" when she wrote. She was also aware of the "political intrigue surrounding the persecution of the Bábís and the manipulation of governmental affairs by clergy and corrupt officials." And she was, as we have had abundant occasion to note, an unabashed and brilliant actress-improviser in her own passion play, the drama of her life within the unfolding grander passion play of the Advent that "she regarded as a momentous point of transition in religious history."[3]

A prime example of the political intrigue that she sensed was the meeting of Amír Kabír with Bahá'u'lláh in early June, 1851. Amír Kabír had recently strengthened his ties to the shah by becoming his brother-in-law and was feeling quite secure in his authority, but although he had summoned Bahá'u'lláh to his presence and was arrayed in his pearl-studded robe of state, he was, as always, rather on the defensive with Bahá'u'lláh, the slight, elegant aristocrat he knew as Ḥusayn 'Alí of Nur.[4]

He'd heard rumors of Bahá'u'lláh's mystic perspicacity and His detachment from His inherited position. He knew that Bahá'u'lláh was a Bábí leader. Having engineered the execution of the Báb and the slaughter of so many of His followers, he, like many other enemies of the new faith, couldn't rid himself of one fear: what if the Báb were right? What if this were the destined day, and the Báb was, in truth, the Lord of the Dawn? What if he himself, the prime minister, was simply a pawn of prophecy? He asked Bahá'u'lláh if the Qur'án made any mention of himself, the Great Commander?[5]

"Yes," Bahá'u'lláh answered, "where it says . . ." And he partially quoted Sura 19, verse 18: "'I take refuge in the God of Mercy from thee! if thou art Taqí . . .'"[6]

Amír Kabír's given name was Taqí. (One is irresistibly reminded of Ṭáhirih's Uncle Taqí.) If Amír Kabír knew his Qur'án, he knew this was a quote from one of the Prophet's retellings of the Annunciation, and that it didn't literally apply to him. Yet Bahá'u'lláh's meaning was plain, especially since *taqí* as an epithet often inferred false piety.[7]

Completely infuriated, the prime minister then asked if the Qur'án made any reference to his father. As a cook in the shah's kitchen, Amír Kabír's father had been legendarily jealous of people who were more highly placed. Bahá'u'lláh cited a verse castigating the covetous.[8]

Amír Kabír, now even angrier than before, discarded most of his pretended friendliness. He told Bahá'u'lláh that he was aware of all His activities, particularly His material aid and His advice to the Bábís at Ṭabarsí. What a pity, he opined, with false remorse, that such a resourceful person as Bahá'u'lláh didn't have a greater opportunity to serve His king and country. He said the shah was going on a journey and suggested that Bahá'u'lláh also take a little trip, perhaps to Karbala, thus implying that Bahá'u'lláh should prove Himself a devout Shiite. When Bahá'u'lláh (thus cleansed) returned to Iran, the prime minister went on, He would be named head of the shah's court.[9]

Bahá'u'lláh knew this was an effort to bribe Him. And He saw that Amír Kabír intuited some of His importance to the Bábís, but not all of it. He later wrote, ". . . had he been aware of my true position, he would certainly have laid hold on me. He exerted the utmost effort to discover the real situation, but was unsuccessful. God wished him to be ignorant of it."[10]

Perhaps Bahá'u'lláh's own heart held intimations of His "true position." He had maintained close correspondence with the Báb, and before His execution, the Báb had sent Him, via one of the surviving Letters of the Living, a box containing certain documents, His seals, and His agate rings. One of the treasures in the box was a scroll of delicate pale blue paper. On it, the Báb had written, in His exquisite calligraphy, in the shape of a five-pointed star, 360 derivatives of the word *Bahá*.[11]

Bahá'u'lláh also recognized, behind the apparent geniality of the prime minister's gesture, an order of banishment—a dangerous order. Karbala swarmed with Iranians who would jump at the chance to profit by spying on Him and even murdering Him. Undaunted, He arranged to go to Karbala accompanied only by two relatives. Just before He left, the sepulchered remains of the Báb and His faithful disciple arrived in Tehran. Bahá'u'lláh told His brother, Músá, and another friend to place them safely in a secret place.[12]

Bahá'u'lláh reached Karbala in August and found the Bábís there under the sway of a man who claimed to incarnate the Holy Ghost. His prize student had been one of Ṭáhirih's chief converts. Bahá'u'lláh, with no fear of the prime minister or his spies, persuaded the alleged Holy Ghost to revoke his claim, won the prize student over again as a Bábí, and began enlivening and uniting the Bábís in Karbala and its surroundings.[13]

He stayed in the Shiite shrine cities for nine months until, in 1852, the slippery sands of power moved and changed shape in Iran. The seemingly invincible Amír Kabír was murdered by orders of the shah; Násiri'd-Dín's mother had never liked the prime minister, and then suspicions arose about his connections with Russia.[14]

So it was that a long-time rival of Amír Kabír's became the prime minister. He was Mírzá Áqá Khán. He came from Nur, the home province of Bahá'u'lláh, and he was a distant relative and old friend of Bahá'u'lláh's family. Now he took a title that meant *the Greatest One.* However, as minister of war to the previous shah, he'd fallen from favor and had been bastinadoed and banished. At that time, when he was wounded and in dire financial straits, Bahá'u'lláh helped him more than once, and in fact, he credited Bahá'u'lláh with curing him of "an assertedly incurable illness." In 1848, while he was in exile, Ṭáhirih, at Bahá'u'lláh's request, had been sheltered by the women of his family, led by his sister, in one of his houses in Tehran.[15]

During his exile, Áqá Khán studied the faith of the Báb and promised his Bábí teacher that if he regained his governmental influence, he'd do all he could to protect the Bábís. His teacher reported this to the Báb, who wrote to Áqá Khán saying he would soon find himself in Tehran in a position of power second only to the king, and he must not forget his promise. In response, the exile fervently repeated the promise.[16]

In 1850, he was back in Tehran as a trustee of the government. The Báb had been executed. Áqá Khán told Bahá'u'lláh he didn't think the Bábí Faith would outlive the death of its founder, and in fact he hoped for its quick extinction, given the religious dissension it produced. Bahá'u'lláh replied, "... You can be certain that the flame that has been kindled will, by this very act [the execution of the Báb], blaze forth more fiercely than ever ..."[17]

Now Áqá Khán, formerly disgraced exile and almost-Bábí, was "the Greatest One." Despite his hope for the demise of the Bábí Faith, he had tremendous reverence for Bahá'u'lláh, recognizing His charisma. At one time, his son had asked him whether he agreed that the unworldly Bahá'u'lláh had disappointingly failed to live up to the traditions of His courtier father. "... Do you really believe him to be an unworthy son of his father?" Áqá Khán had answered. "All that either of us can hope to achieve is but a fleeting and precarious allegiance which will vanish as soon as our days are ended ... Not so ... with [Ḥusayn 'Alí, Bahá'u'lláh]. Unlike the great ones of the earth, whatever be their race or rank, he is the object of a love and devotion such as time cannot dim nor enemy destroy."[18]

As newly-appointed prime minister, Áqá Khán at first made a show of remembering his promise to the Báb. He claimed he wanted to try to reconcile the Bábís and the authorities, and said he felt Bahá'u'lláh would be the best person to represent the Bábís, He issued a pardon to Bahá'u'lláh and ordered Him home from Karbala to Tehran.[19]

Bahá'u'lláh left Karbala in the spring of 1852 and rode toward Iran. He loved the outdoors, high mountains and flowers, and now He could admire stunning vistas along with cyclamen, crocus, narcissus, and pale pink almond blossoms, and relish the scents of fresh herbs and grasses. By May, He passed through Karand, one of the villages that had been so receptive to Ṭáhirih, then Kermanshah and Hamadan. From Kermanshah He sent a gift of sweets to His children. By the time the hot summer months descended, He and His family had made their way to the mountains above Tehran.[20]

Whether or not Ṭáhirih had been able to visit with Bahá'u'lláh and His family in Tehran, she no doubt heard of these happenings through her Bábí contacts and was happy to know that Bahá'u'lláh was safe. She, meanwhile, continued her dauntless efforts to educate her sisters of all kinds and classes. One of them was Shams-i Jahan Qajar, a princess who was a granddaughter of Fatḥ-'Alí-Sháh. She had been fascinated by the claims of the Báb during the 1840s and now was encouraged by a tutor in her household, a Bábí who had been among Ṭáhirih's escort during her travels, to go and meet Ṭáhirih. The princess was a poet with the pen-name Fitna.* She became a Bábí and later a Bahá'í, and she wrote a lyric poem describing her meeting with Ṭáhirih.[21]

The princess had heard much of Ṭáhirih's impressive presence and her declaration that it was the time of the Advent. Ṭáhirih was still strictly confined in the little upstairs chamber when the princess succeeded in catching a glimpse of her and talking with her. She said she strolled with her attendants in the direction of the mayor's house, and when she reached it, she prayed, "O God, if this Cause is true, make Qurratu'l-'Ayn come forward and let me see her." Then, she wrote, ". . . the window of the top story suddenly opened and Qurratu'l-'Ayn, like a brilliant sun, looked out and called to me, 'What do you want, Princess?'"[22]

Astonished at this efficacious answer to her prayer, the princess stared at the sunlike face smiling down at her and burst into tears. Ṭáhirih laughed. It struck the princess that this was very strange: she herself was free, walking in a garden, yet she was weeping, while a woman imprisoned in one room, under threat of death, was so happy as to be laughing.[23]

---

* Fitna is a telling pen-name. To Shiites, al-Fitna al-Akhir al-Zaman is the uprising at the end of time, i.e., the messianic revolution prophesized to be led by the Mahdi (Amanat, *Resurrection and Renewal*, p. 418).

"My lady," she addressed Ṭáhirih, "I would like to know why you're imprisoned."

"Because I have spoken the truth. Why did the descendents of Muḥammad fall into captivity? Because they, also, spoke the truth."

"Where is the truth?"

"The center of truth appeared in the world and they killed him."

"Is it the one they killed in Tabriz?"

"Yes. He was our Promised One—your Promised One and mine—and they martyred him."

The princess asked, "Who were those people in the Fortress of Ṭabarsí?"

"They, also, were his disciples." Then Ṭáhirih suddenly added, "Go, Princess, or you'll be in trouble." She shut her window and withdrew a moment before the mayor's guards encircled the princess and asked what she was doing.

"I came here for a walk," she haughtily told them.

They knew why she'd really come, but they chose to believe her excuse. "Very well. Now that you've finished your walk, kindly leave."[24]

The princess obeyed them, but she wept for days afterward, praying to see Ṭáhirih again. Once more, her prayer was answered. She attended the wedding of one of the mayor's sons and was with the women in the andarun, celebrating, when a guest expressed an interest in Ṭáhirih. Others joined her, and soon all were curious. Was this famously lovely woman truly an infidel? If she was, how and why had she become one? Or was she insane? Or (deliciously) evil, depraved? Finally, the women sent a message to the mayor asking him if they might, for a wedding present, see his prisoner.[25]

Ṭáhirih was brought from her small, barren room. Her presence more than filled the big, ornate andarun and lifted the spirits of all the women there. One of the guests recalled, "When I saw her my heart was filled with happiness. When Qurratu'l-'Ayn entered the room, she was so beautiful and so dignified, and when she spoke it was with such power that we . . . gradually turned to her and came and listened to her and forgot all about the wedding."[26]

Sweets, bells, drums, dances, and songs all became unimportant background as Ṭáhirih walked about the room, effortlessly radiating her sunlike attraction, making the ladies weep as she told the sorrows of her solitude, making them laugh with humorous anecdotes, now and then chanting her own verses and, no doubt, quotations from the writings of the Báb. Many of the ladies, including the princess, became Bábís.[27]

Ṭáhirih's influence extended to the serving women in the house of the mayor. One of them, a Muslim maid, recounted, "The prisoner's habit was to rise at the time of the *seher* (a little before dawn), while everyone else was still asleep. She made her ablutions, all the while softly chanting prayers and spontaneous praises of God. During the day she did not leave the room in which she was installed, which she kept in a state of scrupulous cleanliness. Nobody was admitted to her presence without having first obtained her permission. Alone, she was always carefully dressed and held herself as if she was in the midst of assembled company without letting anything go. Sometimes she arose and walked in her room while praying. The women who came to see her, after having received clearance, were all captivated by the charm of her beauty and her eloquence: they were won over and transported in their admiration of her.'"[28]

Apparently Ṭáhirih was "accustomed to" leaving her room at night, when she could take some exercise. She would walk in the courtyard (it must have been the courtyard of the andarun), where she could bathe herself as well.[29]

The mayor's wife, like the other women of the household, was keenly attuned to Ṭáhirih's sweet profundity, if not to the faith that caused it. She actively invited "the flower of womanhood in Tehran" to come and meet Ṭáhirih, acted as her hostess, and "never failed to contribute her share in deepening her influence among her womenfolk."[30]

Perhaps Ṭáhirih could have continued indefinitely in this relatively genteel confinement. The shah was rather fascinated with her. His new prime minister's sister, wife, and other female family members were even "accused of being her sympathizers" ever since she'd taken refuge with them in his house years before.[31]

It is said that her older son visited her in Tehran and came away reporting that she was praying and reading the Qur'án. He apparently didn't know that Bábís venerated and read the Qur'án and other holy books, and habitually prayed. Perhaps he was trying to get her to recant and save her life, not to mention the family honor; in later years, he said she'd died a Muslim.[32]

Of course we know this was far from the truth. She never hid her beliefs. Her inevitable martyrdom occurred in a bloodbath of persecution against the Bábís that broke out after some sadly misguided Bábís attempted to assassinate the shah.

As we've seen, the Bábí community had fallen into disarray in Karbala, and it took Bahá'u'lláh to restore it. As may be imagined, confusion also reigned in other locales following the execution of the Báb, the public torture and murders of so many of His followers, and the tragedies of Ṭabarsí, Nayriz, and Zanjan.

Intuiting the future position of Bahá'u'lláh and knowing the despair of the Bábís, Ṭáhirih prayed in poems and other writings that Bahá'u'lláh would disclose His position and heal all the rifts in the community. In one letter she wrote, "'O my God! O my God! The veil must be removed from the face of the Remnant of the Lord.* O my

* A title for Bahá'u'lláh symbolizing His role as a Manifestation of God.

God! Protect Husayn,* the mystery of Muḥammad, and advance the day of reunion with Him . . . Make the point of Bahá, O my God, to circulate . . . protect all who circumambulate the twin points† and keep them steadfast in Thy most Great Cause, so that they might behold the point sending forth light upon them.'"[33]

But Bahá'u'lláh disclosed nothing. In subtle and not-so-subtle ways, the Báb had signaled that Bahá'u'lláh was the one to whom the Bábís should turn after His death, but "there were a number of Bábís who had the temerity to see themselves as leaders of the community, and who displayed various levels of spiritual and intellectual capacity, which in their own minds logically gave them the position of the Báb's successor. No less than twenty-five Bábís ultimately asserted their pretensions to leadership." One of these was a half-brother of Bahá'u'lláh's who took advantage of the fact that the Báb had made reference to him among a number of people he called "'mirrors' among his outstanding disciples." All this despite the fact that the Báb had clearly said there would be no "successor" to Himself "in this Dispensation"; He said His purpose was to foretell "Him Whom God will make Manifest," and that person was not His "successor" per se, but a new revelator.[34]

A Bábí with successorship in mind became leader of a cult in Tehran. He hatched a plot to assassinate the shah in revenge for the death of the Báb. Then he went to Bahá'u'lláh to win His support for the scheme. Bahá'u'lláh told him in no uncertain terms to abandon it and also give up his claim of being the the Báb's successor, for, He said, it would all lead to an abyss of unmitigated disaster.[35]

---

* A reference to Bahá'u'lláh's given name, Ḥusayn 'Alí, and also to the revered Imam Ḥusayn.

† The Báb and Bahá'u'lláh, regarded as two guiding stars shining at the same time, are often called the twin points.

The ambitious Bábí disregarded the advice. On the morning of August 15, 1852, three of his co-plotters waylaid the shah in hill country where he was on a partridge-hunting expedition. He was riding a bit ahead of his guards and his entourage of over one hundred people when the three, dressed as gardeners, approached him in the servile manner of petitioners. However, this lasted only an instant because they then attacked.[36]

One of them grabbed the bridle of the shah's horse and fired the first shot. The other two also fired. They were so daft that they had only loaded their guns with birdshot, not enough to accomplish murder, but they succeeded in wounding the shah and knocking him off balance. Two of the would-be assassins dragged the shah from his horse and raised their daggers.[37]

The shah defended himself, the horse careened wildly, and within those seconds of confusion the stunned retinue regained its wits and closed in to protect the king. A guard cut down one of the attackers with a sword while his two fellow conspirators were disarmed and tied up. They cried out that they were avenging the death of the Báb and all their martyred brethren. Then they fell silent, and remained so. Soon afterward, one died with molten lead poured down his throat; the second underwent public torture and execution; and the body of the one killed by the guard was cut in half and hung from the Tehran city gates.[38]

The shot that hit the shah struck his loins, but the wound was only "skin-deep." The shah also might have been wounded mildly in his mouth and thigh. According to another account, the buckshot "riddled . . . the right arm and back of the king" and "cut the collar of pearls adorning" the royal horse's neck. The shah's European physician declared "there were not the slightest grounds for alarm," but word flew to Tehran that the shah was dead, and panic ensued.[39]

A contemporary historian wrote, "No one thought himself safe . . . Every bush was a Bábí, or concealed one . . ." A special issue of the government's newspaper appeared immediately, trumpeting the shah's safety, and he received the British envoy, Sir Justin Sheil, and the Russian Prince Dolgorokov that very afternoon. Nevertheless, mob panic continued. The sight of the body of one of the attackers "tied to the tail of a mule and dragged over the stones as far as Tehran" did nothing to assuage it. Stores were shut, and bread supplies gave out. Sheil, fearing an attack on the British embassy, sought the protection of Afghan horsemen.[40]

He and Dolgorokov noted that the shah was pale when they saw him, but it seemed more with fury than anything else. The shah said there was no precedent in Iranian history for such an attempt at regicide, and he was right. In the past, Iranian kings had been murdered by internal agents, but none of the populace had ever thought to try it. It was similar to "contemporary European examples."[41]

The shah was terrified, thinking there must be a huge conspiracy against him that was receiving help from inner circles. His suspicions were augmented by the momentary inaction of his guards during the first minutes of the attack. Rivals of the new prime minister lost no chance to implicate him in the plot, given his past association with the family of Bahá'u'lláh and the attachment that the women of his household had for Ṭáhirih.[42]

In response, Áqá Khán cracked down hard on the Bábís, and a bloodbath began. Among the first ten Bábís killed, three suffered "the exceptionally barbarous method of sham'ajin (candle decoration)." Holes were gouged into their bodies, lighted candles were stuck into the holes, and then they were led through gaily adorned bazaars to the accompaniment of celebratory music. The custom was to finally halve the still-living victim with a hatchet, but one of the three was taken to the same location where the shah had been attacked and shot in the head. This was the *qisas*, or *retaliation by blood.* But it wasn't enough. Blood retaliation went on and on. However, the Bábís would have sung with Hafez: "My spilled blood freed me from the pain of love . . ."[43]

In the midst of the nightmare, Ṭáhirih also met her death—or, depending on one's view, her freedom. Prince Dolgorukov reported to his superior, "For a long time there has been imprisoned in Tehran under the surveillance of Mahmud Khan, Chief of Police,* a Bábí woman. In spite of this she apparently found means daily to gather around herself many members of her sect. She was strangled in a garden . . ."[44]

She'd been subject to seven interrogations by two leading mujtahids and had refused to recant her faith, instead "sharply criticizing" the "ignorance and backwardness" of the learned doctors.[45]

Then, as a French biographer of the Báb, A. L. M. Nicolas, recorded, the friendly maid in the mayor's house recalled that Ṭáhirih left her room one night, "as she was accustomed to doing. I was awake and I saw her go into the courtyard where she washed her whole body. Then she returned to her room, where she changed into all white clothing. She perfumed herself while singing, and I had never seen her so content and so joyous. She spoke to all the women of the household and begged them to pardon the discomforts which her presence had brought upon them and the wrongs she had committed towards them. She acted, in a word, exactly like someone who is going to undertake a great journey."[46]

Another history records that the wife of the mayor said Ṭáhirih "kissed me . . . (and) placed in my hand the key to her chest, in which she had left for me a few trivial things as a remembrance of her stay in my house." Ṭáhirih told her friend, "Whenever you open this chest and behold the things it contains, you will, I hope, remember me and rejoice in my gladness." Within the chest was a small vial of scent, a rosary, and three rings, one turquoise, one cornelian, and one ruby. Ṭáhirih also

---

* *Kalantar*, Mahmud's Khan title, can be translated as *Chief of Police* and also as *Mayor.*

gave the mayor's wife a small package to entrust to a woman who would call for it on the third day after her death. The woman duly appeared at the house and received the package.[47]

According to the maid, after bidding everyone farewell as she deemed fit, Ṭáhirih "wrapped herself in a chador. Her joy . . . was so strange that we began to weep, for we loved her on account of her goodness and her inexhaustible benevolence. But she smiled at us and said: 'Tonight I am going to undertake a great, a very great voyage.' At that moment there was a knock on the door to the street. 'Run and open it,' she said, 'It is me they have come for.'"[48]

"It was the kalantar who entered. He came into her room and said to her: 'Come, madam, for you have been summoned.'[49]

"'Yes,' she said, 'I know where I will be taken; I know what will be done to me. But, remember well, a day will come when your master will in turn kill you.'" (This prediction was realized in short order.) Ṭáhirih also reportedly said to the kalantar, "You can kill me as soon as you like, but you cannot stop the emancipation of women."[50]

She was murdered with great secrecy. Perhaps that is why we do not know the exact date of her death, except that it occurred in August, 1852. The son of the kalantar recalled that "an ordinance was published forbidding the inhabitants of the city from remaining in the streets later than three hours after sunset . . ."* He said that he soon received "the order to establish a cordon of policemen from the house of the kalantar to the Garden of Ilkhani . . . Four hours after sunset, the kalantar . . . conducted me to his house. He entered alone into the andarun and returned soon afterwards accompanied by Qurratu'l-'Ayn."[51]

---

* According to A. L. M. Nicolas, the young man was the mayor's nephew, but more sources refer to him as the mayor's son, so we'll call him that.

The kalantar gave his son a sealed envelope and told him to bring Ṭáhirih to the garden and deliver her into the hands of ʻAzíz Khán Sardár, the Minister of War. The son mounted her on a horse and threw his coat over her so her figure in the night shadows would resemble a man's. He had troops with him, yet he feared that if the Bábís got wind of what was happening and tried to free Ṭáhirih, all his men would flee "so much did the Bábís inspire terror."[52]

He was extremely relieved to finally reach the garden. He put Ṭáhirih in a room beneath the entryway and set his guards around her, then went to find the minister of war, who sat alone, waiting for him. "Nobody knows who you have brought here?" he asked. "Nobody," the son assured him, "and now that I have fulfilled my mission, give me the release form for my prisoner." This request was refused. The minister insisted that the son assist in the execution.[53]

There are various versions of how Ṭáhirih died, essentially the same in essence but differing in details. In one, Ṭáhirih had said to her friend, the kalantar's wife, "I would request you to allow your son to accompany me to the scene of my death and to ensure that the guards and executioner . . . will not compel me to divest myself of this attire . . ."[54]

However it occurred, the young man was present when the minister of war "summoned a Turkish domestic manservant . . . a young man with a very handsome face . . . gave him many compliments and said to him . . . 'Take these twenty pieces of gold, spend them as you wish, and soon I will find you a good job. But while waiting, take this silk handkerchief and go down with the officer. He will conduct you into a room where you will find a young infidel woman who turns away the believers from the path of Muhammad. Strangle her with this handkerchief—in this way you will render a great service to God, and I will recompense you generously."[55]

The son took the servant into the room where Ṭáhirih waited. She was "prostrated and praying." The servant approached her. "Then she raised her head, looked him straight in the eye, and said to him, 'Young man! It would be unworthy for your hand to soil itself with this murder.'"[56]

The servant "ran off like a madman" and told the minister of war that he couldn't kill Ṭáhirih. "I will lose your protection," he said, "I will lose myself. Do with me whatever you wish, but I will not touch this woman."[56]

So he vanished into the night, and the minister of war summoned one of his horsemen who, as a punishment for some undisciplined act, was being forced to work in the kitchen. ". . . I think you are worthy of winning back my affection," the minister told him. "It must have very much bothered you to go so long without being able to drink spirits. Here, take a large glass and drink . . ." He then presented the man with another handkerchief and sent him to do away with Ṭáhirih.[57]

This man had no hesitation: "As soon as he entered, he attacked . . . put the handkerchief around her neck and pulled it several times" until she "fell to the ground. Then he put a knee on her back and pulled on the handkerchief with all his might. As he was roused up and afraid, he did not allow her time to exhale. He took her up in his arms in a swoon and carried her behind the wall of the icehouse. There was a well there into which he pitched her alive. We called some men, and we hastily filled up the well, because dawn was approaching."[58]

So the seemingly dauntless sun of Ṭáhirih's life was at last eclipsed. Apparently, she was silenced, veiled forever, extinguished. The kalantar's wife recounted her grief in full at the loss of Ṭáhirih, and various Europeans reported the death, among them Dr. Jacob Polak, an ophthalmologist and surgeon from Austria who at the time taught medicine in the school that had been established by the now-deposed reformist prime minister. He said he witnessed the execution and "That beautiful lady suffered her slow death with superhuman fortitude." Prince Dolgorukov wrote of the murder in a critique of the shah and his government, and the Times of London reported Ṭáhirih's death on October 13, 1852, under the headline, "Fair Prophetess of Kazoeen" (Qazvin).[59]

Ṭáhirih's mother, Amina, had died in 1851, her sympathetic Uncle 'Alí died in 1852, and her father didn't outlive her by very long. Heartbroken by her death and increasingly pressured in Qazvin, he went to Karbala, where he died at the shrine of the Imam Ḥusayn in 1854. Her maternal uncle, 'Abdu'l-Vahhab, the father of her brother-in-law and fellow Letter of the Living who died at Ṭabarsí, was also unable to go on and retreated to the Shrine of Imam 'Alí, where he passed away in 1853. Ṭáhirih's former husband, now the Friday Imam and the inheritor of all his father's "aggressiveness, browbeat the remainder of the family into at least outward compliance with Usuli orthodoxy."[60]

It seems that Ṭáhirih's daughter, Zaynah, said by some to have been with her until the time of her execution, maintained that her mother died a Shiite. Ṭáhirih's sister, Marḍíyyih, who died in 1896, reportedly taught theology and even gave fatwas, but the truth of her inner convictions is unknown. A family member tried to expunge the fact that Uncle 'Alí was a Bábí, only stating in a short biography of him that <u>Sh</u>ay<u>kh</u> Aḥmad was one of his teachers. Ṭáhirih's assassinated uncle / father-in-law was given the title Shahid-i Thalith, the Third Martyr, after two Shiite martyrs of medieval times, and his descendants took the surname *Shahidi.* Her father's descendants took the surname *Salihi,* while her Uncle 'Alí's descendants became the *Alawis.* Some of these relatives were so proud of their connection with the Third Martyr that they added Shahidi to their names.[61]

Yet, despite the efforts of the Friday Imam to make the family close ranks and annihilate her memory, references to Ṭáhirih in Iran and other parts of the world continued over the coming century, and her reputation refuses to die. Farzanieh Milani writes, "Her life is probably the best documented of nineteenth-century Iranian women." In *Touba and the Meaning of Night*, published in 1989 in Iran and more recently in the United States in English, the novelist Shahrnush Parsipur refers to Ṭáhirih without even the need to mention her name: "Haji thought to himself that women think. Unfortunately, they think. Not like ants or tree particles. Not like specks of dust. But more or less like himself . . . After all didn't that rebellious woman cause a lot of trepidation and disorder during his childhood? They said she was a loose woman but a scholar too. A lot of rumors about her circled around. He even recalled hearing a man tell his father excitedly that she is the Proof of the Age."[62]

But the event that Ṭáhirih would have hailed as her chief vindication and joy occurred in 1863, in Baghdad: Bahá'u'lláh, an exile soon to be a prisoner of the Ottoman Empire, established the Bahá'í Faith, and with it the fulfillment, as she would have seen it, of the Báb's sacrifice and mission, and of her own life and death.[63]

Now, as the Bahá'í Faith is universally disseminated, her name, story and spirit endure not just in history but in humanitarian foundations, social service projects, and the lives of countless female artists, writers, lawyers, teachers, doctors, and other heroines and servants of humanity in Iran and throughout the world. In them, Ṭáhirih, immortal dawn-breaker, glitteringly answers the question—

When will a woman symbolize the sun?
When will she step down, full of fire,

to blaze glory over the earth?
When will she bid the moon bow down

and command the stars to scatter?
Just because she wants to see

diamonds scattered. Knowing
there will always be more.[64]

With profligate disregard for conventions and superstitions, Ṭáhirih conquered immense limitations in her lifetime, and she continues to conquer. Like Laylí, she was kept veiled in a tent of tradition, a steel-strong fabric of black and white calligraphies—over a thousand years of scripture. Yet as Saba, the East Wind, carried Majnún's ecstatic songs to Laylí, so Ṭáhirih received, through the interstices of the ancient words that were her walls, the fragrance and color of the essence of love. For Ṭáhirih that was divine love as manifested in her "secret of secrets"—progressive revelation, the oneness of all faiths and fulfillment of all prophecy—that she found in the teachings of the Báb, her longed-for Friend. She read His words, lived them, rent the veils asunder, rejoiced.

In Arabic mythos, *al saba* is "a breeze that started blowing from the sea's dark western horizon . . ." but became "the Eastern Breeze that bears blessings" through its whirling progress over the desert sands of Najd. It is said in Islamic tradition that "never has God sent a prophet without sending with Him the East Wind . . ."[65]

Ṭáhirih likened herself to Saba, one of the Báb's and Bahá'u'lláh's ushers and voices for the recreation of humanity, and her spectacular effect was a recasting of woman's role despite both subtle and violent restraints imposed upon her, including the restraint of death. 'Abdu'l-Baha wrote of her last moments, "Ṭáhirih rejoiced; she had heard with a light heart the tidings of her martyrdom; she set her eyes on the supernal Kingdom and offered up her life." And of her enduring spirit, He said, "Salutations be unto her, and praise. Holy be her dust, as the tiers of light come down on it from Heaven . . ."[66]

But currently there can be no marker for Ṭáhirih's grave. Then let us leave her standing enshrined in her most famous song, one that whispers like Saba wafting constantly across the deserts and mountains of Iran—

The Solitude of the Sun

If by chance I see Thee face to face,
 I'll tell Thee my travail in minute detail,
Nuance by nuance, trace by trace.

To see Thy face, like Saba I wander
 Door to door, street to street and lane to lane,
From dwelling-place to dwelling-place.

Dying of distance from Thee I cry tears of blood,
 Tigris upon Tigris, stream upon stream,
well-spring upon well-spring, sea upon sea.

Where is the ambergris line of Thy cheek,
 And Thy lips' budding roses?—rose within rose,
Scent within scent, tulip in tulip.

Eyebrow and eye and mole of Thee—appear!
 That the bird of Thy heart may prey upon mine,
Love upon love, mood upon mood, intensity upon intensity.

My poor heart is wrung with anguish for Thee
 That binds my breast to the very stuff of life,
Filament by filament, vein by vein, artery by artery.

Tahereh traverses her deep heart's core parting
 Veil from veil, absence from absence, and finds
Only presence, only Thee—Thee, and Thee alone.[67]

Notes

PREFACE

1. Nabíl-i-A'ẓam, *The Dawn-Breakers,* pp. 294–95; Ruhe, *Robe of Light,* pp. 84, 86–87.
2. Women's Rights National Historic Park, http://nps.gov/wori/historyculture/the-first-womens-rights-convention.htm; The European Revolution of 1848, http://age-of-the-sage.org, p. 3; Sprachman, *Language and Culture in Persian,* p. 43.
3. "2003 Nobel Peace Prize," OnlineNewshour, http://www.pbs.org/newshour/bb/middle_east/july-dec03/nobel_10-10.html.
4. Ṭáhirih Justice Center, "About Us," http://www.tahirih.org/tahirih/about-us.
5. Milani, *Veils and Words,* p. 90.
6. Arberry, *Classical Persian Literature,* p. 202; Hatcher and Hemmat, *The Poetry of Ṭáhirih,* no. 27, translated from the Persian by Janet Ruhe-Schoen.
7. Shoghi Effendi, *God Passes By,* p. 73.
8. Hatcher and Hemmat, *The Poetry of Ṭáhirih,* no. 27, translated from the Persian by Janet Ruhe-Schoen.

1 / NEWS OF THE BIRTH OF A FEMALE CHILD

1. Amanat, *Resurrection and Renewal,* p. 295; Nabíl-i-A'ẓam, *The Dawn-breakers,* p. 84.
2. Shoghi Effendi, *God Passes By,* p. 73; Milani, *Veils and Words,* p. 82.

3. 'Abdu'l-Bahá, *Memorials of the Faithful*, p. 190; Mernissi, *The Veil and the Male Elite*, p. 118; Walther, *Women in Islam*, p. 224; Mernissi, *The Veil and the Male Elite*, p. 115; Mohabbat, *Paisajes del Alma*, p. 120, translated by Janet Ruhe-Schoen.
4. Nabíl-i-A'ẓam, *The Dawn-breakers*, p. xxvii.
5. Bird, *Neither East Nor West,* p. 94; Milani, *Veils and Words*, p. 5.
6. Steingass, *A Comprehensive Persian-English Dictionary*, p. 308.
7. Nabíl-i-A'ẓam, *The Dawn-breakers*, p. 83; Milani, *Veils and Words*, p. 77.
8. Steingass, *A Comprehensive Persian-English Dictionary*, p. 963.
9. Mohabbat, *Paisajes del Alma*, p. 127; Amanat, *Resurrection and Renewal*, p. 296; Momen, "Usuli, Akhbari, Shaykhi, Bábí," pp. 322, 327.
10. Ali, Muhammad, "Let Us Learn Our Inheritance," AACAR Bulletin, Fall 1989, p. 7, http://vlib.iue.it/carrie/texts/carrie_books/paksoy-4; Stevens, *The Land of the Great Sophy*, pp. 140–41.
11. "Qazvin," http://www.iranchamber.com; "Qazvin," http://www.absoluteastronomy.com; "Qazvin," http://www.rockclimbing.com/routes/Asia/Iran/Qazvin/.
12. Chardin, *Travels in Persia,* p. 134.
13. Bird, *Neither East Nor West*, p. 52.
14. Momen, "Usuli, Akhbari, Shaykhi, Bábí," pp. 296, 327–28.
15. Wright, *The English Amongst the Persians*, p. 12; Nabíl-i-A'ẓam, *The Dawn-breakers*, p. xxvi.
16. Wilber, *Persian Gardens and Garden Pavilions*, p. 141; Stevens, *The Land of the Great Sophy*, p. 141; Bird, *Neither East Nor West*, p. 344.
17. Sackville-West, *Passenger to Teheran,* pp. 107–8.
18. Gail, *Persia and the Victorians*, p. 37.
19. Balyuzi, *The Báb: The Herald of the Day of Days*, p. 8; Bird, *Neither East Nor West*, p. 267.
20. Gail, *Persia and the Victorians*, pp. 88, 89.
21. Ibid., p. 89.
22. Chardin, *Travels in Persia*, pp. 171–72; Stevens, *The Land of the Great Sophy*, p. 141.
23. Bird, *Neither East Nor West*, pp. 182–83.
24. Bayat, *Mysticism and Dissent,* p. 61.
25. Gail, *Dawn Over Mount Hira*, p. 82.
26. "Qazvin," http://www.absoluteastronomy.com/topics/Qazvin and "Qazvin," http://rockclimbing.com/routes/Asia/Iran/Qazvin/.
27. Momen, "Usuli, Akhbari, Shaykhi, Bábí," p. 319.

28. Amanat, *Resurrection and Renewal*, pp. 33–47.
29. Momen, "Usuli, Akhbari, Shaykhi, Bábí," p. 327.
30. "Qazvin," http://www.iranchamber.com; Mernissi, *The Veil and the Male Elite*, p. 195.
31. Walther, *Women in Islam*, p. 73.
32. Momen, "Usuli, Akhbari, Shaykhi, Bábí," pp. 322, 327; Milani, *Veils and Words*, p. 83.
33. Milani, *Veils and Words*, pp. 327–28.
34. Ibid., pp. 326–27; Ruhe, *Robe of Light*, p. 78; Bahrampour, "Persia on the Pacific," http://www.irandokht.com.
35. Wilber, *Persian Gardens and Garden Pavilions*, p. 21.
36. Muhammad-Hoseini, *Hadrat-i-Táhirih*, p. 128; Momen et al., *Iranian Studies*, p. 327.
37. Farmaian, *Daughter of Persia*, p. 154.
38. Walther, *Women in Islam*, p. 74; Chebel, *Symbols of Islam*, pp. 32, 80.
39. The Holy Qu'rán, Sura 16:57.
40. Ibid., Sura 81:8–9.
41. Nabíl-i-Aʻẓam, *The Dawn-breakers*, p. 84, note 1.
42. Momen, "Usuli, Akhbari, Shaykhi, Bábí," pp. 323–24.

2 / WINE CUP IN THE WILDERNESS

1. Vogelsang-Eastwood, *An Introduction to Qajar Dress*, p. 49; Mangol Bayat, *Mysticism and Dissent*, p. 37.
2. Bayat, *Mysticism and Dissent: Socioreligious Thought in Qajar Iran*, pp. 2–11.
3. Ibid.
4. Ibid., p. 38; Nabíl-i-Aʻẓam, *The Dawn-breakers*, p. 2.
5. Burke and Elliot, *Lonely Planet Iran*, pp. 230, 2–5.
6. Hafez, *The Garden of Heaven*, p. 55; Bayat, *Mysticism and Dissent*, p. 38; Saiedi, *Gate of the Heart*, p. 148.
7. Amanat, *Resurrection and Renewal*, p. 15.
8. Bayat, *Mysticism and Dissent*, p. 51.
9. Amanat, "From ijtihad to wilayat-i-faqih," p. 4; *The ʻAválim*, quoted in Bahá'u'lláh, The Kitáb-i-Íqán, ¶270; Ṣádiq, quoted in Bahá'u'lláh, The Kitáb-i-Íqán, ¶270.
10. Amanat, *Resurrection and Renewal*, p. 421; Hafez, quoted in Gray, *The Green Sea of Heaven*, p. 143.

11. The Holy Qur'án, p. 691, Sura 17:49–52, p. 708.
12. Nabíl-i-A'ẓam, *The Dawn-breakers*, pp. 4, 12.
13. Bayat, *Mysticism and Dissent*, p. 51.
14. Momen, "Usuli, Akhbari, Shaykhi, Bábí," pp. 323–24.
15. Hillmann, *A Lonely Woman: Foroogh Farrokhzaad and Her Poetry*, pp. 66–67.
16. Amanat, "Messianism and Millenarianism in Islam," p. 2. http://iranica.com.
17. Babayan, *Mystics, Monarchs, and Messiahs*, pp. 121–50.
18. Ibid., pp. 3–4.
19. Ibid., pp. 20–21.
20. Nabíl-i-A'ẓam, *The Dawn-breakers*, pp. 4, 12.
21. Amanat, *Resurrection and Renewal*, p. 99.
22. Ibid., pp. 84–85.
23. Ibid., p. 88.
24. Ibid., pp. 44–46.
25. The Holy Qur'án, Sura 6:71–82, pp. 308–11; Amanat, *Resurrection and Renewal*, p. 47.
26. Amanat, *Resurrection and Renewal*, pp. 46, 99, 97.
27. Ibid., pp. 82–83.
28. Ibid., pp. 70–75.
29. Helminski, *Women of Sufism*, pp. 132–36.
30. Ibid., p. 320; Amanat, *Resurrection and Renewal*, p. 318.
31. Stevens, *The Land of the Great Sophy*, p. 142.
32. The Holy Qu'rán, Sura 62:9; Chebel, *Symbols of Islam*, pp. 76–77.
33. Amanat, "From ijtihad to wilayat-i-faqih," p. 5; Tullio, *The Interpretation of Dialogue*, pp. 140–41.
34. Amanat, *Resurrection and Renewal*, p. 318.
35. Ibid., pp. 317–18.
36. Bird, *Neither East Nor West*, p. 227.
37. Nabíl-i-A'ẓam, *The Dawn-breakers*, pp. 82–83, note 2.
38. The Holy Qur'án, Sura 113, p. 1808.
39. Amanat, *Resurrection and Renewal*, p. 319.
40. Amanat, "From ijtihad to wilayat-i-faqih," p. 6.
41. Amanat, *Resurrection and Renewal*, p. 297.
42. Bayat, *Mysticism and Dissent*, p. 39.
43. Chardin, *Travels in Persia*, pp. 237–38, 15; Batjmanglij, *A Taste of Persia*, p. 28.

44. Chardin, *Travels in Persia,* p. 12; Nabíl-i-Aʻẓam, *The Dawn-breakers,* pp. 82–83, note 2.
45. Bayat, *Mysticism and Dissent,* p. 39.

3 / THE HARP OF LOVE AND PAIN

1. Nizami, *The Story of Layla and Majnún,* p. 11.
2. Ibid., pp. 12–13.
3. Ibid., p. 222; Hatcher and Hemmat, *The Poetry of Ṭáhirih,* p. 2; Bahá'u'lláh, *The Seven Valleys and the Four Valleys,* p. 11; Ṭáhirih, quoted in Hatcher and Hemmat, *The Poetry of Ṭáhirih,* poem no. 14, unpaginated Persian text, translated by Janet Ruhe-Schoen.
4. Nizami, *The Story of Layla and Majnún,* pp. 40–41.
5. Ibid., p. 128
6. Ibid.
7. Ibid., p. 168.
8. Ibid., pp. 169–73.
9. Bahá'u'lláh, *The Seven Valleys and the Four Valleys,* p. 11; Attar, *The Conference of the Birds,* pp. 172, 172–73.
10. Hafez, *The Garden of Heaven,* p. 1; Bird, *Neither East Nor West,* p. 18; Hafez, *The Garden of Heaven,* pp. 21, 26, 23.
11. Hafez, *The Garden of Heaven,* p. 23.
12. Afaqi, *Ṭáhirih in History: Perspectives on Qurratu'l-'Ayn from East and West,* p. 193; Hatcher and Hemmat, *The Poetry of Ṭáhirih,* p. 2.
13. Muḥammad Irshad, quoted in Afaqi, *Ṭáhirih in History: Perspectives on Qurratu'l-'Ayn from East and West,* p. 37.
14. Afaqi, *Ṭáhirih in History: Perspectives on Qurratu'l-'Ayn from East and West,* p. 37.
15. From a translation by Susan Manek, quoted in ibid., p. 194; from a translation by Janet Ruhe-Schoen of Persian text no. 6 in Hatcher and Hemmat, *The Poetry of Ṭáhirih.*
16. Shoghi Effendi, *God Passes By,* p. 72; Root, *Táhirih the Pure,* p. 102; 'Abdu'l-Bahá, *The Promulgation of Universal Peace,* p. 75.
17. Nabíl-i-Aʻẓam, *The Dawn-breakers,* p. 84, note 1.
18. Hatcher and Hemmat, *Adam's Wish,* pp. 7, 58, note 81, p. 57, note 77.
19. Nabíl-i-Aʻẓam, *The Dawn-breakers,* p. 75; 'Abdu'l-Bahá, *Memorials of the Faithful,* p. 191.

20. Momen, "Usuli, Akhbari, Shaykhi, Bábí," p. 328; Afaqi, *Ṭáhirih in History: Perspectives on Qurratu'l-'Ayn from East and West,* p. 42, note 33; Momen, "Usuli, Akhbari, Shaykhi, Bábí," p. 328.
21. Khatibi and Sijelmassi, *The Splendor of Islamic Calligraphy,* pp. 52, 74, 96, 148; Arberry, *Classical Persian Literature,* p. 55.
22. The Holy Qur'án, Sura 96:3–5.
23. Arberry, *Classical Persian Literature,* pp. 40, 42; Sciolino, *Persian Mirrors,* p. 141.
24. Sciolino, *Persian Mirrors,* p. 143.
25. Arberry, *Classical Persian Literature,* p. 101.
26. Ibid., p. 101; Afaqi, *Ṭáhirih in History: Perspectives on Qurratu'l-'Ayn from East and West,* p. 242.
27. Momen, "Usuli, Akhbari, Shaykhi, Bábí," p. 328; Hasan, quoted in Afaqi, *Ṭáhirih in History: Perspectives on Qurratu'l-'Ayn from East and West,* p. 71.
28. 'Abdu'l-Bahá, *Memorials of the Faithful,* p. 190; Gail, *Dawn Over Mount Hira,* p. 81.
29. Wiebke, *Women in Islam,* p. 79.
30. Vogelsang-Eastwood and van Doorn, *An Introduction to Qajar Era Dress,* pp. 33–59.
31. Ibid.
32. Najafi and Hinckley, *Persia is My Heart,* pp. 85–86.
33. Milani, *Veils and Words,* p. 48.
34. Ibid., p. 85.
35. The Holy Qu'rán, Sura 33:53.
36. Milani, *Veils and Words,* p. 79.
37. Khanam and Samiyeddin, *Muslim Feminism and Feminist Movement,* p. 198.
38. Helminski, *Women of Sufism,* pp. 137–38.
39. Smith, *Rab'ia the Mystic,* p. 4; ibid., note 20.
40. Hirschfield, *Women in Praise of the Sacred,* p. xx; The Holy Qur'án, Introduction, pp. 9–10, 8.
41. Brooks, *Nine Parts of Desire,* p.168; Helminski, *Women of Sufism,* pp. 1–12; Brooks, *Nine Parts of Desire,* p. 88.
42. French, Marilyn, *From Eve to Dawn: A History of Women in the World,* p. 279; "Women in Medicine" and "Warrior Women," *Islamic Center Newsletter,* Vol. 10, Issue 3, http://www.icnef.org/newsletters/2004/Mar2004.pdf.

43. Milani, *Veils and Words*, p. 51; Wiebke, *Women in Islam*, p. 72.
44. Milani, *Veils and Words*, p. 27.
45. Schimmel, *Islam: An Introduction*, quoted in The Wisdom Fund, "Slavery in Islam," http://www.twf.org.
46. The Holy Qur'án, Sura 49:13, 24:30.
47. Milani, *Veils and Words*, p. 20.
48. Ibid., pp. 209, 214, 211.
49. Nafisi, *Reading Lolita in Tehran*, p. 192.
50. Bahá'u'lláh, *The Seven Valleys and the Four Valleys*, p. 10.

4 / DRUMS OF CEREMONY

1. Hume-Griffith, *Behind the Veil in Persia and Turkish Arabia*, pp. 84–86; Saghaphi, In the Imperial Shadow, p. 57.
2. "Calendar," http://www.iranchamber.com; Molnar, Michael, *The Star of Bethlehem*, http://books.google.com.
3. Bird, *Neither East Nor West*, p. 112; E. G. Browne, quoted in Bird, *Neither East Nor West*, p. 8.
4. Walther, Wiebke, *Women in Islam*, p. 97; Burke and Elliot, *Iran*, p. 50; George, "*Zurkhaneh: The Persian House of Strength*," Black Belt, March 1977, pp. 55–57, http://books.google.com; Kian-Ersi, "Ebadi: Children [sic] Rights Are the Same as Human Rights," *Persian Morning Daily*, Oct. 9, 2003, NetIran, http://thewe.cc.
5. Najafi and Hinckley, *Persia is My Heart*, pp. 15–16.
6. Esposito, *Oxford History of Islam*, pp. 78–82; The Richard E. Wright Research Reports, "Karbala Stones," Vol. 1, #4, Nov. 1983, http://richardewright.com/8311_karbala.html.
7. Esposito, *Oxford History of Islam*, pp. 78–82.
8. Hatcher and Hemmat, *Adam's Wish*, p. 171; Bird, *Neither East Nor West*, p. 165; Browne, *A Literary History of Persia,* 3:524–25; Hatcher and Hemmat, *Adam's Wish*, p. 171.
9. Chebel, *Symbols of Islam*, pp. 44–46; The Holy Qur'án, Sura 97:3–5.
10. Fernea, *Guests of the Sheik*, pp. 115–17; Saghaphi, *In the Imperial Shadow*, pp. 125, 115–17.
11. Browne, *A Literary History of Persia,* 1:131–32.
12. Faizi, *The Prince of Martyrs*, pp. 35–40.
13. Fernea, *Guests of the Sheik*, pp. 242–43.

14. Chelkowski, Peter, "Time Out of Memory: Ta'ziyeh, the total Drama," htpp://www.asiasociety.org.
15. Mottahedeh, Negar, "Karbala Drag Kings and Queens," htpp://www.asiasociety.org.
16. Daneshvar, Simin, *Savashun*, Mage Publishers, Washington, DC, 1990, p. 260.
17. Hatcher and Hemmat, *Adam's Wish*, p. 171.
18. Boyce, *Zoroastrians: Their Religious Beliefs and Practices*, p. 1; Boyce, *Textual Sources for the Study of Zoroastrianism*, pp. 12–14, 70.
19. Bird, *Neither East Nor West*, p. 369; Kianush, K., "The Festival of Noe-Rooz" and "A Brief History of Noe-Rooz," Iransaga, http://www.art-arena.com; Sprachman, *Language and Culture in Persian*, p. 146.
20. Sackville-West, *Passenger to Teheran*, pp. 83–90.
21. Ibid.
22. Wilber, *Persian Gardens and Garden Pavilions*, pp. 155, 22–23.
23. Stevens, *The Land of the Great Sophy*, p. 141; "No-Rooz, the Iranian New Year at Present Times" [sic], Culture of Iran, http://www.iranchamber.com.
24. Wilber, *Persian Gardens and Garden Pavilions*, p. 40.
25. Gail, *Dawn Over Mt. Hira*, p. 82.

5 / IDEAL COUPLE, OPPORTUNE MARRIAGE, IRRESISTIBLE MOON

1. Beck and Nashat, *Women in Iran from 1800 to the Islamic Republic*, pp. 42, 39.
2. Ibid., p. 38.
3. Ibid., pp. 38–39; Saghaphi, *In the Imperial Shadow*, p. 32; Beck and Nashat, *Women in Iran from 1800 to the Islamic Republic*, p. 42.
4. Arberry, *Classical Persian Literature*, p. 399; Walther, *Women in Islam*, p. 90.
5. Walther, *Women in Islam*, pp. 40, 41.
6. Robertson, Stephen, "Age of Consent Laws," http://www.chm.gmu.edu/cyh/teaching-modules/49; "Married Women's Property Act," http://womenshistory.about.com.
7. Beck and Nashat, *Women in Iran from 1800 to the Islamic Republic*, p. 46.
8. Ibid., p. 47; Hume-Griffith, *Behind the Veil in Persia and Turkish Arabia*, p. 101; Najafi and Hinckley, *Persia is My Heart*, p. 122.

9. Beck and Nashat, *Women in Iran from 1800 to the Islamic Republic*, pp. 46–47.
10. Momen, “Usuli, Akhbari, Shaykhi, Bábí,” p. 328; Vogelsang-Eastwood, *An Introduction to Qajar Dress*, Illustration, p. 48; Gail, *The Greatest Holy Leaf*, p. 17.
11. Gail, *The Greatest Holy Leaf*, p. 48.
12. Beck and Nashat, *Women in Iran from 1800 to the Islamic Republic*, p. 78.
13. Amanat, *Resurrection and Renewal*, p. 297.
14. Ibid., p. 417.
15. Munier, *Iraq: An Illustrated History and Guide*, pp. 124–25.
16. Ibid., pp. 126–27.
17. ‘Alí, quoted in Gail, *Dawn Over Mt. Hira*, p. 12; Munier, *Iraq: An Illustrated History and Guide*, p. 126; Gail, *Dawn Over Mt. Hira*, p. 13.
18. Munier, *Iraq: An Illustrated History and Guide*, pp. 128–29; Daneshvar, *Savushun*, p. 89.
19. Fernea, *Guests of the Sheik*, pp. 229–30.
20. Amanat, *Resurrection and Renewal*, p. 159.
21. ‘Abdu’l-Bahá, *Memorials of the Faithful*, 191.
22. Ibid., p. 298.
23. Kian-Ersi, “Ebadi: Children [sic] Rights Are the Same as Human Rights,” *Persian Morning Daily*, Oct. 9, 2003, NetIran, http://thewe.cc; Momen, “Usuli, Akhbari, Shaykhi, Bábí,” pp. 328–29; Amanat, *Resurrection and Renewal*, p. 298; Momen, “Usuli, Akhbari, Shaykhi, Bábí,” pp. 328–29.
24. Muhammad-Hoseini, *Hadrat-i-Táhirih*, p. 128; Amanat, *Resurrection and Renewal*, p. 297.
25. ‘Abdu’l-Bahá, *Memorials of the Faithful*, p. 191.
26. Ibid., p. 192.
27. Bayat, *Mysticism and Dissent*, p. 52.
28. Ibid.
29. Ibid., p. 53; The Holy Qur’án, Sura 39:22–23, 3:84.
30. The Holy Qur’án, Sura 3:85; ibid, p. 145, note 418.
31. Bayat, *Mysticism and Dissent*, pp. 52–54.
32. Nabíl-i-A‘ẓam, *The Dawn-breakers*, p. 33.
33. Ibid., p. 25.
34. Ibid., p. 38.
35. ‘Abdu’l-Bahá, *Memorials of the Faithful*, p. 189.
36. Ibid.
37. Ibid., p. 190.

38. Ibid., pp. 191–92; Nabíl-i-A'ẓam, *The Dawn-breakers*, pp. 40–41.
39. Saghaphi, *In the Imperial Shadow*, p. 113.
40. Root, *Táhirih the Pure*, pp. 54–55.
41. Milani, *Veils and Words*, p. 109.

6 / 1844, IRAQ

1. Najafi and Hinckley, *Persia is My Heart*, p. 235.
2. Behranpour, *To See and See Again*, p. 194.
3. Mohabbat, *Paisajes del Alma*, p. 129.
4. Nabíl-i-A'ẓam, *The Dawn-breakers*, p. 28.
5. Amanat, *Resurrection and Renewal*, p. 68.
6. Nabíl-i-A'ẓam, *The Dawn-breakers*, pp. 36–45.
7. Ibid.
8. Mehrabkhani, *Mullá Ḥusayn: Disciple at Dawn*, pp. 1–2, 7–10, 20–21, 33–34.
9. Ibid., pp. 33, 41.
10. Ibid., pp. 50–51; Attar, *The Conference of the Birds*, pp. 35–50.
11. Bahá'u'lláh, *The Seven Valleys and the Four Valleys*, pp. 5–7; Mehrabkhani, *Mullá Ḥusayn: Disciple at Dawn*, p. 53; Browne, *A Year Amongst the Persians*, p. 326, http://www.Bahai-library.com/books/ayatp/.
12. Burke and Elliot, *Iran*, pp. 268–69; "Shiraz," http://www.iranchamber.com; Curzon, *Persia and the Persian Question*, p. 96.
13. Daneshvar, *Savashun*, pp. 275–79.
14. Mehrabkhani, *Mullá Ḥusayn: Disciple at Dawn*, p. 54.
15. Amanat, *Resurrection and Renewal*, pp. 136, 138–39.
16. Amanat, *Resurrection and Renewal*, p. 136; Nabíl-i-A'ẓam, *The Dawn-breakers*, pp. 30, 26.
17. Ibid., p. 27.
18. Amanat, *Resurrection and Renewal*, p. 299; Nabíl-i-A'ẓam, *The Dawn-breakers*, p. 240.
19. Amanat, *Resurrection and Renewal*, p. 299; Root, *Táhirih the Pure*, p. 57.
20. Mohabbat, *Paisajes del Alma*, p. 129.
21. 'Abdu'l-Bahá, *Memorials of the Faithful*, p. 193.
22. Root, *Táhirih the Pure*, pp. 121–22.
23. Hatcher and Hemmat, *Adam's Wish*, p. 169, note 1; The Holy Qur'án, Sura 7:72.

24. Hafez, *The Garden of Heaven*, p. 80.
25. Bahá'u'lláh, *The Seven Valleys and the Four Valleys*, p. 7.
26. Afaqi, *Ṭáhirih in History: Perspectives on Qurratu'l-'Ayn from East and West*, p. 254.

7 / 1844, EUROPE, AND THE UNITED STATES

1. Shelley, *A Defence of Poetry*, http://www.bartleby.com/27/23.
2. Shelley, *The Revolt of Islam*, http://www.books.google.com, pp. 116–17, 170–72.
3. Ibid., pp. 170, 117.
4. "Claude Henri de Rouvroy, Comte de Saint-Simon" http://www.1911.encyclopedia.org.
5. Enfantin, Barthelemy Prosper, http://www.newworldencyclopedia.org; Forget, "Saint-Simonian Feminism," *Feminist Economics*, March, 2001, pp. 79–96, http://www.informaworld.com; Bell and Offen, *Women, the Family, and Freedom*, p. 143, http://books.google.com.
6. Revelations 12:1–2.
7. Campion, *Mother Ann Lee: Morning Star of the Shakers*, pp. 31, 7, http://www.books.google.com; "The True Story of Joanna Southcott," Joanna Southcott Website, http://www.btinternet.com/~joannasouthcott/ and "Gale Encyclopedia of Occultism and Parapsychology: Joanna Southcott," http://www.answers.com/topic/joanna-southcott.
8. Sheridan, *The Rivals*, http://books.google.com, p. 16; Austen, *Northanger Abby*, http://books.google.com, p. 130.
9. Anderson, *Joyous Greetings: The First International Women's Movement, 1830–1860*, p. 69, http://books.google.com.
10. Ibid., pp. 36–41, 31–32.
11. Ibid., pp. 41–45.
12. Gilbert and Gruber, *The Madwoman in the Attic*, pp. 24, 23.
13. 1 Corinthians 14:34–35; Gilbert and Gruber, *The Madwoman in the Attic*, p. 120.
14. Axelrod, Roman, and Travisano, *The New Anthology of American Poetry*, pp. 355–56.
15. Anderson, *Joyous Greetings: The First International Women's Movement, 1830–1860*, pp. 123–24.

16. Simkin, John, "William Lloyd Garrison," Spartacus Educational Web site, http://www.Spartacus.schoolnet.co.uk/; Venet, *Neither Ballots nor Bullets*, p. 3, http://book.google.com; Anderson, *Joyous Greetings: The First International Women's Movement, 1830–1860*, p. 118.
17. Lewis, Jone Johnson, "Seneca Falls 1848 Women's Rights Convention," http://womenshistory.about.com/od/suffrage1848/a/seneca_falls.htm.
18. Document 4 (1:53–62): World's Anti-Slavery Convention, London, June, 1840, http://www.sscnet.ucla.edu/history/dubois/classes/995/98F/doc4.html.
19. Dureka, Derek, "Elaw, Zilpha," http://pabook.libraries.psu.edu/palitmap/bios/Elaw_Zilpha.html; Elizabeth, *Memoir of Old Elizabeth, A Coloured Woman*, p. 17, http://womenshistory.about.com/od/aframer18631900/l/bl_old_elizabeth.htm.
20. Harper, "Emancipation in New York," http://www.slavenorth.com/nyemancip.htm; "Sojourner Truth biography," *Women in History*, Lakewood Public Library, http://www.lkwdpl.org/wihohio/trut-soj.htm.
21. Anderson, *Joyous Greetings: The First International Women's Movement, 1830–1860*, pp. 48–49, 52.
22. Fuller, "Gale Group," http://www.encyclopedia.com, 1997.
23. Fuller, *Woman in the 19th Century*, p. 97; http://www.lkwdpl.org/wihohio/trut-soj.htm.
24. Ibid., p. 157.
25. "The Burned-Over District," http://www.history.sandiego.edu/GEN/civilwar/01/burned.
26. Amanat, *Resurrection and Renewal*, p. 11.
27. Bliss, *Memoirs of William Miller*, p. 256, http://books.google.com.
28. Nichol, *The Midnight Cry*, pp. 248–50, http://books.google.com; Knight, *Millennial Fever and the End of the World*, p. 218.
29. Cecil, *Cults in 19th Century Britain*, http://www.i-c-r.org.uk/publications/monographarchive/Monograph27.pdf.
30. Media History Project, 1830–1839, University of Minnesota, http://www.mediahistory.umn.edu/; Adams, Henry, *The Education of Henry Adams*, p. 2, http://books.google.com.
31. Moholy, Lucia, *100 Years of Photography*, p. 78, http://books.google.com; Gardner, J. B., *The Daguerreotype Process*, http://daguerre.org/index.php.
32. Marx, *Critique of Hegel's Philosophy of Right*, p. 141, http://books.google.com.

33. "A Passage from Flora Tristan's l'Union Ouvriere," translated by Doris and Paul Beik, http://www.mtholyoke.edu/courses/rschwart/hist255/at/tristan_text.html.
34. Ibid.
35. Grogan, *Flora Tristan,* pp. 198, 205.
36. "Dominican War of Independence," http://www.nationmaster.com/encyclopedia/Dominican-War-of-Independence; Douglass, *Narrative of the Life of Frederick Douglass,* p. 118, http://books.google.com.
37. Psalm 137:1; Ami Isseroff, "Biography of Rabbi Yehudah Alkalai," http://www.zionism-israel.com/bio/alkalai_biography.htm.

8 / 1844, IRAN

1. Burke et al., *Iran,* pp. 288–89; Ruhe, *Robe of Light,* pp. 55–56.
2. Richards, *A Persian Journey,* pp. 130–31.
3. "Joseph Wolff," http://www.1911encyclopedia.org; Amanat, *Resurrection and Renewal,* p. 83, note 59.
4. Amanat, *Resurrection and Renewal,* pp. 26, 23.
5. Amanat, *Pivot of the Universe,* p. 29.
6. Amanat, *Resurrection and Renewal,* pp. 21–23.
7. Nabíl-i-A'ẓam, *The Dawn-breakers,* pp. 54, 52.
8. Ibid., pp. 52–53.
9. Ibid., pp. 53–54.
10. Ibid., p. 55.
11. Ibid., pp. 55–56.
12. Ibid., p. 57.
13. Ibid.
14. Ibid.
15. Ibid.
16. Ibid.
17. Ibid.
18. Ibid., p. 59.
19. Ibid.
20. Ibid., pp. 60–61.
21. Genesis 37–50.
22. The Holy Qur'án, Sura 7:172.
23. Genesis 27:29.

24. The Holy Qur'án, Sura 12:111; Bahá'u'lláh, *The Seven Valleys and the Four Valleys*, pp. 7–8.
25. Saiedi, *Gate of the Heart*, pp. 142, 98, 108.
26. Nabíl-i-A'ẓam, *The Dawn-breakers*, p. 61; The Holy Qur'án, Sura 7:172.
27. Saiedi, *Gate of the Heart*, p. 131.
28. Nabíl-i-A'ẓam, *The Dawn-breakers*, pp. 61–63.
29. Bahá'u'lláh, *The Seven Valleys and the Four Valleys*, pp. 7–8; Afnan, *Black Pearls: Servants in the Households of the Báb and Bahá'u'lláh*, editor's note, plus an excerpt from the book, http://bahai-library.com/articles/black.pearls.html.
30. Nabíl-i-A'ẓam, *The Dawn-breakers*, p. 63.
31. Ibid.
32. Ibid., p. 65.
33. Mehrabkhani, *Mullá Ḥusayn: Disciple at Dawn*, pp. 69, 73–74; Amanat, *Resurrection and Renewal*, p. 175.
34. Mehrabkhani, *Mullá Ḥusayn: Disciple at Dawn*, pp. 74–75; Saiedi, *Gate of the Heart*, pp. 124, 51.
35. Mehrabkhani, *Mullá Ḥusayn: Disciple at Dawn*, pp. 74–75; Amanat, *Resurrection and Renewal*, p. 212.
36. Nabíl-i-A'ẓam, *The Dawn-breakers*, pp. 66–67.
37. Ibid., p. 67.
38. Mehrabkhani, *Mullá Ḥusayn: Disciple at Dawn*, pp. 74–79.
39. Nabíl-i-A'ẓam, *The Dawn-breakers*, p. 82; Amanat, *Resurrection and Renewal*, p. 299; Nabíl-i-A'ẓam, *The Dawn-breakers*, p. 80; Amanat, *Resurrection and Renewal*, pp. 179, 183.
40. Amanat, *Resurrection and Renewal*, pp. 179, 184, 182–83.
41. Ibid., pp. 188, 183.
42. Nabíl-i-A'ẓam, *The Dawn-breakers*, pp. 69–70; Mehrabkhani, *Mullá Ḥusayn: Disciple at Dawn*, p. 80.
43. Nabíl-i-A'ẓam, *The Dawn-breakers*, p. 70; Saiedi, *Gate of the Heart*, pp. 156, 20.
44. Saiedi, *Gate of the Heart*, p. 133; Amanat, *Resurrection and Renewal*, pp. 213, 299.
45. 'Abdu'l-Bahá, *Memorials of the Faithful*, p. 193; the Báb, *Selections from the Writings of the Báb* 2:34:1.
46. Saiedi, *Gate of the Heart*, pp. 50, 148, 52.
47. Ṭáhirih, poem no. 27, Persian, in Hatcher and Hemmat, *The Poetry of Ṭáhirih*, translated by Janet Ruhe-Schoen.

48. 'Abdu'l-Bahá, *Memorials of the Faithful*, p. 193; Mohabbat, *Paisajes del Alma*, p. 131; Shoghi Effendi, *God Passes By*, p. 71; Bahá'u'lláh, *The Seven Valleys and the Four Valleys*, p. 15.

9 / AS A SLAVE SITTING UNDER A SWORD

1. Nabíl-i-A'ẓam, *The Dawn-breakers*, pp. 89, 87.
2. Saiedi, *Gate of the Heart*, p. 140; The Holy Qur'án, pp. 8–9, 12; Amanat, *Resurrection and Renewal*, p. 214.
3. Amanat, *Resurrection and Renewal*, pp. 125–26.
4. Cutsinger, James S., *Paths to the Heart: Sufism and the Christian East,* p. 215, http://google.books.com; The Holy Qur'án, Sura 12:88–93.
5. The Holy Qur'án, Sura 97:3; Saiedi, *Gate of the Heart*, p. 47.
6. Balyuzi, *The Báb: The Herald of the Day of Days*, p. 61; Amanat, *Resurrection and Renewal*, pp. 216–17.
7. Balyuzi, *The Báb: The Herald of the Day of Days*, p. 60.
8. Ibid., pp. 60–61.
9. Ibid., p. 68.
10. The Báb, *Selections from the Writings of the Báb*, 2:24:1, 2:33:3.
11. Ibid., 2:27:3.
12. Nabíl-i-A'ẓam, *The Dawn-breakers*, p. 85; Amanat, *Resurrection and Renewal*, pp. 307, 299; Nabíl-i-A'ẓam, *The Dawn-breakers*, p. 286; Jami, quoted in Browne, *A Literary History of Persia*, 2:441.
13. Shoghi Effendi, *God Passes By*, p. 6; Amanat, *Resurrection and Renewal*, pp. 120–21; Nabíl-i-A'ẓam, *The Dawn-breakers*, pp. 72–73; Amanat, *Resurrection and Renewal*, p. 123.
14. Amanat, *Resurrection and Renewal*, p. 111; Mohabbat, *Paisajes del Alma*, p. 197; Balyuzi, *The Báb: The Herald of the Day of Days*, p. 32.
15. Balyuzi, *The Báb: The Herald of the Day of Days*, pp. 34–35.
16. Ibid., p. 35.
17. Ibid., p. 34.
18. Ibid., p. 36.
19. Amanat, *Resurrection and Renewal*, p. 114; Balyuzi, *The Báb: The Herald of the Day of Days*, p. 39.
20. Amanat, *Resurrection and Renewal*, p. 129; Balyuzi, *The Báb: The Herald of the Day of Days*, p. 39.
21. Amanat, *Resurrection and Renewal,* p. 114.
22. Balyuzi, *The Báb: The Herald of the Day of Days*, p. 40.

23. Nabíl-i-A'ẓam, *The Dawn-breakers*, pp. 77–78, 80; Amanat, *Resurrection and Renewal*, p. 135.
24. Amanat, *Resurrection and Renewal*, pp. 121–22.
25. Balyuzi, *The Báb: The Herald of the Day of Days*, p. 41; Amanat, *Resurrection and Renewal*, pp. 147–50.
26. Mohabbat, *Paisajes del Alma*, p. 197; Balyuzi, *Khadíjih Bagum*, p. 2.
27. Balyuzi, *Khadíjih Bagum*, pp. 5–7.
28. Ibid., pp. 6–17
29. Ibid.
30. Ibid.
31. Ibid.
32. Ibid.
33. Ruhe, *Robe of Light*, pp. 21–22.
34. Momen, *Bahá'u'lláh: A Short Biography*, p. 8; The Holy Qur'án, Sura 33:26, notes 3703, 3704; Momen, *Bahá'u'lláh: A Short Biography*, p. 8.
35. Bahá'u'lláh, *The Summons of the Lord of Hosts*, "Lawḥ-i-Ra'ís," ¶11–16.
36. Momen, *Bahá'u'lláh: A Short Biography*, pp. 23–30; Balyuzi, *Bahá'u'lláh: The King of Glory*, p. 18.
37. Saghaphi, *In the Imperial Shadow*, p. 177; Taherzadeh, *The Revelation of Bahá'u'lláh*, 4:29–30.
38. Ruhe, *Robe of Light*, pp. 33–49.
39. Ibid.
40. Ibid.
41. Ibid.
42. Ibid.
43. Ibid.
44. Ibid.
45. Ibid.
46. Ibid.
47. Nabíl-i-A'ẓam, *The Dawn-breakers*, pp. 104–7.
48. Ibid.
49. Ibid.
50. Ibid.
51. Ruhe, *Robe of Light*, p. 65.
52. Shoghi Effendi, *The Promised Day is Come*, p. 12.

10 / FIRE AND ICE

1. Ṭáhirih, quoted in Amanat, *Resurrection and Renewal,* pp. 301–3.
2. Yusuf Ali, in The Holy Qur'án, p. 24, note 48; 'Abdu'l-Bahá, quoted in Thompson, *The Diary of Juliet Thompson,* p. 90.
3. Ṭáhirih, quoted by 'Abdu'l-Bahá in Thompson, *The Diary of Juliet Thompson,* p. 91.
4. 'Abdu'l-Bahá, quoted in Juliet Thompson, *The Diary of Juliet Thompson,* p. 90; Bahá'u'lláh, *Prayers and Meditations,* p. 304.
5. Bahá'u'lláh, *Gleanings from the Writings of Bahá'u'lláh,* no. 27.2.
6. Ibid., no. 27.3–4.
7. Ibid., no. 27.4.
8. Bayat, *Mysticism and Dissent,* pp. 53–54; Ṭáhirih, quoted in Amanat, *Resurrection and Renewal,* p. 301; 'Abdu'l-Bahá, *Selections from the Writings of 'Abdu'l-Bahá,* no. 221.7.
9. Saiedi, *Gate of the Heart,* p. 149.
10. The Báb, *Selections from the Writings of the Báb,* 2:44:2, 2:51:1.
11. Saiedi, *Gate of the Heart,* p. 122; Bankier and Lashgari, *Women Poets of the World,* p. 76.
12. The Holy Qur'án, Sura 12:39–40; the Báb, *Selections from the Writings of the Báb,* 2:12:1.
13. Amanat, *Resurrection and Renewal,* p. 230.
14. Ibid.
15. Ibid., pp. 232–33.
16. The Báb, quoted in Balyuzi, *The Bab: The Herald of the Day of Days,* p. 84.
17. Amanat, *Resurrection and Renewal,* p. 234; Major Rawlinson, quoted in Balyuzi, *The Bab,* p. 67.
18. Nabíl-i-A'ẓam, *The Dawn-breakers,* note 1, pp. 91–92; Amanat, *Resurrection and Renewal,* p. 237.
19. Nabíl-i-A'ẓam, *The Dawn-breakers,* p. 89.
20. Amanat, *Resurrection and Renewal,* pp. 238–39.
21. Ibid., pp. 251–52.
22. Saiedi, *Gate of the Heart,* p. 22.
23. Ibid., p. 252.
24. The Báb, *Selections from the Writings of the Báb,* 2:19:2.
25. Balyuzi, *The Báb: The Herald of the Day of Days,* pp. 76–77.
26. Ibid., pp. 77–78.
27. Nabíl-i-A'ẓam, *The Dawn-breakers,* p. 146.

28. Ibid., pp. 145–47.
29. Balyuzi, *The Báb: The Herald of the Day of Days*, p. 88.
30. The Holy Qur'án, Sura 49:6.
31. Balyuzi, *The Báb: The Herald of the Day of Days*, pp. 84–89; Afnan, *Black Pearls: Servants in the Households of the Báb and Bahá'u'lláh*, pp. 11–15.
32. Mohabbat, *Paisajes del Alma*, p. 131.
33. Kjeilen, Tore, "Ashura," http://www.i-cias.com/e.o/ashura.htm.
34. Benlafquih, Christine, "Day of Ashura," at http://www.suite101.com/content/day-of-ashura-a87975; Brunner, Borgna, "Major Islamic Holidays," http://www.infoplease.com/spot/islamicholidays.html.
35. The Báb, *Selections from the Writings of the Báb*, 2:47:2–3.
36. Shoghi Effendi, *God Passes By*, p. 38; information that the poem is used on the Báb's birthday courtesy of Mali Davachi Teymoorian, author's notes from personal conversation, 2008. Translation by Janet Ruhe-Schoen from Hatcher and Hemmat, *The Poetry of Ṭáhirih*, poem #8, unpaginated Persian text.
37. Amanat, *Resurrection and Renewal*, pp. 300–305.
38. Ibid., p. 306.
39. Ibid., p. 307.
40. Ibid.
41. Ibid., p. 308; Mohabbat, *Paisajes del Alma*, p. 133.
42. Milani, *Veils and Words*, pp. 91–92.
43. Amanat, *Resurrection and Renewal*, pp. 308, 420, 245, note 237; The Holy Qur'án, Sura 3:61.
44. Ibid., p. 138, note 400.
45. 'Abdu'l-Bahá, *Memorials of the Faithful*, pp. 178–80.
46. Ibid., p. 194; Amanat, *Resurrection and Renewal*, p. 308.
47. 'Abdu'l-Bahá, *Memorials of the Faithful*, p. 194; Amanat, *Resurrection and Renewal*, p. 308.
48. Root, *Táhirih the Pure*, p. 61.
49. Amanat, *Resurrection and Renewal*, p. 309.
50. Ibid., p. 309, note 93.
51. Fogg, *Arabistan*, pp. 212–13, 218.
52. Ibid.
53. Layard, *Autobiography and Letters*, pp. 343–44.
54. Ibid., Fogg, *Arabistan*, p. 223.
55. Root, *Táhirih the Pure*, p. 62.
56. Ibid., p. 61; Gail, *Dawn over Mount Hira*, p. 83.

57. Saiedi, *Gate of the Heart*, p. 69.
58. Ibid., pp. 74, 71.
59. Ibid., pp. 104, 103.
60. Nabíl-i-A'ẓam, *The Dawn-breakers*, note 1, p. 175; Lamden, *Sinaitic Mysteries: Studies in Honor of the Late Hasan M. Balyuzi*, p. 104; Mohabbat, *Paisajes del Alma*, p. 133.
61. 'Abdu'l-Bahá, *Memorials of the Faithful*, pp. 191–92.
62. Amanat, *Resurrection and Renewal*, pp. 309–10.
63. Mohabbat, *Paisajes del Alma*, p. 134; Root, *Táhirih the Pure*, p. 63.
64. Amanat, *Resurrection and Renewal*, pp. 310 and 311, note 100.
65. 'Abdu'l-Bahá, *Memorials of the Faithful*, pp. 192–93.
66. Ibid., p. 195; Amanat, *Resurrection and Renewal*, p. 311.
67. Amanat, *Resurrection and Renewal*, p. 311.
68. Ibid., p. 313.

11 / MURDER

1. Gail, *Dawn Over Mt. Hira*, p. 84; *Amanat, Resurrection and Renewal*, p. 312; Root, *Tahirih the Pure*, p. 64.
2. Glassé, *The New Encyclopedia of Islam*, pp. 31–32; Ruhe, *Robe of Light*, p. 170; Amanat, *Resurrection and Renewal*, p. 86.
3. Ruhe, *Robe of Light*, p. 170; Amanat, *Resurrection and Renewal*, pp. 312, 313, note 15; Nabíl-i-A'ẓam, *The Dawn-breakers*, p. 272, note 2.
4. Burke et al., *Lonely Planet Iran*, p. 195 and p. 195, note 3.
5. Amanat, *Resurrection and Renewal*, p. 313.
6. 'Abdu'l-Bahá, *Memorials of the Faithful*, p. 196; Amanat, *Resurrection and Renewal*, p. 313; 'Abdu'l-Bahá, *Memorials of the Faithful*, p. 196.
7. Nabíl-i-A'ẓam, *The Dawn-breakers*, p. 272, note 3; Mohabbat, *Paisajes del Alma*, p. 136.
8. The Circle of Ancient Iranian Studies website, http://www.cais-soas.com.
9. Harris, *Inside Iran*, pp. 147–48; Eliassian, "Esther's Iranian Tomb Draws Pilgrims of all Religious Stripes," http://www.iran-heritage.org/interestgroups/Judaism-monument.htm.
10. Sciolino, *Persian Mirrors*, p. 217.
11. Amanat, *Resurrection and Renewal*, p. 315, note 124.
12. Ibid., pp. 313–14.
13. Ibid., pp. 313–14; Root, *Táhirih the Pure*, p. 66; Mohabbat, *Paisajes del Alma*, pp. 137–39.

14. Shoghi Effendi, *God Passes By,* p. 74.
15. Amanat, *Resurrection and Renewal,* p. 315; Shoghi Effendi, *God Passes By,* p. 74.
16. Amanat, *Resurrection and Renewal,* pp. 316, 301.
17. Ibid., pp. 320, 256.
18. Browne, *A Literary History of Persia,* 4:371.
19. Nabíl-i-A'ẓam, *The Dawn-breakers,* p. 273; 'Abdu'l-Bahá, *Memorials of the Faithful,* p. 190.
20. Wallbridge, "Essays and Notes on Babi and Bahai History," http://www.h-net.org/~bahai/bhpapers/vol6/waless/chap2.htm.
21. Nabíl-i-A'ẓam, *The Dawn-breakers,* pp. 273–75; Milani, *Veils and Words,* p. 85.
22. 'Abdu'l-Bahá, *Memorials of the Faithful,* p. 197.
23. Root, *Tahirih the Pure,* pp. 69–70.
24. Ibid.
25. Ibid., Nabíl-i-A'ẓam, *The Dawn-breakers,* p. 275, note 2.
26. Brill, *E. J. Brill's First Encyclopedia of Islam,* p. 439; Milani, *Veils and Words,* pp. 81–82.
27. Nabíl-i-A'ẓam, *The Dawn-breakers,* pp. 276–78.
28. Ibid.
29. Ibid.
30. Ibid.
31. Ibid.
32. Root, *Táhirih the Pure,* pp. 72–73.
33. Ibid.
34. Ibid., pp. 73–74, 72.
35. Ibid., p. 74.
36. Ibid.
37. Ibid., pp. 74–75.
38. Ibid.
39. Amanat, *Resurrection and Renewal,* p. 324; Root, *Táhirih the Pure,* p. 102.
40. Amanat, *Resurrection and Renewal,* p. 322.
41. Ibid., p. 323.
42. Ruhe, *Robe of Light,* pp. 79–80.
43. Ibid., Nabíl-i-A'ẓam, *The Dawn-breakers,* p. 280.
44. Ibid., and Amanat, *Resurrection and Renewal,* p. 323 (including note 169).
45. Nabíl-i-A'ẓam, *The Dawn-breakers,* p. 282.
46. Amanat, *Resurrection and Renewal,* p. 323, note 172.

47. Ruhe, *Robe of Light*, p. 78; Mohabbat, *Paisajes del Alma*, p. 142; Amanat, *Resurrection and Renewal*, p. 324; 'Abdu'l-Bahá, *Memorials of the Faithful*, p. 199.
48. Wallbridge, "Essays and Notes on Babi and Bahai History," http://www.h-net.org/~bahai/bhpapers/vol6/waless/chap2.htm; Nabíl-i-A'ẓam, *The Dawn-breakers*, p. 284.
49. Nabíl-i-A'ẓam, *The Dawn-breakers*, p. 284.
50. Gray, *The Green Sea of Heaven*, p. 123.
51. Nabíl-i-A'ẓam, *The Dawn-breakers*, p. 285; Momen, "Usuli, Akhbari, Shaykhi, Bábí," p. 334.
52. Milani, *Veils and Words*, p. 77.

12 / THE PRICE OF A CASHMERE SHAWL

1. Saiedi, *Gate of the Heart*, p. vii.
2. Balyuzi, *Khadíjih Bagum: The Wife of the Báb*, pp. 16–22.
3. Ibid.
4. Ibid.
5. Ibid.
6. Nabíl-i-A'ẓam, *The Dawn-breakers*, pp. 191–92.
7. Ibid., pp. 194–95.
8. Balyuzi, *The Báb: The Herald of the Day of Days*, pp. 104–5.
9. Balyuzi, *Khadíjih Bagum: The Wife of the Báb*, pp. 16–22.
10. Ibid., pp. 103, 106–7.
11. Nabíl-i-A'ẓam, *The Dawn-breakers*, pp. 209–17.
12. Ibid.
13. Ibid.
14. Ibid.
15. Ibid.
16. Ibid., pp. 172–76; Balyuzi, *The Báb: The Herald of the Day of Days*, p. 94.
17. Nabíl-i-A'ẓam, *The Dawn-breakers*, pp. 223–28.
18. Ibid.
19. Ibid.
20. Ibid.
21. Ibid.
22. Ibid., pp. 230–31; Balyuzi, *The Báb: The Herald of the Day of Days*, p. 123.
23. Nabíl-i-A'ẓam, *The Dawn-breakers*, pp. 230–32, including notes 2–3.

24. Ibid.
25. Ibid., p. 235; Momen, "Usuli, Akhbari, Shaykhi, Bábí," p. 331; Nabíl-i-A'ẓam, *The Dawn-breakers*, p. 235, note 2.
26. Momen, "Usuli, Akhbari, Shaykhi, Bábí," p. 331.
27. Nabíl-i-A'ẓam, *The Dawn-breakers,* p. 235, note 2; Balyuzi, *The Báb: The Herald of the Day of Days*, p. 125.
28. Balyuzi, *The Báb: The Herald of the Day of Days*, pp. 124, 126–27.
29. Ibid., pp. 128–29.
30. Ibid., Reiss, *The Orientalist*, p. 10.
31. Reiss, *The Orientalist,* pp. 13–16.
32. Ibid.

13 / 1848, IRAN—LOVE'S AMPLITUDE

1. Mohabbat, *Paisajes del Alma*, p. 142; 'Abdu'l-Bahá, *Memorials of the Faithful*, p. 199.
2. Bahá'u'lláh, quoted in Hatcher and Hemmat, *The Poetry of Ṭáhirih*, p. 2.
3. Ṭáhirih, quoted in Hatcher and Hemmat, *The Poetry of Ṭáhirih*, poem #22 in Persian, translated by Janet Ruhe-Schoen.
4. Ṭáhirih, quoted in Hatcher and Hemmat, *The Poetry of Ṭáhirih*, p. 2; Gail, *Dawn Over Mount Hira*, p. 81.
5. 'Abdu'l-Bahá, *Memorials of the Faithful*, p. 200.
6. Ibid.
7. Momen, *Bahá'u'lláh: A Short Biography*, p. 8; "Stevens, Ethel Stefana (1879–1972)," at Bahá'í Tributes, http://bahaitributes.wordpress.com; Afnan, Mírzá Habibu'llah, "The Báb in Shiraz," http://www.h-net.org/~bahai/trans/vol1/babshir1.htm.
8. Ruhe, *Robe of Light*, p. 82.
9. Nabíl-i-A'ẓam, *The Dawn-breakers,* p. 269.
10. Mehrabkhani, *Mullá Ḥusayn: Disciple at Dawn*, pp. 123–24.
11. Nabíl-i-A'ẓam, *The Dawn-breakers,* pp. 286–87.
12. Ibid.
13. Mírzá Músá, quoted in Nabíl-i-A'ẓam, *The Dawn-breakers,* pp. 286–87.
14. Sackville-West, *Passenger to Teheran,* p. 143; Mehrabkhani, *Mullá Ḥusayn, Disciple at Dawn*, pp. 134–37
15. Mehrabkhani, *Mullá Ḥusayn, Disciple at Dawn*, pp. 134–37.
16. Ibid.
17. Ibid.

18. Ibid.; Nabíl-i-A'ẓam, *The Dawn-breakers,* p. 285, note 1.
19. Mehrabkhani, *Mullá Ḥusayn: Disciple at Dawn*, pp. 134–37.
20. Balyuzi, *The Báb: The Herald of the Day of Days*, pp. 129–30.
21. 'Alí Khán, quoted in Nabíl-i-A'ẓam, *The Dawn-breakers,* p. 256.
22. Ibid., p. 257.
23. Mehrabkhani, *Mullá Ḥusayn: Disciple at Dawn*, pp. 138–40.
24. Balyuzi, *The Báb: The Herald of the Day of Days*, pp. 132–33.
25. Mehrabkhani, *Mullá Ḥusayn: Disciple at Dawn*, pp. 134–42.
26. Ibid.
27. Nabíl-i-A'ẓam, *The Dawn-breakers,* p. 258, note 1.
28. Mehrabkhani, *Mullá Ḥusayn: Disciple at Dawn*, p. 143.
29. Ibid., p. 149.
30. Balyuzi, *The Báb: The Herald of the Day of Days*, pp. 131–32.
31. Nabíl-i-A'ẓam, *The Dawn-breakers,* pp. 260–63.
32. Ibid.
33. Mehrabkhani, *Mullá Ḥusayn: Disciple at Dawn*, pp. 148–52.
34. Ibid.
35. Ibid.
36. Ibid., pp. 153, 157.
37. Ibid., p. 158.
38. Curzon, *Persia and the Persian Question*, pp. 153–157.
39. Ibid.
40. Ibid.
41. Curzon, *Persia and the Persian Question*, p. 148.
42. Mehrabkhani, *Mullá Ḥusayn: Disciple at Dawn*, pp. 159–60.
43. Ibid.
44. Ibid., p. 162–68.
45. Ibid., p. 174–76.
46. Ibid.
47. Ibid.
48. Ibid.
49. Ibid., pp. 162–68.
50. Ibid., pp. 174–76.
51. Ibid.
52. Ibid.
53. Ibid., pp. 174–76.

14 / 1848, IRAN—THE GOLDEN LOOKING GLASS

1. Ruhe, *Robe of Light,* pp. 83–85.
2. Ibid.
3. Shoghi Effendi, *God Passes By,* pp. 19–20.
4. Ibid., p. 31.
5. Ibid., p. 25.
6. Ibid.; 'Abdu'l-Bahá, *Promulgation of Universal Peace,* pp. 104–5.
7. Shoghi Effendi, *God Passes By,* p. 32; Nabíl-i-A'ẓam, *The Dawn-breakers,* pp. 293, 294, note 1; Shoghi Effendi, *God Passes By,* p. 50.
8. Quddús, quoted in Nabíl-i-A'ẓam, *The Dawn-breakers,* p. 294.
9. Shaykh Abú-Turáb, quoted in Nabíl-i-A'ẓam, *The Dawn-breakers,* p. 294.
10. Ibid.
11. Ibid., p. 294.
12. Nabíl-i-A'ẓam, *The Dawn-Breakers,* p. 294, note 2.
13. Shoghi Effendi, *God Passes By,* p. 12; Bahá'u'lláh, quoted in Nabíl-i-A'ẓam, *The Dawn-breakers,* pp. 460; Mírzá Áqá Ján, quoted by Bahá'u'lláh in *The Dawn-breakers,* pp. 460–61.
14. Nabíl-i-A'ẓam, *The Dawn-breakers,* p. 295.
15. Ibid., p. 296; Ṭáhirih, quoted in ibid., p. 296.
16. The Holy Qur'án, Sura 56:1–5, 25–26.
17. Bahá'u'lláh, quoted in Ruhe, *Robe of Light,* pp. 88–89.
18. Ṭáhirih, quoted in Ruhe, *Robe of Light,* pp. 88–89; Ruhe, *Robe of Light,* pp. 88–89.
19. Nabíl-i-A'ẓam, *The Dawn-breakers,* pp. 297–98; Ruhe, *Robe of Light,* p. 91; Nabíl-i-A'ẓam, *The Dawn-breakers,* pp. 297–98.
20. Nafis, *Reading Lolita in Tehran,* p. 324.
21. Bahá'u'lláh, *Gleanings from the Writings of Bahá'u'lláh,* 131.3.
22. Ruhe, *Robe of Light,* pp. 91–92.
23. Bahá'u'lláh, quoted Nabíl-i-A'ẓam, *The Dawn-breakers,* p. 275.
24. Ibid.
25. Ruhe, *Robe of Light,* pp. 91–92.
26. Afaqi, *Táhirih in History: Perspectives on Qurratu'l-'Ayn from East and West,* pp. 196–97
27. Ibid.
28. Ibid.
29. Khatibi and Sijelmassi, *The Splendor of Islamic Calligraphy,* p. 131.
30. Hatcher and Hemmat, *The Poetry of Ṭáhirih,* no. 35, unpaginated Persian, translated by Janet Ruhe-Schoen.

31. 'Abdu'l-Bahá, *Selections from the Writings of 'Abdu'l-Bahá*, no. 222.1.
32. The Báb, *Selections from the Writings of the Báb*, 3:15:1; Hatcher and Hemmat, *The Poetry of Ṭáhirih*, no. 12, unpaginated Persian, translated by Janet Ruhe-Schoen.

15 / 1848, IRAN—UNDER THE TIGER'S EYE

1. Farmaian and Munker, *Daughter of Persia*, p. 85.
2. Amanat, *Pivot of the Universe*, p. 81; Balyuzi, *The Bab*, pp. 139–40; Amanat, *Resurrection and Renewal*, p. 387.
3. Amanat, *Pivot of the Universe*, pp. 100–102, 42, 25.
4. Ibid., pp. 43, 36.
5. Saghaphi, *In the Imperial Shadow*, pp. 172–73; Amanat, *Pivot of the Universe*, p. 77.
6. Ibid., p. 74; Burke and Elliot, *Iran*, pp. 146–47.
7. Burke and Elliot, *Iran*, pp. 146–47.
8. Amanat, *Pivot of the Universe*, pp. 74–75.
9. Ibid.
10. Bird, *Neither East Nor West*, p. 238; Amanat, *Pivot of the Universe*, p. 75.
11. Amanat, *Pivot of the Universe*, p. 81; Balyuzi, *The Báb: The Herald of the Day of Days*, p. 137.
12. "Urmia (Urumiyeh), The Cradle of Civilization," Cais Archeological and Cultural News, Oct. 25, 2003, Circle of Ancient Iranian Studies, http://www.cais-soas.com; Burke and Elliot, *Iran*, p. 131.
13. Nabíl-i-A'ẓam, *The Dawn-breakers*, p. 309.
14. Ibid., p. 311.
15. Amanat, *Resurrection and Renewal*, pp. 386–87.
16. Ibid., pp. 387–88.
17. Nabíl-i-A'ẓam, *The Dawn-breakers*, pp. 314–15.
18. See Amanat, *Resurrection and Renewal*, pp. 389–90.
19. See Nabíl-i-A'ẓam, *The Dawn-breakers*, pp. 315–17.
20. Amanat, *Pivot of the Universe*, p. 86.
21. See Nabíl-i-A'ẓam, *The Dawn-breakers*, pp. 318–19.
22. Ibid., p. 320.
23. Amanat, *Resurrection and Renewal*, p. 391.
24. Nabíl-i-A'ẓam, *The Dawn-breakers*, pp. 320–22, note 1.
25. Dr. Cormick, quoted in Nabíl-i-A'ẓam, *The Dawn-breakers*, pp. 320–22, note 1.

26. Balyuzi, *The Báb: The Herald of the Day of Days*, pp. 146–47.
27. Nabíl-i-A'ẓam, *The Dawn-breakers*, p. 323.

16 / 1848, THE UNITED STATES AND EUROPE— THE SPRINGTIME OF THE PEOPLES

1. Rynder, "All Men and Women are Created Equal," http://www.historynet.com/all-men-women-are-created-equal-cover-page-april-99-american-history-feature.htm.
2. Stanton, *Eighty Years and More*, Chapter 2, http://www.digital.library.upenn.edu; "Modern History Sourcebook: the Declaration of Sentiments, Seneca Falls Conference, 1848, http://www.fordham.edu/halsall/mod/Senecafalls.html.
3. Rynder, "All Men and Women are Created Equal," http://www.historynet.com/all-men-women-are-created-equal-cover-page-april-99-american-history-feature.htm; Anderson, *Joyous Greetings: The First International Women's Movement, 1830–1860*, p. 168, http://books.google.com; Rynder, "All Men and Women are Created Equal," http://www.historynet.com/all-men-women-are-created-equal-cover-page-april-99-american-history-feature.htm.
4. Stanton, *Eighty Years and More*, Chapter 9; Frances Osgood, *The New Anthology of American Poetry*, Vol. 1, pp. 350, 354.
5. Rynder, "All Men and Women are Created Equal," http://www.historynet.com/all-men-women-are-created-equal-cover-page-april-99-american-history-feature.htm.
6. Wagner, *Sisters in Spirit*, pp. 44, 42–43.
7. Ibid., p. 48; E. C. Stanton quoted in Holbrook, M. L., *Parturition Without Pain*, p. 112.
8. Anderson, *Joyous Greetings: The First International Women's Movement, 1830–1860*, pp. 16, 167, http://books.google.com.
9. Ibid., pp. 155–57.
10. Ibid.
11. Ibid.
12. Ibid.
13. "The Quaker Influence on the Seneca Falls Convention," http://www.nps.gov/wori/historyculture/index.htm.
14. Rynder, "All Men and Women are Created Equal," http://www.historynet.com/all-men-women-are-created-equal-cover-page-april-99-american-

history-feature.htm; Anderson, *Joyous Greetings: The First International Women's Movement, 1830–1860,* p. 168, http://books.google.com.
15. Stanton et al., *History of Woman Suffrage,* pp. 68–75, http://books.google.com.
16. Ibid.
17. Ibid.
18. Rynder, "All Men and Women are Created Equal," http://www.historynet.com/all-men-women-are-created-equal-cover-page-april-99-american-history-feature.htm.
19. Ibid.
20. Ibid.
21. Anderson, *Joyous Greetings: The First International Women's Movement, 1830–1860,* p. 172, http://books.google.com.
22. Rynder, "All Men and Women are Created Equal," http://www.historynet.com/all-men-women-are-created-equal-cover-page-april-99-american-history-feature.htm.
23. Ibid.; McLean, "This Month in History," p. 16.
24. Anderson, *Joyous Greetings: The First International Women's Movement, 1830–1860,* p. 170, http://books.google.com.
25. Rynder, "All Men and Women are Created Equal," http://www.historynet.com/all-men-women-are-created-equal-cover-page-april-99-american-history-feature.htm.
26. Stanton et al., *History of Woman Suffrage,* p. 76.
27. Ibid., pp. 115–16.
28. Ibid.
29. Ibid.
30. Ibid.
31. Ibid.
32. Ibid.
33. Ibid.
34. Ibid.
35. Anderson, *Joyous Greetings: The First International Women's Movement, 1830–1860,* pp. 21–22, http://books.google.com.
36. Ibid., pp. 155–57, 16.
37. Margaret Fuller, quoted in Kornfield, *Margaret Fuller: A Brief Biography with Documents,* p. 57.
38. Ibid., pp. 57, 58.
39. Margaret Fuller, quoted in ibid., pp. 58, 62, 211.

40. Ibid., p. 220.
41. Ibid.
42. Ibid., pp. 220–21.
43. Kornfield, *Margaret Fuller: A Brief Biography with Documents*, pp. 220–21.
44. Margaret Fuller, quoted in ibid., p. 222.
45. Ibid.
46. Kornfield, *Margaret Fuller: A Brief Biography with Documents*, p. 222.
47. Ibid., p. 231.
48. Ibid., p. 235.

17 / "AND I WILL BURY MY SOUL WITH MY OWN HAND"

1. Sa'adi, quoted in Van Doren, *Anthology of World Poetry*, p. 145.
2. Amanat, *Resurrection and Renewal*, p. 329; Milani, *Veils and Words*, p. 98.
3. The Holy Qur'án, Sura 2:190–91.
4. Amanat, *Resurrection and Renewal*, p. 328; Nabíl-i-A'ẓam, *The Dawn-breakers*, pp. 350–51.
5. Curzon, *Persia and the Persian Question*, p. 380; Mehrabkhani, *Mullá Ḥusayn: Disciple at Dawn*, p. 189.
6. Amanat, *Resurrection and Renewal*, p. 348; Nabíl-i-A'ẓam, *The Dawn-breakers*, p. 351.
7. Ruhe, *Robe of Light*, p. 93.
8. Ibid.
9. Amanat, *Resurrection and Renewal*, p. 329.
10. Nabíl-i-A'ẓam, *The Dawn-breakers*, title page.
11. Mehrabkhani, *Mullá Ḥusayn: Disciple at Dawn*, p. 181.
12. Ibid., p. 178.
13. Ibid., pp. 182–83.
14. Ibid.
15. Ibid., pp. 181–83 and 187–88.
16. Ibid., pp. 187–88.
17. Ibid., pp. 185–92.
18. Ibid.
19. Ibid.
20. McCarry, *Old Boys*, p. 318.
21. Mehrabkhani, *Mullá Ḥusayn: Disciple at Dawn*, p. 196.
22. Ibid.
23. Ibid., pp. 197–210.

24. Ibid.
25. Ibid.
26. Ibid.
27. Ibid.
28. Ibid., pp. 213–14.
29. Ibid., pp. 226–27.
30. Ibid.
31. Nabíl-i-A'ẓam, *The Dawn-breakers*, pp. 352–53.
32. Ibid.
33. Ibid.
34. Ibid., pp. 358–59.
35. Ibid.
36. Ibid.
37. Ibid., pp. 359–61.
38. Ibid.
39. Ibid.
40. Ibid., p. 362.
41. Mehrabkhani, *Mullá Ḥusayn: Disciple at Dawn*, p. 247.
42. Ibid., p. 248.
43. Nabíl-i-A'ẓam, *The Dawn-breakers*, p. 368.
44. Ibid.
45. Mehrabkhani, *Mullá Ḥusayn: Disciple at Dawn*, pp. 249–50.
46. Ibid., pp. 352–60.
47. Ibid.
48. Ibid.
49. Ibid.
50. Ruhe, *Robe of Light*, p. 104.
51. Ibid.
52. Curzon, *Persia and the Persian Question*, p. 383; Ruhe, *Robe of Light*, pp. 105–8.
53. Ruhe, *Robe of Light*, pp. 105–8.
54. Ibid.
55. Ibid.
56. Ibid.
57. Ibid.
58. Ibid.
59. Ibid.
60. Nabíl-i-A'ẓam, *The Dawn-breakers*, p. 378.

61. Dolgorukov, "Excerpts from dispatches Written during 1848–1852 by Prince Dolgorukov," *World Order* 1, no. 1 (1966): 19–20.
62. Nabíl-i-A'ẓam, *The Dawn-breakers*, pp. 379–82.
63. Ibid.
64. Ibid.
65. Ibid.
66. Ibid.
67. Ibid.
68. Mehrabkhani, *Mullá Ḥusayn: Disciple at Dawn*, pp. 272–75.
69. Ibid.
70. Nabíl-i-A'ẓam, *The Dawn-breakers*, pp. 384–87.
71. Ibid.
72. Ibid.
73. Ibid., pp. 388–407; Mehrabkhani, *Mullá Ḥusayn: Disciple at Dawn*, pp. 284–85; Dolgorukov, "Excerpts from dispatches Written during 1848–1852 by Prince Dolgorukov," *World Order* 1, no. 1 (1966): 21.
74. Root, *Táhirih the Pure*, p. 59; Nabíl-i-A'ẓam, *The Dawn-breakers*, pp. 411–12; Amanat, *Resurrection and Renewal*, p. 388, note 196.
75. Nabíl-i-A'ẓam, *The Dawn-breakers*, pp. 414–26; Mehrabkhani, *Mullá Ḥusayn: Disciple at Dawn*, pp. 285–86.
76. Ibid., pp. 430–32.
77. Ibid.
78. Amanat, Resurrection and Renewal, p. 329.

18 / THRALLS OF YEARNING LOVE

1. Amanat, *Resurrection and Renewal*, p. 329.
2. Gale Encyclopedia of Biography, "Mirza Taqi Khan Amir-e Kabir," at http://www.answers.com/topic/amir-kabir; Elton, *The History of Iran*, pp. 110–11.
3. "The Bábí-State Conflicts of 1848–1853," http://bahai.haifa.ac.il/Moghaddam/S_Z_Moghaddam_Abstract.pdf
4. Amanat, *Pivot of the Universe*, pp. 10, 31.
5. Sheil, Lady Mary, "Glimpses of Life and Manners in Persia," p. 123, http://bahai-library.com/shiel_glimpses_life_persia&chapter=8.
6. Milani, *Veils and Words*, p. 88.
7. Amanat, *Pivot of the Universe*, p. 68; Bird, *Neither East Nor West*, p. 159.

8. Root, *Táhirih the Pure*, pp. 95–96; Ṭáhirih, quoted in Milani, *Veils and Words*, p. 88.
9. Násiri'd-Dín Sháh, quoted in Root, *Táhirih the Pure*, p. 95.
10. Nabíl-i-A'ẓam, *The Dawn-breakers*, pp. 446–47; Balyuzi, *The Báb: The Herald of the Day of Days*, pp. 182–83.
11. Nabíl-i-A'ẓam, *The Dawn-breakers*, p. 447.
12. Ibid., pp. 447–48.
13. Ibid., pp. 447–48; Ruhe, *Robe of Light*, p. 113; Nabíl-i-A'ẓam, *The Dawn-breakers*, p. 448.
14. Nabíl-i-A'ẓam, *The Dawn-breakers*, pp. 448–49.
15. Ibid., pp. 449–52.
16. Ibid., p. 452.
17. Ibid.
18. Ibid.
19. Ibid., p. 453.
20. Ibid., pp. 462–63.
21. Dolgorukov, "Excerpts from dispatches Written during 1848–1852 by Prince Dolgorukov," *World Order* 1, no. 1 (1966): 21.
22. Nabíl-i-A'ẓam, *The Dawn-breakers*, p. 463.
23. Ibid., pp. 171–77, 465.
24. Ibid., pp. 475–99.
25. Ibid.
26. Ibid.
27. Ibid.
28. Ibid.
29. Ibid.
30. Nafisi, *Reading Lolita in Tehran*, p. 76.
31. Bird, *Neither East Nor West*, pp. 240–41.
32. Nabíl-i-A'ẓam, *The Dawn-breakers*, pp. 504–13.
33. Ibid.
34. Ibid.
35. Ibid.
36. Ibid.
37. Ibid.
38. Ibid.
39. Hume-Griffith, *Behind the Veil in Persian and Turkish Arabia*, p. 118, http://www.muhammadanism.org/Hume-Griffith/hume-griffith_illustrations.pdf.

40. "The Báb, Forerunner of Bahá'u'lláh," at http://info.bahai.org/the-bab-forerunner.html.
41. Nabíl-i-A'ẓam, *The Dawn-breakers*, pp. 504–24.
42. Ibid.
43. Ibid.
44. Ibid.
45. Ibid.
46. Ibid.
47. "The Báb, Forerunner of Bahá'u'lláh," at http://info.bahai.org/the-bab-forerunner.html; Momen, *Early Western Accounts of Bahá'í (and Bábí) Faith*, http://www.northill.demon.co.uk/relstud/bfwestac.htm.
48. Nabíl-i-A'ẓam, *The Dawn-breakers*, pp. 525–26.
49. Ibid., p. 527, note 1; Burke et al., *Iran*, p. 167.
50. Burke et al., *Iran*, p. 268.
51. Nabíl-i-A'ẓam, *The Dawn-breakers*, p. 529.
52. Ibid.
53. Balyuzi, *The Báb: The Herald of the Day of Days*, p. 100; Amanat, *Resurrection and Renewal*, p. 101; Balyuzi, *The Báb: The Herald of the Day of Days*, pp. 100–102.
54. Balyuzi, *The Báb: The Herald of the Day of Days*, p. 100.
55. Nabíl-i-A'ẓam, *The Dawn-breakers*, pp. 534–35.
56. Ibid., pp. 537–39, 439–40.
57. Ibid., p. 541–59.
58. Ibid.
59. Ibid.
60. Ibid.
61. Ibid.
62. Ibid.
63. Ibid., p. 563, note 1.
64. Ibid., pp. 573–79.
65. Ibid.

19 / THE SOLITUDE OF THE SUN

1. Hatcher and Hemmat, *The Poetry of Ṭáhirih*, no. 13, translated from the Persian by Janet Ruhe-Schoen.
2. Hatcher and Hemmat, *Adam's Wish*, p. 10, pp. 81–82.
3. Ibid., pp. 81–82.

4. Ruhe, *Robe of Light*, pp. 123–24.
5. Ibid.
6. Ibid.
7. Ibid.
8. Ibid.
9. Ibid.
10. Bahá'u'lláh, quoted in ibid.
11. Ruhe, *Robe of Light*, p. 115.
12. Ibid., pp. 125–26.
13. Ibid., pp. 128–29.
14. Ibid.
15. Ibid., p. 129.
16. Ibid., pp. 118–19.
17. Bahá'u'lláh, quoted in ibid.
18. Ruhe, *Robe of Light*, pp. 118–19.
19. Ibid., p. 129.
20. Ibid., pp. 133–34.
21. Cole, *Modernity and the Millennium*, p. 169, http://books.google.com.
22. Avirih, "The Story of the Princess," vol. 14, no. 11, 1924.
23. Ibid.
24. Ibid.
25. Ibid.
26. Ibid.
27. Ibid.
28. Afaqi, *Ṭáhirih in History*, p. 109.
29. Ibid.
30. Nabíl-i-Aʻẓam, *The Dawn-breakers*, p. 622.
31. Amanat, *Resurrection and Renewal*, p. 329, note 200.
32. Momen, "Usuli, Akhbari, Shaykhi, Bábí," p. 334.
33. Faizi, *Explanation of the Emblem of the Greatest Name*, http://bahai-library.com/books/greatest.name/.
34. Ruhe, *Robe of Light*, p. 122.
35. Ibid., pp. 135–36.
36. Ibid.
37. Ibid.
38. Ibid.
39. Amanat, *Pivot of the Universe*, pp. 208–11; Perigord, *Translation of the French Footnotes of the Dawn-breakers*, p. 72.

40. Amanat, *Pivot of the Universe*, pp. 208–11; Perigord, *Translation of the French Footnotes of the Dawn-breakers*, p. 74.
41. Amanat, *Pivot of the Universe*, pp. 208–11.
42. Ibid.
43. Ibid.; Hafez, *The Green Sea of Heaven*, p. 83.
44. Dolgorukov, "Excerpts from dispatches Written during 1848–1852 by Prince Dolgorukov," *World Order* 1, no. 1 (1966): 23.
45. Ruhe, *Robe of Light*, p. 150.
46. Nabíl-i-A'ẓam, *The Dawn-breakers*, pp. 625–28.
47. Ibid.
48. Afaqi, *Ṭáhirih in History*, pp. 109–10.
49. Ibid.
50. Ibid.; Shoghi Effendi, *God Passes By*, p. 75.
51. Nabíl-i-A'ẓam, *The Dawn-breakers*, p. 628, note 1; Afaqi, *Ṭáhirih in History*, p. 110.
52. Afaqi, *Ṭáhirih in History*, pp. 110–11; Ruhe, *Robe of Light*, p. 151.
53. Afaqi, *Ṭáhirih in History*, pp. 110–11.
54. Nabíl-i-A'ẓam, *The Dawn-breakers*, p. 623.
55. Afaqi, *Ṭáhirih in History*, pp. 111.
56. Ṭáhirih, quoted in Afaqi, *Ṭáhirih in History*, p. 111.
57. Afaqi, *Ṭáhirih in History*, pp. 111–12.
57. Ibid.
58. Ibid.
59. Dr. Jacob Polak, quoted in Ruhe, *Robe of Light*, p. 151; Dolgorukov, "Excerpts from dispatches Written during 1848–1852 by Prince Dolgorukov," *World Order* 1, no. 1 (1966): 23; Amanat, *Resurrection and Renewal*, p. 330.
60. Momen, "Usuli, Akhbari, Shaykhi, Bábí," pp. 333–34.
61. Ibid.
62. Milani, *Veils and Words*, pp. 80, 98.
63. Shoghi Effendi, *God Passes By*, p. 155.
64. Janet Ruhe-Schoen, "When Will a Woman Symbolize the Sun?", 2002.
65. Stetkevych, *The Zephyrs of Najd*, pp. 132, 125.
66. 'Abdu'l-Bahá, *Memorials of the Faithful*, p. 203.
67. Hatcher and Hemmat, *The Poetry of Ṭáhirih*, no. 27, translated from the Persian by Janet Ruhe-Schoen.

Bibliography

WORKS OF BAHÁ'U'LLÁH

Gleanings from the Writings of Bahá'u'lláh. Translated by Shoghi Effendi. Wilmette, IL: Bahá'í Publishing, 2005.

The Hidden Words. Translated by Shoghi Effendi. Wilmette, IL: Bahá'í Publishing, 2002.

The Kitáb-i-Íqán: The Book of Certitude. Translated by Shoghi Effendi. Wilmette, IL: Bahá'í Publishing, 2003.

The Seven Valleys and the Four Valleys. Translated by Marzieh Gail in consultation with Ali Kuli Khan. Wilmette, IL: Bahá'í Publishing Trust, 1991.

WORKS OF THE BÁB

Selections from the Writings of the Báb. Compiled by the Research Department of the Universal House of Justice and translated by Habib Taherzadeh with the assistance of a Committee at the Bahá'í World Center. Wilmette, IL: Bahá'í Publishing Trust, 2006.

WORKS OF 'ABDU'L-BAHÁ

Memorials of the Faithful. New ed. Translated by Marzieh Gail. Wilmette, IL: Bahá'í Publishing Trust, 1996.

Promulgation of Universal Peace: Talks Delivered by 'Abdu'l-Bahá during His Visit to the United States and Canada in 1912. Compiled by Howard MacNutt. Wilmette, IL: Bahá'í Publishing Trust, 2007.

Selections from the Writings of 'Abdu'l Bahá. Compiled by the Research Department of the Universal House of Justice. Translated by a Committee at the Bahá'í World Center and Marzieh Gail. 1st pocket-size ed. Wilmette, IL: Bahá'í Publishing, 2010.

WORKS OF SHOGHI EFFENDI

God Passes By. New ed. Wilmette, IL: Bahá'í Publishing Trust, 1974.

The Promised Day Is Come. 1st pocket-size ed. Wilmette, IL: Bahá'í Publishing Trust, 1996.

OTHER WORKS

Adams, Henry. *The Education of Henry Adams.* Mineola, NY: Dover Publications, 2002. http://books.google.com.

Afaqi, Sabir, ed. *Ṭáhirih in History: Perspectives on Qurratu'l-'Ayn from East and West.* Los Angeles: Kalimát Press, 2004.

Afnan, Abu'l-Qasim. *Black Pearls: Servants in the Households of the Báb and Bahá'u'lláh.* Los Angeles: Kalimat Press, 1990.

Afnan, Mirza Habibu'llah. "The Báb in Shiraz," translated by Ahang Rabbani, (revised ed. 2004). H-Bahá'í: Translation of Shaykhí, Bábíand Bahá'í Texts, no. 11 (October, 1997). http://www.h-net.org/~bahai/trans/vol1/babshir1.htm.

al-Farid, Umar Ibn. *Umar Ibn al-Farid: Sufi Verse, Saintly Life.* Translated by Th. Emil Homerin. Mahwah, NJ: Paulist Press, 2001.

Ali, A. Yusuf, translator and commentator. *The Holy Qur'án.* Elmhurst, NY: Tahrike Tarsile Qur'án, Inc., 2001.

Ali, Muhammad. "Let Us Learn Our Inheritance: Get to know Yourself." *AACAR Bulletin.* Vol. 2, no. 3, (Fall 1989). http://vlib.iue.it/carrie/texts/carrie_books/paksoy-4.

Amanat, Abbas. "From itihad to wilayat-i-faqih: The Evolving of the Shi'ite Legal Authority to Political Power." *Logos, A Journal of Modern Society and Culture,* no. 2.3, (Summer, 2003). http://www.logosjournal.com/amanat.htm.

———. "Islam in Iran v. Messianic Islam in Iran." Encyclopaedia Iranica, digital edition. New York: Columbia University, 2009–2010.

———. *Pivot of the Universe.* Los Angeles: University of California Press, 1997.

———. *Resurrection and Renewal: The Making of the Babi Movement in Iran, 1844–1850.* Ithaca, NY: Cornell University Press, 1989.

Anderson, Bonnie S. *Joyous Greetings: The First International Women's Movement, 1830–1860.* New York: Oxford University Press, 2000. http://books.google.com.

Arberry, A. J. *Classical Persian Literature.* London: George Allen & Unwin Ltd., 1967.

———. *Discourses of Rumi.* London: Routledge Curzon, 2004.

———. *The Legacy of Persia.* London: Oxford University Press, 1963.

Attar, Farid Ud-Din. *The Conference of the Birds.* Translated by Afkham Darbandi and Dick Davis. New York: Penguin Books, 1984.

Austen, Jane. *Northanger Abbey.* London: Richard Bentley, 1833. http://books.google.com.

Avirih, Jinab-i. "The Story of the Princess." *Star of the West* 14, no. 11 (February, 1924).

Axelrod, Steven, Camille Roman, and Thomas Travisano. *The New Anthology of American Poetry.* Vol. 1. Picataway, NJ: Rutgers U. Press, 2003.

Babayan, Kathryn. *Mystics, Monarchs, and Messiahs: Cultural Landscape of Early Modern Iran,* Cambridge, MA: Harvard University Press, 2002.

Balyuzi, H. M. *Bahá'u'lláh: The King of Glory.* Oxford: George Ronald, 1980.

———. *The Báb: Herald of the Day of Days.* Oxford: George Ronald, 1973.

———. *Khadíjih Bagum: The Wife of the Báb,* Oxford: George Ronald, 1981.

Bamdad, Madr ol-Moluk. *Darkness into Light.* Hickville, NY: Exposition Press, 1977.

Bankier, Joanna and Deirdre Lashgari, eds. *Women Poets of the World.* New York: MacMillan Publishing, 1983.

Batjmanglij, Najmieh K. *A Taste of Persia.* Washington, DC: Mage Publishers, 1999–2000.

Bayat, Mangol. *Mysticism and Dissent: Socioreligious Thought in Qajar Iran.* Syracuse: Syracuse University Press, 1982.

Beck, Lois and Guity Nashat. *Women in Iran from 1800 to the Islamic Republic.* Urbana and Chicago: University of Illinois Press, 2004.

Behranpour, Tara. *To See and See Again: A Life in Iran and America.* Los Angeles: University of California Press, 1999.

Bell, Gertrude. *Persian Pictures.* New York: Boni and Liveright, 1928.

Bell, Susan G. and Karen M. Offen. *Women, the Family, and Freedom: The Debate in Documents.* Stanford: Stanford University Press, 1983. http://books.google.com.

Bird, Christiane. *Neither East Nor West: One Woman's Journey Through the Islamic Republic of Iran.* New York: Washington Square Press, 2001.

Bliss, Sylvester. *Memoirs of William Miller.* Boston: Joshua V. Himes, 1853. http://books.google.com.

Boyce, Mary. *Textual Sources for the Study of Zoroastrianism.* Chicago: The University of Chicago Press, 1984.

———. *Zoroastrians: their Religious Beliefs and Practices.* London: Routledge, Taylor, and Francis Group.

Brill, E. J. *E. J. Brill's First Encyclopedia of Islam*. Leiden, The Netherlands: printed by author, 1987. http://books.google.com.

Brooks, Geraldine. *Nine Parts of Desire: The Hidden World of Islamic Women.* New York: Anchor Books, 1995.

Browne, Edward Granville. *A Literary History of Persia.* Vol. I. New York: Charles Scribner's Sons, 1902.

———. *A Literary History of Persia.* Vol. 3. Cambridge: Cambridge University Press, 1984.

———. *A Literary History of Persia.* Vol. 4. Cambridge: Cambridge University Press, 1969.

———. *A Year Amongst the Persians.* Cambridge: Cambridge University Press, 1927. http://www.bahai-library.com/books/ayatp.

Burke, Andrew, Mark Eliot, and Kamin Mohammadi. *Iran.* Footscray, Victoria, Australia: Lonely Planet Publications Pty Ltd, 2004.

Campion, Nardi Reeder. *Mother Ann Lee: Morning Star of the Shakers.* Hanover, NH: The University Press of New England, 1990. http://books.google.com.

Chardin, Sir John. *Travels in Persia: 1673–1677.* Mineola, NY: Dover Publications, 1988.

Chebel, Malek. *Symbols of Islam.* New York: Barnes and Noble, 2003.

Chelkowski, Peter. *Ta'ziyeh: Ritual and Drama in Iran.* New York: New York University Press, 1979.

"Claude Henri de Rouvroy, Comte de Saint-Simon" and "Joseph Wolff." http://www.1911.encyclopedia.org.

Cole, Juan. *Modernity and the Millennium: The Genesis of the Bahá'í Faith in the Nineteenth-Century Middle East.* New York: Columbia University Press, 1998.

Collier-Thomas, Bettye. *Daughters of Thunder: Black Women Preachers and Their Sermons.* San Francisco: Jossey-Bass Publishers, 1998.

Cowen, J. M., ed. *The Hans Wehr Dictionary of Modern Written Arabic (Arabic-English).* Urbana, IL: Spoken Language Services, 1994.

Curzon, George N., *Persia and the Persian Question.* Vol. 1. New York: Barnes and Noble, 1966.

Cutsinger, James S. *Paths to the Heart: Sufism and the Christian East.* Bloomington, Ind.: World Wisdom, Inc., 2002.

Daneshvar, Simin. *Savushun: A Novel about Modern Iran.* Washington, DC: Mage Publishers, 1990.

Daniel, Elton L. *The History of Iran.* Westport, CT: Greenwood Press, 2001.

Douglass, Frederick. *Narrative of the Life of Frederick Douglass.* 2007. http://books.google.com.

Dureka, Derek. "Elaw, Zilpha." http:///pabook.libraries.psu.edu/palitmap/bios/Elaw_Zilpha.html.

Eliassian, Helen. "Esther's Iranian Tomb Draws Pilgrims of all Religious Stripes," March, 2005. http://www.iran-heritage.org/interestgroups/Judaism-monument.htm.

Elizabeth. *Memoir of Old Elizabeth, A Coloured Woman.* http://womenshistory.about.com/od/aframer18631900/l/bl_old_elizabeth.htm.

Elwell-Sutton, L. P. *Persian Grammar.* Cambridge: Cambridge University, 1963.

Esposito, John L., ed. *Oxford History of Islam.* New York: Oxford University Press, 1999.

Faizí, Abu'l-Qásim. "Explanation of the Symbol of the Greatest Name." Bahá'í Library Online. http://bci.org/prophecy-fulfilled/grstname.htm.

———. *The Prince of Martyrs.* Oxford: George Ronald, 1999.

Farman-Farmaian, Sattareh, and Dona Munker. *Daughter of Persia.* New York: Anchor Books, 1962.

Fernea, Warnock Elizabeth. *Guests of the Sheik.* Garden City, NY: Doubleday, 1965.

French, Marilyn. *From Eve to Dawn: A History of Women in the World.* New York: Feminist Press at the University of New York, 2008.

Fogg, William Perry. *Arabistan.* Hartford: Dustin, Gilman and Co., 1875.

Forget, Evelyn L. "Saint-Simonian Feminism." *Feminist Economics* 7, no. 1. Houston: Rice University, March 2001. http://www.informaworld.com.

Friedl, Erika. *Women of Deh Koh: Lives in an Iranian Village.* Washington, DC: Smithsonian Institution Press, 1989.

Gail, Marzieh. *Arches of the Years.* Oxford: George Ronald, 1991.

———. *Bahá'í Glossary.* Wilmette, IL: Bahá'í Publishing Trust, 1955.

———. *Dawn Over Mount Hira.* Oxford: George Ronald, 1976.

———. *Persia and the Victorians.* London: George Allen and Unwin Ltd., 1951.

———. *The Greatest Holy Leaf.* Oxford: George Ronald, 1982.

———. *The Sheltering Branch.* Oxford: George Ronald, 1959.

"Gale Encyclopedia of Occultism and Parapsychology: Joanna Southcott." http://www.answers.com/topic/joanna-southcott.

Gardner, J. B. "The Daguerreotype Process." From the *Anthony's Photographic Bulletin* 20 (13 April 1889). http://daguerre.org/index.php.

George, Deveral D. "Zurkhaneh: The Persian House of Strength." *Black Belt,* (March, 1997). http://books.google.com.

Gilbert and Gruber. *The Madwoman in the Attic.* New Haven, CT: Yale University Press, 1979.

Glassé, Cyrill. *The New Encyclopedia of Islam.* Lanham, MD: Rowman and Littlefield, 2008. http://books.google.com.

Grogan, Susan K. *Flora Tristan: Life Stories.* New York: Routledge, 1998. http://books.google.com.

Grousset, René. *The Civilizations of the East.* Vol. 2. New York: Alfred A. Knopf, 1931.

Hafez. *The Garden of Heaven.* Translated by Gertrude Bell. Mineola, NY: Dover Publications, 2003.

"History of Telecommunications in the World, in Iran, and in Tehran." Telecommunication Company of Tehran. http://www.tct.ir.

———. *The Green Sea of Heaven.* Translated by Elizabeth T. Gray, Jr. Ashland, OR: White Cloud Press, 2002.

Harris, Mark. *Inside Iran.* San Francisco: Chronicle Books, 2008.

Hatcher, John S. and Amrollah Hemmat. *Adam's Wish: The Unknown Poetry of Ṭáhirih.* Wilmette, IL: Bahá'í Publishing, 2008.

———. *The Poetry of Ṭáhirih.* Oxford: George Ronald, 2002.

Helminski, Camille Adams. *Women of Sufism.* Boston: Shambala, 2003.

Hillman, Michael. *A Lonely Woman: Forugh Farrokhzaad and her Poetry.* Washington, DC: Mage Publishers, 1987.

Hirshfield, Jane, ed. *Women in Praise of the Sacred.* New York: HarperCollins, 1994.

The Holy Scriptures. Philadelphia: The Jewish Publication Society of America, 1958.

Holbrook, M. L., MD. *Parturition without Pain.* New York: Holbrook, 1891. http://books.google.com.

Hume-Griffith, M. E. *Behind the Veil in Persia and Turkish Arabia.* Philadelphia: J. B. Lippencott Co., 1909. http://muhammadanism.org.

Kazemzadeh, Firuz. "Excerpts from dispatches Written during 1848–1852 by Prince Dolgorukov." *World Order* 1, no. 1 (1966).

Keats, John. *The Complete Poems of John Keats.* New York: Modern Library, 1994.

Khanam, R. and A. Samiyeddin. *Muslim Feminism and Feminist Movement.* Delhi, India: Global Vision Publishing House, 2002. http://books.google.com.

Khatibi, Abdel Kebir and Mohammad Samiyeddin. *The Splendor of Islamic Calligraphy*. New York: Thames and Hudson, 2001.

Kian-Ersi. "Ebadi: Children [sic] Rights Are the Same as Human Rights." *Persian Morning Daily.* Oct. 9, 2003. NetIran, http://thewe.cc.

Kianush, K. "The Festival of Noe-Rooz" and "A Brief History of Noe-Rooz." Iransaga. http://www.art-arena.com.

Knight, George R. *Millennial Fever and the End of the World.* Boise, Idaho: Pacific Press, 1993.

Kornfeld, Eve. *Margaret Fuller: A Brief Biography with Documents.* Boston: Bedford Books, 1997.

Lambden, Stephen. *Sinaitic Mysteries: Studies in Honor of the Late Hasan M. Balyuzi.* Los Angeles: Kalimat Press, 1988. http://books.google.com.

Layard, Sir A. Henry. *Autobiography and Letters.* London: John Murray, 1903. http://google.books.com.

"Letters of the Living (Hurúf-i-Hayy)." The Bahá'í Encyclopedia Project. National Spiritual Assembly of the Bahá'ís of the United States, 2009. http://www.bahai-encyclopedia-project.org.

Lewis, Jone Johnson. "Seneca Falls 1848 Women's Rights Convention." http://womenshistory.about.com/od/suffrage1848/a/seneca_falls.htm.

Marx, Karl. *Critique of Hegel's Philosophy of Right.* New York: Cambridge University Press, 1982. http://books.google.com.

Masamian, Farnez and Bijan. *Divine Educators.* Oxford: George Ronald, 2005.

McCarry, Charles. *Old Boys.* New York: Overlook Press, 2004.

McLean, Alison. "This Month in History." *Smithsonian Magazine* (July, 2008).

Mehdevi, Anne Sinclair. *Persian Adventure.* New York: Alfred A. Knopf, 1953.

Mehrabkhani, R. *Mullá Ḥusayn: Disciple at Dawn.* Los Angeles: Kalimat Press, 1987.

Memoir of Old Elizabeth, A Coloured Woman. "Documenting the American South." Philadelphia: Collins Press, 1863. http://docsouth.unc.edu/neh/eliza1/eliza1.html.

Mernissi, Fatima. *The Veil and the Male Elite.* Reading, MA: Perseus Books, 1991.

Milani, Farzanieh. *Veils and Words.* Syracuse, NY: Syracuse University Press, 1992.

Mohabbat, Navid. *Paisajes del Alma.* Barcelona: Bahá'í Editorial of Spain, 2007.

Mohammad-Hoseini, Nosratollah. *Hadrat-i-Ṭáhirih.* Dundas, Ontario: Association for Bahá'í Studies in Persian, 2000.

Momen, Moojan. *Bahá'u'lláh: A Short Biography.* Oxford: Oneworld, 2007.

———. "Usuli, Akhbari, S͟hayk͟hi, Bábí: The Tribulations of a Qazvin Family." *Iranian Studies* 36, no. 3 (September, 2003).

Munier, Gilles. *Iraq: An Illustrated History and Guide.* Northampton, MA: Interlink Books, 2004.

Nabíl-i-A'ẓam. *The Dawn-breakers: Nabíl's Narrative of the Early Days of the Bahá'í Revelation.* Translated from the original Persian and edited by Shoghi Effendi. Wilmette, IL: Bahá'í Publishing Trust, 1932.

Najafi, Najmeh and Helen Hinckley. *Persia is My Heart.* New York: Harper and Brothers, 1953.

Nafisi, Azar. *Reading Lolita in Tehran.* New York: Random House, 2003.

National Park Service., U.S. Dept. of the Interior. "The Quaker Influences on the Seneca Falls Convention." Seneca Falls, NY: Women's Rights National Historic Park, 2005.

New World Encyclopedia. http://www.newworldencyclopedia.org.

Nichol, Francis D. *The Midnight Cry: A Defense of the Character and Conduct of William Miller.* Brushton, NY: TEACH Services, Inc., 2000. http://books.google.com.

Nizami. *The Story of Layla and Majnún.* Translated by Gelpke, Mattin, and Hill. New Lebanon, NY: Omega Publications, 1997.

"No-Rooz, the Iranian New Year at Present Times" [sic]. Culture of Iran. http://www.iranchamber.com.

The New American Desk Encyclopedia. New York: Penguin Books USA, 1993.

Palmer, E. H. *A Concise Dictionary of the Persian Language.* London: Rutledge and Kegan Paul, 1949.

Pendlebury, David, trans. and ed. *Jami: Yusuf and Zulaikha.* London: The Octagon Press, 1980.

Perigord, Emily McBride, trans. *Translation of the French Footnotes of the Dawn-breakers.* Wilmette, IL: Bahá'í Publishing Trust, 1970.

"Qazvin" and "Shiraz." http://www.iranchamber.com.

Reiss, Tom. *The Orientalist.* Prince Frederick, MD: RB Large Print, 2005.

Richards, Fred. *A Persian Journey.* London: Jonathan Cape, 1932.

Root, Martha. *Ṭáhirih the Pure.* Los Angeles: Kalimat Press, 1981.

Royal Persian Paintings: The Qajar Epoch, 1785–1925. New York: I. B. Taurus Publishers with Brooklyn Museum of Art, 1998.

Ruhe, David S. *Robe of Light.* Oxford: George Ronald, 1994.

Rumi, Jalalu'l-Din. *Selected Poems of Rumi.* Translated by Reynold A. Nicholson. Mineola, NY: Dover Publications, 2001.

Rynder, Constance. "All Men and Women are Created Equal." *American History Magazine* (April, 1999). http://historynet.com/all-men-women-are-created-equal-cover-page-april-99-american-history-feature.htm.

Sackville-West, Vita. *Passenger to Teheran.* New York: HarperCollins, 1992.

Saghaphi, Mirza Mahmoud Khan. *In the Imperial Shadow: Page to the Shah.* Garden City: Doubleday, Doran and Company, 1932.

Saiedi, Nader. *Gate of the Heart: Understanding the Writings of the Báb.* Canada: Wilfrid Laurier University Press, 2008.

Schimmel, Annemarie. *Islam: An Introduction.* New York: State University of New York Press, 1992.

———. "Karbala." *Al-Serat: A Journal of Islamic Studies.* Vol. XII. http://www.al-islam.org/al-serat/karbala-schimmel.htm.

Sciolino, Elaine. *Persian Mirrors.* New York: Simon and Schuster, 2000.

"Sections of Anahita Temple at Kangavar Destroyed by New Construction." The News Section, Circle of Ancient Iranian Studies Web site (January 20, 2010). http://www.cais-soas.com.

Sheil, Lady Mary Leonora Woulfe. *Glimpses of Life and Manners in Persia.* London: John Murray, 1856. http://bahai-library.com/shiel_glimpses_life_persia.

Shelley, Percy Bysshe. *The Complete Poetical Works of Shelley.* Boston: Houghton Mifflin Co., 1901.

Sheridan, Richard Brinsley. *The Rivals: A Comedy in Five Acts.* London: A. Millar, W. Law, and R. Cater, 1797. http://books.google.com.

Simkin, John. "William Lloyd Garrison." Spartacus Educational Web site. http://www.Spartacus.schoolnet.co.uk/.

Smith, Margaret. *Rabi'a Basri: The Mystic and Her Fellow-saints in Islam.* New Delhi: Kitab Bhavan, 2003.

"Sojourner Truth biography." *Women in History.* Lakewood Public Library. http://www.lkwdpl.org/wihohio/trut-soj.htm.

Sprachman, Paul. *Language and Culture in Persian.* Costa Mesa, CA: Mazda Publishers, Inc., 2002.

Stanton, Elizabeth Cady, Susan Brownhell Anthony, and Matilda Joslyn Gage. *History of Woman Suffrage.* New York: Fowler and Wells, 1881. http://books.google.com.

Stetkevych, Jaraslav. *The Zephyrs of Najd.* Chicago: University of Chicago Press, 1993.

"Stevens, Ethel Stefana (1879–1972)." Appreciations of the Bahá'í Faith. *Bahá'í Tributes.* http://bahaitributes.wordpress.com.

Stevens, Sir Roger. *The Land of the Great Sophy.* London: Methuen and Company, 1971.

Stokes, Jim. "The Story of Joseph in the Bábí and Bahá'í Faiths." *World Order* 29, no. 2 (Winter, 1997–98).

———. "The Story of Joseph in Five Religious Traditions." *World Order* 28, no. 3 (Spring, 1997).

Taherzadeh, Adib. *The Revelation of Bahá'u'lláh, Mazra'ih and Bahjí: 1877–92.* Vol. 4. Oxford: George Ronald, 1987.

"The True Story of Joanna Southcott." Joanna Southcott Website. www.btinternet.com/~joannasouthcott/.

Thompson, Juliet. *The Diary of Juliet Thompson.* Los Angeles: Kalimat Press, 1983.

Tullio, Maranhao, ed. *The Interpretation of Dialogue.* Chicago: University of Chicago Press, 1990. http://books.google.com.

Tyler, Alice Felt. *Freedom's Ferment: Phases of American Social History to 1860.* Minneapolis: The University of Minnesota Press, 1944.

"Urmia (Urumiyeh), The Cradle of Civilization." *Cais Archeological and Cultural News.* Oct. 25, 2003. Circle of Ancient Iranian Studies. http://www.cais-soas.com.

Van Doren, Mark. *Anthology of World Poetry.* New York: Harcourt, Brace and World, Inc., 1936.

Venet, Wendi Armand. *Neither Ballots nor Bullets.* Charlottesville, VA: University Press of Virginia, 1991. http://book.google.com.

Vobelsang-Eastwood, Gillian. and L. A. F. Barjesteh van Waawijk van Doorn. *An Introduction to Qajar Dress.* Rotterdam: Barjesten van Waalwijk van Dloorn and Co.'s Uitgeversmaatschappij, 2002.

Wagner, Sally Roesch. *Sisters in Spirit.* Summertown, TN: Native Voices, 2001.

Walther, Wiebke. *Women in Islam.* Princeton, NJ: Markus Weiner Publishers, 1999.

Wilbur, Donald N._*Persian Gardens and Garden Pavilions.* Rutland, VT: Charles E. Tuttle Co., 1962.

Wright, Denis. *The English Amongst the Persians.* London: I. B. Taurus, 2001.

Index

Bahá'í
PUBLISHING

Bahá'í Publishing and the Bahá'í Faith

Bahá'í Publishing produces books based on the teachings of the Bahá'í Faith. Founded over 160 years ago, the Bahá'í Faith has spread to some 235 nations and territories and is now accepted by more than five million people. The word "Bahá'í" means "follower of Bahá'u'lláh." Bahá'u'lláh, the founder of the Bahá'í Faith, asserted that He is the Messenger of God for all of humanity in this day. The cornerstone of His teachings is the establishment of the spiritual unity of humankind, which will be achieved by personal transformation and the application of clearly identified spiritual principles. Bahá'ís also believe that there is but one religion and that all the Messengers of God—among them Abraham, Zoroaster, Moses, Krishna, Buddha, Jesus, and Muḥammad—have progressively revealed its nature. Together, the world's great religions are expressions of a single, unfolding divine plan. Human beings, not God's Messengers, are the source of religious divisions, prejudices, and hatreds.

The Bahá'í Faith is not a sect or denomination of another religion, nor is it a cult or a social movement. Rather, it is a globally recognized independent world religion founded on new books of scripture revealed by Bahá'u'lláh.

Bahá'í Publishing is an imprint of the National Spiritual Assembly of the Bahá'ís of the United States.

For more information about the Bahá'í Faith,
or to contact Bahá'ís near you,
visit http://www.bahai.us/
or call
1-800-22-UNITE

Other Books Available from Bahá'í Publishing

COMPASSIONATE WOMAN
The Life and Legacy of Patricia Locke
John Kolstoe
$21.00 U.S. / $23.00 CAN
Hardcover
ISBN 978-1-931847-85-8

Compassionate Woman shares the captivating life of Patricia Locke, a Lakota Indian, who dedicated her life to righting injustices on behalf of indigenous peoples, as well as all of humanity. She was awarded the MacArthur Fellowship, was the first American Indian to serve as a senior officer on the National Spiritual Assembly of the Bahá'ís of the United States, and was posthumously inducted into the National Women's Hall of Fame.

This fascinating biography of Patricia Locke, who was given the name *Compassionate Woman*, gives us a glimpse into the life of someone dedicated to restoring justice and helping those in need. Her life of service began in Anchorage, Alaska, when she founded a community center aimed at assisting Native Americans, Eskimos, and Aleuts—who had moved to the city from villages—to cope with the many problems they encountered. She then went on to work for the Western Interstate Counsel for Higher Education, where she focused much of her energy on establishing colleges on Reservations. She was particularly concerned with improving education for American Indians, and worked hard toward advancing education on Reservations so that Native American culture and language could be woven into the curriculum. She also spent many years as a freelance writer, instructor at various universities, and activist on behalf of the poor and oppressed. In addition to the MacArthur Fellowship, Locke was the first American Indian to serve as a senior officer on the National Spiritual Assembly of the Bahá'ís of the United States, and was posthumously inducted into the National Women's Hall of Fame. Patricia Locke was wholeheartedly committed to serving the needs of others, and her indomitable spirit lives on through her legacy of service and loving compassion for all peoples of the world.

THE QUICKENING
Unknown Poetry of Ṭáhirih
John S. Hatcher and Amrollah Hemmat
$18.00 U.S. / $20.00 CAN
Trade Paper
ISBN 978-1-931847-83-4

A new priceless collection of previously unpublished poems by the renowned nineteenth-century poetess, Ṭáhirih.

The Quickening is a newly translated collection of stirring poems by the renowned nineteenth-century poetess Ṭáhirih that deal with a subject that has challenged religious scholars throughout the ages. Among the world religions, no theme has attracted more attention or caused more controversy than the concept of a last judgment or end of time. The Bahá'í view of the "Resurrection," or the "Quickening," as the term is translated here, stands in bold contrast to many traditional views. It is seen as a prelude to a glorious outcome—the galvanizing of our collective will to bring about a just and lasting peace and the unification of humankind. In addition to the beautifully crafted English translation of Ṭáhirih's poems, this volume also includes her work in the original Persian and Arabic.

SPIRIT OF FAITH
The Oneness of Religion
Bahá'í Publishing
$12.00 U.S. / $14.00 CAN
Hardcover
ISBN 978-1-931847-81-0

Spirit of Faith: The Oneness of Religion is a compilation of writings and prayers that focus on the inherent oneness of all the world's great religions. Spiritual seekers of all faiths will relish these uplifting passages that underscore the unity of thought that helps us define our place within a single, unfolding, and divine creation. This collection contains writings from Bahá'u'lláh, the Báb, and 'Abdu'l-Bahá.

The *Spirit of Faith* series will explore a range of topics—such as the unity of humanity, the eternal covenant of God, the promise of world peace, and much more—by taking an in-depth look at how the writings of the Bahá'í Faith view these issues. The series is designed to encourage readers of all faiths to think about spirituality, and to take time to pray and meditate on these important topics.

TALKS BY 'ABDU'L-BAHÁ
THE ETERNAL COVENANT
'Abdu'l-Bahá
$14.00 U.S. / $16.00 CAN
Hardcover
ISBN 978-1-931847-82-7

Spiritually uplifting and thought-provoking collection of talks from one of the central figures of the Bahá'í Faith.

Talks by 'Abdu'l-Bahá is a collection of talks given by 'Abdu'l-Bahá—the son and appointed successor of Bahá'u'lláh, the Prophet and Founder of the Bahá'í Faith—during his historic journey to North America in 1912. Speaking in front of diverse audiences, 'Abdu'l-Bahá offered profound insights on a number of topics in a simple manner accessible to anyone who listened with an open heart. The talks included in this volume all relate to the theme of the eternal covenant of God, one of the central themes of the teachings of the Bahá'í Faith. According to this covenant, God never leaves humankind alone without guidance but rather makes His will and purpose known to us through the appearance of His Prophets or Manifestations, Who appear periodically throughout history in order to advance human civilization.